"eighth sister no more"

Alan R. Sadovnik and Susan F. Semel
General Editors

Vol. 56

The History of Schools and Schooling series is part of the Peter Lang Education list.
Every volume is peer reviewed and meets
the highest quality standards for content and production.

PETER LANG
New York • Washington, D.C./Baltimore • Bern
Frankfurt • Berlin • Brussels • Vienna • Oxford

ERRATA

All photo credits to the Connecticut College Archives should instead be credited to the Linda Lear Center for Special Collections and Archives, Connecticut College.

PAUL P. MARTHERS

"eighth sister no more"

THE ORIGINS & EVOLUTION
OF CONNECTICUT COLLEGE

PETER LANG
New York • Washington, D.C./Baltimore • Bern
Frankfurt • Berlin • Brussels • Vienna • Oxford

Library of Congress Cataloging-in-Publication Data

Marthers, Paul P.
"Eighth sister no more": the origins and evolution of Connecticut College / Paul P. Marthers.
p. cm. — (History of schools and schooling; v. 56)
Includes bibliographical references and index.
1. Connecticut College—History. I. Title.
LD1281.C322M37   378.746'5—dc22   2010023356
ISBN 978-1-4331-1221-8 (hardcover)
ISBN 978-1-4331-1220-1 (paperback)
ISSN 1089-0678

Bibliographic information published by **Die Deutsche Nationalbibliothek.**
Die Deutsche Nationalbibliothek lists this publication in the "Deutsche
Nationalbibliografie"; detailed bibliographic data is available
on the Internet at http://dnb.d-nb.de/.

The paper in this book meets the guidelines for permanence and durability
of the Committee on Production Guidelines for Book Longevity
of the Council of Library Resources.

© 2011 Peter Lang Publishing, Inc., New York
29 Broadway, 18th floor, New York, NY 10006
www.peterlang.com

Printed in the United States of America

CONTENTS

LIST OF ILLUSTRATIONS

ACKNOWLEDGMENTS

This historical investigation would not have been possible without the cooperation of officials at Connecticut College, nor would it have been undertaken without the support I received from Reed College (chiefly its president Colin Diver)
that enabled me to attend the University of Pennsylvania. Connecticut's President
Leo Higdon and members of his staff, Wendy Mahon and Patricia Carey, assisted
my efforts to gather information from Connecticut College's historical files and
from people associated with the College. Special thanks are due to Nova Seals,
College Archivist, Laurie Deredita, Director of Special Collections, and Brian
Rogers, Emeritus College Librarian; without their assistance, this project never
would have made it past the idea stage.

Numerous others listened to developing, sometimes incoherent, thoughts
about the project, asked poignant questions, or made valuable suggestions regarding avenues of inquiry to pursue or avoid. Talking to those individuals sharpened
my focus. Those helpful individuals to whom I am grateful are Mary Linda Arma-
cost, Hilton Hallock, and Marvin Lazerson of the University of Pennsylvania;
Helen Horowitz of Smith College; and Sally Schwager of Harvard University's
Graduate School of Education. I am also grateful to Larry Shall of Oglethorpe
University and Elissa Tenney of Bennington College for their guidance. I am
grateful especially to Marybeth Gasman of the University of Pennsylvania, who
gave generously of her time to read drafts, made suggestions for revisions, and bol-
stered my growing confidence in my research and writing skills.

Many others made themselves available for interviews and gave generously of
their time. For their invaluable assistance, I thank Oakes Ames, Jane Bredeson,
Thyra Briggs '92, Lisa Brownell, Liz Cheney '92, Marion Doro, Anthony Enders,
Elizabeth Enders '62, Linda Eisenmann '75, Margaret Carpenter Evans '44, Nor-
man Fainstein, David Fenton, Torrey Fenton '59, '90(MAT), '94(MA), Jim
Garvey '79, Claire Gaudiani '66, the late Richard Goodwin, Dirk Held, Jeanette
Hersey, Pamela Gwynn Herrup '65, Frances Hoffmann, Philip Jordan, Eric Kap-
lan '85, Charlie Luce, Martha Merrill '84, Lynda Munro '76, Jeff Oshen '76, Dan
Parrish, Nancy Rubsam, Margaret Sheridan '67, Agnes Underwood '63, George
Willauer, and Susan Young.

None of this work would have been possible without the love, support, and
patience of my wife Janet and son Reed. Both endured numerous nights and
weekends when I was present but immersed in the world of Connecticut College,
women's history, Wesleyan University, the Seven Sister colleges, coeducation, and
the history of higher education. Little Reed helped keep his father grounded while
Janet asked sharp questions and provided excellent editorial advice and constructive criticism. Visits by my mother-in-law, Lynne Platt, kept Janet sane and Reed
happy while I was off in Philadelphia attending classes or in New London or Mid-

dletown searching through archives. Lastly, I thank my parents, Philip Marthers and Marjorie Berten, for fostering a love of learning, which for me has been a life-changing force.

CHAPTER ONE

Why Study Connecticut College?

Connecticut College for Women would not have been established in 1911 if
Wesleyan University had not stopped admitting women in 1909. From 1868 to
1909, Wesleyan University had been the only college opportunity for women in
Connecticut. But in 1909 Wesleyan ceased its "forty-year experiment in coeducation," leaving no college for women in Connecticut.[1] In response, Elizabeth
Wright, a Wesleyan alumna, along with other concerned members of the Hartford College Club, formed a committee to bring Connecticut a women's college.
Lacking the funds to establish a college on their own, but not lacking in initiative
and will, Elizabeth Wright and her fellow clubwomen took their cause across the
state of Connecticut, to civic leaders, other women's clubs, philanthropists, and
college officials.

The townspeople of New London, led by high school principal Colin Buell,
raised $134,000 to convince Wright and her committee to choose New London
over the hometown favorite Hartford and several other competing towns. A local
heir to a shipping fortune, Morton Plant, followed with a million-dollar endowment gift that secured a future for the new college. Although local in character,
Connecticut College for Women was, from its opening for classes in 1915, national in its aspirations, drawing its first president (Frederick Sykes) from Columbia University and many of its early faculty from prominent institutions, including
Barnard, Brown, Smith, Vanderbilt, Vassar, and the University of Wisconsin.[2]

In the nascent stages of this project, I was drawn to the story of the forty-year
"experiment" in coeducation at Wesleyan University, because my parents and sib-
lings were born in Middletown, Connecticut, and my father grew up across the
street from the Wesleyan campus. My father's grandfather was a maintenance man
in charge of Wesleyan's Shanklin Science Laboratory, where he died tragically on
the job in 1943. My father's mother worked for a time as a cook in a Wesleyan
fraternity house. No one in my father's family ever attended Wesleyan, let alone
graduated from college. Still, while I was growing up in the Connecticut River
Valley, before moving to Vermont in the ninth grade, I saw Wesleyan as the symbol of college writ large: it became the original source of inspiration that sparked
me to end up as the first and, sadly, the only four-year college graduate in my family. Focusing on Wesleyan, which is not my alma mater—although I took a graduate writing course there in 1995—struck me as a chance to make a symbolic and
intellectual journey home.

As I read more about Wesleyan and spoke with the University's archivist, I discovered that its brief foray into coeducation had been covered extensively, first by Louise Wilby Knight's 1972 Wesleyan honors thesis and later by David Potts' 1994 history of Wesleyan's first one hundred years.[3] Upon closer examination, the topic began to look too thin to sustain further study. I also began to wonder whether Wesleyan officials would be receptive to someone reawakening and shining a spotlight on a less-than-admirable aspect of the University's history. My decision to forgo the story seemed fortuitous when in April 2007 I encountered, in Wesleyan's archives, a woman writing a dissertation on 19th century coeducation efforts at three Methodist institutions: Boston University, Northwestern University, and Wesleyan University.

Still, Wesleyan's aborted experiment in coeducation fascinated me, not because of what happened at Wesleyan but because of what one of its alumnae did in response. How could one not be impressed by the initiative of Elizabeth Wright and the Hartford College Club, whose big dreams and strong wills led to the founding of Connecticut College for Women in New London? The more I followed that thread in the Wesleyan coeducation saga, the more it became apparent that the founding story of Connecticut College held promise as a topic for full examination and analysis. When I turned my attention from Wesleyan University to Connecticut College, I realized that the younger college's grassroots founding and initial reason for being as a women's college was a story worth telling, perhaps even a story unlike other founding tales of women's colleges.

Connecticut College, like Wesleyan University, is not my alma mater. But Connecticut College and I, like Wesleyan University, have a historical family connection. That connection, at least in part, prompted my interest in pursuing the turn of the Wesleyan story toward the eventual founding of Connecticut College. Genealogical research my wife (Janet) and I conducted in the summer of 2004 on my father's family led back to New London, Connecticut, where the trail ended at the marriage of James Marthers to Anne Stark in 1775, both of New London. In addition, one of the lines of the James Marthers to Paul Marthers family tree branches over to the Rogers family that owned some of the land that became the Connecticut College campus. As a result, the study held a personal as well as a scholarly interest.

There is scant mention of Connecticut College in scholarship on higher education history. What is available about Connecticut College's origin and development comes primarily from "house histories." Former dean of faculty Gertrude Noyes '25 (1982), first decade faculty member Irene Nye (1943), and retired director of libraries Brian Rogers (1999) have written thorough histories of Connecticut College—albeit ones published by the College, which may render them less than objective.[4] Patricia Sullivan's 1982 Ph.D. dissertation study (for Boston

College) of Rosemary Park's presidencies at Connecticut College and Barnard College supplements the insider historical accounts and the materials found in alumni magazines and college guides.[5] Still, none of the insider histories contextualizes Connecticut College for Women's origin story and pioneering contribution to women's higher education. And none of them critically assesses the curricular tensions between the liberal arts and vocational subjects that existed at Connecticut College into the 1950s, the mission-altering move to coeducation in 1968, the complicated relationship between the College and New London, or the ambitious and tumultuous 1988-2001 presidency of Claire Gaudiani '66.

Numerous women's colleges (and former women's colleges) can lay claim to the title of "Eighth Sister" to the Seven Sisters: Barnard College, Bryn Mawr College, Mount Holyoke College, Radcliffe College, Smith College, Vassar College, and Wellesley College. The defunct Pembroke College of Brown University was one of three coordinate colleges for women in the Ivy League. Wheaton College of Massachusetts is older than each of the Seven Sisters and was often the next best choice for women who did not get admitted by the likes of Vassar and Wellesley. Wells College is older than all but Mount Holyoke among the Seven Sisters and was often seen as a respected alternative to them. Although younger and somewhat different from a curricular standpoint, Skidmore College and William Smith College of Hobart deserve consideration. Catholic families of the northeastern United States thought of Manhattanville College as the Catholic equivalent of a Sister college, while Midwestern Catholics thought the same thing about Saint Mary's of Indiana. As the women's college counterpart to Rutgers University, Douglass College patterned itself after the Seven Sisters; for example, its namesake and other early deans graduated from Sister colleges. Many southerners saw Goucher College, Agnes Scott College, Sweet Briar College, Hollins College, Randolph Macon Women's College, and Sophie Newcomb College of Tulane University as analogues to the Seven Sisters in the North. Among America's historically black colleges and universities, Spelman College has always been regarded as the institution most parallel to a Seven Sister college. Mills College, which drew many early faculty and curricular ideas from Seven Sisters, was the West Coast's best claim on "Eighth Sister" before Scripps College opened in 1926. And while there were women's colleges at or near Miami University, the University of Rochester, Tufts University, and Western Reserve University, none of them were as frequently equated with the Seven Sisters as Connecticut College for Women and most of the other colleges just listed.

By putting the label "Eighth Sister" on Connecticut College, I am not suggesting that it was more worthy of that designation than any of its other high quality women's college counterparts. To do so might be to pick an unnecessary argument with those devoted to other women's colleges, but especially with the partisans of

Pembroke, Wells, and Wheaton, as those were colleges not infrequently selected over Connecticut College by women seeking their best alternative to a Seven Sisters education. I have affixed the term "Eighth Sister" to Connecticut College because it is a descriptive phrase that came up repeatedly in archival materials and interviews with alumni, faculty, and staff. Archival documents revealed that Connecticut College for Women officials were always acutely conscious of the Seven Sister colleges and often shaped its programs and policies to follow those older standard bearers in women's education. Not coincidentally, Connecticut College's first woman president (Katharine Blunt) was a Vassar graduate. Blunt's protégé and Connecticut College's other legendary female president, Rosemary Park, graduated from Radcliffe. The act of calling Connecticut College the "Eighth Sister" is thus a way of saying no more and no less than that it was one of America's women's colleges that sought to run in the same league as the Seven Sisters. Others more versed in women's college history can decide which women's college really was the "Eighth Sister."

Although there is room for an updated comprehensive history of Connecticut College, writing one was not my intention in undertaking this study. Instead I sought to understand the founding circumstances and vision for Connecticut College for Women, reasoning that investigating how it came to exist would help place it in the history of women's higher education in America. Looking at the founding of Connecticut College presented a frame that revealed the importance of three key defining aspects: its ties to New London, its hybrid curriculum of liberal arts and vocational subjects, and its mission to expand higher education opportunities for women. As I examined those three key themes, not just at Connecticut College's founding moment, but also at critical points during the institution's evolution, I kept in mind the question, would its founders and early shapers recognize their Connecticut College for Women in the coeducational Connecticut College that is approaching its second century, and if so how?

The origin of Connecticut College warrants close examination because it represents an example of a grassroots college founding; in fact, it is one of the few colleges launched by the women's club movement in America's progressive era.[6] The vocational elements in its initial curriculum set Connecticut College for Women apart from its prominent northeastern sisters (such as Bryn Mawr) and heralded a different model for women's education, one that fit the progressive era's emphasis on career preparation for women. Connecticut College for Women joined three other women's colleges founded in the progressive era—Skidmore (1903), William Smith (1908), and Douglass (1918)—that offered majors in liberal arts and home economics. While its vocational edges set its curriculum apart from the Seven Sister colleges during its first fifty years, Connecticut College (and its progressive era sisters) gradually embraced the liberal arts to the exclusion of majors such as home economics—a curricular evolution that became a representative pattern in women's higher education.

Connecticut College is also noteworthy as an example of a prominent women's college (with Vassar) that embraced coeducation in the late 1960s, leading the way for numerous other northeastern women's and men's colleges. Many of Connecticut College's northeastern sisters, such as Smith, rejected coeducation, while several others, such as Wells and Wheaton, waited twenty or more years to become coeducational, only doing so in the face of enrollment or student quality declines, or both. And finally, Connecticut College is noteworthy because it is making its way, as it approaches its second century, with an institutional identity that, due to the ways coeducation altered it, is only peripherally reminiscent of the college that opened in 1915.

"Eighth Sister No More does not attempt to recount or analyze all of Connecticut College's history; rather, the primary focus is on the College's founding decade, including the critical events, people, decisions, programs, societal developments, and social forces that led to its establishment. The story of Connecticut College's evolution could be told in linear, start-to-finish fashion like most institutional historiographies. To do so, however, might mask the elements that both parallel and set apart Connecticut College's origins from college founding patterns in America. A straight telling might also give short shrift to the ways in which three prominent progressive movements shaped Connecticut College's founding circumstances and reasons for being. Last of all, no one but alumnae and other devotees to Connecticut College would be likely to pay much attention to a book that told the story of one particular women's college without trying to answer questions such as did Connecticut College represent a continuation of the type of women's colleges that came before it, or did it introduce a significant modification to the already established model? The opportunity to address such contextual and institutional identity questions was a chief motivation in undertaking this historical investigation.

The chapter following this introduction tells the story of Connecticut College for Women's founding. The focus is on the College's founding decade, particularly how Hartford College Club member Elizabeth Wright, New London educator and booster Colin Buell, founding president Frederick Sykes, and chief benefactor Morton Plant helped give birth to the College. Because Connecticut College has always been linked historically to the three oldest colleges in its home state, the chapter also focuses attention on the state of Connecticut's earliest and enduringly prominent trio of liberal arts institutions, Trinity, Wesleyan, and Yale. Chapter two further seeks to contextualize Connecticut's founding mission within the New England Small College Athletic Conference (NESCAC), a set of colleges that now comprise its aspirational peers and competitors.[7] Examining

Connecticut's founding in a comparative context helps clarify whether that founding was unique, representative of a common tradition, or a hybrid of different founding models.

Like most institutions, Connecticut College was at the moment of its origin a product of the ideas that had the most currency at the time. To understand, analyze, and contextualize Connecticut College at its point of origin, I devote the third chapter to three movements (women's clubs, vocational education, and home economics) that influenced thinking about education for women in America's progressive era (1890–1920). Each of those three progressive era movements helped shape the new women's college that opened in New London, Connecticut, in 1915.

The aim of the fourth chapter is to place Connecticut College's founding vision and mission within the context of women's college history, particularly against the Seven Sister colleges, because they set the tone for women's higher education up to and after Connecticut College's founding. The fourth chapter further contrasts Connecticut College's founding reason for being with that of seven later women's colleges: Bennington College, Douglass College, Sarah Lawrence College, Scripps College, Simmons College, Skidmore College, and William Smith College, three of which are now coeducational like Connecticut. Contextualizing Connecticut College in relation to other prominent women's colleges helps answer questions regarding the kind of women's college Connecticut was before it became coeducational in 1969. Was Connecticut the proverbial "Eighth Sister"? Was it in the progressive wave of women's colleges that included Bennington, Sarah Lawrence, and Scripps? Or was it something entirely different in the constellation of women's colleges, a progressive-era liberal arts college with a practical bent?

The next several chapters examine and analyze critical points in the evolution of Connecticut College. The first development essential to an understanding of the evolution of Connecticut College is the curriculum reform that occurred in the 1950s and early 1960s. That effort, led by President Rosemary Park, eliminated vocational courses of study, such as the home economics major, and underscored the primacy of the liberal arts. Park's curricular reforms solidified Connecticut College's growing academic stature, aligned it more closely with the Seven Sister colleges (fortifying the College's claim on the moniker "eighth sister"), and, by placing greater emphasis on the sciences, prepared the way for coeducation.

Following the movement of its curriculum toward a pure liberal arts focus, Connecticut College made an even more radical alteration to its founding mission. The College voted in 1968 to begin admitting men in 1969. Understanding Connecticut College's evolution as an institution is impossible, or at best incomplete, without consideration of the institution's historic, and surprisingly uncontroversial, move to coeducation. A full chapter discusses that momentous decision and its effect on Connecticut College.

Connecticut College's identity and mission have been bound up with its hometown of New London from the beginning. Inherent in the central role that New London played in the founding of the College is a kind of promise owed to the local community. To shed light on how the College has or has not kept that promise, one chapter examines the Connecticut College Arboretum, which has provided research and teaching opportunities to students and faculty for nearly 80 years and has existed historically as a bridge to the New London community. The same chapter examines Connecticut College's sponsorship of the American Dance Festival from 1948 to 1978, assessing the benefit that program brought to the greater New London community and the College. Another chapter describes and assesses the attempts made in the 1990s by President Claire Gaudiani—the only alumna to hold that post at Connecticut—to breathe new life into the town-gown partnership so central to the College's founding story.

Connecticut College is a relatively young institution, not yet one hundred years old. Yet in less than a century Connecticut College has filled a gap in educational opportunity for women and become a coeducational institution that dropped "for women" from its name. Following coeducation, Connecticut College has grown to serve 1,900 students, offer 55 undergraduate majors and six master's degree programs, and operate six centers for interdisciplinary study. Connecticut College has also emerged as one of America's forty leading liberal arts colleges. Understanding the evolution of Connecticut College requires an examination of scholarship related to mission and organizational development in higher education. Concepts such as institutional mission and organizational saga, ethos, and culture provide a theoretical context for determining whether Connecticut College's mission has stayed constant, whether it has adapted with the times, or whether Connecticut College has an organizational saga that expresses a distinctive identity. The concluding chapter also looks at Connecticut College's current mission statement and institutional priorities for its second century in order to determine if they embody elements of the College's founding mission and original vision. The concluding chapter pays close attention to aspects of the founding mission and vision that still are prominent as Connecticut College looks forward to its second hundred years.

From its inception Connecticut College has been a liberal arts college focused overwhelmingly on the education of undergraduates.[8] The liberal arts college has been a historically important breed in American higher education. But with the 20th century growth of a public university sector that stresses access and the more recent emergence of for-profit colleges that offer convenience, small liberal arts colleges, in aggregate, now enroll less than 10 percent of all students in American higher education, and represent a shrinking share of the educational marketplace.[9]

These facts beg the question, why study a single liberal arts college such as Connecticut College?

One reason is because liberal arts colleges are arguably the archetypal institution in American higher education.[10] America's first institutions of higher education, such as Harvard and Yale, before they became multidimensional universities, were small liberal arts colleges. Liberal arts colleges have historically been curious mixtures of tradition and innovation, providing models for the collections of colleges that comprise large universities.[11] Liberal arts colleges have frequently been the bellwethers of change, the indicator species that signals the health and fragility of the overall higher education landscape.[12]

Despite their historical significance, liberal arts colleges continue to face threats to their survival from vocational majors, large university honors programs, declining percentages of students able or willing to pay for a liberal arts education, for-profit universities, and the increasing bottom line orientation of students and parents demanding an immediate payoff after graduation.[13] The process of how the liberal arts, as a guidepost for study, and the colleges singularly focused on the traditional arts and sciences curriculum, such as Connecticut College, adapt or differentiate their missions to survive is potentially instructive for all of higher education, not just for small colleges.[14]

Understanding the evolution of a college like Connecticut College requires a familiarity with documents, descriptions, and memories provided by the people who built and shaped the institution. Unfortunately, none of Connecticut College's founders are around to recount the institution's beginnings. Regrettably, few of the key individuals who shepherded Connecticut College through its critical first fifty years are still alive. What has survived as the voice of those key individuals, however, is the historical record of reports, letters, and speeches as preserved in the Connecticut College Archives, and found in newspaper articles, histories, and documents produced by Connecticut College such as alumni magazines, brochures, catalogs, and annual reports.

This book examines a process, the founding of a college and key points in its subsequent evolution. Understanding that process required archival research and oral history interviews with individuals familiar with the founding and evolution of Connecticut College, individuals whose positions at or longevity there, or both, required them to think critically and often about the College in a historical and comparative context.[15] The investigation took me through archival documents in the Connecticut College and Wesleyan University libraries. Oral history interviews with alumni and current and former staff and faculty of Connecticut College, especially individuals who invested a significant portion of their lives there, brought the story off the dusty shelves and out of the yellowed pages of history.

The oral history interviews enabled me to probe the enduring significance of Connecticut College's founding story. The interviews elicited connections to memories of the past, bridges to individuals present in the early years as well as reflections on and opinions about decisions, individuals, forces, and circumstances that have shaped the development of Connecticut College over its first one hundred years. In addition, the writings on women's clubs, home economics, the vocational movement, the progressive era, women's colleges, New England colleges, coeducation, higher education history, mission, and organizational ethos and saga provided useful frames for understanding Connecticut College's evolution.

I hope that the findings of this book will augment the collective understanding of the history of American colleges as well as the history of women in higher education. The fact that Connecticut College's mission changed in 1969 when it became a coeducational institution is especially salient because countless small liberal arts colleges were altered by coeducation in the late 1960s or early 1970s. Researchers of higher education history may also find informative the focus on how a college's founding shapes its evolution.

To survive, colleges have always adapted to meet the needs of changing times or have transformed themselves in anticipation of future challenges and opportunities.[16] This study examines the importance of the past, particularly the institutional birth process and how it influences colleges as they go forward to what all hope will be an existence into perpetuity. Holding up a lens in 2009 to a college such as Connecticut College provides an unobstructed view into the liberal arts segment of American higher education at a time when most liberal arts colleges struggle for sustainability, distinctiveness, attention, and resources. Rediscovering and understanding their founding raison d'etre is a potentially useful tool that small liberal arts colleges might utilize in the course of institutional self-assessment, attempts at renewal, preparations for the future, and efforts to gain competitive advantage.

Notes

1   David B. Potts, *Wesleyan University, 1831–1910: Collegiate Enterprise in New England* (New Haven: Yale University Press, 1992). See also Louise W. Knight, "The Quails," (B.A. honors thesis, Wesleyan University, 1972). WUA, Louise Knight File. Wesleyan trustees had voted to admit women in 1871. Although the reversal of coeducation vote occurred in 1909, there were women finishing up their degrees at Wesleyan through 1911.

2   *Connecticut College for Women First Annual Announcement, 1915–1916* (New London, CT: Connecticut College for Women, 1915), 6-9.

3   Potts, *Wesleyan University, 1831–1910: Collegiate Enterprise in New England*. See also Knight, "The Quails."

4   Gertrude Noyes, *History of Connecticut College* (New London, CT: Connecticut College, 1982). See also Brian Rogers, "From the Beginning," In *Connecticut College: The Long View*, ed. Lisa

Brownell, William Mercer, Catherine Phinizy, and Brian Rogers (New London, CT: Connecticut College, 1999), 15–32; Irene Nye, *Chapters in the History of Connecticut College During the First Three Administrations, 1911–1942* (New London: Connecticut College, 1943).

5   Patricia Sullivan, "Rosemary Park: A Study of Educational Leadership During the Revolutionary Decades" (Ph.D. dissertation, Boston College, 1982).

6   The other prominent example is Douglass College of Rutgers University, launched by the clubwomen in New Jersey. See George P. Schmidt, *Douglass College: A History* (New Brunswick, NJ: Rutgers University Press, 1968).

7   William G. Bowen and Sarah A Levin, *Reclaiming the Game: College Sports and Educational Values* (Princeton, NJ: Princeton University Press, 2003), 39. The NESCAC colleges are Amherst, Bates, Bowdoin, Colby, Connecticut, Hamilton, Middlebury, Trinity, Tufts, and Wesleyan.

8   David Breneman, *Liberal Arts Colleges: Thriving, Surviving, or Endangered?* (Washington, DC: Brookings Institution, 1994). See also Hugh Hawkins, "The Making of the Liberal Arts College Identity," *Daedalus* (Winter 1999), 1–25.

9   Ibid. See also Michael Delucchi, "Liberal Arts" Colleges and the Myth of Uniqueness," *The Journal of Higher Education* (July-August 1997), 414–426; Michael S. McPherson & Morton O. Shapiro, "The Future Economic Challenges for the Liberal Arts Colleges," in *Distinctively American: The Residential Liberal Arts College*, ed. Steven Koblik & Stephen R. Graubard (New Brunswick, NJ: Transaction Publishers, 2000), 47–75.

10   Matthew Hartley, *A Call to Purpose: Mission-Centered Change at Three Liberal Arts Colleges* (New York: RoutledgeFalmer, 2002), 5.

11   Warren Bryan Martin, "Adaptiveness and Distinctiveness," *Journal of Higher Education* (March-April, 1984), 286–296.

12   Hartley, *A Call to Purpose*, 6.

13   Richard H. Hirsch, "Generating Ideals and Transforming Lives: A Contemporary Case for the Residential Liberal Arts College," in *Distinctively American: The Residential Liberal Arts College*, 173–194. See also McPherson & Shapiro, "The Future Economic Challenges for the Liberal Arts Colleges" and Paul Neely, "The Threats to Liberal Arts Colleges," in *Distinctively American: The Residential Liberal Arts College*, 27–45.

14   Hawkins, "The Making of the Liberal Arts College Identity." See also Neely, "The Threats to Liberal Arts Colleges."

15   John W. Creswell, *Educational Research: Planning, Conducting, and Evaluating Quantitative and Qualitative Research* (Upper Saddle River, NJ: Pearson/Merrill Prentice Hall (2nd ed.), 2005).

16   Robert Zemsky, Gregory R. Wegner, & William F. Massey, *Remaking The American University: Market-Smart And Mission-Centered* (New Brunswick, NJ: Rutgers University Press, 2005).

CHAPTER TWO

The Founding of Connecticut College for Women

The origin story of Connecticut College is that of a grassroots founding, the product of enthusiasm tied to a powerful idea: the belief that Connecticut, as the only New England state without one in 1911, needed a college option for women.[1] Propelled by that belief, Elizabeth Wright and the Hartford College Club "simply went ahead with unbounded confidence that an institution so badly needed must come, and that helpers would be raised up to make it a certainty."[2] The Hartford College Club, as Elizabeth Wright explained in 1911, intended "to awake public sentiment in favor of the new college and to find out whether influential people would help the movement."[3] One of those influential people Wright and her Hartford College Club awoke was Colin Buell, a New London schoolmaster who had long dreamed of a women's college in his hometown. In Buell's estimation, the members of the Hartford College Club were "women of great faith and vision," an inspired group that "made the thing work; perhaps as much to their own surprise as to that of many others."[4]

What spurred the grassroots movement that resulted in New London landing Connecticut College for Women? The single biggest factor was a 1909 decision by Wesleyan University in Middletown forty miles to the north. That year Wesleyan's trustees decided to stop enrolling women, with the result that Connecticut's remaining three colleges (Trinity College, Wesleyan, and Yale University) were for men only, a situation some called "a disgrace to the state."[5] Wesleyan's decision set in motion the events that led Elizabeth Wright, her fellow members of the Hartford College Club, Colin Buell, and New London civic leaders to collaborate in establishing Connecticut College for Women in 1911.[6]

The founding of Connecticut College for Women was more complex than it appears at first glance. Some have characterized Connecticut College for Women's founding as the righting of a wrong or the correcting of an injustice, because when the new institution opened in 1915, it filled a statewide need for women seeking higher education.[7] Others have labeled it a defensive or reactive founding—emphasizing that Connecticut College might not exist had Wesleyan not stopped educating women.[8] To be sure, the notion of a defensive or reactive college founding is not as attractive an origin story as the inspirational notion of a band of relatively ordinary women and one man, working tirelessly to create a college. There is no reason, save for the positive spin instinct of public relations, to choose whether to characterize the founding of Connecticut College as either the result of grassroots idealism (joined to local boosterism) or defensive activism; it was a mixture of both.

Understanding Connecticut College's founding requires knowing something about the prominent institutions that had shaped the local college landscape that the new college for women entered in 1911. Three men's colleges, Trinity, Wesleyan, and Yale, had long defined college in Connecticut, the former two especially in the small liberal arts bracket Connecticut College for Women joined. Of related interest are the roots of the colleges that now comprise the New England Small College Athletic Conference (NESCAC), in which Connecticut College competes and to which it has been compared since coeducation in 1969.[9] A later chapter (chapter four) examines Connecticut College for Women's founding place among the northeast's influential women's colleges.

The Influence of Yale University

At the time of Connecticut College for Women's founding in 1911, Trinity and Wesleyan were Connecticut's best-known small liberal arts colleges, but Yale University was known far beyond Connecticut, as it had established itself for a time in the early 19th century as America's leading university.[10] Already more than two hundred-years-old by the time of Connecticut College for Women's founding, Yale cast a big shadow that extended through Hartford, Middletown, and even to New London.

There is no evidence that Yale served as the founding model for Connecticut College the way the Ivy League men's colleges had for the Seven Sister women's colleges, such as Vassar and Wellesley. Yet Yale was influential during Connecticut College for Women's founding decade in a number of indirect but significant ways. The founders of Connecticut College for Women modeled its charter after that of Yale (and a similar charter at Trinity) to give the new college "the maximum privileges and exemptions due a higher education institution in the state of Connecticut."[11]

Perhaps Connecticut College for Women's charter reflected Yale's not just because Yale was the state's oldest college (founded in 1701), but also because the men with college degrees who served on Connecticut College's first board of trustees were Yale graduates.[12] Yale also figured prominently into Connecticut College for Women's founding due to the efforts of Yale alumnus Colin Buell, who took his long-held dream of a women's college for New London to his fellow sons of Yale, hoping to enlist them to contribute to the new college.[13] In letters and a Yale alumni magazine article he penned, Buell called upon "the patriotism and chivalry of Yale men," hoping his entreaty would "summon them to place a building on the campus of Connecticut College for Women to be called 'Yale Hall,' the gift of the eldest brother to the only sister."[14] The hoped-for Yale Hall never materialized, but Connecticut College, itself, might never have been born, and it certainly would not have come to be located in New London, without the efforts of Yale man Colin Buell.

Founding trustee and second board chair Frank Valentine Chappell attended Yale, as did his brother, whose architecture firm designed and constructed Connecticut College for Women's first buildings.[15] George S. Palmer, Yale 1878, chaired the New London fundraising campaign before becoming a member of Connecticut College for Women's first board of trustees.[16] Another Yale graduate and original Connecticut College trustee, Oliver Gildersleeve, visited America's "best colleges for women" from which he gathered "helpful suggestions and other interesting data" to assist the College's trustee committee on sites and campus plans.[17]

The lone academic on Connecticut College for Women's first board of trustees was not an official from Wesleyan or Trinity but Yale alumnus Henry P. Wright, the former Dean of Yale College.[18] Dean Wright chaired the trustee committee that admitted Connecticut College for Women's first class.[19] Due to Dean Wright's presence and the many Yale alumni connections, Connecticut College for Women's earliest trustee meetings were held in New Haven on the Yale campus. For example, an April 1911 letter from Colin Buell confirmed that a meeting of the organizers of Thames College was to occur in Osborn Hall at Yale University on April 29 at 2:15 p.m.[20]

In terms of alumni affiliation, the two institutions that had the most influence on the new college were Yale, whose alumnus Colin Buell devoted his life to female education as head of New London's Williams Memorial Institute, then later served on one of the incorporators and original board members of Connecticut College for Women, and Wesleyan, through its disenfranchised female graduates, such as Elizabeth Wright (class of 1897). The fact that so many Yale alumni helped steward its origins suggests that implicitly Connecticut College for Women was as much the distaff counterpart to Yale as it was to Wesleyan or Trinity.

The city of New London had something the other towns in Connecticut lacked, a committed advocate for women's higher education, Colin Buell. Aside from Elizabeth Wright, no individual did more to make Connecticut College for Women a reality than Buell. Buell is widely credited as the originator of the idea of a women's college for New London, the first person who "planted the seed of Connecticut College which germinated" and "grew into a more or less conscious belief that New London would some day possess such an institution."[21] Buell's position as principal of Williams Memorial Institute (WMI), a New London secondary school for girls, made him keenly aware of the need for a women's college for Connecticut. His desire for a women's college for New London originated in 1891, fully twenty years before the founding of Connecticut College for Women.[22] His hope had been for a college that graduates of his Williams Memorial Institute could attend, perhaps even one attached to the Institute itself.[23]

When Colin Buell and Elizabeth Wright discovered in 1910 that they were of like minds, neither was to be denied in making the dream of establishing a college for women in Connecticut come true.

Several years before Wesleyan University "closed its doors to the girls," Buell had asserted at the 1894 WMI commencement that a women's college for Connecticut was needed, inevitable, and something the city of New London should seek to attract.[24] Buell considered it an embarrassment that Massachusetts had "five colleges for women while Connecticut has none."[25] He hoped that the people of his native nutmeg state would "remedy their defect" and "repair the breach in their walls" by turning to the "'Old Harbor Town'" of New

Figure 2.1. Colin Buell

London as "the choicest place for the location of a [women's] college."[26] Buell believed that New London's strategic location, "almost equally distant from Barnard, Smith, Mt. Holyoke, Wellesley, and Radcliffe," made it the ideal spot in the state of Connecticut for a women's college.[27] Prior to the convergence of Buell's grand dreams for New London with Elizabeth Wright's initiatives on behalf of the Hartford College Club, Buell made several failed attempts to secure a benefactor to finance his dreamed-of women's college.[28] At one point, he even found a financier (Mrs. J.N. Harris), who agreed to fund the expansion of WMI into a women's college.[29] Mrs. Harris' offer was contingent on approval of a charter change by WMI's trustees.[30] That charter change never happened. Buell forever lamented the fact that "petty jealousy on the part of well-meaning but misguided individuals set the plan back and the capitalist [Harris] died soon after, before any definite action had been secured."[31]

Buell further claimed that he and a wealthy New Londoner, Sebastian Lawrence, outlined a plan in 1907 for a women's college, agreeing that it "should not bear the name of any one person, but should be called "Connecticut College for Women."[32] Buell claimed that he and Lawrence wrote down the plan and submitted a request for funds to the Rockefeller Foundation's General Education Board (GEB).[33] The GEB denied that request.[34] Buell lost the request letter, but claims to have given the denial letter to Connecticut College, a copy of which I did not find in the Connecticut College Archives—although I did find the GEB's 1910 denial letter to Elizabeth Wright (which made no reference to a previous request by Buell).[35] Whatever the case, Sebastian Lawrence eventually concluded that Buell's plan for a women's college in New London was "magnificent, but it can't be done, it will cost too much."[36]

Figures 2.2. & 2.3. Elizabeth Wright

After meeting each other in 1910, Buell and Wright worked tirelessly to raise funds for the proposed college. Buell exhorted New London officials and residents to show the state, the Hartford College Club's planning committee (chaired by Wright), and the world that their city was the best place for the new college. Enthusiasm was so high that residents of New London surpassed the $100,000 goal, raising nearly $135,000. Newspaper articles, books, and the College's own descriptions of its founding tell tales of children raiding their piggybanks and working-class men and women contributing a few dollars in hopes that their daughters might someday go to the new college.[37]

Figure 2.4. Morton Plant

The unexpected outpouring of funds by New Londoners impressed and surprised the Hartford College Club's planning committee, which had been waiting for its home city to make a bid. New London upstaged Hartford and closed the deal by providing not only $135,000 but also a hilltop tract of land with a view of the historic former whaling port and Long Island Sound. As a result, the Connecticut Legislature chartered Thames College in 1911. Within a year, the fledgling women's college had secured one million dollars in funds for endowment from a wealthy summer resident of New London, Morton Plant, and had changed its name to Connecticut College for Women—to emphasize its importance to its home state and to honor the wishes of Plant.[38]

In recognition of the generosity of its home city, Connecticut College for Women's founding board of trustees chose to name one of the three original campus buildings New London Hall. The new college adopted as its seal a depiction of a tree and a body of water framed by the Latin motto of *Tanquam lignum quod plantatum est secus decursus aquarum* (Like a tree planted by rivers of waters that bringeth forth its fruit in its season)—symbols acknowledging the institution's local environs: the picturesque view of Long Island Sound from campus, and the college grounds donated by and purchased from New London residents.[39]

Despite the vigorous and successful efforts of Yale alumnus Colin Buell, it would not be accurate to say that Yale, as an institution, took anything but a curious interest in Connecticut College for Women. Yale's highest official, for example, discouraged Elizabeth Wright when she contacted him on behalf of the Hartford College Club. President Arthur Twining Hadley of Yale told Elizabeth Wright in a letter dated April 16, 1910, that he disapproved of her plans to mount a public subscription program to fund her proposed women's college.[40] Citing his "good deal of experience about the conditions under which money can or cannot be raised," Hadley advised Wright and her fellow clubwomen to wait to canvass publicly for donations until they had raised at least one million dollars privately.[41] Because Wright's public fundraising plan seemed to him premature, Hadley further predicted that it and the whole venture to establish a women's college in Connecticut would fail.[42]

Elizabeth Wright and her Hartford College Club, thus, regarded Yale primarily as a source of funds and a powerful endorser of the women's college idea. Yale was a potential generous rich and powerful uncle to the proposed women's college. Wright and the Hartford College Club sought Yale's approval and moral support just as they sought and received the same from Connecticut's governor, congressmen, senators, and state DAR chapters.[43] For example, Wright boasted in a 1910 report to the Hartford College Club that the *Yale Daily News* "is ready at any time to write up the subject" of the proposed women's college; and despite his letter to the contrary, said that President Hadley of Yale endorsed the project.[44] But it was individual Yale alumni, like Colin Buell, rather than the institution itself, that ended up providing vital energy to make the proposed college grow from dream to reality.

Elizabeth Wright recognized the potential import of her dream and thus was undeterred by President Hadley's condescending paternalistic rebuke. Reading between the lines of Hadley's letter to Wright, it is not difficult to imagine that sure-of-himself guardian of the established male elite chuckling condescendingly at what he saw as the ill-informed actions of a clumsy woman. Wright's letter from Hadley, like the responses she received from the Rockefeller Foundation and its General Education Board, show that the wealth behind American higher education in the earliest decades of the twentieth century was at best indifferent to and at worst dismissive of her drive to establish a woman's college. In a March 25, 1910, letter to Elizabeth Wright, Wallace Buttrick, Secretary of the Rockefeller Fund of the General Education Board, explained that "The General Education Board has repeatedly declined to participate in the founding of new institutions."[45] On many levels such attitudes exemplify the underdog status of women and the lack of respect accorded to an enterprising woman, like Wright, in the America of 1911. In other ways having nothing to do with gender discrimination, the lack of enthusiasm Elizabeth Wright encountered as she canvassed among the elites was not surprising. Almost no colleges up to that time had been founded without the backing of at least one of the following: a fortune with a namesake benefactor, a church or denomination, a state appropriation, or a devoted group of civic leaders.

The Founding of Trinity and Wesleyan's "Experiment" in Coeducation

If Yale was Connecticut College for Women's indifferent uncle, then Wesleyan and Trinity were its brothers. Elizabeth Wright's letters on behalf of the Hartford

College Club indicate that each of the three institutions showed some interest in having the proposed women's college serve as a coordinate college in the Radcliffe College of Harvard University model.[46] Despite that interest, the Hartford College Club never considered the coordinate college idea very seriously.[47]

Certainly Wright's alma mater, Wesleyan, and Trinity—her hometown college—were well known to the Hartford College Club and perhaps closer referents, in envisioning a new liberal arts college for women, than the university model of Yale.[48] Over the course of Connecticut College's history and development, particularly following coeducation when the College joined the New England Small College Athletic Conference (NESCAC), Connecticut has been grouped with and compared against Trinity and Wesleyan.[49] Officials in Hartford, Middletown, and New London were also competitors long before the founding of NESCAC.

The city of New London, for example, vied, along with Middletown and Hartford to be the location of what became Connecticut's second college—Washington College, later named Trinity.[50] The location decision for Trinity came down to Hartford versus Middletown, with Hartford pledging more of the $30,000 sought by the planners to establish the Episcopalian college.[51] The losing cities of New London and Norwich were quite bitter about that choice; as a result Eastern Connecticut became an especially infertile region for fundraising by Trinity's first president, Bishop Thomas Brownell.[52] Although nearly ninety years would pass before Connecticut College for Women's founding, it is arguable that some memory of and shame over losing Trinity lingered in New London when the Hartford College Club was searching for a site for its proposed women's college.

Less than a decade after losing Trinity College to Hartford, Middletown landed a college of its own. Wesleyan University, founded in 1831 by Methodists and community leaders, used as its early campus the abandoned buildings in Middletown left by a defunct military academy.[53] The all-male Wesleyan began conferring degrees in 1833.[54] Some thirty years later, primarily due to enrollment declines and challenging economic conditions in post-Civil War America, Wesleyan turned to Methodist organizations for support.[55] Always at least somewhat Methodist in character, Wesleyan became even more Methodist in 1870, when it changed its charter to bring it under denominational control.[56] The new charter required Wesleyan's president and a majority of its faculty members and trustees to be Methodists.[57] The transformed Wesleyan became a Methodist institution dedicated to providing liberal education in service to church and country.[58] Wesleyan began to think of itself less as a New England college and instead as the only college in America where Methodists could get proper training.[59]

Women had no college option in Connecticut until 1872 when four women entered Wesleyan University.[60] A number of factors influenced Wesleyan to admit women. For one, its newer Methodist counterparts in the northeast, Boston University and Syracuse University, had chosen coeducation.[61] Boston University's President William Warren asserted that it was time for the idea of higher education for men only to be "retired to the museum of pedagogical paleontology."[62] Other New England colleges, such as Bates and Colby (and later Middlebury in 1883), had recently adopted coeducation to forestall declines in application quality and enrollment as well as to address financial strains similar to the ones Wesleyan was experiencing.[63] In addition, Wesleyan's president, Joseph Cummings, had become interested in coeducation after hearing Oberlin College's President James Fairchild speak of its benefits at a conference in 1867.[64] Wesleyan officials subsequently investigated the feasibility of coeducation, then moved in 1869 toward decisions that led to the enrollment three years later of the four women who became Wesleyan's first female students.[65] Hartford College Club leader Elizabeth Wright, an 1897 graduate, attended Wesleyan as a result of the turn to coeducation.[66]

Coeducation never achieved wide acceptance at Wesleyan. Male students, alumni, and not a small number of faculty members resented the presence of women, feeling that coeducation had been foisted upon them by a misguided administration.[67] The "older graduates" who had attended Wesleyan before coeducation were bothered by the presence of women; in their opinion, coeducation had brought a "general loosening of moral restraint in the student life" of the campus.[68] Numerous influential Wesleyan faculty members also found coeducation "Undesirable in general or...undesirable under the special conditions of Wesleyan University."[69] Wesleyan men found especially troublesome the fact that the women won a disproportionate share of the academic honors—the same thing occurred at Middlebury following coeducation.[70] Louise Knight's 1972 undergraduate honors thesis further notes that Wesleyan men seen talking to Wesleyan women were beaten, that women were barred from campus clubs, and that women's pictures were not allowed in the University's yearbook.[71] Lecture halls found women sitting on one side of the room, men on the other.[72]

Wesleyan men were not alone in their hostility to women students. Opposition to coeducation resulted at Wesleyan and elsewhere from the belief that the presence of women downgraded a formerly male institution.[73] In the early decades of the twentieth century, such anxiety about the feminization of American culture was not uncommon, even in supposedly enlightened spaces such as college campuses.[74] For example, as female enrollment rose at Iowa's Grinnell College, fear that the campus would be feminized resulted in segregation of the women into separate housing and social organizations.[75] Similar fears led Stanford University to freeze female enrollment at 500, Boston University to launch a "More Men Movement," Middlebury students to start a club to discourage coeducation, and the University of California at Berkeley to provide separate, compensatory facilities and organizations for women.[76]

Figure 2.5. Women students at Wesleyan, 1896

It was no surprise, then, when Wesleyan's trustees voted in 1909 to cease co-education. That trustee decision came to be known as the "vote of exclusion."[77] According to the trustee vote, the class of 1913 was to be the last Wesleyan class to include women.[78] Officials, such as William North Rice—an 1865 graduate of Wesleyan and a geology professor who had served as acting president from 1907 to 1909—cited as justification for reversing course "symptoms of a tendency adverse to coeducation" in the colleges of the Middle West and a strong sentiment against coeducation at the other colleges in New England.[79] Rice may have been referring to the movements toward separation at Grinnell and Oberlin, problems at Boston University and Middlebury, and the fact that Amherst and Williams, for example, had recently reaffirmed their all-male status.[80]

The presence of just three women in the 1909 Wesleyan freshman class that numbered 104 in full led William North Rice to speculate that the situation for those three women must be "decidedly disagreeable."[81] Referring to the alumnae that had preceded the three brave female freshmen of 1909, Rice chafed at the thought that Wesleyan's move out of coeducation would in effect "disinherit two hundred of the very best of our children."[82] Rice made it clear that he sympathized with the women students of Wesleyan but that he also believed it was unwise to continue the failed coeducation experiment, even if it meant that Wesleyan would be "the only college in the world that ha[d] once admitted women and then closed its doors against them."[83]

Rice may not have known that Princeton University had abandoned its short-lived college for women (Evelyn) before the end of the 19th century.[84]

Even as they voted to end coeducation, the Wesleyan trustees endorsed the idea of establishing a coordinate college for women alongside its men's college and pledged to establish one as soon as "the money therfor (sic) could be obtained."[85] Wesleyan's move toward a coordinate women's college paralleled a similar attempt—but one that failed due to insufficient funds—just a few years earlier (1902) at Middlebury.[86] Wesleyan's trustees and President Shanklin further stated that establishing a coordinate women's college was not financially feasible unless "a considerable sum of money can be got to start the thing."[87] Wesleyan's leadership, according to Professor Rice, was especially concerned that the women's college have "a solid financial basis" with "no risk of its collapsing after being once started."[88]

Some Wesleyan officials and faculty, such as Professor Rice, even hoped for a "transition from the one arrangement [coeducation] to the other [a coordinate college] without any break."[89] Rice himself strongly favored coeducation in general as well as for Wesleyan, but he recognized that the coordinate women's college idea was the most politically palatable solution in 1909 for the University.[90] In response to the many women writing letters critical of Wesleyan's "vote of exclusion," Professor Rice emphasized that Wesleyan's board of trustees had not just stated their approval of the coordinate women's college idea but had additionally voted to create a committee of seven trustees and five faculty members to investigate the feasibility of establishing one.[91]

The closing of Wesleyan's doors to women inflamed Elizabeth Wright and her fellow alumnae, so much so that Wright and the Hartford College Club launched its women's college campaign soon after Wesleyan's announcement. William North Rice actually contacted Wright in 1910, on behalf of President Shanklin, to broach the possibility of locating in Middletown, alongside Wesleyan, the new women's college that the Hartford College Club was proposing.[92] In his letter to Elizabeth Wright, Professor Rice emphasized that Wesleyan's trustees, as well as the "coeducationalists and anticoeducationalists" on the University's faculty, were strongly in favor of a coordinate women's college and had approved a resolution and formed a committee to establish one "as soon as the necessary funds are provided."[93] Wesleyan was ready, according to Rice, to offer use of its library, museum, and "other [unspecified] educational facilities" to help establish a coordinate women's college.[94] Rice further suggested that "It would also be practicable, to a considerable extent, for the same instructors to teach in the two institutions."[95]

Rice's offer on behalf of Wesleyan had one major catch. Wesleyan would provide no money of its own to help establish a coordinate women's college. President Shanklin, Rice explained, was engaged in persuading Wesleyan alumni to contribute to a campaign to raise $1 million to meet the terms of a challenge grant from the Rockefeller Foundation's General Education Board.[96] To establish a coordinate women's college would require at least $400,000 according to the calculations of Wesleyan's trustees.[97] But Rice made it clear to Wright that the $400,000 in needed funds would have to "come from parties outside of the constituency to which the President will naturally appeal for the general endowment."[98]

Recognizing that Rice was saying that Wesleyan wanted a women's college but would only establish one if the new college could bring its own money, Wright rejected Professor Rice's overture.[99] In turning down Rice, Wright used strong language that indicated that she and other alumnae of Wesleyan still smarted from the slights they endured at alma mater.[100] What guarantee, Wright asked, could Wesleyan give that after a few years it "would not vote to abolish the co-ordinate college and devote to other purposes the money raised for that object?"[101] What assurances, Wright wondered, could

Figure 2.6. William North Rice

Wesleyan offer that "the girls of the new college would be protected from the sort of treatment which women students during the past few years have endured at the hands of the [male] undergraduates?"[102] And even if the hazing of women ceased, would the women of the new coordinate college get to "share in the scholarships, prizes, honors, privileges, etc" of Wesleyan that had been denied Wright and her sister alumnae of the University?[103] Wright was skeptical.

The general public sentiment, Wright told Rice, was "not in favor of a coordinate college."[104] To be persuasive, Wesleyan would need, in Wright's estimation, "a very attractive offer—something more than library and museum privileges.[105] Trinity and Yale, she asserted (embellishing the truth—in the case of Yale—to her advantage), are "both ready to furnish these, and beautiful sites, one over *a mile* long, have been offered near these colleges."[106] In closing her letter to Rice, Wright could not pass up the opportunity to scold Wesleyan for its past mistreatment of women, telling him that "Wesleyan should endeavor, for its own good, to create a better public sentiment in the matter."[107] Wright's emphatic no to Rice must have been cathartic, as it slammed the door shut on Wesleyan just like the University had done earlier to her and other women. Wright and her fellow Hartford College Club members decided that the amount of money Wesleyan wanted for a coordinate women's college would be better invested in a new college, one that would put women at its center, not off to the side.

The "Booster College" and Connecticut College for Women

Most American colleges were from the beginning local institutions, designed for and supported by their home communities.[108] Community-driven initiative resulted in what could be called the enterprise college founding, that is, the phenomenon of colleges established to boost the growth and development of newly settled towns as America moved west. The American college was often a frontier college, an expression of the aspirations of newly settled or growing towns.[109] Numerous colleges can trace their location back to an initial subsidy or a donation of property from its founding town.[110] Colleges were considered an asset that would attract settlers to frontier towns; thus, practically every community wanted one.[111]

A fundamental element in college founding in the 19th century, particularly in the story of sectarian colleges, was the alliance forged between the promoters of the college and the leaders of the town or county.[112] Here is where piety often joined with the profit motive.[113] College promoters and church leaders usually agreed to locate the college in a particular community in return for the promise that its members would raise a sum of money.[114] Such colleges often began with an offer of land and the quid pro quo understanding that both college and town would benefit.[115] The resulting colleges became community enterprises, interwoven into the fabric of the town, tied closely to local, cultural, and economic ambitions.[116] The town and nearby communities supplied a large percentage of the students, local residents attended college events, and townspeople contributed to operating expenses, construction of buildings, and endowment funds.[117] The community-focused booster colleges, which ranged from Bates and Williams in New England to Carleton, Grinnell, and Oberlin in the Midwest, widely dispersed cultural resources, increased public demand for higher education, and brought with them great expectations that they would become, even more so than the church, the center of religious enlightenment and culture for the community.[118]

The founding of Connecticut College mirrored that of the 19th century booster college in a number of ways.[119] In a real sense, the institution was New London's college. The vast majority of Connecticut College's students over the early decades came from within its home state, helping fulfill its founding promise. Like the booster colleges, most of the members of Connecticut College for Women's first board of trustees were local businessmen and prominent city officials, including the mayor of New London.[120] Like the booster colleges, Connecticut College for Women represented the grand dreams of town officials and promoters—as new or ambitious towns, like New London, pinned their hopes on the allure of a college that might bestow on the community the aura of Athens, Rome, or Oxford.[121]

Luring, or founding a college, like Connecticut College for Women, tended to elevate a town's stature and boost its civic pride.[122] Because colleges promised to attract students, educate the local workforce, and bring economic benefit to the region, rival communities fought to land new colleges.[123] Elizabeth Wright showed that she knew this when she speculated to her fellow members of the Hartford College Club "that almost any town in the state would be willing to offer a suitable site for the sake of the advantages to the town of having such a college located in it."[124] Wright was prescient. The idea of a women's college for Connecticut generated much enthusiasm across the state. Twenty towns and cities competed to be the location, offering campus sites and money. The Connecticut towns that campaigned for the proposed women's college, including Berlin, Gildersleeve, Hartford, Meriden, Middletown, New London, Rockville, Waterford, West Hartford, and Willimantic.[125]

The forces that led New London to respond so readily and generously with donations arose from a classic booster belief stated by Colin Buell in a 1910 letter to *The* (New London) *Day*.[126] Buell exhorted his fellow citizens of New London to act, because "the town which secures this proposed institution will at once be placed on the high road to prosperity and greatness."[127] Echoing the civic-minded champions of the 19th century booster colleges, Buell called upon New Londoners to "wake up and go after it [the proposed college], for a college is not going to beg New London, or any other place, to take it in out of the cold."[128] Buell has also been credited as the person most responsible for initiating and cultivating Morton Plant's $1 million gift that endowed the fledgling women's college.[129]

Civic leaders were eager to land the proposed college. Reports by Elizabeth Wright to the Hartford College Club cite interest from businessmen's associations in Meriden and West Hartford, the Connecticut Farmer's League, and the Willimantic board of trade.[130] New London, for example, appointed a committee to make its case to Wright's Hartford College Club. Writing on behalf of that committee in November 1910, New London mayor Bryan Mahan outlined nineteen reasons why his city should be chosen as the location of Connecticut's women's college.[131] New London, according to Mahan, was willing to offer $50,000 and 280 acres (land later estimated by Colin Buell to have been worth $115,000) for the proposed college's site.[132] Mahan also cited New London's pleasant climate, historic neighborhoods, the fact that numerous wealthy families called the city home, and its proximity to New Haven, Providence, and the established women's colleges of the East.[133] Underlying Mayor Mahan's push to draw the proposed women's college to New London was the implicit assumption that winning out over rival towns would help restore civic pride in a city that had been declining since the whaling era.[134]

Booster colleges were more likely to land in towns that had, as Colin Buell said about New London, "a strong undercurrent of ambition for better and greater things."[135] Behind every booster college were true believers convinced that their town was as significant as the larger towns in the region and would be even more significant if it was to land a college. Boosters were frequently indefatigable promoters like Buell, whose fundraising drive motivated 6,000 people from a city of 19,500 to make donations.[136] That level of participation alone could not have failed to impress upon the Hartford College Club that New London was a worthy, if not the superior, location for the new college.

New London's success at securing Connecticut College for Women indeed owed much to the galvanizing fund drive that Buell devised. In a move that must have seemed as risky as it was bold, Buell proposed to secure $100,000 for the proposed college in ten days.[137] To do so, Buell formed an executive committee of five leaders, a citizens committee of ten, and a campaign committee of eleven teams, each headed by a captain who selected five members to solicit funds.[138] At two o'clock each afternoon of the ten-day fund drive, the committee posted up-to-date results on a 24-foot-wide clock and a 30-foot-high thermometer.[139] Following each posting of new and higher tallies, the campaign organizers would sound the city's fire alarm for all to hear.[140] The announcement on the tenth day that the campaign had exceeded its goal by $35,000 inspired a "monstrous celebration," during which officials at the nearby fort fired an 18-gun salute and campaign workers, donors, and other celebrants paraded triumphantly through downtown New London.[141]

"Securing the college was not the only result of the campaign," according to Colin Buell.[142] Buell saw other benefits for his city, noting that "a new civic pride had been awakened; a new city spirit had been born; a new unity of purpose had been engendered."[143] Connecticut College for Women's first descriptive brochure cited as the new institution's "most valuable asset the attitude of New London people toward the college."[144] "The New London people," according to the brochure, "have shown a spirit of good will towards the college which is bound to make it a grand success."[145]

Although Morton Plant intended his $1 million gift that endowed and named Connecticut College for Women as a way to give something lasting to his adopted city of New London, the motives of college boosters were not always based just on giving back to the community or promoting their town's fortunes. Economic self-interest was often part of the calculation. More often than not, boosters saw an opportunity to line their own pockets through contracts with the colleges. This happened in Connecticut College for Women's case with the

Chappell family that included Alfred H. Chappell, a founding incorporator, and his son, Frank Valentine Chappell, the institution's second board chair.[146] In its first decade of operation, the new college became a source of revenue for the Chappell businesses.[147] The Chappell architecture firm, operated by Alfred's son and Frank's brother, for example, designed and constructed the campus. The Chappell coal company supplied the College's fuel for many years. These kinds of entanglements of the early trustees in College affairs displeased Connecticut College's first president, Frederick Sykes, culminating in a conflict that led to Sykes' removal by the board in 1917—a story described in the following chapter.[148]

Several other original trustees of Connecticut College for Women, such as Frank Palmer and William Reeves, not to mention Mayor Bryan Mahan, had interests in New London business and civic agendas.[149] Even Elizabeth Wright and Colin Buell profited personally from the new college: Wright with a sinecure for herself as bursar as well as a position for her sister, Mary.[150] Both Wrights retired from the College after more than thirty years of service. Colin Buell held the post of trustee secretary of Connecticut College until his death in 1938.[151] Buell also served as a member of the College's first faculty, teaching the one mathematics course offered at Connecticut during 1915–1916.[152] Fittingly, Buell's mathematics class met on the fourth floor of New London Hall, the building that had been constructed to commemorate the $135,000 fund drive that he led to establish the College.[153] Buell routinely showed up to teach math at Connecticut, or to attend faculty meetings, after working a full day at Williams Memorial Institute, where he served as principal from 1891 until 1937.[154] It was during an early Connecticut faculty meeting that Buell proposed the first system used at the College for keeping class records.[155] For his service and devotion, Connecticut College awarded Buell an honorary Master of Arts degree in 1935. The Williams Memorial Institute honored Buell by naming a building for him in 1934.

Characterizing the Founding of Connecticut College

To the extent that New London leaders campaigned against more than a dozen rival Connecticut towns, and its townspeople contributed $134,000 to secure what became Connecticut College for Women, the College's founding exhibited elements of boosterism. In other respects, Connecticut College for Women's founding did not fit the booster pattern. Booster colleges generally popped up where the idea for them originated, and their founding usually fulfilled the dreams of leaders in one particular town. The founding of Connecticut College for Women, on the other hand, filled a need for the women of a whole state. The idea of the college germinated in not one but in two places: in New London in the mind of Colin Buell, and in West Hartford in the minds of Elizabeth Wright and her fellow members of the Hartford College Club.

If Connecticut College for Women was a booster college, it was one that boosted its whole state nearly as much as its hometown. That is not the general booster pattern, which tended to be more specific to a single community. What fit the booster pattern, however, was the process of selecting the location for Connecticut College for Women. The competition that occurred between Connecticut towns mirrored the 19th century booster college founding pattern, as New London officials, such as Mayor Bryan Mahan, believed that the new college would enhance the economic fortunes and future development prospects for their city.

Unlike so many of its peer colleges, Connecticut College for Women did not get founded as a monument to a major benefactor.[156] Morton Plant's $1 million endowment gift made a huge difference for the fledgling college, but it was not the equivalent in sustaining largesse that had stood behind colleges such as Vassar, whose founder, millionaire brewer Matthew Vassar, aspired in 1861 to create a "monument more lasting than the pyramids."[157] From the beginning, Connecticut College for Women was a tuition-driven institution. Connecticut College and New London officials also knew that the College had needed its home city for support in getting started, and thus could not adopt an aloof and haughty self-sufficient cast from atop its campus hill.

Had Morton Plant donated considerably more than $1 million, Connecticut College might have experienced a transformation in resources that would have put it on par with wealthier institutions such as Vassar. There is, in fact, a tale, perhaps an apocryphal one, that says a Mrs. Harkness (of the Harkness fortune) offered a substantial sum to the College in the 1930s on the condition that it move its campus to her estate in Waterford.[158] Katharine Blunt, Connecticut's third president, refused the offer, attracting instead from Mrs. Harkness a donation to build the College's chapel. The Harkness property eventually became a Connecticut State Park, and the bulk of the Harkness family fortune went to Yale.

In its non-sectarian aspect, Connecticut College for Women diverged from the local-in-character 19th century college. Lack of religious ties made Connecticut College for Women an anomaly in comparison not just to Trinity, Wesleyan, and Yale but also when compared to its other New England small college peers: Amherst (Congregational), Bates (Baptist), Bowdoin (Congregational), Colby (Baptist), Middlebury (Congregational), Trinity (Episcopal), Wesleyan (Methodist), and Williams (Congregational).[159] Even the Seven Sister colleges were religious in character, if not explicitly tied to a denomination.[160] Vassar had Baptist leanings. Quakers founded Bryn Mawr. The Unitarianism of the evangelical Henry Durant shaped the early character of Wellesley. The pious Sophia Smith established Smith College in consultation with her minister. And its Episcopal brother institution, Columbia, influenced Barnard's founding ideals, as did its indefatigable Jewish early promoter, Annie Meyer Nathan.[161]

Yet by the time of Connecticut College for Women's founding, some of the denominational linkages were weakening in New England. At Wesleyan, greater academic specialization, including the rise of science, combined with alumni and trustee influence from New York, drew the University away from Methodism.[162] In 1907 Wesleyan altered its charter to prevent denominational tests for trustees, officers, and faculty.[163] Ironically, Wesleyan's movement away from conservative and controlling Methodism coincided with its cessation of coeducation.

The founding of Connecticut College for Women does not fit neatly into the traditional founding patterns in American higher education. It was not a church-related founding, not a monument to an individual, not an attempt to prove women intellectually worthy of men, and not a coordinate women's branch of an established men's college. In many respects, Connecticut College's founding resembled the booster college pattern. But while the process of founding Connecticut College had clear booster elements, it would be inaccurate to categorize it as just a booster college. The idea that launched Connecticut College came instead from the non-commercial, idealistic, social justice tradition of righting past wrongs and providing options for underserved, underdog elements of society. In merging boosterism with equality and access, Connecticut College's founding represented a distinctive origin model.

Notes

1 Elizabeth C. Wright, "Report on Women's College to the Hartford College Club" (May 14, 1910). CCA, Elizabeth Wright File.

2 Colin S. Buell, "Thames College, A College for Women to be Located in New London, Connecticut" (no date, estimated 1911). CCA, Colin Buell File.

3 Elizabeth C. Wright to Mr. Nelson Wild (July 1911). CCA, Elizabeth Wright File.

4 Colin Buell, "Rome Was Not Built in a Day" (1915). CCA, Colin Buell File.

5 Elizabeth C. Wright, "A College for Women in Connecticut: Report to the Hartford College Club" (July 1910). Connecticut College Archives (hereafter identified as CCA), Elizabeth Wright File.

6 Noyes, *History of Connecticut College*. See also Irene Nye, *Chapters in the History of Connecticut College*.

7 Jane Bredeson (23 January 2007), Lisa Brownell (22 January 2007), Torrey Fenton (24 April 2007), interviews by author (interviews in possession of author).

8 Frances Hoffmann, interview by author 12 June 2007 (interview in possession of author).

9 The NESCAC colleges are Amherst, Bates, Bowdoin, Colby, Connecticut, Hamilton, Middlebury, Trinity, Tufts, and Wesleyan. Discussed in Bowen and Levin, *Reclaiming the Game: College Sports and Educational Values*.

10 Donald Tewksbury, *The Founding of American Colleges and Universities Before the Civil War* (New York: Archon, 1965). See also John R. Thelin, *A History of American Higher Education* (Baltimore: Johns Hopkins University Press, 2004).

11 Elizabeth C. Wright to Colin Buell (12 March 1911). CCA, Elizabeth Wright File. Histories of Connecticut College by Noyes and others always note the similarity of Connecticut's charter to Yale's, but fail to mention that Trinity's charter also emulated Yale's--perhaps another example of Connecticut gaining stature by selective association with quality and prestige.

12 Trustee Files of Colin Buell, F.V. Chappell, Oliver Gildersleeve, George S. Palmer, and Henry P. Wright. CCA.

13 Colin S. Buell, "Thames College: An Account of the Struggle by a Yale Graduate to Found a Woman's College in Connecticut," *Yale Alumni Weekly* (21 April 1911), 751. CCA, Colin Buell File.

14 Colin S. Buell, "Letter of Appeal to Fellow Graduates of Yale" (March 1914). CCA, Colin Buell File.

15 "Frank Valentine Chappell, Former Regatta Day Chief, Is Dead at the Age of 86," *The Day* (19 February 1962). CCA, F.V. Chappell File.

16 Buell, "Thames College: An Account of the Struggle by a Yale Graduate to Found a Woman's College in Connecticut."

17 *The Connecticut College for Women* (New London, CT: Connecticut College for Women, 1911), 10.

18 Noyes, *History of Connecticut College*.

19 Nye, *Chapters in the History of Connecticut College*, 25.

20 Colin S. Buell to Edward D. Robbins (21 April 1911). CCA, Colin Buell File.

21 Colin S. Buell, "Rome Was Not Built in a Day" (1915). See also "Prof. Colin S. Buell, '77, Dies; Principal of W.M.I. and Connecticut College Trustee," *The Day* (31 January 1938). CCA, Colin Buell File.

22 Buell, "Thames College, A College for Women to be Located in New London, Connecticut." See also Buell, "Thames College: An Account of the Struggle by a Yale Graduate to Found a Woman's College in Connecticut," 751.

23 Buell, "Rome Was Not Built in a Day."

24 Colin S. Buell, "New London Should Try to Bring College Here," *The Day* (13 September 1910). CCA, Colin Buell File.

25 Buell, "Thames College, A College for Women to be Located in New London, Connecticut."

26 Ibid.

27 Ibid.

28 Ibid.

29 Buell, "Rome Was Not Built in a Day."

30 Ibid.

31 Buell, "Thames College, A College for Women to be Located in New London, Connecticut."

32 Buell, "Rome Was Not Built in a Day."

33 Ibid.

34 Ibid.

35 Ibid.

36 Ibid.

37 Nye, *Chapters in the History of Connecticut College*. See also Noyes, *History of Connecticut College*.

38 Ibid.

39 Ibid.

40 Arthur Twining Hadley to Elizabeth C. Wright (16 April 1910). CCA, Elizabeth Wright File.

41 Ibid.

42 Ibid.

43 Wright, "Report on Women's College to Hartford College Club." See also Governor Frank Weeks to Elizabeth C. Wright (13 May 1910). CCA, Elizabeth Wright File; Buell, "New London Should Try to Bring College Here."

44 Wright, "Report on Women's College to Hartford College Club."

45   Wallace Buttrick to Elizabeth Wright (25 March 1910) CCA, Elizabeth Wright File. See also
     Starr J. Murphy to Elizabeth Wright (22 March 1910), CCA, Elizabeth Wright File. Murphy,
     an assistant to John D. Rockefeller, referred Miss Wright's plea for funds for the proposed
     "women's college in Connecticut" to the General Education Board.

46   Elizabeth C. Wright to Professor William North Rice of Wesleyan (26 July 1910), CCA, Eliza-
     beth Wright File.

47   Ibid.

48   Noyes, *History of Connecticut College*. See also Nye, *Chapters in the History of Connecticut Col-
     lege*; Wright, "Report on Women's College to Hartford College Club."

49   Bowen and Levin, *Reclaiming the Game: College Sports and Educational Values*, 39.

50   Ibid.

51   Ibid.

52   Ibid.

53   Rudolph, *The American College and University*. See also Potts, *Wesleyan University, 1831-1910*.

54   Tewksbury, *The Founding of American Colleges and Universities Before the Civil War*.

55   George Peterson, *The New England College in the Age of the University* (Amherst, MA: Am-
     herst College Press, 1964).

56   Ibid. See also Potts, *Wesleyan University, 1831–1910*.

57   Ibid.

58   Ibid.

59   Peterson, *The New England College in the Age of the University*.

60   Ibid. See also Knight, "The Quails."

61   Ibid.

62   Rosalind Rosenberg, "The Limits of Access: The History of Coeducation in America," in
     Women and Higher Education in American History, ed. John Mack Faragher & Florence Howe
     (New York: W.W. Norton & Company, 1988), 107–129.

63   Potts, *Wesleyan University, 1831-1910*. See also Rudolph, *The American College and Uni-
     versity*; Florence Howe, "Myths of Coeducation," in *Myths of Coeducation: Selected Essays,
     1964–1983* (Bloomington: Indiana University Press, 1984), 206–220, 212. According to
     Leslie Miller-Bernal, *Separate by Degree: Women Students' Experiences in Single-Sex and Co-
     educational Colleges* (New York: Peter Lang Publishing, 2000), 45, the financial exigency
     caused by Middlebury's enrollment decline to 38 students led to the admission of women in
     1883.

64   Potts, *Wesleyan University, 1831–1910*.

65   Ibid. See also Knight, "The Quails;" William North Rice to Miss Moore (9 January 1909)
     WUA, William North Rice File.

66   Noyes, *History of Connecticut College*. See also Nye, *Chapters in the History of Connecticut Col-
     lege*; Potts, *Wesleyan University, 1831–1910*.

67   Potts, *Wesleyan University, 1831-1910*. See also Knight, "The Quails;" Rosenberg, "The Limits
     of Access," 112.

68   Crandall J. North to William North Rice (14 January 1908). WUA, William North Rice File.
     North was, at the writing of the letter, the Corresponding Secretary for the Endowment Fund
     of the New York East Conference of the Methodist Episcopal Church.

69   Rice to Miss Moore.

70   Potts, *Wesleyan University, 1831–1910*. Regarding Middlebury, see Miller-Bernal, *Separate by
     Degree*, 51.

71   Knight, "The Quails," 30–47.

72   Ibid.

73   Rosenberg, "The Limits of Access," 126.

74   Miller-Bernal, *Separate by Degree*, 52.

75   Ibid., 118. See also Joan G. Zimmerman, "Daughters of Main Street: Culture and the Female Community at Grinnell, 1884–1912, in *Woman's Being, Woman's Place: Female Identity and Vocation in American History*, ed. Mary Kelley (Boston: G.K. Hall & Company, 1979), 154–170.

76   Lynn D. Gordon, "Co-education on Two Campuses: Berkeley and Chicago, 1890–1912," in *Woman's Being, Woman's Place: Female Identity and Vocation in American History*, ed. Mary Kelley (Boston: G.K. Hall & Co., 1979), 171–193. See also Rosenberg, "The Limits of Access," 116; Miller-Bernal, *Separate by Degree*, 52; David M. Stameshkin, *The Town's College: Middlebury College, 1800–1915* (Middlebury, VT: Middlebury College Press, 1985).

77   William North Rice to Miss Bass (16 June 1909). WUA, William North Rice File. See also Knight, "The Quails."

78   William North Rice to Mrs. Cummings (4 March 1909). WUA, William North Rice File.

79   Rice to Miss Moore.

80   Ibid.

81   Ibid.

82   Ibid.

83   Ibid.

84   Alexander Leitch, "Evelyn College," *A Princeton Companion* (Princeton, New Jersey: Princeton Univerity Press, 1978). See also Sonia Fernandez, "Decades Before Coeducation, Sister School Let Women Into Princeton" *The Daily Princetonian* (13 December 1999); Schmidt, *Douglass College: A History*.

85   Rice to Mrs. Cummings.

86   Miller-Bernal, *Separate by Degree*, 52–53.

87   Rice to Miss Bass.

88   Rice to Mrs. Cummings.

89   Rice to Miss Bass.

90   Rice to Miss Moore, Mrs. Cummings, and Miss Bass.

91   Rice to Mrs. Cummings.

92   William North Rice to Elizabeth Wright (22 July 1910). WUA, William North Rice File.

93   Ibid; See also Rice to Miss Moore.

94   Rice to Elizabeth Wright. Note that in an earlier draft of the letter Rice had written "laboratories," not "other educational facilities."

95   Ibid.

96   Ibid.

97   Rice, Draft of Letter to Elizabeth Wright (14 July 1910). WUA, William North Rice File.

98   Rice to Elizabeth Wright.

99   Elizabeth C. Wright to William North Rice (26 July 1910). WUA, William North Rice File.

100 Ibid.

101 Ibid.

102 Ibid.

103 Ibid.

104 Ibid.

105 Ibid.

106 Ibid.

107 Ibid.

108 Boorstin, "Higher Education in Place of Higher Learning." See also Hawkins, "The Making of the Liberal Arts College Identity."

109 Ibid.

110 Hawkins, "The Making of the Liberal Arts College Identity."

111 Boorstin, "Culture With Many Capitals." See also J.S. Brubacher & W. Rudy, *Higher Education in Transition: A History of American Colleges and Universities* (3rd ed.) (New York: Harper & Row, 1997); Hawkins, "The Making of the Liberal Arts College Identity;" Mabel Newcomer, *A Century of Higher Education for Women* (New York: Harper & Brothers, 1959), 23.

112 Daniel J. Boorstin, "Culture with Many Capitals: The Booster College," In *The Americans: The National Experience* (New York: Vintage Books, 1965), 152–161. See also Potts, "American Colleges in the Nineteenth Century."

113 Wilcox, "Piety and Profit in College Building."

114 Potts, "American Colleges in the Nineteenth Century."

115 Wilcox, "Piety and Profit in College Building."

116 Boorstin, "Culture With Many Capitals." See also Potts, "American Colleges in the Nineteenth Century;" Wilcox, "Piety and Profit in College Building."

117 Potts, "American Colleges in the Nineteenth Century."

118 Ibid.

119 Boorstin, "Culture with Many Capitals: The Booster College." See also *Connecticut College for Women: Preliminary Announcement* (New London, CT: Connecticut College for Women, 1914). Connecticut's first board of trustees included Bryan Mahan, the Mayor of New London, Morton and Nellie Plant of nearby Groton, Colin Buell, head of New London's Williams Memorial Institute, and three prominent New London businessmen: F. Valentine Chappell, Frank Palmer, and William Reeves. Also on Connecticut's first board were Simeon Baldwin, the Governor of Connecticut, Henry Wright, the former dean of Yale University, Louis Cheney, Mayor of Hartford, Edwin Milner of Moosup, Connecticut, Edward Robbins of New Haven, Edward Smith of Hartford, President Frederick Sykes, and four members of the Hartford College Club: Mary Clark Mitchell, Mary Partridge, Frances Scudder Williams, and Elizabeth Wright.

120 Ibid.

121 Boorstin, "Culture With Many Capitals." See also Daniel J. Boorstin, "A Higher Learning for All," in *The Americans: The Democratic Experience* (New York: Vintage Books, 1973), 478–490.

122 Boorstin, "Culture With Many Capitals."

123 Ibid. See also Brubacher & Rudy, *Higher Education in Transition*; Newcomer, *A Century of Higher Education for Women*, 23.

124 Wright, "Report on Women's College to the Hartford College Club."

125 Wright, "A College for Women in Connecticut."

126 Buell, "New London Should Try to Bring College Here."

127 Ibid.

128 Ibid..

129 "Prof. Colin S. Buell, 77, Dies; Principal of W.M.I. and Connecticut College Trustee."

130 Wright, "A College for Women in Connecticut."

131 Bryan Mahan, "To the Committee Appointed to Select a Site, and to Establish a Women's College in Connecticut" (5 November 1910). CCA, Elizabeth Wright File.

132 Ibid. See also Colin S. Buell, "Appeal to the People of Connecticut and Statement of Policy by the Trustees of Thames College" (3 June 1911). CCA, Colin Buell File.

133 Bryan Mahan, "To the Committee Appointed to Select a Site, and to Establish a Women's College in Connecticut" (5 November 1910). CCA, Elizabeth Wright File.

134 Noyes, *History of Connecticut College.*

135 Buell, "Thames College: An Account of the Struggle by a Yale Graduate to Found a Woman's College in Connecticut," 751.

136 Buell, "Thames College: An Account of the Struggle by a Yale Graduate to Found a Woman's College in Connecticut," 751.

137 Buell, "Thames College, A College for Women to be Located in New London, Connecticut."

138 Ibid.

139 Ibid.

140 Ibid.

141 Ibid.

142 Ibid.

143 Ibid.

144 *The Connecticut College for Women* (New London, CT: Connecticut College for Women, 1911), 7.

145 Ibid, 7.

146 *Connecticut College for Women, Preliminary Announcement: Foundation, Organization, Site, and Plans* (New London, CT: Connecticut College for Women, 1914).

147 W.W. Harris, "College's Fate Hangs in Balance," *The Day* (20 March 1917). CCA, Frederick Sykes File.

148 Harris, "College's Fate Hangs in Balance." The trustees claimed that Sykes was an ineffective manager of Connecticut College's business affairs. Sykes and his defenders argued that Sykes' removal came because he would not be a pawn to trustee business interests. Despite opposition from the trustees, Sykes had the support of students and faculty. Sykes' removal by the trustees foreshadowed a pattern that would play out many times thereafter for succeeding presidents of Connecticut College. I found ample evidence in the Connecticut College Archives, Gertrude Noyes' history of the College, and the numerous interviews I conducted to conclude that only Katharine Blunt and Rosemary Park, and (maybe) Charles Shain did not get urged to leave by trustees, faculty, or both.

149 Files of William Reeves and Frederick Sykes, CCA.

150 Elizabeth Wright File. CCA.

151 Irene Nye, John E. Wells, and David D. Leib, "Faculty Resolution in Regard to Mr. Buell" (7 February 1931). CCA, Colin Buell File.

152 Ibid.

153 Ibid.

154 Ibid.; "Professor Colin S. Buell, 77, Dies; Principal of W.M.I. and Connecticut College Trustee."

155 Nye, Wells, and Leib, "Faculty Resolution in Regard to Mr. Buell."

156 Frederick Rudolph, *The American College and University: A History* (New York: Alfred A. Knopf, 1962).

157 Helen Horowitz, *Alma Mater: Design and Experience in the Women's Colleges from Their Nineteenth-Century Beginnings to the 1930s* (New York: Knopf, 1984). See also Elaine Kendall, *Peculiar Institutions: An Informal History of the Seven Sister Colleges* (New York: G.P. Putnam's Sons, 1975).

158 Jane Bredeson (23 January 2007) and Laurie Deredita (31 July 2007), interviews by author (interviews in possession of author).

159 Peterson, *The New England College in the Age of the University*. See also Potts, "American Colleges in the Nineteenth Century;" Donald Tewksbury, *The Founding of American Colleges and Universities Before the Civil War*.

160 Kendall, *Peculiar Institutions*. See also, Rudolph, *The American College and University*.

161 Ibid.

162 Potts *Wesleyan University, 1831–1910*.

163 Ibid.

CHAPTER THREE

How Three Progressive Era Movements Shaped Connecticut College for Women

The key individuals and underlying forces that influenced the founding of Connecticut College for Women converged in New London, Connecticut, between 1910 and 1915 to create a type of women's college that had not been seen in 19th century America. Connecticut College for Women emerged during an era when women were opening previously closed doors, pushing at the boundaries of their traditional roles, and emerging into public life in unprecedented numbers.[1] During the decade of Connecticut College's founding, when a woman sought a college education it meant (more than it had in the past) that she intended to work afterwards.[2] The woman of 1910—compared to her predecessors—found the range of occupations open to her expanding.[3] Although women in 1910 were still largely excluded from business and the other established male professions, "they proved to be inventive and creative in developing alternative work."[4]

Three significant progressive era movements helped forge Connecticut College's pioneering identity as a liberal arts college with vocational and practical edges to its curriculum: the women's club movement, the vocational education movement, and the home economics movement. The Hartford College Club to which one of Connecticut College's founders (Elizabeth Wright) belonged sprung from the women's club tradition. And founding president Frederick Sykes drew ideas that shaped Connecticut College for Women's original curricular vision from the vocational education and home economics movements operating in America's progressive era (1890–1920).

The Influence of the Clubwoman

The turn of the 19th to the 20th century heralded the so-called "new woman" of the progressive era with her enhanced sense of self, gender, and mission.[5] The new woman wanted a chance to contribute to society and an opportunity to wield influence beyond her home.[6] Using her newfound ambitions and energies, the woman of the progressive era began to find paths to power and fulfillment through greater participation in public life.[7] Out of this climate sprang the women's club movement. It became common for the typical middle class American woman of the progressive era to belong to some sort of voluntary society, perhaps a church group, a literary discussion circle, an alumnae association, or a social welfare project.[8] Women of the progressive era utilized single-sex organizations, such as clubs, to penetrate public affairs. Their clubs and associations became a means to promote better social conditions and an instrument to advance women's special interests.[9]

The women's club tradition of the late 19th and early 20th centuries helped build the foundation for the establishment of Connecticut College for Women in 1911. In America during the progressive era, before women had the right to vote, women's clubs provided opportunities for the so-called second sex to exercise leadership and influence in the societal spheres within which they primarily operated.[10] Because men were busy in their traditional power realms of commerce and politics, women had the opportunity to take up social causes and community improvement efforts through the activities of their clubs, which became an important civic sphere outside male power channels.

Club affiliation often provided the solace of a shared predicament, as clubwomen sought freedom from domestic duties or needed to express discontent with their lives as wives and mothers.[11] Their involvement in clubs taught women how "to cooperate with each other, to organize, speak out at meetings, publish newspapers, and wield influence in the public sphere."[12] With their newfound solidarity came the recognition that women could aspire to promote reforms of societal injustices and clean up the corruption created by the men of the industrial era.[13] Clubwomen frequently worked to bring about a more rational and just society. As they did so, they found themselves in the advance guard of the progressive movement in the United States.[14] Numerous major reform initiatives trace their gestation to efforts of clubwomen. For example, clubwomen endorsed the federal suffrage amendment as early as 1914.[15] Clubwomen helped bring about the Pure Food and Drug Act of 1908 and the Children's Bureau of the Labor Department in 1912.[16] Collectively clubwomen also campaigned to end child labor, protect their factory worker sisters, and safeguard the food supply.[17]

Participation in women's clubs helped develop and strengthen the belief among pioneering feminists that woman's sphere was as important as man's.[18] Clubs, for example, spurred women to act on their own behalf, to establish scholarships or undertake even grander programs such as the Hartford College Club's campaign to establish the state of Connecticut's first women's college.[19] Yet overall, most clubs sponsored non-controversial local initiatives that few would even think of opposing, such as planting trees and building hospitals, libraries, and playgrounds.[20]

Many of the leaders of the women's clubs, like Elizabeth Wright, were college-educated women trying to reconcile their careers and their private lives.[21] Following her graduation from Wesleyan in 1897, Wright, for example, had worked as a teacher and then as an assistant principal in the Portland, Connecticut, schools.[22] As a single woman who never married, Wright did not represent the typical profile of the clubwoman.[23] But being single brought with it some advantages. The single woman's lack of children meant that she could join clubs at an earlier age and devote more of her time to club activities. For such women, clubs provided a supportive and necessary sisterhood.[24] Yet in a world that revered women for their childbearing capabilities, single women, like Wright, no matter how welcoming their women's clubs may have seemed, were always outsiders.[25]

In many communities, there also tended to be a social hierarchy of clubs. Careful screening of prospective members kept most clubs "overwhelmingly Yankee."[26] Clubs rarely included women who were of Central European, Eastern European, Mediterranean, or Jewish descent.[27] Even some clubwomen who appeared to be of Yankee descent had a more complicated lineage. For example, Elizabeth Wright's middle name was Caramossi, after her Italian mother, who was the daughter of a Count Muzzarelli.[28] The fact that her surname was Anglo Saxon may have made the Hartford College Club friendlier to Wright, although her royal claim, if known to the club members, may also have mitigated discrimination against her Italian ancestry.

By 1910 the General Federation of Women's Clubs that existed across America comprised one million members.[29] The Hartford College Club to which Wright belonged exemplified the women's club movement that had become an American institution by 1911. Like most women's clubs, the Hartford College Club's members shared a common background, in this case, college attendance. In early 20th century America, female college graduates were still not plentiful, but they were organized. College clubs for women existed all over the state of Connecticut in 1910 when Elizabeth Wright, Mary Clark Mitchell, Mary Morgan Partridge, and Frances Scudder Williams set out with determination to bring their sisters a women's college.[30] Many of the Hartford College Club's members had degrees from Seven Sister colleges. Mary Clark Mitchell, for example, who served as the Hartford College Club's first president, graduated in 1883 from Smith College.[31] The daughter of a missionary, Frances Scudder Williams long served her alma mater (Wellesley College) as president of its alumnae association.[32] In addition to her term presiding over the Hartford College Club, Williams is credited with making the first monetary contribution toward the founding of Connecticut College for Women.[33] Club members, like Williams, tended to be intensely loyal, remaining in the organization year after year, and often taking turns hosting meetings.[34] The Hartford College Club, for example, held its first discussion of the plan to establish a women's college in the West Hartford home of club member Harriet Wadsworth.[35]

Because women's clubs tended to operate according to parliamentary procedure and to rotate the chairmanship or presidency so that every member could gain leadership experience, it was Frances Scudder Williams' turn in 1910 to serve at the helm of the Hartford College Club.[36] The Club had taken notice in 1909 when Wesleyan University announced that it would no longer enroll women.

Wesleyan's decision had meant that women in Connecticut would no longer have an in-state college option. President Williams reacted to Wesleyan's cessation of coeducation by appointing a committee (with Elizabeth Wright as chair) to establish a college for women in Connecticut. Wright and two other committee members, Mary Clark Mitchell and Mary Morgan Partridge, took on the task of promoting the women's college cause to potential benefactors across the state of Connecticut. Wright and her fellow Hartford College clubwomen presented their case to civic leaders, other women's clubs, philanthropists, and college officials in the nearly two-dozen Connecticut towns that vied to be the chosen location for the proposed women's college.[37]

Wright framed the argument for a women's college by citing demographic changes affecting women in the northeastern United States. In a May 1910 report to the Hartford College Club, Wright referenced a *New York Times* article that had said there was "Not room enough for girls in Eastern Colleges."[38] Wright noted that the number of women attending college in the United States had grown 800 percent between 1890 and 1910—from 10,761 in 1890 to 84,909 in 1910.[39] Wright could have noted as well that in 1900 fully 36 percent of college students were women (up from 20 percent in 1870), that women outnumbered men in liberal arts courses and liberal arts colleges, and that in 1910 women comprised 40 percent of all college students in America.[40] Wright could also have correctly predicted that the enrollment of women in United States colleges would keep increasing. By the end of Connecticut College's first decade (1920), women would comprise nearly 50 percent of all college students in the United States.[41]

As she made her case for a women's college for Connecticut, Wright pointed out that between 1890 and 1910, the number of men attending college had also increased at a high rate (250 percent), but one still outpaced three to one by women.[42] Men's colleges had been able, Wright asserted, to keep up with enrollment increases, whereas the Seven Sister colleges, such as Vassar, were at their enrollment limits and could take on no more students.[43] Statistics compiled by Wright and stated in Connecticut College for Women's first promotional bulletin showed that Bryn Mawr, Smith, Vassar, and Wellesley combined had 1,592 more potential willing students than spaces available.[44] That there was excess demand for higher education by women in the northeastern United States helped justify the founding of a new women's college in New England.

The situation was especially disadvantageous for the young women of Connecticut, because the state's three senior colleges (Trinity, Wesleyan, and Yale) only admitted men. The state of Connecticut suffered by comparison to neighboring Massachusetts, where women were nearly four times as likely to attend college—having numerous options that included coeducational Boston University, and six senior women's colleges: Mount Holyoke, Radcliffe, Simmons, Smith,

Wellesley, and Wheaton.[45] By contrast, the young women of Connecticut had to go out of state for college, most frequently to Smith—which in 1913 had 102 students from Connecticut—or to Vassar, which had 54 Connecticut women.[46] Connecticut's leading newspaper, *The Hartford Courant*, took notice of the situation, stating in an October 4, 1910, article that "Connecticut, although it has always enjoyed the reputation of being foremost in education, is far behind her neighbors in this respect."[47] That quote from *The Hartford Courant* later appeared in the first brochure promoting Connecticut College for Women.[48]

Echoing notions of republican motherhood, Wright and *The Hartford Courant* further argued that having no college for women in Connecticut portended troublesome implications for the education of its children.[49] Children, they noted, were most likely to be educated by women, whether in the classroom or at home, so for the State of Connecticut to neglect the college education of its women meant that its children's opportunities would also suffer.[50] Similarly *The Hartford Courant* believed it "desirable that [Connecticut's children] should receive at least as good advantages as are offered in other states."[51] Connecticut, thus, needed a women's college to meet the needs of both the young women and the children in the state, and to bring the state up to the level of its New England counterparts, all of which had colleges open to women.[52]

Wright took an additional tack in making the case to the Hartford College Club. She cited the social mobility function of a college education, noting that not having a women's college in Connecticut would keep higher education "beyond the reach of the poor girl who needs it most."[53] Wright explained, "To a wealthy girl, higher education is an adornment: to a poor girl it is a source of income, for she depends on her brains for her living."[54] Establishing a college for women in Connecticut would stand, in Wright's estimation, as an egalitarian gesture. Wright envisioned Connecticut's first college solely for women as one that would be useful to the state, because it would train women to better their economic situations, which in turn would uplift society.

The Hartford College Club launched its women's college campaign soon after Wesleyan University's announcement that only male students were welcome there. Wesleyan's move angered Elizabeth Wright, in particular, on multiple grounds. First, Wright, an 1897 graduate of Wesleyan, felt betrayed by her alma mater. Second, Wright believed the issue warranted the Hartford College Club's attention because the move had not only forsaken her and her fellow Wesleyan alumnae sisters, but had also left the young women of Connecticut bereft of an in-state college option.[55] Wright and the Hartford College Club hoped for a new college for women or at least a coordinate college with an already established institution such as Trinity, Wesleyan, or Yale. Yale showed no interest in a coordinate college.[56] Trinity was of natural interest to the Hartford College Club, due to its nearby location, but no serious negotiations transpired.

Hearing of the Hartford College Club's plans, officials at Wesleyan approached Wright to propose a coordinate women's college and offer use of its library, its museum, some of its "educational facilities" and access to a portion of its teaching faculty.[57] But the Wesleyan proposal lacked one essential element: financial support. Wesleyan officials made it clear that funds to launch and sustain the coordinate women's college would have to come from sources external to the University.[58] Wright and her clubwomen rejected Wesleyan's proposal.[59] Wright was still bitter at Wesleyan for mistreating its female students and then closing its doors on them altogether. She did not trust Wesleyan to treat women any better in a coordinate college.[60]

Wright and the Hartford College Club chose instead to take the risk of going ahead with the idea of a stand-alone women's college. That effort generated much enthusiasm. Towns and cities from around Connecticut competed to be the location of the new college, offering campus sites and money. One Connecticut town, New London, had something the others lacked, a committed advocate for women's higher education, Colin Buell, who had been working to establish a women's college since the early 1890s.[61] When Buell and Elizabeth Wright discovered in 1910 that they were of like minds, neither was to be denied in making their dream of a college for women in Connecticut come true. Buell rallied New Londoners to raise $135,000 to secure the former whaling port as the location for the women's college. Another New London benefactor, Morton Plant, whose family shipping fortune had helped launch the University of Tampa, contributed a $1 million endowment gift, thus ensuring that the Hartford College Club's wishful visions would take shape in the form of a college for the women of Connecticut.[62]

Successful at making the dreams of a small women's club a reality, Elizabeth Wright and her fellow Hartford College Club leaders Mary Clark Mitchell, Mary Morgan Partridge, and Frances Scudder Williams served ultimately as incorporators of Connecticut College for Women as well as members of its original board of trustees.[63] Williams became a longtime supporter of the Connecticut College Arboretum.[64] Her contributions resulted in a tract of land in the Arboretum named in her honor.[65] Elizabeth Wright went from visionary volunteer to first secretary of Connecticut College's board of trustees. From an office in downtown New London's Mohican Hotel, Wright worked diligently with first president Frederick Sykes and her fellow trustees to bring Connecticut College for Women into being.[66] After the College opened in 1915, Wright acted as its first registrar. Thereafter Wright became bursar and assistant treasurer, remaining in the latter position, alongside her sister Mary, until their joint retirements in 1943.[67] In recognition of her many contributions, Connecticut College awarded Wright an honorary Master of Arts degree in 1935.[68]

Following her retirement, Elizabeth Wright published a novel entitled *The Force of Circumstances* that chronicled a poor Irish American World War Two veteran's struggles against class prejudice and social superiority.[69] In 1961, two years before Wright's death in 1963 at the age of 86, Connecticut College named a residence hall for her.[70] Both Wesleyan University and Connecticut College cited Wright in 1968 when announcing a student exchange program between the two soon-to-be-coeducational institutions.[71] Wright's name is still invoked whenever the founding story of Connecticut College gets told. It is no exaggeration to say that Connecticut College for Women would never have become a reality without the efforts of Wright and the other women who comprised the Hartford College Club in the first decade of the 20th century. Connecticut College, along with Douglass College of Rutgers University, stands as one of the few colleges in America founded by the clubwomen of the progressive era.[72]

Frederick Sykes and the Vocational Education Movement

At the turn of the 20th century on through its first decade, it became apparent to some that America needed a college for women "different from...anything in existence, a college that should be something more than an imitation of the type of men's colleges that prevailed 25 years ago."[73] According to its proponents, this new type of women's college should not simply copy the Seven Sisters, with their emphasis on "the conventional cultural studies," that is, the liberal arts and sciences.[74] Strict study of the liberal arts was seen as too unspecific for the progressive era woman, who needed a more vocational education that would prepare her to be useful in the world.[75]

Proponents of the new type of higher education for women hoped for "a college [that] would turn out graduates really fitted to help in the work of the world, and [ready] to assume places of immediate usefulness."[76] The college they envisioned would have a utilitarian as well as an intellectual mission.[77] It would be "a college that from the first, by reason of its ideals and aims, by reason of its faculty even if small, [would] be...wholly worth while in its usefulness to a purposeful working world."[78] It would be a college that looked forward to where women's education was heading, not backward to where it had been.[79] One of the stalwarts of the new approach to higher education for women was Columbia University's Frederick Sykes, making him, even though he had no prior inkling, "just the man to head the new college" that would be founded in New London, Connecticut, in 1911.[80]

Even before there was any possibility that he would be Connecticut College for Women's first president, Frederick Sykes had thought and written about changing trends in women's education.[81] Sykes' role at Teachers College of Columbia University's Division of the Practical Arts, following experience teaching in the secondary schools of his native Ontario, Canada, gave him a vantage point from which to assess currents in secondary and higher education.[82] The post at Teachers College also gave Sykes a bully pulpit from which to suggest curricular innovations. As a result, he was better fitted than most college officials of the time to serve as the founding president of an innovative college for women. Because it was a brand new institution and because he was hired as its president before it had a curriculum or a faculty, Frederick Sykes had an unusual opportunity to shape Connecticut College for Women's curriculum in ways that represented a new current in women's higher education in the United States when it opened for classes in 1915.

Figures 3.1 and 3.2. President Frederick Sykes

In choosing Frederick Sykes as its first president, Connecticut College for Women got an unusually practical academic, one whose interests ranged beyond English literature, the field in which he earned his doctorate at Johns Hopkins University, to industrial education and architecture.[83] To his new post, Sykes brought a "cosmopolitan approach to problems of education."[84] Before Sykes became president of Connecticut, he had advocated for an education that met "the demands of life."[85] As director of the household and practical arts division of Columbia University's Teachers College—the leading program in that emerging vocational field, Sykes had made an exhaustive study of the vocational schools of Europe, the findings of which had led him to promote technical education in the

United States.[86] Sykes had also examined the kindergarten, manual training, household arts, and vocational education movements in the United States.[87] Drawing on his findings, Sykes subsequently organized the departments of university extension teaching, industrial arts, and household arts within Columbia University's Teachers College.[88] Under his direction, Teachers College's practical arts division—comprised primarily of female students—aimed to provide an education that made the act of living beautiful, efficient, and humane.[89]

While at Columbia, Sykes gave speeches and wrote articles on the importance of vocational training in primary and secondary schools. He asserted that America's public schools were not sufficiently equipped to train students to enter vocational fields. In a 1911 article, Sykes cited statistics showing that fewer than 20 percent of all American public school students continued their studies beyond the age of fourteen.[90] Ironically for someone with a Ph.D. in English who would soon become president of a liberal arts college, Sykes criticized America's public schools for teaching a college preparatory curriculum to all despite the fact that relatively few students in the United States pursued higher education.[91]

During the years Sykes worked at Teachers College, the ideas of educator and philosopher John Dewey inspired a utilitarian outlook that dominated the thinking about secondary education in the United States.[92] Dewey's conception of the "new education" emphasized the importance of learning as preparation for life and career.[93] Vocational education seemed essential to meet the needs of America's industrial economy, especially because the elimination of apprenticeship programs had left the working classes with few ways to gain skills.[94] By the time Sykes became president of Connecticut College for Women (1913), the vocational movement in the United States was ascendant and perhaps even at its zenith.[95] The United States, for example, had 142 industrial schools, and in New England's largest city (Boston) nearly half of the secondary school students were enrolled in vocational training programs.[96]

Sykes advocated vocational education because he recognized the critical societal need for both efficient and proficient workers.[97] In Sykes' estimation, schools could not and should not ignore the persistent question that had also occupied the attention of John Dewey, "Do you prepare for life and livelihood?"[98] One of Sykes' core beliefs was that elementary and secondary school instruction was too abstract and needed "to be made more concrete, more real, more vital."[99] Sykes wondered why more educators could "not recognize the worth and dignity of vocational purpose in education...[as] an asset of the highest educational value?"[100] Vocational education was a necessary response, according to Sykes, to basic economic facts and industrial needs.[101] Gone were the days, Sykes argued, when the public school system could rest on the belief that "the best or only possible training given to students by the state was a general academic education."[102] Like Dewey, Sykes believed that the new education required doing in addition to thinking, because the child "prefers doing the thing to mere hearing about it."[103] Sykes admired the fact that Dewey's new type of education had a practical end and that it offered "an adjustment of the school to life," rather than the reverse.[104]

Propelling the vocational education movement was the widespread belief that America's youth at the turn of the 20th century lacked the skills required to drive further industrial growth for the nation.[105] Applying a vocational model to public education was expected to help the United States "build for national efficiency."[106] The new education, according to Sykes, would aim "to train our people to meet the problems of livelihood and living—to apply science and art, craft and machinery, method and organization to make possible a higher achievement of living for all."[107] The new education also attracted Sykes because he saw it as not merely technical but also as providing the foundation for a civil society, that is, "the hygiene, the civics and the law that concern every workman as a man and a citizen."[108]

Perhaps because he had taken his doctorate at America's first German-style research university (Johns Hopkins), Sykes admired Germany as "the most remarkable example among all the nations, of the immediate economic benefits of specialized education applied to the needs of a newly developing nation."[109] Sykes believed that an emphasis on technical education had transformed Germany from a poor country into the richest and most powerful nation in Europe.[110] The United States, in Sykes' opinion, needed to emulate Germany and the other nations that had made household and industrial arts central to the standard curriculum offered in the public schools.[111] The lesson Sykes drew from Germany, and the other thriving countries in Europe, was that further industrial development depended on the technical education and training that would meet the needs of life and its changing economic conditions.[112] To enact a German-style system of industrial education, the United States would need, in Sykes' estimation, to invest in elementary trade and commercial schools, cooperative and part-time industrial schools, and technical and arts schools at the junior high and high school levels.[113]

The shift in emphasis that Sykes recommended for pre-college education toward more vocational opportunities held implications for America's colleges and universities. Sykes speculated that "we shall have colleges of a new type established that will unite the so-called cultural studies with training in the technical arts."[114] Sykes foresaw the need for colleges that would train women for work in civic activities and social service—colleges that would aim to improve the general health and welfare of society, colleges that would be powerhouses for human betterment.[115] He would later bring an emphasis on those characteristics to his leadership of Connecticut College for Women.

Concurrent with Connecticut College for Women's founding in 1911 was the reality that more women than ever were self-supporting—drawing inspiration from organizations such as the Equality League of Self-Supporting Women that had been founded in 1907 by Harriot Stanton Blatch, daughter of pioneering feminist Elizabeth Cady Stanton.[116] Educators like Frederick Sykes anticipated that a new type of college would be needed to train such women who aspired to take on greater responsibility in the world.[117] But at the same time it was still widely supposed that a woman's education would necessarily be different from a man's.[118] Indeed, if men had always been educated to achieve, then the new woman would need an education that prepared her to serve.[119] Sykes, for example, envisioned a type of education that readied women to serve on boards protecting the health and general welfare of children, the home, and the community.[120] Sykes also expected that social service and civic activities would require trained women workers and that those women would be needed in laboratories, domestic architecture firms, and the administration of institutions.[121]

The early decades of the 20th century brought unprecedented employment opportunities for American women. By the time of Connecticut College for Women's founding in 1911, women were a growing presence in the professions: they held 8,596 patents, they argued cases before the Supreme Court, they made up 12 percent of newspaper reporters, they practiced architecture and medicine (comprising 5 percent of all U.S. physicians in 1900), and they numbered two-thirds of all librarians.[122] Between 1900 and 1910, the number of female managers in the United States increased by 180 percent from 77,214 to 216,537, and women represented 41.3 percent of all professional workers, a 6.1 percent increase from levels in 1900 and a share of the professional workforce that held steady for the next forty years.[123] Half of the women professionals in the United States were schoolteachers, but a growing number were appearing as college professors.[124] In 1910 there had been 2,928 women serving as college faculty members and administrators; by 1920 their numbers totaled 9,974—just over 25 percent of all college faculty members—although most taught at women's colleges or coeducational land grant universities beyond the northeast.[125]

By 1911 hospitals and schools in the United States relied on 80,000 women working as nurses and 500,000 women working as teachers.[126] A 1912 survey of alumnae of five women's colleges showed 54 percent working as teachers.[127] In addition to offering programs in nursing and teaching, colleges were increasingly necessary to train women for other emerging vocations like dietetics and social work that came to be dominated by women, including a growing number of women who hoped to combine marriage and a professional career.[128] More employed women, including those with college educations, were getting married.[129] For example, in the 1910 to 1920 decade of Connecticut College for Women's founding, the proportion of married professional women in America rose from 12.2 percent to 19.3 percent.[130]

Despite the array of new careers open to them even if they got married, American women of the progressive era found life after college exceedingly difficult.[131] Graduating women often felt tension between what Jane Addams called the "social claim—the responsibility of college women to the world at large—versus the family claim—parents' demands that their daughters forego their opportunities to work outside the home."[132] After graduating from Seven Sister colleges such as Vassar, many women transitioned back to the traditional domestic sphere by taking home economics classes.[133] A 1910 Vassar College theater production dramatized the conflicting tensions Addams had described. In "Victoria Vassar, or After College, What?" the female lead, choosing between a career in social work or marriage to a Yale man, chooses the latter with no small degree of ambivalence.[134] Other more enterprising women channeled their desire for an occupation into creating new structures for women like themselves; for example, Marion Talbot formed the Association of Collegiate Alumnae (following the same premise of the Hartford College Club) not long after she graduated from Boston University.[135] Still, others applied their energies to the women's suffrage movement. Smith graduate Gertrude Weil, for example, returned home after college and became president of the North Carolina Equal Suffrage League.[136]

The vocationally inspired ideas expressed by Frederick Sykes, and others, about women's higher education signified a break, even if not a radical one, with the path that had been trod by the Seven Sister colleges since Vassar's opening for classes in 1865. Sykes' notions reflected, to a large degree, the thinking that was emerging in the first two decades of the 20th century in America regarding the new roles women would have in society. The spirit of those middle decades of the progressive era heralded a greater interest in vocational schooling and a growing consciousness that women's education could serve a valuable societal purpose.[137] Yet rather than judge the Seven Sisters' curriculum inadequate, Sykes sought to perfect its liberal arts model by joining to it a curriculum that would also prepare women to fulfill new roles as working professionals.[138]

Sykes seems to have drawn upon the more practical bent of Columbia's Extension School as well as on the vocational curriculum he saw young women taking in Canada at prominent secondary schools such as Ontario's DeMill Ladies College and Alma College, when he worked for the Ontario Department of Education.[139] Sykes helped devise for Connecticut a curriculum that joined traditional liberal arts classes, of the sort approved by the existing eastern colleges of high standing, to vocational offerings that would train graduates to work in expanding fields open to women such as nutrition and dietetics, home economics, and teaching.[140] A Connecticut College education combined a rigorous intellectual foundation in the liberal arts subjects offered at the Seven Sister colleges with practical training that recognized that women could have useful roles in the world of work.

Sykes wanted Connecticut College students to be women who viewed the world as a place for work and service.[141]

The Home Economics Movement

The home economics movement began as part of a broader campaign for reform taking place in America's progressive era. As it developed, the home economics movement attached to the vocational training movement advocated by education reformers—like Frederick Sykes—who wanted a curriculum for middle and high school students better suited to training workers.[142] Education reformers, like Sykes, attacked the traditional college preparatory Greek and Latin curriculum on the grounds that classical learning provided poor preparation for work in industry or on the farm.[143] Capitalizing on these trends, the home economics movement, thanks to its pioneering proponent Ellen Swallow Richards, devised socially acceptable ways for a woman to use her education—such as running her home efficiently or tending to health and sanitary problems in schools.[144] Richards accomplished this by recasting the home, and the skills needed to operate it, in a scientific frame. Because she believed that running the home required scientific methods, Richards proposed that all women's colleges offer domestic economy courses, and many, such as Connecticut College for Women, did.[145]

Home economics solidified its standing as a profession with its own national conventions—held in Lake Placid, New York, between 1899 and 1907, own *Journal of Home Economics*, own professional organization, the American Home Economics Association, and an endorsement by the General Federation of Women's Clubs.[146] With home economics' maturity as a field came a growing recognition that the individual household was a complex institution needing the application of scientific principles.[147] University of Chicago Dean of Home Economics, Marion Talbot, for example, declared the home a center of consumption.[148] Frederick Sykes, likewise, saw the home having an economic production function, an industrial center that revolved around household chores like cooking and cleaning, as well as an educational role, serving as the chief school for children, where they learned words, reading, manners, and character.[149]

Home economics intended to be a practical science that would improve domestic life. Studying domestic science fields, for example, gave mothers tools to combat infant mortality and childhood diseases.[150] Making the home the subject of study also gave it scientific legitimacy and imbued women's traditional roles with newfound value and significance.[151] Sykes and other home economics partisans even speculated that the application of science to the household might lead to a homemaking parallel to the concept of preventive medicine.[152] The home economics movement also spawned new occupations for women, one example being dietetics.[153] Dietitians trained in home economics programs at colleges, such as

Connecticut College for Women, helped nurses and hospital administrators prepare meals for patients and served as consultants for physicians prescribing diet therapies.[154] Dietitians became especially sought after following the expansion (in 1909) of nursing education in hospitals.[155] When hospitals subsequently needed women who could teach dietetics to nurses, college home economics programs scrambled to meet the demand.[156] The field arrived as a profession with the establishment of the American Dietetic Association in 1917, two years after the opening of Connecticut College for Women.[157]

Even more than their counterparts in education and nursing, the faculty members who taught in home economics departments made strong efforts to find jobs for their graduates.[158] Home economics professors—such as longtime Connecticut College professor Margaret Chaney—recognized that gainfully employed graduates were the best promoters of the field.[159] Women with home economics degrees found careers as social workers, factory inspectors, orphanage managers, private school heads, nutritionists, teachers, and operators of test kitchens for companies.[160] When the Smith-Lever Act established the Cooperative Extension Service in 1914, it created a new career option for home economics graduates— that of providing domestic science instruction to women on farms.[161] Textiles and nutrition also emerged between 1910 and 1920 as promising areas of employment for home economics graduates.[162]

In the early decades of the 20th century, child development also came to occupy a prominent place in the home economics curriculum.[163] A 1917 survey revealed, for example, that 80 percent of college-educated women wanted home economics programs to include courses in child study—a curricular expansion that occurred at Connecticut College for Women as its home economics program developed.[164] Those decades also brought the first White House Conference on Children (1909), the establishment of the United States Children's Bureau (1912), and marked the ascendancy of child-centered professions such as child psychology and pediatrics.[165] Home economists of the period re-conceptualized mothering as professional labor requiring education and expertise.[166] The modernization of mothering was supposed to usher traditional women's work into the 20th century and cast childrearing as a more intellectually challenging undertaking that would appeal to the bright and curious women entering college.[167]

Progressive era women, just as they had a salutary effect on the individual home, began to be counted on to "make the larger home, to civilize the city."[168] In Frederick Sykes' estimation, leadership in managing the living conditions of the future would come from women who welcomed their new responsibilities and their new opportunities for training, including the accompanying challenges that both posed. Democracy, in Sykes' view, depended on social justice realized by happy, busy, beneficent, effective human beings.[169] Bringing such conditions about was the work of the truly educated, and women would play a central role in the transformation.[170]

The task of socializing and civilizing society had come to be owned by women in the years leading up to the founding of Connecticut College for Women.[171] Jane Addams had established the settlement house movement and, in doing so, had turned the field of social work into an important career option for women with college training.[172] Social work became the earliest profession to offer significant opportunities for leadership to women.[173] By the year of Connecticut College's opening (1915), social work was the third most common occupation of women who had attended college.[174] Although the founders of Connecticut College for Women hoped to establish "technical schools" for the "professional training of women" in fields like social work, those ideals were not realized, leaving Simmons College the opportunity to become a pioneer in social work education.[175]

Preparing women for their civilizing and socializing roles in the larger world and in the home provided the motivating force for the new type of education that Frederick Sykes believed women needed, regardless of whether those women were going to be social workers, dietitians, or homemakers.[176] Yet despite all the changing currents in education and society, when Sykes stepped back and took stock of women's evolving responsibilities and opportunities, he concluded that the new occupations—which Connecticut College's programs in dietetics, household economy, and the teaching of home economics prepared women for—were "only the old ones writ large," for mothers had always been a child's first nurse, teacher, book provider, housekeeper, and charity worker.[177]

Sykes' analysis of women's changing opportunities and occupations also echoed the emerging concept of "municipal housekeeping," which implied an even grander purpose than had previously been imagined for women's traditional roles. Municipal housekeeping rested on the notion that "women possessed special moral qualities which ought to be applied outside the home."[178] Those, like Sykes, who promoted the concept of municipal housekeeping, regarded the community as an extension of the home and as an appropriate place for women to apply their special sensibilities to civic reform and the welfare of humanity.[179] Women were to use their home economics education and the scientific principles it inculcated to "improve the larger world."[180] Because homemaking was seen as a cornerstone of the modern social order, it became the responsibility of the educated homemaker to keep the larger world figuratively neat and well ordered.[181] Proponents of municipal housekeeping believed that "women's function, like charity, begins at home and then, like charity, goes everywhere."[182]

Inspired by Ellen Richards, the home economics movement transformed domesticity into a vehicle to expand women's political power.[183] The field of home economics provided an outlet for the talents and energies of educated women like

Richards and those who would follow, such as Katharine Blunt, a Vassar and Chicago-trained chemist who would become—in 1930—Connecticut College's first woman president.[184] Recasting the home as a site of scientific importance redefined it and encouraged women to take the expertise they had developed in the domestic sphere out into the larger arenas of social reform and political action.[185] By stretching the definition of the home to encompass the larger household, that is, the city (through municipal housekeeping), Richards both challenged the doctrine of domesticity and made the idea of the home synonymous with woman's moral authority and power.[186] Woman's moral authority, joined to her domestic skills, enabled her to "move into a male world and clean it up, as if it were no more than a dirty house."[187]

What did all this mean for the soon-to-be-established Connecticut College for Women? It meant that the new college that opened for classes in 1915 owed its existence to Elizabeth Wright and her fellow members of the Hartford College Club. It meant that Connecticut College for Women's curriculum gave expression to progressive era notions about vocational education and the education and training needs of the new woman. It meant that the home economics movement's imprint was on Connecticut College for Women's original curriculum, a course of study that placed dietetics and household economy alongside the liberal arts. Overall, it meant that Connecticut College for Women was not a mere copy of the Seven Sisters, but a new college shaped in tangible ways by some of the dominant currents of the progressive era.

The Fate of Frederick Sykes

Founding president Frederick Sykes' association with Connecticut College for Women ended in controversy. The practical and industrious Sykes had worked tirelessly and without pay from his appointment in 1913 to the fall of 1915 when Connecticut College for Women opened. Arguably, Sykes gave the college its "vital soul."[188] Nearly all aspects of the new college had his imprint when it opened in 1915. He designed the first seal of Connecticut College, hired every faculty member, and had a significant hand in determining the domestic Tudor, English manor style of architecture of the first campus buildings.[189] Sykes believed that "the good that counts is good in action" and exhorted Connecticut students to reach toward the future, to "press toward the mark for the prize of the high calling of your womanhood."[190]

But unlike Colin Buell and Elizabeth Wright, Sykes did not have a long career at the College. Connecticut College's trustees voted in February 1917 to oust Sykes, who fought them until relenting in June 1917.[191] Sykes' resignation followed months of bad relations between him and the board. The trustees accused Sykes of "business inefficiency," claiming that he was an ineffective manager whose mishandling of business affairs spurred several threatened lawsuits from suppliers and builders.[192] The trustees claimed that Sykes lectured and browbeat them into getting his way.[193] Months before asking for his resignation, the board began holding meetings without Sykes present, and a committee of trustees (led by Frank Chappell and William Reeves) took over management of the day-to-day business affairs of the College.[194]

Throughout the controversy, students, faculty, and some New London civic organizations supported Sykes.[195] The *New London Telegraph* asserted that Connecticut College for Women's board was ill equipped to visualize and comprehend the "purposes of the institution as they were created by the master mind [Sykes] to which they themselves had delegated its building."[196] To some, the result of the trustees driving away Sykes effectively meant that "the soul had gone out of the college."[197] The *New London Telegraph*'s "Commentator" poignantly observed:

> "The college is not the walls and roofs that house it. It is not the charter nor the funds, nor yet the faculty and student body. It is the purpose and the aim, and the processes by which these are attained. It is the light that burns in the minds and the love that fills the hearts. It is the creed, the ethical law, the intent, always kept in sight, to guide to a harbor of lofty and splendid idealism. And it was this that Dr. Sykes built."[198]

A handful of faculty members left Connecticut College for Women because of the controversy.[199] Sykes's supporters alleged that graft hastened his departure, that the president had opposed nepotism in hiring, thus making enemies of Elizabeth Wright (who wanted the College to hire her sister Mary) and other trustees with relatives up for jobs.[200] Sykes' supporters pointed out that the Chappell family of New London had benefited greatly from the College, as board chair Frank Chappell's company supplied the College's coal, while his brother's firm designed the buildings.[201] Sykes had dared to criticize the Chappell Coal Company for price gouging when the firm raised coal prices from $6 per ton to $9 per ton.[202] Sykes also haggled with the Chappell architecture firm over construction cost overruns and errors.[203] Sykes' objections led Connecticut College's board eventually to prohibit contracts between the College and companies owned or run by trustees and to bar trustees from holding administrative jobs at the College.[204] Neither of those governance reforms took effect in time to help Sykes keep his job.

Connecticut's trustees turned to a solid and steady minister, Benjamin Marshall, to follow Sykes. In Marshall the trustees got the stylistic opposite of Sykes. Ministers, unlike career faculty members, come to their first college presidency knowing that they depend on the connections and goodwill of board members to secure life-giving resources. The board that chose Marshall likely knew this. Marshall came to Connecticut College from his alma mater, Dartmouth, where he was chaplain and professor of biblical history and literature.[205] His inaugural address reassured the college community that he had no plans for radical change. If change occurred on his watch, it would be the result of an evolutionary process.[206] Marshall had a far longer tenure than Sykes, eleven years in all, and he is credited with restoring stability, advancing the young college's prestige, and further developing the academic programs and facilities.[207] Despite Marshall's steadying hand and accomplishments, it appears that trustees forced him to resign in 1928 to the dismay of alumnae and students.[208]

Regardless of what precipitated it, the removal of Frederick Sykes was the culmination of a power struggle between a president and a board of trustees. Sykes departed devoted to Connecticut College for Women's students and faculty yet bitter about the way its board of trustees had treated him. His experience as the intellectual and inspirational life-giving force of Connecticut College for Women reflected his observation on the day that the new college opened that "our heads were in the clouds"; but his humiliation by the trustees mirrored the end clause of that opening day statement, "though our feet were in the mud."[209] Petty disputes had indeed dragged the sublime Sykes into the mud. Less than six months later, Sykes died suddenly from a heart attack at the age of fifty-four. He will forever be remembered in New London as one of the primary shapers of Connecticut College. But Frederick Sykes should also be remembered as an influential thinker who helped fashion a type of women's college that (as the following chapters demonstrate) was just beginning to emerge in American higher education during the early decades of the 20th century.

Notes

1   Karen Manners Smith, "New Paths to Power: 1890-1920," in *No Small Courage*, ed. Nancy F. Cott (New York: Oxford University Press, 2000), 353–412, 402.

2   Rosenberg, "The Limits of Access," 122.

3   This analysis focuses on white middle class women, because they were the group most likely to attend colleges like Connecticut College for Women. Barbara Sicherman, "College and Careers: Historical Perspectives on the Lives and Work Patterns of Women College Graduates," in *Women and Higher Education in American History*, ed. Faragher and Howe (New York: W.W. Norton, 1988), 130–164, 156.

4   Sarah Stage and Virginia B. Vincenti, *Rethinking Home Economics: Women and the History of a Profession* (Ithaca: Cornell University Press, 1997), 97.

5   Nancy Woloch, *Women and the American Experience* (Boston: McGraw Hill, 2006), 269.

6   Rosalind Rosenberg, *Divided Lives: American Women in the Twentieth Century* (New York: Hill and Wang, 1992), 57.

7   Manners Smith, "New Paths to Power," 358, 365.

8   Woloch, *Women and the American Experience*, 270.

9   Ibid., 296; Blair, *The Clubwoman as Feminist: True Womanhood Redefined, 1868-1914*, ed. Karen J. Blair (New York: Holmes and Meier, 1980), 61.

10 Annette K. Baxter, "Preface," in *The Clubwoman as Feminist*, xi–xv.

11 Blair, *The Clubwoman as Feminist*, 61.

12 Ibid, 8.

13 Ibid., 8. See also William D. Jenkins, "Housewifery and Motherhood: The Question of Role Change in the Progressive Era," in *Woman's Being, Woman's Place: Female Identity and Vocation in American History*, ed. Mary Kelley (Boston: G.K. Hall & Company, 1979), 142–153.

14 Baxter, "Preface," xiv.

15 Blair, *The Clubwoman as Feminist*, 5.

16 Freedman, "Separatism as Strategy," 512–529, 517. See also Woloch, *Women and the American Experience*, 299.

17 Ibid., 270. See also Kohlstedt,"Single Sex Education and Leadership," 94.

18 Blair, *The Clubwoman as Feminist*, 107.

19 Ibid., 71.

20 Woloch, *Women and the American Experience*, 289.

21 Ibid., 23.

22 Biographical notes in Elizabeth Wright File, CCA.

23 Ibid., 60.

24 Ibid., 37.

25 Ibid. 61.

26 Blair, *The Clubwoman as Feminist*, 63.

27 Ibid., 63.

28 " Miss Elizabeth Wright Dies; College Founder, First Bursar," *Conn Census* (28 February 1963). Connecticut College Archives (hereafter identified as CCA), Elizabeth Wright File. See also "Founder of Connecticut College Writes First Novel," Exposition Press, Press Release (1950). Wright's mother, Aurelia Muzzarelli, was an Italian Countess. Both of Wright's parents were prominent painters; in fact Wright's father, George F. Wright, painted several portraits of Abraham Lincoln as well portraits of 18 governors of Connecticut and 13 governors of Illinois.

29 Freedman, "Separatism as Strategy," 512–529, 517.

30 Elizabeth Wright to Colin Buell (8 July 1913). CCA, Colin Buell File. Wright enclosed with the letter to Buell a list of 22 different women's clubs in Connecticut that she had canvassed for support. Examples included the Association of Collegiate Alumnae of New Haven, the Bristol College Club, the Greenwich College Club, the Monday Reading Club of Hartford, the Motherhood Club of Hartford, and the Putnam D.A.R.

31 "Mrs. Mary Clark Mitchell Dies, Long Leader in Many Educational, Religious and Civic Movements," *Hartford Courant* (17 December 1936).

32 "College Founder, Honorary Trustee Dies at Age of 93" *(Conn Census,* 8 May 1958). CCA, Frances Scudder Williams File.

33 "Mrs. Williams is Retiring From Board: Connecticut College Trustee was Among Institution Founders" *(Hartford Courant,* 21 May 1949).

34 Ibid., 63.

35 Staying in the Connecticut College guesthouse in January 2007, I noticed its living room holds a portrait of Harriet Wadsworth, with an inscription on the frame which notes that in Wadsworth's home Elizabeth C. Wright and other women from the Hartford College Club held the first of the meetings that led to the founding of Connecticut College.

36 "Mrs. Williams is Retiring From Board," *The Day* (21 May 1949). See also "A Founder of College, Mrs. S.H. Williams," *Connecticut College 1958* (Summer 1958), 4; "College Founder, Honorary Trustee Dies at Age of 93," *Conn Census* (8 May 1958). CCA, Frances Scudder Williams File.

37 Wright, "Report of Women's College to the Hartford College Club." See also Elizabeth C. Wright, "A College for Women in Connecticut."

38 Wright, "Report of Women's College to the Hartford College Club."

39 Wright, "A College for Women in Connecticut."

40 Newcomer, *A Century of Higher Education for Women*. See also Rosenberg, *Divided Lives*, 26; Woloch, *Women and the American Experience*, 274.

41 Manners Smith, "New Paths to Power," 389. See also Newcomer, *A Century of Higher Education for Women*.

42 Wright, "A College for Women in Connecticut."

43 Wright, "Report of Women's College to the Hartford College Club."

44 *The Connecticut College for Women*, 3.

45 Wright, "A College for Women in Connecticut."

46 "Women's College President Talks," *New Haven Union* (April 6, 1913). CCA, Frederick Sykes File.

47 *The Connecticut College for Women*, 3.

48 Ibid.

49 Wright, "A College for Women in Connecticut."

50 Ibid.

51 *The Connecticut College for Women*, 3.

52 Ibid.

53 Wright, "Report of Women's College to the Hartford College Club."

54 Ibid.

55 Elizabeth C. Wright, "Report of Women's College to the Hartford College Club."

56 Yale University president Arthur Twining Hadley to Elizabeth C. Wright (16 April 1910). CCA, Elizabeth Wright File.

57 Rice to Elizabeth Wright. Note that in an earlier draft of the letter Rice had written "laboratories," not "other educational facilities."

58 Rice to Elizabeth Wright.

59 Elizabeth C. Wright to William North Rice (26 July 1910). WUA, William North Rice File.

60 Ibid.

61 Buell, "Thames College: An Account of the Struggle by a Yale Graduate to Found a Woman's College in Connecticut," 751.

62 Nye, *Chapters in the History of Connecticut College*. See also Noyes, *A History of Connecticut College*.

63 Ibid.

64 Richard Goodwin to Mrs. S.H. Williams (11 May 1949), CCA, Frances Scudder Williams File.

65 Rosemary Park to Mrs. S.H. Williams (20 October 1950), CCA, Frances Scudder Williams File.

66 Noyes, *History of Connecticut College*.

67 Margaret B. Chaney, "Memorial Resolution—Miss Elizabeth C. Wright" (February 1963). See also "Miss Elizabeth Wright dies; College Founder, First Bursar" *Conn Census* (28 February 1963). CCA, Elizabeth Wright File.

68 "Notes to File, Miss Elizabeth C. Wright, Retired Bursar" (19 March 1959). CCA, Elizabeth Wright File.

69 Exposition Press News Release, "Founder of Connecticut College Writes First Novel" (1950). CCA, Elizabeth Wright File.

70 Connecticut College Office of Press Relations (15 February 1963). CCA, Elizabeth Wright File.

71 "Connecticut and Wesleyan Plan Resident Student Exchange," *CC News* (Spring 1968). See also "Notes From College Row: Right Again," *The Wesleyan Alumnus* (October 1968), 4.

72 George P. Schmidt, *Douglass College: A History* (New Brunswick, NJ: Rutgers University Press, 1968).

73 William Welton Harris, "Some Personal Reminiscences of Dr. Sykes," *Connecticut College News* (26 October 1917). CCA, Frederick Sykes File. Harris had known Sykes before he was selected as Connecticut's first president. Harris, who sent a daughter to Connecticut College for Women, believed from his first notice of the new college that Sykes was the perfect man to lead it into being.

74   Ibid.
75   Roberta Frankfort, *Collegiate Women: Domesticity and Career in Turn-of-the-Century America* (New York: New York University Press, 1977), 109.
76   Harris, "Some Personal Reminiscences of Dr. Sykes." See also Frederick H. Sykes, "The Social Basis of the New Education for Women," *Teachers College Record* (May 1917), 227; "A Canadian President for Connecticut College" (no author, no date), 31. CCA, Frederick Sykes File; "Dr. Sykes to Head Woman's College, *The Day* (14 February 1913). CCA, Frederick Sykes File.
77   Ibid.
78   Ibid.
79   Nye, *Chapters in the History of Connecticut College*, 21.
80   Harris, "Some Personal Reminiscences of Dr. Sykes."
81   Frederick H. Sykes, "The Social Basis of the New Education for Women."
82   "A Canadian President for Connecticut College."
83   Ibid.
84   Nye, *Chapters in the History of Connecticut College*, 21.
85   Frederick H. Sykes, "Industrial Arts Education and Industrial Training," *Teachers College Record* (September 1911), 197.
86   "Dr. Sykes to Head Woman's College." See also Stage and Vincenti, *Rethinking Home Economics*, 76.
87   Sykes, "Industrial Arts Education and Industrial Training," 199.
88   Ibid, 199.
89   Sykes, "The Social Basis of the New Education for Women," 227.
90   Sykes, "Industrial Arts Education and Industrial Training," 214.
91   Ibid., 214.
92   Jenkins, "Housewifery and Motherhood," 142–153. See also John Dewey, "My Pedagogic Creed," *School Journal* (January 1897), 77–80; Lee Benson, Ira Harkavy, and John Puckett, *Dewey's Dream: Universities and Democracies in an Age of Education Reform* (Philadelphia: Temple University Press, 2007); John L. Rury, "Vocationalism for Home and Work: Women's Education in the United States, 1880-1930," *History of Education Quarterly* (Spring, 1984), 40.
93   Ibid., 144–145.
94   Kohlstedt, "Single Sex Education and Leadership," 95.
95   Kohlstedt, "Single Sex Education and Leadership," 95.
96   Ibid, 95; See also Jenkins, "Housewifery and Motherhood," 145.
97   Sykes, "Industrial Arts Education and Industrial Training," 200.
98   Ibid. See also Dewey, "My Pedagogic Creed;" Benson, Harkavy, and Puckett, *Dewey's Dream: Universities and Democracies in an Age of Education Reform*, 35.
99   Ibid., 199.
100 Ibid., 201.
101 Ibid., 202.
102 Ibid., 203.
103 Ibid., 204. See also Dewey, "My Pedagogic Creed;" Benson, Harkavy, and Puckett, *Dewey's Dream*.
104 Ibid., 206.
105 Rury, "Vocationalism for Home and Work," 23.
106 Sykes, "Industrial Arts Education," 220.
107 Ibid., 220.
108 Ibid., 213. Sykes echoes Dewey's belief that school is preparation for citizenship and that education must try to raise human society to a higher level. See also Dewey, "My Pedagogic Creed;" Benson, Harkavy, and Puckett, *Dewey's Dream*, 35–39.
109 Ibid., 212.

110 Ibid., 215.

111 Ibid., 215.

112 Ibid., 210-211.

113 Ibid., 216-218.

114 Ibid., 218.

115 Ibid, 218. Also Brownell, interview. Brownell, the editor of *CC: Connecticut College Alumni Magazine*, supplied the "powerhouse for human betterment" quote.

116 Manners Smith, "New Paths to Power," 398.

117 "A Canadian President for Connecticut College" (no author, no date), 31.

118 Ibid. See also Kohlstedt, "Single Sex Education and Leadership," 96.

119 Ibid.

120 "A Canadian President for Connecticut College, 31.

121 Ibid., 31.

122 Frank Stricker, "Cookbooks and Law Books: The Hidden History of Career Women in Twentieth-Century America," in *A Heritage of Her Own: Toward a New Social History of American Women*, ed. Nancy F. Cott and Elizabeth Hofkin Pleck (New York: Simon & Schuster, 1979), 482.

123 Ibid.

124 Ibid.

125 Ibid., 483. See also Rosenberg, "The Limits of Access," 96.

126 Sykes, "The Social Basis of the New Education for Women," 229

127 Geraldine Joncich Clifford, "Women's Liberation and Women's Professions: Reconsidering the Past, Present, and Future," in *Women and Higher Education in American History*, ed. Faragher and Howe (New York: W.W. Norton, 1988), 165–182, 173.

128 Stricker, "Cookbooks and Law Books," 486.

129 By 1905 the woman who attended college hoped to have a career and a marriage in her future, according to Patricia A. Palmieri's *In Adamless Eden: The Community of Women faculty at Wellesley* (New Haven, CT: Yale University Press, 1995), 218.

130 Ibid., 486.

131 Joyce Antler, "After College What?": New Graduates and the Family Claim," *American Quarterly* (Autumn 1980), 409–434, 410.

132 Ibid., 412.

133 Ibid., 417.

134 Ibid., 419.

135 Ibid, 411.

136 Joan Marie Johnson. *Southern Women at the Seven Sister Colleges: Feminist Values and Social Activism, 1875–1915*. Athens: University of Georgia Press, 2008.

137 Frankfort, *Collegiate Women*.

138 Harris, "Some Personal Reminiscences of Dr. Sykes."

139 Laura Suchan, "Useful Ornaments: Form and Function at an Ontario Ladies College," Presentation at the History of Education Society's Annual Conference, St. Petersburg, Florida (7 November 2008). See also Demill Ladies' College Annual Calendar, 1881–1882, Oshawa Community Museum & Archives, Oshawa, Ontario, Canada; Johanna Selles-Roney, 'Manners or Morals?' Or 'Men in Petticoats?' Education at Alma College, 1871–1898 in *Gender and Education in Ontario*, ed. R. Heap and A. Prentice (Toronto: Scholar's Press, 1991), 249–272.

140 *Connecticut College for Women: Preliminary Announcement*.

141 Frederick H. Sykes, "Commencement Address," *Connecticut College News* (20 June 1917).

142 Stage, "Home Economics: What's in a Name?" 3, 8.

143 Ibid., 23.

144 Frankfort, *Collegiate Women*, 109. See also Sarah Stage, "Ellen Richards and the Social Significance of the Home Economics Movement," in *Rethinking Home Economics: Women and the History of a Profession*, 17–33.

145 Frankfort, *Collegiate Women*, 109.

146 Jenkins, "Housewifery and Motherhood," 146–147. See also Stage, "Home Economics: What's in a Name?" 5; Rima D. Apple, "Liberal Arts or Vocational Training?: Home Economics Education for Girls," in *Rethinking Home Economics: Women and the History of a Profession*, 79–95, 80; Virginia B. Vincenti, "Chronology of Events and Movements Which Have Defined and Shaped Home Economics," in *Rethinking Home Economics: Women and the History of a Profession*, 321–330, 322.

147 Jenkins, "Housewifery and Motherhood," 150; See also Sykes, "The Social Basis of the New Education for Women," 235.

148 Woloch, *Women and the American Experience*, 293.

149 Sykes, "The Social Basis of the New Education for Women," 233–234.

150 Rosenberg, "The Limits of Access," 99.

151 Manners Smith, "New Paths to Power," 365. See also Woloch, *Women and the American Experience*, 292.

152 Sykes, "The Social Basis of the New Education for Women," 238.

153 Lynn K. Nyhart, "Home Economists in the Hospital," in *Rethinking Home Economics: Women and the History of a Profession*, 125–144, 128.

154 Nyhart, "Home Economists in the Hospital," 128. See also *Connecticut College for Women, First Annual Announcement, 1915–1916*, 17, 32.

155 Ibid., 132.

156 Ibid., 132.

157 Ibid., 128. See also *Connecticut College for Women First Annual Announcement, 1915–1916*.

158 Kathleen R. Babbitt, "Legitimizing Nutrition Education: The Impact of the Great Depression," in *Rethinking Home Economics: Women and the History of a Profession*, 145–162, 145.

159 Margaret S. Chaney to Home Economics Alumnae (14 January 1957). CCA, Home Economics File.

160 Babbitt, "Legitimizing Nutrition Education," 145; See also Stage, "Home Economics: What's in a Name?" 11.

161 Ibid., 146.

162 Nancy Tomes, "Spreading the Germ Theory: Sanitary Science and Home Economics, 1880-1930," in *Rethinking Home Economics: Women and the History of a Profession*, 34-53, 49.

163 Julia Grant, "Modernizing Mothers: Home Economics and the Parent Education Movement, 1920–1945," in *Rethinking Home Economics: Women and the History of a Profession*, 57.

164 Ibid., 57. See also *Connecticut College Bulletin, 1925–1926* (New London, CT: Connecticut College for Women, 30 March 1925).

165 Ibid., 57.

166 Ibid., 56.

167 Ibid., 57.

168 Sykes, "The Social Basis of the New Education for Women," 240.

169 Ibid., 242.

170 Ibid., 242.

171 Ibid., 240.

172 Rosenberg, *Divided Lives*, 29. See also Manners Smith, "New Paths to Power," 390.

173 Sicherman, "College and Careers," 155.

174 Ibid., 155.

175 *Connecticut College Announcement 1917–1918* (New London, CT: Connecticut College for Women, 20 June 1917). See also Kohlstedt, "Single-Sex Education and Leadership," 99; Mark, *Delayed by Fire*, 38.

176 Sykes, "The Social Basis of the New Education for Women," 240.

177 Ibid., 240.

178 Ibid., 74.

179 Ibid., 74.

180 Apple, "Liberal Arts or Vocational Training?" 94. See also Stage, "Home Economics: What's in a Name?" 25, 33.

181 Rury, "Vocationalism for Home and Work," 23. See also Woloch, *Women and the American Experience*, 293.

182 Blair, *The Clubwoman as Feminist*, 106.

183 Ibid., 19.

184 Stage, "Ellen Richards and the Social Significance of the Home Economics Movement," 17-33. See also Grant, "Modernizing Mothers: Home Economics and the Parent Education Movement, 1920–1945," 57. Grant notes that in 1926 Katharine Blunt was president of the American Home Economics Association.

185 Ibid., 19.

186 Stage, "Home Economics: What's in a Name?" 30. See also Stage, "Ellen Richards and the Social Significance of the Home Economics Movement," 17–33.

187 Ibid.

188 Sykes, "Students of Dear C.C."

189 Nye, *Chapters in the History of Connecticut College*, 28.

190 Sykes, "Students of Dear C.C."

191 Elizabeth Wright, "Notes on Connecticut College Board Meeting of February 1917," CCA, Elizabeth Wright File.

192 "President Sykes Comments on Action of Trustees," *The Day* (19 April 1917). See also "College President Sykes Asked to Resign; May Fight Trustees' Attempt to Remove Him," *The Day* (14 March 1917).

193 "F.V. Chappell Says Dr. Sykes' Charge is Unqualified Falsehood," *The Day* (17 March 1917).

194 Ibid.

195 Margery S. Rowe '19, "To Dr. Sykes: 'Lives of Great Men all Remind Us, We Can Make Our Lives Sublime,'" *Connecticut College News* (20 June 1917). See also Winona Young, Marion Kofsy, Esther Batchelder, Sadie Coit, Ruth Trail, Luise Ansley, Juline Warner, Alice Horrax, Marenda Prentis, "Students' Mass Meeting Passes Resolutions: Appreciate President Sykes' Work with and Attitude Towards Students Body," *Connecticut College News* (20 June 1917); Frederick H. Sykes to Mrs. George Fenner (9 June 1917)—Sykes is responding to the Equal Franchise League's resolution in support of him; "A Disavowal." All from CCA, Frederick Sykes File.

196 "The Commentator's Column: Being Personal Opinions on Events, Conditions and People Here and Elsewhere," *New London Telegraph* (Fall 1917).

197 Ibid.

198 Ibid.

199 "College President Sykes Asked to Resign; May Fight Trustees' Attempt to Remove Him," *The Day* (14 March 1917).

200 Walter W. Conklin, "Would Reorganize College Trustees," Letter to the Editor, *The Day* (19 March 1917). See also "How College Controversy Appears in Other Cities," *The Day* (19 March 1917). Both in CCA, Frederick Sykes File.

[201] Ibid. Walter W. Conklin observed, "while the college might be a good thing for the city of New London, it certainly was a mighty good thing for the Chappell family." See also "Suit for Slander to be Brought Against Dr. Sykes; Yonkers Man Who Interests Self in College Affairs Got Sykes His Job," *Waterbury Herald* (25 March 1917).

[202] "President Sykes Gives Reasons Why His Trustees Oppose Him," *The Day* (15 March 1917).

[203] Ibid.

[204] "President Sykes Comments on Action of Trustees."

[205] Nye, *Chapters in the History of Connecticut College*, 41. See also Noyes, *History of Connecticut College*, 47.

[206] Benjamin Marshall, *Inaugural Address* (23 November 1917), CCA Benjamin Marshall File.

[207] Nye, *Chapters in the History of Connecticut College*, 49. See also Noyes, *History of Connecticut College*, 83.

[208] "Student Government Resigns in Tribute to Pres. Marshall: Records Approval of Policy," *The Day* (Spring 1928), CCA Benjamin Marshall File. See also Letter to the Alumnae, from members of the New London Chapter of Connecticut College Alumnae (7 March 1928), CCA Benjamin Marshall File.

[209] Nye, *Chapters in the History of Connecticut College*, 23.

CHAPTER FOUR

The "Eighth Sister" or a New Type of Women's College?

In July 1910, Elizabeth Wright told her fellow members of the Hartford College Club, "If the girls are to have only one college, let it be a good one."[1] Later that same month, Wright wrote Professor William North Rice of Wesleyan University to say that "the time has come" "when the girls of Connecticut should have a first class college, *second to none.*"[2] Wright was correct. The time had indeed come for a high quality college for women in Connecticut, but the time had also come for a college that, when it opened its doors for classes in September 1915, was not simply a copy of the other successful women's colleges. The time had come for "a new college with new methods and with a different purpose from that of any existing colleges for women," what Connecticut College's founding president Frederick Sykes would label "the next step in women's education."[3]

Connecticut College for Women opened in 1915 with a curriculum that joined liberal arts classes, "of the sort approved by the existing Eastern colleges of high standing," to vocational offerings that would train graduates to work in expanding fields open to women such as nutrition and dietetics, home economics, and teaching.[4] The Connecticut College curriculum combined a rigorous intellectual foundation in the traditional liberal arts subjects found at the Seven Sister colleges with practical training that recognized that women could have useful roles in the world of work. Consistent with a college founded to fill both a local and a larger societal need for greater educational and career opportunities for women, Connecticut College for Women sought to prepare its students to make contributions to and take action in the communities beyond its campus boundaries. Founding President Frederick Sykes described Connecticut College students as women who viewed the world as a place for work and service.

Comprehending Connecticut College for Women's difference at its founding moment requires some background understanding of the pace-setting colleges for women that preceded it. In telling the story of women's colleges in America, virtually all historians agree that the most influential group has been the Seven Sister colleges.[5] Each of the Seven Sisters was an attempt to establish a college that would show women capable of measuring up to the same challenging academic curriculum required at the best men's colleges.[6] Despite the presence of coeducational Bates College, Boston University, and Middlebury College as well as the coordinate women's colleges at Brown (Pembroke) and Tufts (Jackson), the Seven Sister colleges provided the dominant model of women's higher education available in Connecticut's home region of New England. All new colleges for women could not help but be conscious of the Seven Sisters. Yet to grasp Connecticut College for Women's founding context fully, it is also necessary to consider other women's colleges established during America's "progressive era," as well as the later women's colleges that have worn the label "progressive."[7]

Setting the Standard: The Seven Sister Colleges

Many scholars of women's higher education break the founding of women's colleges into two eras.[8] The Romantic Period (1820–1860) brought the female seminary, exemplified by Mary Lyon's creations at Mount Holyoke (1837) and Wheaton (1834) and the daughter seminaries like Rockford College (1847) in Illinois, the alma mater of social work pioneer Jane Addams.[9] Female seminaries rested on the belief that women needed to be educated differently and separately from their brothers.[10] A seminary education, which was generally offered at the pre-college level, aimed to enable young women to become schoolteachers and be self-supporting until marriage.[11] Mary Lyon intended Mount Holyoke graduates, for example, to be teachers and missionaries, not homemakers.[12] More than 80 percent of Mount Holyoke graduates between 1838 and 1850 worked as schoolteachers for at least a year after leaving the South Hadley campus.[13] The female seminaries made a point of educating the daughters of the working classes.[14] By contrast, the students who attended the later Sisters, such as Smith and Vassar, were predominantly the daughters of upper middle class and upper class professionals.[15]

Mount Holyoke's female seminary model of one monumental building in which the whole of college education and life took place became the model for the campuses of Vassar and Wellesley.[16] The founders of Mount Holyoke, Vassar (1861), and Wellesley (1870) believed that women needed special settings for their education as well as more guidance and protection than men.[17] Wellesley's ornate and palatial College Hall to some eyes made all the existing women's colleges look like textile mills.[18] Smithsonian Institution architect James Renwick's Main Hall at Vassar—a sprawling building that served as the entirety of the college until expansion near the dawn of the twentieth century—evoked "a Victorian age when unmanaged imaginations flourished."[19]

The Era of Reform (1860–1890) was a time of "I can do anything that you can do" feminism.[20] Bryn Mawr (1885), Smith (1871), Vassar, and Wellesley sought to prove to the world that women were mentally and physically capable of successfully negotiating the rigors of the curriculum found at the elite men's colleges of the day.[21] Matthew Vassar envisioned his new college as the women's equivalent of Harvard, Yale, and Princeton.[22] When Vassar opened in 1865, it was the first women's college with a significant endowment and the first to cause the world to take notice of women's education.[23] Smith, like Vassar before it, aspired to be the equal of any men's college.[24] When it opened in 1875, Smith's academic standards were higher than any of the other women's colleges.[25] Wellesley's founder Henry Durant likewise believed that women were up to the scholastic challenge of a men's curriculum, and he wanted to give them a chance to prove it.[26] The education of women, in Durant's opinion, was part of a larger and broader battle for women's rights embedded within a great crusade for human justice.[27]

But Wellesley took an important step beyond the other Seven Sister colleges when it became the first women's college to have a woman president, a faculty comprised entirely of women, and a large representation of women on the board of trustees.[28] Like Vassar College before it, Wellesley College aimed to give "young women who seek a collegiate education opportunities fully equivalent to those usually provided for young men."[29] Founder Henry Durant envisioned his Wellesley as "a female Harvard."[30] Wellesley would show that women could "shed and ultimately disavow the ethos of frail and ornamental womanhood."[31] With its all female faculty and youthful, charismatic president (Alice Freeman), Wellesley proclaimed to the world that women could run their own college.[32] Wellesley stood as an emancipator of women, the exemplar of "the possibilities of individual and societal transformation through the regeneration of women," an institution that confirmed the progress society was making in late 19th century America.[33] Like the other Seven Sister colleges, Wellesley adopted a strong intellectual emphasis on the liberal arts in its curriculum but stood somewhat apart from the others with its ethos of service.[34] Despite Wellesley's mission to produce graduates who would make useful contributions to society, the College anchored its curriculum solely in the liberal arts, so that it would not be misunderstood as a college to prepare women for specific professions and technical careers.[35]

Perhaps because it opened after its sister women's colleges had achieved success, Bryn Mawr College had the opportunity to carve out its own distinctive institutional character, becoming a special example of a women's aristocracy of wit and brains.[36] The force of President M. Carey Thomas, whose father and uncle were among the group of socially prominent Quakers who founded Bryn Mawr, imprinted a lasting identity on the institution, molding its direction and image in the early years toward one of academic rigor.[37] The first woman with a Ph.D. to head a college, Thomas never compromised high standards; she wanted to turn out scholars, preferably future professors, rather than cultured ladies.[38] Thomas wanted the Bryn Mawr woman to become as well known and as respected a type as England's Oxford and Cambridge man.[39] Thomas believed that women's education should be identical to men's in order to demonstrate that a woman's capacity of mind was equal to that of a man.[40]

Although it was a women's college in the mold of the Seven Sisters, Bryn Mawr felt the influence of the new German-inspired Johns Hopkins University. Most of Bryn Mawr's founding trustees (including Thomas' father) had served on the board at Johns Hopkins.[41] A teenage Carey Thomas had been disappointed when her father told her that Johns Hopkins did not intend to admit female undergraduates—a decision that made it necessary for Thomas to go elsewhere (the coeducational Cornell University) for college.[42] In addition, a cadre of early faculty imported from Johns Hopkins shaped the serious scholarly atmosphere that developed throughout Bryn Mawr's stark, Gothic campus.[43] So many Bryn Mawr graduates pursued doctoral study at Johns Hopkins that Bryn Mawr came to be nicknamed "Jane Hopkins."[44]

The Bryn Mawr student culture that developed held to the belief that women there belonged to a very special society demarked by superior intellect.[45] Bryn Mawr women were often contemptuous of male institutions, referring to Haverford College "boys" and Princeton University as the "Bryn Mawr Annex!"[46] Bryn Mawr represented a clear departure from female educational institutions that molded subservient wives and mothers.[47] In shaping Bryn Mawr's indelible character during her long reign as president (1894–1922), M. Carey Thomas rejected domesticity for women and sought to educate independent, competitive women who would never succumb to passivity.[48] She opposed the idea of a special curriculum for women built around fields like domestic science, and she did not favor teaching existing subjects from a woman's point of view.[49]

M. Carey Thomas' high aims for Bryn Mawr students reflected the changes occurring in the progressive era in women's higher education.[50] Women of the progressive era evinced interest in social activism and were far more likely to enter college.[51] In 1870 women had been just 21 percent of the total undergraduate enrollment in America, but by 1910, women were 40 percent of all undergraduate students, and by 1920 they comprised 47 percent.[52] From 1890 to 1920, the number of women enrolled in United States colleges increased 405 percent, from 56,000 to 283,000.[53] By the beginning of the second decade of the 20th century, the decade of Connecticut College's founding, women outnumbered men in liberal arts majors.[54]

New Models: Connecticut and Its Analogues

The early decades of the 20th century in America continued the era of workplace specialization and the industrialization of everyday life. Underlying the advance of industrialization was the progressive era belief that social conditions could be improved through the application of specialized expertise.[55] During the progressive era decades, the Association of Collegiate Alumnae (ACA) devoted much energy to the question, what should women do?[56] The ACA speculated that women needed a college education that joined traditional womanhood to intellectual training.[57] For it had begun to be an accepted notion in the years preceding Connecticut College's founding in 1911 that colleges for women could offer a curriculum that went beyond cultural and scholarly subjects.[58] At the same time, coeducational universities, such as Cornell and Wisconsin, offered career preparation and the college diploma for both men and women became sought after for its utility.[59] Greater numbers of women entered college hoping to prepare for work beyond the home in the growing numbers of occupations available to them.[60]

Although teaching and raising children had long constituted the most acceptable occupations for women, as the 20th century opened, American women began to receive encouragement to train for work in domestic science, libraries, pottery, bookbinding, landscape architecture/gardening, nursing, typing, stenography, and social welfare work in settlement houses.[61] Laura Drake Gill, the president of Barnard College, stated in 1908, for example, that social service was an area better adapted to women than even the established male-dominated professions of law, medicine, and theology that Seven Sister graduates had proven themselves capable of entering.[62] Concurrently, the introduction of vocational subjects such as home economics and child study in American high schools and colleges represented a new emphasis on giving women formal and scientific training for their domestic roles.[63] While vocational subjects, such as home economics, drew criticism for lacking academic rigor, home economics graduates had uncommon success at finding jobs.[64]

The founding of Connecticut College for Women rested on the necessity of educating women for the changing times.[65] Connecticut College's approach to education would, according to its early shapers, "take cognizance of the great change in the status of women, their new opportunities and enlarged responsibilities."[66] Progressive era America needed colleges, in the estimation of founding trustee and school principal Colin Buell, "for the purpose of providing the facilities to prepare women for their work in the life of the world."[67] Some years later at her inauguration in 1930, Katharine Blunt stated Connecticut College's founding difference succinctly: "the right of women to a higher education and their ability to profit by it having been proved, we are now free to experiment. We can attempt to adapt the curriculum to the special interests of women."[68] Connecticut College, indeed, aimed to experiment, as it offered an education that would "cover the principal activities of modern life for which women are peculiarly adapted."[69]

Connecticut College for Women's chief proponents had bold aims and frequently stated those aims with inflated rhetoric. Connecticut College, in the estimation of its founding president Frederick Sykes, would not be "just another college," but would be "one of the most valuable schools for the training of young women to be found in America," a pioneering institution with its own defined individuality and character.[70] Sykes saw for Connecticut College a "high destiny in the education of women" and wanted it to provide an education that enabled women "to see truth in its relation to life."[71] He envisioned a college that would

achieve "the union of the old education with the new ideals of culture and character united with technical training, social direction and human sympathy."[72] Sykes
and Colin Buell were united in the belief that "woman has a place to fill that she
alone can fill" and that "many occupations are open to her for which she needs the
most careful preparation."[73] They wanted a college that would prepare women to
assume places of immediate usefulness in the world.[74]

Connecticut College sought to move women's education beyond the exclusively
academic focus of the Seven Sister colleges, by training women "for the kind of life
that most of them are to lead after they leave college."[75] Colin Buell hoped that the
new college's educational program would "involve reforms in curriculum and
method that will eventuate in the establishment of the true relations between
women and their environment."[76] Buell and Frederick Sykes believed that it was
false to give women an education that separated the cultural from the vocational.[77]
They believed that the study of culture and the study of the arts and sciences should
not be encapsulated from life or simply serve as preparation for life but should be
related to the concerns of living itself.[78] Their Connecticut College would provide
an education "to solve the problem of woman's preparation for the work demanded
of her to-day."[79] But unlike the strictly vocational colleges, Connecticut College
would also stress culture and liberal arts, making its mission a union of the old and
the new currents in women's education.[80] Connecticut College's educational plan
would be "thoroughly modern, while thoroughly scholarly."[81]

Connecticut College aimed to provide a liberal arts education that fit
women's interests and activities.[82] Colin Buell, for example, wanted Connecticut
College to "embody the best and most advanced ideas in education, [to be]
broadly conservative in its purposes and untrammeled by the conditions that have
shown up around the older colleges."[83] The architects of Connecticut College's
original curriculum were wary of the limitations of the traditional offerings of
men's colleges and the older women's colleges; they believed that the higher education of women could "be obtained, just as truly through the so-called modern and
practical occupations as through the classical subjects of a dead past."[84] They
wanted their new college to offer subjects for study that were being "more and
more demanded by women, and which differentiate the life-work of women from
that of men."[85] Connecticut College's curriculum, by design, was not limited to
the traditional classical course of study offered at men's colleges or the liberal arts
courses of study found at the Seven Sister colleges.[86]

Like the Seven Sister colleges, Connecticut College for Women was primarily a
liberal arts institution. Early announcements of the College stated that "there will be
ample opportunity for studying all subjects approved by the colleges of best standing."[87] "Colleges of best standing" meant, of course, the Seven Sisters. When Connecticut College opened for classes in 1915, its academic program consisted of the

following liberal arts divisions: literatures and languages; philosophy, psychology, and education; history and the social sciences; mathematical and physical sciences; chemistry; biological sciences; design in the fine and applied arts; and music.[88] The majors and courses offered at Connecticut College included liberal arts staples such as English, Latin, and Greek and ranged to botany, economics, physics, politics, and zoology.[89]

In contrast to the Seven Sister colleges, which had already demonstrated that women could handle the same college curriculum as men, Connecticut College took an alternate tack. When it opened in 1915, Connecticut College had the opportunity to present a different, and emerging, model for women's colleges, one that paired the rigorous liberal arts course of study found at the Seven Sisters with programs that prepared women for the growing number of occupations available to them.[90] Connecticut College aimed to "meet the demands of modern times...[by] offer[ing] vocational courses in dietetics, nutrition, library economy, landscape gardening, and secretarial studies, so that students who intend to earn their own living may receive an ideal training in the work for which they are best fitted."[91] Connecticut College's curriculum was a hybrid of what had worked for the Seven Sisters and of vocational approaches that were taking hold in women's education. This differing approach put Connecticut College among the first prominent liberal arts colleges for women to acknowledge that women would be working out in the world.

Connecticut College endeavored "to meet the demands of modern times" by offering "vocational courses so that students who intend to earn their own living may receive an ideal training for the work for which they are best fitted."[92] Stenography courses, for example, stood alongside academic study in recognition that graduates might work out in the business world and need to be self-supporting.[93] Because Connecticut College's founders likewise felt that preparation for homemaking and motherhood should be made as honorable and as important as preparation for any other field or profession, the curriculum included home economics courses to impart to women the new scientific methods of housekeeping.[94] Connecticut College's early announcements also stated an ambitious intention, but one never realized, to establish technical schools "for the professional training of women, in education, applied science, commerce, and the arts."[95] Some hailed Connecticut College for Women for filling a "crying need in this country for such an institution," even going so far as to suggest that it could "blaze new trails" for other women's colleges to follow.[96] Nearly thirty years after Connecticut College's founding, Katharine Blunt opined that its original mission to join the liberal arts with technical training for professional pursuits had been revolutionary.[97]

Despite its curricular differences, the requirements for entry to Connecticut College for Women resembled those at the Seven Sister colleges.[98] Candidates for admission needed to show they had completed at least fifteen high school units of preparation in languages, history, mathematics, science, and the arts.[99] Within the required fifteen units, at least three had to be from English and the languages (preferably Latin), one from history, and two from math or science. Connecticut College's initial curriculum had three aims: (1) provide rigorous study of the traditional liberal arts—the same aim as the Seven Sisters; (2) prepare women to make contributions to the world, including through jobs outside the home; (3) inculcate scientific approaches to women's traditional domestic roles.[100] Connecticut College also sought to emphasize music and art to a greater degree than had most of the established women's colleges.[101]

Connecticut College for Women's first president exhibited the institution's duality between liberal arts and practical training. Founding President Frederick Sykes was a classically trained scholar who held a Ph.D. in English from Johns Hopkins University, had edited Scribner's English Classics Series, and published articles and books on the poetry of Alfred Lord Tennyson and the French elements in Middle English.[102] Sykes was also a poet. Yet before helping launch Connecticut College, Sykes had directed the extension and practical arts divisions at Teachers College, where he was regarded as an accomplished scholar and a "vigorous" administrator.[103] Sykes was a thinker and a doer, exhibiting exactly the union of intellect and industry he hoped to develop in the students of Connecticut College.

The appointment of a serious scholar from an old and elite college (Columbia) as president demonstrated that Connecticut College for Women, at its founding, aspired to be a liberal arts college of the first rank. Working for the coeducational Teachers College of the venerable Columbia enabled Sykes to understand the type of education women needed to prepare for the full extent of her new roles in society.[104] What he observed at Teacher's College helped him fashion a new college that would prepare women to work in the fields of education, applied science, commerce, and the arts.[105] Such preparation was necessary, in Sykes' view, because women of the future would not just direct the operation of the individual home; they would also be the new housekeepers of the city, civilizing society, helping solve problems such as poor living conditions in tenements and unsanitary working environments for laborers—problems created by men due to their "insatiable demand for profits."[106]

Speaking to a Mount Holyoke College Alumnae Association meeting in 1913, Sykes stated Connecticut College's distinctive aims. Women, he noted, were demanding broader training than that offered by the older, established women's colleges.[107] The academic education provided by the Seven Sister colleges was inadequate, Sykes believed, to "fit [women] for the battle of life."[108] The time had come for the education of women to be adapted to the needs of the day; the scope of instruction at women's colleges needed to extend the application of knowledge to functional values.[109] In 1917, he told an audience of Teachers College alumnae something similar, saying that women needed both philosophy and the practical arts in their education.[110] The next step in educating women was to join technical and vocational training onto the traditional academic offerings at women's colleges.[111] Connecticut College sought to do just that.

Just as there had been a revolution in women's education in the middle of the 19th century, there was a revolution occurring in the 20th century. Connecticut College for Women filled, in the opinion of its early shapers like Frederick Sykes, a crying need for technical training for women, in professional areas as well as in household arts and fine arts.[112] The gulf between the liberal arts and practical subjects, like home economics, had been too large, he believed, before the appearance of an institution like Connecticut College. Certainly Sykes believed in the necessity of a strong academic foundation, recognizing that Connecticut College would need a curriculum that would make it "the highest type of college."[113] But Sykes also hoped that Connecticut College would be "the best and noblest example of women's education in all modern phases."[114]

Figure 4.1. Katharine Blunt

The joining of the traditional liberal arts education with the emerging practical arts, such as domestic science, also appeared in the selection of Connecticut College's third president, Katharine Blunt. Like Ellen Richards, Katharine Blunt, Connecticut's first female president, was a Vassar alumna, whose graduate work was in sanitary chemistry, the field developed by Richards. Blunt had come up through the academic ranks in the emerging women's field of home economics, serving as president of the American Home Economics Association (AHEA), the organization founded by Ellen Richards, and becoming dean of the home economics division at the

University of Chicago, where she had taken her doctorate.[115] By the time Blunt assumed the presidency of Connecticut College in 1930, she had achieved success and leadership positions in one of the fields designed by and meant for the kind of new woman that Frederick Sykes had envisioned the College educating.

Douglass, Simmons, Skidmore, and William Smith

The zeitgeist during the decade of Connecticut College for Women's founding led to a college different from the Seven Sisters, a new kind of college devoted to "the sacred cause of the development of woman hood."[116] America's Progressive Era (1890–1920) that heralded the emancipated and economically independent "new woman" brought colleges like Connecticut College for Women that emphasized, or offered career preparation. While Connecticut College was innovative, it was not the only path-breaking women's college to emerge in America's progressive era. Simmons College (1899), Skidmore College (1903), William Smith College (1908), and Douglass College (1918) also emphasized education for the purpose of work and service. One could argue, as the founders of Connecticut College for Women did, that America in the progressive era needed a new type of women's college. Leaving aside the question whether they did represent something heretofore unseen in women's higher education, each of the five new colleges (Connecticut, Douglass, Simmons, Skidmore, and William Smith) sought to provide an alternative to the liberal arts focused Seven Sister colleges that comprised the dominant paradigm in women's higher education in 1911.

Chartered in 1899, Simmons Female College opened for classes in 1902 with the innovative aim to develop women's means to pursue careers and achieve an independent livelihood.[117] In emphasizing "the preparation of young women for life," Simmons sought to be distinctive from the women's colleges nearby, such as Radcliffe and Wellesley.[118] Boston's Simmons College was also decidedly more vocational than the Seven Sisters and Connecticut College for Women. Simmons was the first college in New England to offer a "utilitarian education for girls," with an initial curriculum of Bachelor of Science and certificate programs in domestic science, library studies, secretarial studies, and general science, which later expanded to include teaching and nursing.[119] Liberal arts courses were scant. In 1904 Simmons became a pioneer in the emerging field of social work, administering its program jointly with Harvard University until 1916.[120]

Like Connecticut College for Women, the roots of Simmons College inhere in the women's club movement. At the time of Simmons' founding, Boston's Women's Educational and Industrial Union (WEIU) promoted social service and work opportunities for women.[121] WEIU members ran lunchrooms, a health clinic, a job bureau, and a legal aid center. The Simmons students who directed the WEIU lunchroom on Boylston Street gained experience that would prepare them for careers in food management.[122] The WEIU also ran a school of housekeeping to train women for leadership positions in home economics.[123] Topics studied there included home sanitation, chemistry of foods, home economics, house architecture, cooking, housework, marketing, and household buying.[124] In 1902, Simmons absorbed the WEIU's school of housekeeping.[125] Mary Morton Kehew represented another nexus between Simmons and the WEIU.[126] Kehew served as the WEIU's president from 1899 to 1913 and on the executive committee of Simmons' board of trustees during the College's formative years.[127]

Like Mount Holyoke before it, Simmons did not originate as a school for the wealthy. With its practical curriculum, Simmons sought to provide young women "from families of limited resources" the opportunity for upward economic and social mobility.[128] Because access for all was an early institution-defining goal, Simmons set its tuition at the low amount of $100 and offered ample scholarship support.[129] To attract women with daytime jobs, Simmons also offered evening courses.[130]

Skidmore College in Saratoga Springs, New York, owes its existence to Lucy Scribner Skidmore, who conceived of and endowed the institution.[131] Like Connecticut College for Women and Simmons, Skidmore grew out of the women's club movement of the 1870s to the 1920s.[132] Skidmore began in 1903 as the Young Women's Industrial Club (YWIC) of Saratoga Springs, New York, with a curriculum that included music, folk dancing, performing arts, typewriting, millinery, bookkeeping, sewing, and physical education.[133] The YWIC aimed to "help little girls and young women to become self-supporting."[134] By 1911 the Young Women's Industrial Club had transformed into the Skidmore School of the Arts that offered programs in fine arts, music, and domestic arts and sciences with an aim toward educating elementary, secondary, and college teachers.[135] Marking its maturity as an institution, the School of the Arts became chartered as the B.A.-granting Skidmore College in 1922 by the State of New York—a full decade after Connecticut College for Women's founding in 1911.[136]

Like Connecticut College for Women, whose first president (Frederick Sykes) came from Columbia University's Teachers College, Skidmore had ties to Teachers College. Lucy Scribner Skidmore used the Teachers College School of Industrial Arts as a model when transforming the YWIC into the Skidmore School of the Arts.[137] First president Charles Henry Keyes earned a doctorate at Teachers College and used his connections there to recruit a majority of Skidmore's early faculty and to establish cooperative degree arrangements between Teachers College and Skidmore.[138]

From the beginning, Skidmore College was different from the Seven Sister colleges due to its emphasis on the practical, the professional, and the creative as subjects worthy of college-level study.[139] Skidmore stressed the preparation of young women for careers that would make them useful to society and capable of economic independence.[140] The Skidmore curriculum sought to prepare women for the workforce, in recognition that not all women would marry and raise children.[141] Skidmore's emphasis on the practical was similar to its other progressive era sister colleges, Connecticut College for Women and Simmons. But like Simmons, Skidmore did not emphasize the liberal arts as much as Connecticut did. What Skidmore stressed that set it apart certainly from Simmons, and less so from Connecticut, was its expansive fine and performing arts offerings: music, for example, was the largest of its early programs.[142]

Echoing Simmons and Skidmore, William Smith College, when it opened in 1908 as male Hobart College's coordinate institution for women, purported to provide a modern education that would prepare women for civic life.[143] William Smith College described its educational program for women as "a thoroughly modern education in the arts and sciences, both as the needed introduction to professional or technical training."[144] As early as 1908, William Smith established a department of domestic science and began offering courses in home economics in 1912.[145] Six years later, in 1918, William Smith added a secretarial work department to "enable its graduates to take positions in the business world."[146] Like Connecticut College, the William Smith curriculum was a hybrid of the liberal arts focus found at the Seven Sister colleges and the more vocational thrust distinguishing Simmons.[147] But William Smith also consciously trained women in the social graces to be "ladies," wanting to gives its students "the refining influences of well-ordered homes," an emphasis not found at Connecticut College.[148] In March 1907, the *New York Tribune* called William Smith "the ideal college for women," praising especially its coordinate arrangement within a small country college for men.[149]

The women of the New Jersey State Federation of Women's Clubs founded New Jersey College (NJC) for Women in 1918 with similar motivations to the clubwomen who had established Connecticut College for Women seven years earlier.[150] Mabel Smith Douglass, president of the College Club of New Jersey, believed that her state needed a public college for women, and NJC filled that need when it opened as the coordinate college for Rutgers University.[151] New Jersey College for Women later honored Mabel Smith Douglass, who not only helped found the College but also served as its first dean, with a name change to Douglass College in 1955.[152] Like Connecticut College for Women, Skidmore, and William Smith, Douglass College had a hybrid curriculum. Douglass was primarily a liberal arts college, but one with vocational courses of study to prepare "teachers and secretaries and efficient homemakers."[153]

Connecticut, Douglass, Simmons, Skidmore, and William Smith are distinctive for the prominent vocational elements each college had in its original mission and curriculum. Although service had been a notion embraced by Seven Sister Wellesley College in its motto *non ministrari, sed ministrare* (not to be ministered unto [or be served] but to minister [to serve]), Wellesley, like the other Sister colleges, kept its curriculum largely free of vocational offerings—except for two years in the 1890s when the college offered, then discontinued, home economics.[154] Home economics courses also appeared temporarily at other Seven Sister institutions. In the 1880s Smith offered then canceled a course in household chemistry, and then a decade after Connecticut's founding, Vassar (with its euthenics program) followed the vocational current with a curricular foray into domestic science.[155] Bryn Mawr, on the other hand, never offered domestic science classes.

By the end of Connecticut College's first decade of existence, more than 100 United States colleges offered home economics courses.[156] Liberal arts-oriented women's colleges, such as Mills College (1852) in Oakland, California, and Goucher College (1885) in Baltimore, and coeducational Middlebury College, introduced (between 1909 and 1918) courses and programs in home economics.[157] But the home economics department at Goucher College disbanded after two years, and at Goucher, as at Mills, the emphasis stayed on a Seven Sisters-like liberal arts course of study.[158] The vocational forays at the Seven Sisters, and other women's colleges, tended to exist at the margins of the curriculum rather than as distinguishing elements—as at Connecticut College for Women, Douglass, Simmons, Skidmore, and William Smith.

Serving the Daughters of New London and the "Pauper Scholar"?

Another, less obvious phenomenon, that of the New England pauper scholar, helped shape the development of many of Connecticut College's small college peers. This 19th century phenomenon produced New England colleges largely comprised of students from families that were poorer than those that had traditionally sent sons and daughters to college.[159] The pauper scholars were students from rural New England regions, farm boys and girls of modest means who came to college not due to wealth and prosperity but due to hardship.[160] At college these rough-hewn prospective scholars sought training for the learned professions such as teaching and the ministry.[161]

The decline in farming drove the so-called pauper scholar phenomenon.[162] Often it was the youngest son of a farm family, the one not in line to take over the family farm, who enrolled at one of the eight New England country or "hilltop" colleges that absorbed the pauper scholar enrollment: Amherst, Bowdoin, Brown, Colby, Dartmouth, Middlebury, the University of Vermont, and Williams—all of which were founded between 1765 and 1825.[163] The geographically accessible and financially affordable country colleges provided a proverbial safety valve that reduced pressure on land and families.[164] The pauper students were too poor to make the expensive journeys to Cambridge for Harvard and New Haven for Yale.

As a result, the country colleges enrolled large numbers of local boys who lived at home or in inexpensive off-campus apartments or rooming houses.[165]

Institutional altruism did not drive the emergence of the pauper scholar.[166] Rather, the eight New England country colleges, five of which are now Connecticut College's peers in NESCAC, were struggling to stay afloat financially, and thus were conscious of every tuition dollar available to pay the bills.[167] The country colleges had almost no funds for scholarships.[168] The mingling of the poorer students with their well-to-do classmates brought changes in student demographics and class divisions in housing.[169] The poor student generally could pay tuition for classes, but usually could not afford to live on campus.[170] On average, these self-paying students were older than the traditional-age students and had worked, or were working, to finance their education.[171]

Alone among the Seven Sister colleges, Mount Holyoke drew its students from families in lower socioeconomic brackets, families that were often too poor to support their daughters at the Seminary.[172] Like New England's pauper colleges for men, Mount Holyoke drew the so-called surplus, that is, daughters of large families, working and middle class girls for whom a Mount Holyoke education promised an economic way up, a means to prepare them for occupations (chiefly teaching) that would enable them to support their families until marriage.[173] Mary Lyon intended Mount Holyoke to serve the "common people generally," the daughters of farmers and mechanics, the daughters of the country middle classes.[174] Lyon was not interested in serving the daughters of the wealthy or the gentry; as far as she was concerned, they could "provide for themselves."[175] So she located Mount Holyoke Seminary intentionally in central New England to minimize travel expenses for the small town girls.[176] Lyon also kept tuition costs low to encourage the enrollment of the daughters of large working families with limited means.[177] As a result, Mount Holyoke's students came overwhelmingly from rural New England and New York State; they were not pampered children looking for a finishing-school education but rather young women seeking an education that would provide them with a means of self-support before marriage.[178]

As the New England country small colleges acquired wealth after the Civil War, they took on the air of other institutions with long and venerable histories, and began educating the elite of the nation.[179] The same shift became apparent in the student populations of the later women's colleges. The earliest classes at Smith, which opened in 1875, were largely women whose fathers were doctors, lawyers, or business executives.[180] More than half of the students in Smith's first ten entering classes came from well-off families.[181] Although Elizabeth Wright had hoped that Connecticut College for Women would serve the "poor girl," when it opened in 1915, the majority of its 151 students, like those at its New England liberal arts college peers, were middle class and upper class girls who could pay the not inexpensive tuition (plus room and board) of $500.[182] Wanting to resemble the elite institutions of the day, its founders deliberately set Connecticut College's tuition at a level consistent with "that of other first class colleges for women."[183] There were scholarships available to mitigate the high cost. Benefactors in numerous Connecticut towns, including Bristol, Hartford, Meriden, New London, Norwich, and Willimantic, had provided funds to support students from their communities.[184] Still, it appears that keeping pace with the established and prestigious Seven Sister colleges took precedence over a Simmons-like or early Mount Holyoke-like accessibility for poorer girls.

The demographics of Connecticut College for Women's first classes were true to the local emphasis inherent in its name. Of the 260 women in its first three enrolled classes (the classes of 1919, 1920, and 1921), 204 of the students came from Connecticut.[185] Like the pauper colleges, Connecticut College for Women had a solid representation from nearby towns. But, unlike the pauper colleges, local students were not the majority. In its first three full-time classes, Connecticut College enrolled just 67 (25 percent) of its 267 students from New London and nearby towns: 32/79 (41 percent) in the Class of 1919, 16/99 (16 percent) in the Class of 1920, and 19/82 (23 percent) in the Class of 1921.[186] On the other hand, Connecticut College's part-time students, those who paid no more than the $150 tuition to attend classes, had a decidedly local flavor. Of 53 part-time students enrolled between 1915 and 1919, 48 (91 percent) came from New London or nearby towns.[187]

From the beginning, Connecticut College for Women demonstrated a reach far beyond its hometown, drawing students to its first three classes from England, Illinois, Maine, Maryland, Massachusetts, New Jersey, New York, Ohio, Pennsylvania, and Rhode Island.[188] Ten years after opening for classes, students from the state of Connecticut accounted for just 35 percent (162) of the College's 469 students enrolled in the classes of 1925, 1926, 1927, and 1928.[189] Students came from 27 additional states and the District of Columbia, including faraway states such as California (3), Iowa (4), Michigan (4), Minnesota (3), Missouri (3), West Virginia (3), Wisconsin (3), Arkansas (2), Florida (2), Kansas (1), Nebraska (1), Montana (1), and Oregon (1).[190] After Connecticut, the states most represented in 1925 were Massachusetts (75 or 16 percent), New York (64 or 14 percent), New Jersey (54 or 12 percent), Ohio (22 or 5 percent), Pennsylvania (19 or 4 percent), and Illinois (16 or 3 percent).[191] In its first two decades, Connecticut College for Women had become what founding president Frederick Sykes envisioned, a national college for young women from all over the United States who desired an education that would prepare them "thoroughly for definite work."[192]

Three "Progressive" Women's Colleges

Bennington College, Sarah Lawrence College, and Scripps College have always been interesting to scholars because each of them, from the moment of their founding, so obviously represented a departure from the Seven Sisters model.[193] Each began as an attempt to provide a different brand of education for women, an education more responsive to individual students, a model of learning less dependent on a required curriculum, and a mission not nearly as focused on outdoing the men's colleges.[194] Each of these three later and more progressive-minded women's colleges was, in some respects, an experiment that gave women's higher education something that was previously lacking.[195] Bennington College gave women freedom to explore (including an off-campus fieldwork term) outside the confines of the traditional liberal arts curriculum that reigned at the Seven Sister colleges.[196] Some of the inspiration for the Sarah Lawrence curriculum came from Vassar President Henry Noble McCracken—as McCracken steered Sarah Lawrence toward providing students more academic freedom of choice than Vassar's faculty and trustees had allowed him to achieve in Poughkeepsie.[197] From their beginnings, Sarah Lawrence and Bennington stressed the creative arts more than had been the case at the more traditionally academic Seven Sisters.[198] The arts focus at Bennington and Sarah Lawrence catered primarily to daughters of the wealthy.[199]

Inspired by the ideas of progressive educator John Dewey, Bennington and Sarah Lawrence emphasized educational freedom and fostered independent, experimental learning.[200] Dewey's notion of "learning by doing" influenced the experiential fieldwork term instituted at Bennington and the hands-on approach to learning at Sarah Lawrence.[201] Although Connecticut, Douglass, Simmons, Skidmore, and William Smith originated in the progressive era and responded to dominant currents of the time, it was not until Bennington and Sarah Lawrence that a woman's college organized itself centrally around progressive and even experimental principles.

Less experimental than Bennington and Sarah Lawrence, Scripps followed their lead in providing more curricular freedom and elective choice to its students.[202] Scripps' founding in 1926 filled a need for a women's college counterpart to Pomona College, the eldest of southern California's Claremont Colleges.[203] By the 1920s, the coeducational Pomona faced rising demand from women, which threatened to upset its 60:40 male-female ratio.[204] Scripps was both conservative and progressive.[205] In its curricular design, Scripps emphasized study of the great liberal arts tradition, that is, the acquisition of a common body of knowledge rooted in the traditions of Western civilization.[206] But Scripps also leavened its classic liberal arts emphasis with some progressive notions such as no traditional or disciplinary departmental boundaries, and provided students ample opportunity to explore intellectual interests through elective choice of courses.[207]

By the time they were founded, Bennington, Sarah Lawrence, and Scripps did not need to prove that a women's college could compete with men's colleges.[208] That had already been done. The Seven Sister colleges had demonstrated conclusively that women were up for the same level of academic rigor as men. Some historians even assert that Bennington, Sarah Lawrence, and Scripps were the first women's colleges in America that were intentionally not copies of men's colleges or the Seven Sisters.[209] But to take that assertion too far would be to run up against evidence that Connecticut, Douglass, Simmons, Skidmore, and William Smith did that first as they provided new educational opportunities that met the changing needs of women in America's progressive era.

Was Connecticut College a New Type of Women's College?

Did Connecticut College for Women represent a new type of women's college? Was joining vocational courses of study to a liberal arts core Connecticut College for Women's distinctive innovation in women's higher education, or was it a return to the cult of female domesticity under a different guise?[210] Did Connecticut College for Women, and its progressive era counterparts, represent the realistic recognition that women in 1911 could not reject domesticity altogether but could at least prepare for the new vocations and professions that offered them alternative paths—besides entrance into the male professions, where they faced discriminatory obstacles—to work beyond the home? Or did the vocational edges to the progressive era college curriculum make the intellect subservient to domesticity?[211]

If Connecticut College for Women and its analogues were merely throwbacks to the cult of domesticity and notions of republican motherhood (in other words, a regression in women's higher education), then the hybrid curriculum of liberal arts and vocational subjects did not represent an advance of the progressive era. If, however, the Connecticut College curriculum blazed trails by recognizing that women needed preparation for emerging fields, not just I-can-do-that-too competition with men's colleges, then the new college and its counterparts subverted the domestic ideal by joining it to a liberal arts education and the notion that women would work outside the home. That subversion, if it indeed was one, also expressed Connecticut College for Women's response to the competing and often contradictory demands on women during the progressive era.

There is less room for disputing that the hybrid curriculum that Connecticut College for Women helped introduce set it apart from the Seven Sisters. Soon after it opened, there was recognition that Connecticut College for Women represented a new approach to woman's higher education. For example, the Brooklyn Institute of Arts and Sciences invited Frederick Sykes in 1916 to argue the position "That the curricula of women's colleges follow too closely classical tradition" at a forum that included presidents M. Carey Thomas of Bryn Mawr, Mary Woolley of Mount Holyoke, and Henry Noble McCracken of Vassar.[212] M. Carey Thomas was to argue the opposite position—presumably speaking for her Seven Sister counterparts.[213]

Its critics would argue that Connecticut College for Women's hybrid curriculum enabled women to stay within the limits of domesticity while still justifying their college educations. Yet such a critique fails to deflate the import of the fact that Simmons and Skidmore, but especially Connecticut, Douglass, and William Smith, represented something new and innovative in women's higher education: a curriculum that provided women the classical/cultural education needed to enter the established male professions as well as a course of study designed to prepare women for the occupational fields—that were friendlier to them—emerging in the progressive era. Thus, perhaps Connecticut College and its progressive era sisters are seen most accurately as providing a compromise to alleviate the tensions for women between intellect and domesticity. In effect, Connecticut College showed women how to have both intellect and domesticity in a way that could also lead to self-sufficient work. And because Connecticut College sought to provide a useful education for women, one that acknowledged that women would have jobs outside the home in the emerging women's fields of teaching, home economics, social work, library science, and child development, it, and its counterparts, carved out a distinctive place among enduring notable women's and former women's colleges.[214]

Historians have often left Connecticut College for Women out of the story of American women's colleges. The major chroniclers of women's colleges have tended to skip from the Seven Sisters to the so-called progressive small women's colleges, Bennington, Sarah Lawrence, and Scripps, noting their path-breaking emphasis on curricular freedom of choice and learning by doing. But it has been misleading, to characterize Bennington, Sarah Lawrence, and Scripps as the only progressive counterpoints to the Seven Sisters; instead, it is more accurate to contextualize them as emerging after the first wave of progressive era women's colleges (Connecticut, Douglass, Simmons, Skidmore, and William Smith).[215]

Although they are five colleges that have been relegated to the fine print in the story of women's higher education in America, Connecticut College for Women, Douglass College, Simmons College, Skidmore College, and William Smith College are worthy of study because they pioneered a new kind of college curriculum that fit the changing needs of women during the progressive era. Omitting Connecticut, Douglass, Simmons, Skidmore, and William Smith from the history of women's colleges creates a gap that impedes a full understanding of the subject. Connecticut, Douglass, Simmons, Skidmore, and Williams Smith warrant more attention than they have drawn from historians of women's colleges because they represent innovative colleges fashioned by emerging ideas about the role of women as America entered the 20th century.

Notes

1   Wright, "A College for Women in Connecticut: Report to the Hartford College Club Committee on Women's College."

2   Elizabeth Wright to William North Rice (26 July 1910). CCA, Elizabeth Wright File.

3   "A Canadian President for Connecticut College." See also "Women's College President Talks."

4   *Connecticut College for Women: Preliminary Announcement.*

5   Woody, *A History of Women's Education in the United States.* See also Newcomer, *A Century of Higher Education for Women*; Horowitz, *Alma Mater*; Boas, *Women's Education Begins*; Solomon, *In the Company of Educated Women*; Gordon, *Gender and Higher Education in the Progressive Era.*

6   Ibid.

7   Patricia A. Palmieri, "From Republican Motherhood to Race Suicide: Arguments on the Higher Education of Women in the United States, 1820–1920," in *Educating Women Together: Coeducation in a Changing World*, ed. Carol Lasser (Urbana and Chicago: University of Illinois Press, 1987), 49–64.

8   Palmieri, "From Republican Motherhood to Race Suicide."

9   Ibid.

10 Howe, "Myths of Coeducation," 209–210.

11 Ibid. See also Palmieri, "From Republican Motherhood to Race Suicide."

12 Ibid; See also Horowitz, *Alma Mater.*

13 Ibid., 40.

14 David F. Allmendinger, "Mount Holyoke Students Encounter the Need for Life-Planning, 1837–1850," *History of Education Quarterly* (Spring1979), 27–46. See also Barbara M. Solomon, *In the Company of Educated Women* (New Haven, CT: Yale University Press, 1985) 86–87; Gordon, *Gender and Higher Education in the Progressive Era.*

15 Sarah H. Gordon, "Smith College Students: The First Ten Classes, 1879–1888," *History of Education Quarterly* (Summer 1975), 147–167. See also Gordon, *Gender and Higher Education in the Progressive Era.*

16 Horowitz, *Alma Mater.*

17 Ibid. See also Gordon, "Female Gothic."

18 Kendall, *Peculiar Institutions.* See also Horowitz, *Alma Mater.*

19 Thomas A. Gaines, *The Campus as a Work of Art* (New York: Praeger, 1991), 85.

20 Palmieri, "From Republican Motherhood to Race Suicide." See also Howe, "Myths of Coeducation," 211.

21 Newcomer, *A Century of Higher Education for Women.* See also Horowitz, *Alma Mater*; Gordon, *Gender and Higher Education in the Progressive Era*; Conway, "Perspectives on the History of Women's Education in the United States;" and Woody, *A History of Women's Education in the United States*; Palmieri, "From Republican Motherhood to Race Suicide."

22 Boas, *Women's Education Begins.* See also Boorstin, "A Higher Learning for All," 478–490; Gordon, *Gender and Higher Education in the Progressive Era*; Horowitz, *Alma Mater*; Palmieri, *In Adamless Eden*, 13.

23 Horowitz, *Alma Mater*, 28–41. See also Newcomer, *A Century of Higher Education for Women.*

24 Horowitz, *Alma Mater*, 69–81. See also Kendall, *Peculiar Institutions.*

25 Gordon, "Smith College Students: The First Ten Classes, 1879–1888."

26 Solomon, *In the Company of Educated Women.* See also Howe, "Myths of Coeducation," 214.

27 Ibid.

28   Palmieri, *In Adamless Eden*, xiii, 11. See also Horowitz, *Alma Mater*; Solomon, *In the Company of Educated Women*.

29   Jean Glasscock, *Wellesley College 1875–1975: A Century of Women* (Wellesley, MA: Wellesley College, 1975), 406–407. See also Patricia A. Palmieri, "There was Fellowship: A Social Portrait of Academic Women at Wellesley College, 1895–1920," *History of Education Quarterly* (Summer 1983), 195–214.

30   Palmieri, *In Adamless Eden*, 13. See also Palmieri, "There was Fellowship: A Social Portrait of Academic Women at Wellesley College, 1895–1920," 195.

31   Ibid., 10.

32   Ibid., 11, 19.

33   Palmieri "There was Fellowship: A Social Portrait of Academic Women at Wellesley College, 1895–1920," 196, 197.

34   Frankfort, *Collegiate Women*, 58, 61. See also Palmieri, *In Adamless Eden*, 180, who notes Wellesley's motto of "Non Ministrari sed Ministrare" (Not to Be Served but To Serve).

35   Frankfort, *Collegiate Women*, 107. See also Palmieri, *In Adamless Eden*, 160.

36   Roberta Wein, "Women's Colleges and Domesticity, 1875–1918," *History of Education Quarterly* (Spring 1974), 31–47.

37   Ibid. See also Horowitz, *Alma Mater*, 105–133. See also Solomon, *In the Company of Educated Women*.

38   Boas, *Women's Education Begins*. See also Gordon, *Gender and Higher Education in the Progressive Era*; Newcomer, *A Century of Higher Education for Women*, 164.

39   Helen L. Horowitz, "The Great Debate: Charles W. Eliot and M. Carey Thomas," in *Yards and Gates: Gender in Harvard and Radcliffe History*, ed. Laurel Thatcher Ulrich (New York: Palgrave MacMillan, 2004), 129–137, 134.

40   Ibid., 133, 134.

41   Ibid., 131.

42   Ibid., 133, 134. Harvard President Charles Eliot urged the founders of Johns Hopkins against admitting women, according to Helen Horowitz's account of M. Carey Thomas' 1899 debate with Eliot.

43   Thelin, *A History of American Higher Education*.

44   Ibid. See also Frankfort, *Collegiate Women: Domesticity and Career in Turn of the Century America*, 51.

45   Ibid.

46   Ibid., 49. See also Wein, "Women's Colleges and Domesticity."

47   Ibid.

48   Ibid.

49   Ibid., 134.

50   Palmieri. "From Republican Motherhood to Race Suicide."

51   Gordon, *Gender and Higher Education in the Progressive Era*.

52   Patricia A. Graham, "Expansion and Exclusion: A History of Women in American Higher Education," *Signs: Journal of Women in Culture and Society* (Summer 1978), 759–773. See also Newcomer, *A Century of Higher Education for Women*, 46.

53   Gordon, *Gender and Higher Education in the Progressive Era*. See also Newcomer, *A Century of Higher Education for Women*, 49.

54   Rosenberg, *Divided Lives*.

55   Miller-Bernal, *Separate by Degree*, 123.

56   Rosenberg, *Divided Lives*.

57   Ibid.

58 Ibid., 95.

59 Frankfort, *Collegiate Women*, 98.

60 Ibid., 90. See also Miller-Bernal, *Separate by Degree*, 66.

61 Henry Lefavour, "The Utilitarian in Higher Education," *ACA Publications*, 3 (6), 1903.

62 Laura Drake Gill, "Address of Welcome at the Meeting in 1908," *ACA Publications*, 3 (18) (1908).

63 Ibid.

64 Solomon, *In the Company of Educated Women*, 86–87. See also Miller-Bernal, *Separate by Degree*, 66.

65 "A Canadian President for Connecticut College," 31. See also "Dr. Sykes Heads Woman's College," *The Day* (14 February 1913). CCA, Frederick Sykes File.

66 "A Canadian President for Connecticut College," 31.

67 Buell, "Appeal to Fellow Graduates of Yale on Behalf of Connecticut College for Women's Endowment Committee."

68 "Women's Education Amply Advanced for Experiment in Meeting Special Needs, Says Dr. Blunt at Inaugural, *The Day* (16 May 1930). CCA. Katharine Blunt File. See also Katharine Blunt, "Inaugural Address" (16 May 1930) in Warrine Eastburn, "Miss Katharine Blunt Biographical Material," 3. CCA, Katharine Blunt File.

69 Ibid.

70 Reverend Joseph H. Selden, "Frederick Sykes Memorial Service Address," *Connecticut Colleges News* (26 October 1917). CCA, Frederick Sykes File. See also Nancy Barr Mavity, "To Honor Dr. Sykes," *Connecticut College Alumni Magazine* (December 1951), 10, 11.

71 Frederick H. Sykes, "Students of Dear C.C.," *Connecticut College News* (20 June 1917); "Calls it First Woman's Century," *Buffalo Courier* (31 March 1913)—both from CCA, Frederick Sykes File.

72 William Welton Harris, "Some Personal Reminiscences of Dr. Sykes," *Connecticut Colleges News* (26 October 1917). CCA, Frederick Sykes File; Nye, *Chapters in the History of Connecticut College*, 22.

73 Colin S. Buell, "Appeal to the People of Connecticut and Statement of Policy by the Trustees of Thames College" (3 June 1911). CCA, Colin Buell File.

74 Nye, *Chapters in the History of Connecticut College*, 22.

75 Ibid, 31.

76 Buell, "Thames College: An Account of the Struggle by a Yale Graduate to Found a Woman's College in Connecticut," 751.

77 Katharine Blunt, "Address at Connecticut College for Women's Twenty-Fifth Anniversary Celebration" (12 & 13 October 1940) in Eastburn, "Miss Katharine Blunt Biographical Material," 8. This is Blunt's interpretation of the aims of Sykes, Buell, Wright, etc.

78 Mavity, "To Honor Dr. Sykes," 10, 11.

79 "A Canadian President for Connecticut College."

80 Ibid.

81 Ibid. See also W. W. Harris, "College's Fate Hangs in Balance," *The Day* (20 March 1917). CCA, Frederick Sykes File.

82 Eastburn, "Miss Katharine Blunt Biographical Material," 4. Eastburn paraphrases the words of Frederick Sykes.

83 Buell, "Thames College, a College for Women to be Located in New London, Connecticut."

84 Buell, "Appeal to the People of Connecticut and Statement of Policy by the Trustees of Thames College."

85 Ibid.

86 Ibid.

87   *The Connecticut College for Women*, 11. See also Nye, *Chapters in the History of Connecticut College*, 23.

88   *Connecticut College for Women, Preliminary Announcement: Foundation, Organization, Site, and Plans* (New London, CT: Connecticut College for Women, 1914), 16–19. See also *Connecticut College for Women: First Annual Announcement, 1915–1916*, 14–16.

89   Ibid.

90   *The Connecticut College for Women*. See also *Connecticut College for Women First Annual Announcement, 1915–1916*, 6-9.

91   *The Connecticut College for Women*.

92   *The Connecticut College for Women*.

93   "A Canadian President for Connecticut College," 31.

94   Nye, *Chapters in the History of Connecticut College*, 25, 31.

95   *Connecticut College Bulletin* (New London, CT: Connecticut College for Women, 20 June 1917), 2.

96   Ibid.

97   Blunt, "Address at Connecticut College for Women's Twenty-Fifth Anniversary Celebration," in Eastburn, "Miss Katharine Blunt Biographical Material," 9.

98   "Dr. Sykes Heads Woman's College."

99   *Connecticut College for Women, Preliminary Announcement*, 12-13. See also *Connecticut College for Women, First Annual Announcement 1915–1916*, 10–11.

100 *Connecticut College for Women* (New London, CT: Connecticut College for Women, 1914).

101 "A Canadian President for Connecticut College," 31.

102 Nye, *Chapters in the History of Connecticut College*, 21.

103 Edward W. Sheldon to Morton Plant (15 January 1913). Sheldon relays Columbia President Nicholas Murray Butler's impressions of Sykes. Butler had described Sykes as an "astonishing person, likely to secure an early success for the new institution."

104 Frederick H. Sykes, "Students of Dear C.C."; "Calls it First Woman's Century," *Buffalo Courier* (31 March 1913)—both from CCA, Frederick Sykes File.

105 "WDD, For the National Cyclopedia of American Biography" (1 December 1935). CCA, Frederick Sykes File.

106 Ibid. See also Frederick H. Sykes, "The Social Basis of the New Education for Women," 226–242.

107 "Calls it First Woman's Century."

108 Ibid.

109 "Women's College President Talks." See also Sykes, "The Social Basis of the New Education for Women," 242.

110 Ibid.

111 Ibid.

112 Ibid.

113 Ibid.

114 Ibid.

115 Noyes, *History of Connecticut College*. See also Eastburn, "Miss Katharine Blunt, Biographical Material;" Sarah Stage, "Home Economics: What's in a Name?" in *Rethinking Home Economics: Women and the History of a Profession*, ed. Sarah Stage and Virginia B. Vincenti (Ithaca, NY: Cornell University Press, 1997), 3.

116 Colin S. Buell, "Rome was not Built in a Day," 5.

117 C. Goodwin & J. Wood, "A Brief History of Simmons College," http://www.simmons.edu/resources/libraries/archives/briefhistory.htm (2002). See also Sally G. Kohlstedt, "Single-Sex Education and Leadership: The Early Years of Simmons College," in *Women and Educational*

Leadership, ed. Sari Knopp Biklen & Marilyn Brannigan (Lexington, MA: D.C. Heath & Co., 1980), 93–112; Kenneth L. Mark, *Delayed by Fire: The Early Years of Simmons College* (Privately Published, 1945), 24; Susan L. Poulson, "Simmons College: Meeting the Needs of Women Workers," in *Challenged by Coeducation: Women's Colleges Since the 1960s*, ed. Leslie Miller-Bernal and Susan Poulson (Nashville, TN: Vanderbilt University Press, 2006), 208–234.

118 Mark, *Delayed by Fire*, 44. See also Kohlstedt, "Single-Sex Education and Leadership," 96.

119 Ibid., 94. See also Goodwin and Wood, "A Brief History of Simmons College;" Mark, *Delayed by Fire*, 11, 29 & 30.

120 Kohlstedt, "Single-Sex Education and Leadership," 99. See also Mark, *Delayed by Fire*, 38.

121 Blair, *The Clubwoman as Feminist*, 80.

122 Ibid., 81.

123 Ibid., 83.

124 Ibid., 83.

125 Ibid., 83. See also Mark, *Delayed by Fire*, 27, 31.

126 Kohlstedt, "Single-Sex Education and Leadership," 96.

127 Ibid., 96.

128 Mark, *Delayed by Fire*, 59.

129 Ibid., 59.

130 Ibid., 38, 39.

131 Joseph C. Palamountain, Jr., *Such Growth Bespeaks the Work of Many Hands: The Story of Skidmore College* (New York: The Newcomen Society of North America, 1976). See also Mary C. Lynn, *Make No Small Plans: A History of Skidmore College* (Saratoga Springs, NY: Skidmore College, 2000).

132 Estelle Freedman, "Separatism as Strategy: Female Institution Building and American Feminism, 1870–1930," *Feminist Studies* (Autumn 1979), 512–529.

133 Palamountain, *Such Growth Bespeaks the Work of Many Hands*. See also Lynn, *Make No Small Plans*.

134 Lynn, *Make No Small Plans* 14.

135 Ibid., 8.

136 Ibid., 45–46. Before New York State granted Skidmore College the authority to award baccalaureate degrees, the only way Skidmore diploma holders could receive a bachelor's degree was through 1–2 years of additional study at Teachers College.

137 Ibid., 45.

138 Ibid., 44–47.

139 Ibid. According to Lynn, Skidmore took the approach of trying to provide training for any profession open to women, as long as the quality of its program could be excellent.

140 Ibid., 1.

141 Ibid., 38–39.

142 Ibid., 32, 41. Skidmore offered dance and planned a conservatory of music to be headed by Alfred Hallam of the New York Symphony.

143 *Catalogue of William Smith College 1908–1909.*

144 Ibid., 3.

145 Miller-Bernal, *Separate by Degree*, 81, 88, 90. William Smith offered home economics until 1961. See also *Hobart College Bulletin 1907–08*, HWS Archives.

146 *Catalogue of William Smith College 1918–1919* (Geneva, New York: Hobart College, 1918).

147 Ibid.

148 Miller-Bernal, *Separate by Degree*, 78, 121, 123.

149 Milton H. Turk, "The Ideal College for Women," *New York Tribune* (17 March 1907), HWSCA. See also Miller-Bernal, *Separate by Degree*, 77.

150 Schmidt, *Douglass College: A History*.

151 Ibid., 6-7.

152 Ibid., 195.

153 Ibid., 26–27.

154 Frankfort, *Collegiate Women*, 58. 61. See also Palmieri, *In Adamless Eden*, 180; Newcomer, *A Century of Higher Education for Women*, 83.

155 Frankfort, *Collegiate Women*, 58, 61. See also Newcomer, *A Century of Higher Education for Women*, 83.

156 Miller-Bernal, *Separate by Degree*, 92.

157 Rosalind A. Keep, *Fourscore Years: A History of Mills College* (Oakland: Mills College, 1931), 83, 105, 117. See also Ann Heubeck Knipp and Thaddeus P. Thomas, *The History of Goucher College* (Baltimore, MD: Goucher College, 1938), 417–418. According to Miller-Bernal's *Separate by Degree* (p. 63), Middlebury added home economics courses in 1912 "to meet the special needs of women students."

158 Ibid.

159 David F. Allmendinger, Jr., "New England Students and the Revolution in Higher Education," *History of Education Quarterly* (Winter 1971), 381–389. See also David F. Allmendinger, Jr., *Paupers and Scholars: The Transformation of Student Life in Nineteenth-Century New England* (New York: St. Martin's, 1975)

160 Ibid.

161 Ibid.

162 Ibid.

163 Ibid.

164 Thelin, *A History of American Higher Education*.

165 Allmendinger, "New England Students and the Revolution in Higher Education." See also Allmendinger, *Paupers and Scholars*.

166 Ibid.

167 Ibid.

168 Ibid; Potts, "American Colleges in the Nineteenth Century."

169 Allmendinger, "New England Students and the Revolution in Higher Education." See also Allmendinger, *Paupers and Scholars*.

170 Ibid.

171 Ibid.

172 Allmendinger, "Mount Holyoke Students Encounter the Need for Life Planning," 27–46, 29, 30.

173 Ibid., 35, 36.

174 Allmendinger, "Mount Holyoke Students Encounter the Need for Life Planning," 33.

175 Ibid.

176 Ibid., 40.

177 Ibid.

178 Ibid., 32, 36.

179 Allmendinger, "New England Students and the Revolution in Higher Education." See also Allmendinger, *Paupers and Scholars*.

180 Gordon, "Smith College Students: The First Ten Classes," 147–167.

181 Ibid., 150.

182 Wright, "Report on Women's College to the Hartford College Club." See also *Connecticut College for Women, Preliminary Announcement*, 19; See also *Connecticut College for Women*

First Annual Announcement, 39. Among Connecticut's 151 original students were 99 residential freshmen and 52 special students.

183 *The Connecticut College for Women*, 11.

184 *Connecticut College for Women, Preliminary Announcement*, 19. See also *Connecticut College for Women First Annual Announcement*, 40.

185 *Connecticut College Announcement 1918–1919* (New London, CT: Connecticut College for Women, 29 March 1918), 103–107.

186 Ibid.

187 *Connecticut College Announcement 1918–1919*, 108. See also *Connecticut College Announcement 1917-1918* (New London, CT: Connecticut College for Women, 20 June 1917), 68.

188 *Connecticut College Catalog for 1924–1925* (New London, CT: Connecticut College for Women, 30 March 1925), 172.

189 Ibid.

190 Ibid.

191 Ibid.

192 "Dr. Sykes Heads Woman's College."

193 Horowitz, *Alma Mater*, 319–350. See also Newcomer, *A Century of Higher Education for Women*.

194 Ibid.

195 Horowitz, *Alma Mater*.

196 Ibid.

197 Ibid.

198 Newcomer, *A Century of Higher Education for Women*.

199 Solomon, *In the Company of Educated Women*.

200 Ibid. Regarding John Dewey's philosophy of education, see John Dewey, "My Pedagogic Creed," *School Journal* (January 1897), 77–80; Benson, Harkavy, and Puckett, *Dewey's Dream*.

201 Ibid., 64.

202 Horowitz, *Alma Mater*.

203 Horowitz, *Alma Mater*.

204 Ibid.

205 Ibid.

206 Ibid.

207 Horowitz, *Alma Mater*. See also Newcomer, *A Century of Higher Education for Women*; Studer-Ellis, "Springboards to Mortarboards."

208 Ibid.

209 Brubacher and Rudy, *Higher Education in Transition*.

210 Frankfort, *Collegiate Women*, 74.

211 Ibid., 99.

212 Charles D. Atkins to Frederick Sykes (17 August 1916). CCA, Frederick Sykes File.

213 Ibid.

214 W.D. Jenkins, "Housewifery and Motherhood: The Question of Role Change in the Progressive Era," in *Woman's Being, Woman's Place: Female Identity and Vocation in American History*, ed. Mary Kelley (Boston: G.K. Hall & Company, 1979), 142–153.

215 Horowitz, *Alma Mater*.

CHAPTER FIVE

Curriculum Reform, 1952–1962

At the moment of its founding, Connecticut College for Women was marked by a curricular tension between an emphasis on the liberal arts, which mirrored the elite men's and women's colleges of the day, and vocational aspects, which made it an emerging type of college designed to prepare women for the lives they would lead in 20th century America. Connecticut was a college that simultaneously embraced the established brand of education practiced by its prestigious Seven Sister neighbors and forged its own path by integrating elements of home economics, municipal housekeeping, and professional/clerical training into its academic program. For forty years Connecticut College for Women achieved a balance between those two opposing poles of its curriculum.

By the early 1950s the curricular landscape was changing in the nation and on the Connecticut campus. Post-World War II industrial expansion ushered in a new emphasis on science education on American college campuses. The Truman Commission had declared in 1947 that higher education was in the national interest and had predicted a boom in college enrollment by 1960.[1] Nationally there was a shift from endeavoring to educate a well-rounded generalist to a technically-adept specialist. The major local change was in Connecticut College's leadership. The College's president was no longer Katharine Blunt, whose academic training in chemistry, first at Vassar and then at the University of Chicago, had manifest itself in applications to food science. Blunt had risen in the academy through the narrow lanes open to women of her era, first becoming the president of the American Home Economics Association and then the dean of the University of Chicago's home economics division.[2] Blunt's field of home economics accounted for 60 percent of all women faculty members in higher education at the time of her appointment in 1929.[3] Largely blocked from positions in traditional academic departments such as chemistry, economics, or sociology, women, like Blunt, with training in science and social science fields found that departments and colleges of home economics provided the best, and often the only, opportunity for employment as a professor.[4] With Blunt at the helm, Connecticut College for Women stayed the course with its home economics offerings, even as nationally the field of home economics became increasingly associated with coeducational land-grant universities west of the Alleghenies.

To be sure, even at elite women's colleges such as Vassar there were students who wished their college would teach them how to be household managers and mothers and do better at preparing them for the world of work.[5] According to Vassar College Anthropology Professor Dorothy Lee, some Vassar graduates complained that, because college had taught them it was better to read Plato than to wash diapers, that it was more important to hear a lecture by T.S. Eliot than to stay home with babies after graduation, they had to unlearn what they had learned in college in order to find the value of homemaking or office work.[6] Still, by 1950 the proverbial gold standard for quality in women's higher education had been set by the Seven Sister colleges, like Vassar, all of whom lacked Connecticut College's prominent tension between the liberal arts and the vocational. The Seven Sisters—despite a few minor forays into home economics and euthenics by Smith and Vassar—stood squarely for a traditional and elite liberal arts education.

Rosemary Park Takes on the Curriculum

In historical accounts of Connecticut College for Women, the president who followed the long Katharine Blunt era, Rosemary Park, is frequently heralded for reestablishing the primacy of the liberal arts in the curriculum. If Katharine Blunt was Connecticut's builder-president, then Rosemary Park was its "educator-president."[7] Park and faculty leaders in the 1950s steered Connecticut's curriculum away from the vocational areas that had been offered as major options and minor electives from the College's opening semester in September 1915. At the same time, the Park era shifted the academic emphasis at Connecticut College toward greater depth—accomplished by moving from five courses per semester to four—and toward better prepared freshmen, who arrived at the College having digested a challenging required summer reading list.

When Rosemary Park became Connecticut College for Women's fifth president in 1946, the heart of the College's curriculum consisted of the arts and sciences subjects taught at both the Seven Sisters and at the elite men's colleges of the northeast. There was an additional slant to Connecticut College's curriculum, however, that made it divergent from its prominent brother and sister institutions. Despite the founding insistence on liberal arts, the Connecticut College curriculum had been leavened from the beginning with vocational courses in dietetics, library economy, and secretarial studies.[8] In Park's first year as president, Connecticut College still offered practical majors and courses, including home economics, hygiene, secretarial studies, child study, and retailing, in addition to the traditional liberal arts and sciences core.[9]

Rosemary Park had come to Connecticut College for Women in 1935 from Wheaton College in Massachusetts to teach German. Seeing great potential in Park, Katharine Blunt began to mentor and groom her for higher positions.[10] Under Blunt's tutelage, Park progressed through key administrative posts, taking on the role of dean of freshmen in 1941 and academic dean in 1945. When Blunt's successor Dorothy Shaffter clashed with faculty, trustees, and students, leading to her resignation after less than two years at Connecticut College, Blunt returned as president for an interim year.[11] When Blunt retired permanently in 1946, it seemed prudent to many in the Connecticut College community to appoint someone with an inside familiarity with the institution.[12] The trustees turned to the highly regarded Park for whom the college presidency represented the family business. As the daughter of a former president of Wheaton College in Massachusetts and the sister of the future president of Simmons College, it might have seemed pre-ordained when Park assumed the Connecticut presidency in 1946 at the age of 39.[13] At the time of her appointment, Connecticut College for Women was 35 years old and still had a sense of being a new institution still in formation.

Figure 5.1. Outgoing president Rosemary Park with incoming president Charles Shain at the announcement of his appointment in 1962

Park was a product of Radcliffe, where she took the B.A. and M.A. Like Bryn Mawr's Carey Thomas, Park found her way to Europe for graduate school, earning her Ph.D. in German at the University of Cologne.[14] In that early era of female scholars, women were shut out of many American Ph.D. programs, including those at Harvard and Princeton. Park found Germany, as Thomas had found Zurich, Switzerland, more congenial for doctoral study. The German research university, at the time, was also considered the model for the rest of the world. And, of course, Park's chosen field was the German language and its literature.

Though young compared to other New England liberal arts colleges and the Seven Sisters, the Connecticut College of 1946 had been on the rise. The College, for example, had established a Phi Beta Kappa chapter in 1934, before it had graduated even twenty classes.[15] Connecticut College's 1934 application for a Phi Beta Kappa chapter was one of only four successful petitions from among the 37 submitted that year.[16] The College's Arboretum was emerging as an educational resource for students and the state. Due to the prodigious amount of building that had occurred during Katharine Blunt's two stints as president (1929–1943 and 1945–1946), Rosemary Park took over an established college on a solid foundation, one that had 33 buildings and 848 students from 26 states and eight foreign countries.[17] Connecticut's faculty of 94 professors included impressive scholars of national note such as English literature professor Rosemund Tuve. In short, Connecticut College for Women in 1946 had numerous assets to bolster any claims that it was the proverbial "eighth sister" to the prestigious Seven Sister colleges.

From the beginning of her presidency, Park wrote and spoke against the post-World War II zeitgeist that promoted, in her opinion, an "over-great reverence" for the specialist—a theme she first sounded in her inaugural address.[18] At her inauguration, Park stated her intention to strengthen Connecticut College's mission of liberal education for women.[19] Park specified the need for Connecticut College for Women to undertake a reorganization of its curriculum to achieve a program of study that eschewed specialization.[20] This was because Park was through and through a champion of the liberal arts who favored the generalist approach inherent in traditional liberal learning over focused training to become a specialist. During her sixteen years as president of Connecticut College, a time of unprecedented growth and change in American higher education—including a G.I.-bill inspired enrollment boom and a growing emphasis on science and technology education, Park showed a gift for articulating on a national scale the value of a liberal arts education.[21] She was also skeptical of the progressive educational philosophies that inspired the founding of colleges such as Bennington and Sarah Lawrence, where the emphasis was on curricular freedom of choice.[22] Required courses, in her opinion, were always essential, whether desired by students or not.[23] Colleges, Park believed, were obliged to define and provide the education for the student as its recipient.[24] Park's was the predominant view in the paternalistic era during which she came of age in academia, when the adults in charge determined—with a strong sense of their authority and little interest in negotiation—what was the right course of study to offer students.[25] Such views, however, would break down in higher education in the 1960s as colleges altered their curricular offerings to satisfy changing student interests.[26] Park's privileging of the liberal arts reflected her view of the appropriate education that Connecticut College should provide. Park understood well that the serious elite colleges of the East Coast were liberal arts colleges that did not offer vocational courses of study and had adhered to non-negotiable curricular requirements. The serious elite college she knew best, Radcliffe, certainly had stayed on that traditional path.[27]

During her sixteen years as president of Connecticut College, a time of unprecedented growth and change in American higher education, Park showed a gift for articulating on a national scale the value of a liberal arts education. Park was a faculty president according to the professors and alumni who remember her era. Botany professor Richard Goodwin, for example, praised Park's skill at listening to, supporting, and leading faculty.[28] Faculty like Goodwin appreciated her for keeping the College focused on strengthening its academic core. She exemplified the era of college president as thinker-in-chief. English Professor and Dean Alice Johnson felt that "Rosemary Park enhanced the college in the public eye and constantly supported [its] high standards."[29] Her prominence as a sought-after speaker on a range of issues related to education lent stature to Connecticut College. To the extent that Park became emblematic of Connecticut College for Women, the institution benefited.

Like her predecessor Katharine Blunt, Park exemplified the "strong woman" tradition. But unlike Blunt, who was seen as a ruler type of president, Park was as human and approachable as she was regal and formidable.[30] Park had the ability to persuade faculty to favor and promote, as if it was theirs, the outcomes she preferred.[31] During contentious debates, Park rarely insisted on her own ideas openly but still tended to accomplish her goals. Edward Kranz, a prominent history faculty member during the Park era, observed that "someone else would plant the tree, but it would be planted exactly where she wanted it."[32]

Following the collegial, consensus-building tack of effective small liberal arts college governance, Park led the Connecticut College faculty through curriculum reform in the 1950s. Faculty chaired the Instruction Committee that designed the new curriculum, and in the process Park, although she was pleased with the general outcome, especially the reemphasis on the liberal arts, did not completely get her way.[33] For example, Park thought that students should know marketable skills such as typing, one of the secretarial skills that had been part of the original 1915 curriculum; but the Connecticut faculty did not agree and pushed those courses off into the non-credit extra-curriculum.[34]

In leading the faculty's efforts, Park framed curriculum reform in a larger context that transcended parochial concerns such as which course or department to include or exclude. What was really at stake, according to Park, was the ultimate justification for Connecticut College for Women's existence, that is, the essence of the kind of education the College aspired to provide through its academic program.[35] That ultimate justification, Connecticut's raison d'etre, Park asserted, was the College's educational program, which was in the hands of the faculty.[36] Although Park recognized that crafting a curriculum was in the purview of the College's faculty, she made it clear that whatever was fashioned by them must be a program that would meet the educational needs of the times and its students.[37] The goal for Connecticut College's curriculum was, in Park's estimation, to provide an education that developed in students the capacity to "ask the unanswerable questions which give depth to all of experience."[38] Park stated that in fashioning such an academic program, Connecticut's faculty should not be as concerned with communicating "a wealth of detail" but rather with imparting "a sense of human achievement and of human capacity even in times of complexity and ferment."[39] Park hoped that a Connecticut College education would encourage students to learn "how much one can learn by oneself because one has inclination, ability, and time."[40] In short, Park wanted Connecticut College for Women to encourage its students to become critical thinkers with a desire to learn on their own.

Connecticut College's original curriculum in 1915 had included dietetics (later renamed home economics) and hygiene/physical education in the major areas of study alongside liberal arts staples such as English, history, Latin, and mathematics.[41] Minor courses offered as electives in the 1915 curriculum included education, library economy, secretarial studies, commerce, and horticulture.[42] Non-credit secretarial courses in typewriting and stenography flanked majors in chemistry, English and modern languages.[43] Horticulture and landscape design courses were part of the botany department, and commerce fell under the economics major.[44] Not much had changed between 1915 and 1950. The 1925, 1939, and 1948 Connecticut College course catalogs, for example, listed majors in child development, home economics, and physical education as well as courses in landscape gardening (under botany), stenography, and typing.[45] Home economics courses drew a healthy and steady enrollment. For example, in 1940, home economics 3–4 (principles of food preparation) had an enrollment of 98 students, representing 13% of the College's total enrollment of 755.[46]

By the early 1950s, home economics had become a staple and, in some ways, a distinguishing feature of Connecticut College for Women's curriculum. Founding President Frederick H. Sykes had conceived of Connecticut College as a pioneering women's college, one not modeled after men's colleges, but instead oriented toward the "sphere of women's interests and activities."[47] Women, Sykes hoped, would be trained at Connecticut College to be "true mothers of the home and mothers of the municipality.[48] Toward those ends, Sykes believed that women would need to study food chemistry, nutrition, home planning and decoration, and how to supervise the milk supply.[49]

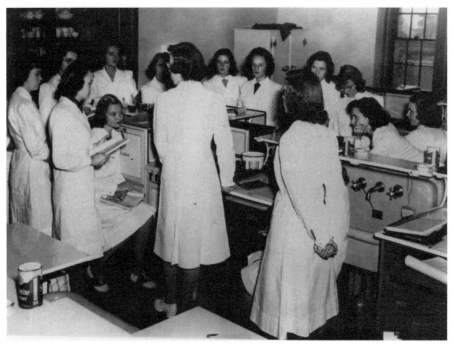

Figure 5.2. A Home Economics class

Connecticut's first woman president, Katharine Blunt, had studied chemistry on the doctoral level and had helped build the home economics department at the University of Chicago—first created by Marion Talbot—into a world-renowned program.[50] Blunt's research in chemistry had been in the applied areas of food safety and sanitary science.[51] In Blunt, Connecticut's home economics department always had a firm supporter, someone who frequently referred to Connecticut College for Women as a "liberal arts college with a vocational slant."[52] Blunt, like Frederick Sykes, believed that Connecticut College should provide an education related to real life.[53] She felt strongly that academic training was always enriched by practical experience.[54] Blunt recognized that at the time of Connecticut's founding the College's intention to provide (alongside the liberal arts) technical training that would prepare women to undertake professional pursuits was revolutionary in higher education.[55] A self-sufficient woman, Blunt wanted Connecticut

College students to have the choice to pursue a career, a traditional path as wife and mother, or both.[56] In advocating careers for her students, Blunt was in the vanguard of women who broke with the prevailing view that preparation for domesticity was the best collegiate plan for women.[57]

Figure 5.3. Connecticut College home economics faculty in the 1950s
(department chair Margaret Chaney is second from right) © Robert Perry

During Blunt's tenure at Connecticut College for Women, the home economics department offered sub-majors in household management and food and nutrition.[58] The household management major encompassed the study of living standards, family finance, and government housing projects.[59] Blunt believed that the home economics department provided "a unique opportunity in research in the social sciences with a woman's slant, along lines which have been underemphasized."[60] At its high point, Connecticut College's home economics department offered as many as 18 courses, including a class introduced in 1933 on marriage and family life.[61] That marriage course was co-taught by Margaret Chaney, longtime chair of Connecticut College's home economics department and the author of a widely used textbook on nutrition.[62] Although she supported home economics as a course of study, Blunt wanted Connecticut College's department to offer fewer courses and to integrate more science into its curriculum.[63] Blunt believed that home economics provided women a scientific understanding of the household environment, and thus she wanted the home economics curriculum at Connecticut College to be regarded as based in science.[64] In Blunt's opinion, the more scientific vocational programs like home economics were, the more they justified their place in the curriculum of a liberal arts college like Connecticut.[65] Blunt's support of home economics as an academic discipline also resulted from her commitment to prepare Connecticut College women for jobs, not just for marriage and motherhood.[66]

Faculty opposition to home economics had been building at Connecticut College for years before the curriculum revisions in the 1950s. A 1946 letter from Home Economics Department Chair Margaret Chaney to Connecticut's Faculty Instruction Committee took issue with a rule for faculty appointments and promotions specifying that instructors must have a Ph.D. degree.[67] Chaney argued that the rule, adopted by the Connecticut College faculty in 1945, placed her department at a hardship, because "there are not enought (sic) women with doctor's degrees to meet the large demand in the field."[68] Chaney pointed out that most non-research-university home economics departments staffed their faculties with master's degree holders.[69] The new rule, Chaney contended, would make it more difficult for Connecticut College for Women's home economics department to fill faculty positions.[70] The new rule also might lead Connecticut's non-Ph.D. faculty in home economics to conclude that reappointment or tenure would be unlikely, thus, "they might as well resign and seek positions elsewhere."[71] In response to Professor Chaney's appeal, the secretary of the Faculty Instruction Committee did not relent on the rule, but did note that Acting President Park had said that "only occasionally should the requirements of the doctorate for the instructorship in Home Economics be enforced."[72]

Two years later (in 1948) Professor Chaney complained to Park again, this time regarding a "student-faculty curriculum committee meeting in which the home economics course, Nutrition A, was condemned so drastically."[73] Chaney's letter to President Park stated that she was upset that the course, a cornerstone of home economics—as well as Chaney's own specialty—had been discussed and criticized by the committee without providing her (or another member of her department) the opportunity to defend it.[74] Chaney was especially bothered that a slanted summary of the discussion appeared in a student newspaper article stating that requiring Nutrition A "was not appreciated by any students."[75] Park in her response to Chaney stated that she was sorry that the student newspaper had made the poor decision to publish such negative remarks that could be verified as a widely held student view.[76] What Park did not say was significant, however. She failed to reassure Professor Chaney by condemning the student criticisms of the nutrition course. Nor did she say that she was sorry for any faculty criticism of the nutrition course.

By the early 1950s, Connecticut College's home economics department was increasingly on the defensive against its detractors on the faculty—so much so that Professor Chaney again asked Park to intercede. Chaney's January 1953 to Park implored her to intervene in faculty curriculum committee decisions that Chaney deemed unfavorable to home economics.[77] Chaney had made a motion in May 1952 to amend Connecticut College's group requirements to include a home economics course among those satisfying the College's science requirements.[78] At that May 1952 faculty meeting, the secretary of the Faculty Instruction Committee had tabled Chaney's motion.[79] Chaney's January 1953 letter stated that many Connecticut College faculty members felt that the tabling of her motion was an arbitrary ruling.[80] Chaney further complained that her subsequent letter asking the Instruction Committee to reconsider was not read at that committee's next meeting.[81] Chaney was understandably distressed that the Faculty Instruction Committee had not allowed full expression of her dissenting view; she likely also understood that the Committee's non-action augured ill for the future of home economics at Connecticut College for Women. President Park did not write a letter of response to Professor Chaney.[82]

Chaney's fears for her department were well founded. The curriculum reforms that occurred in 1953 specified that the home economics major would no longer be offered at Connecticut College after 1958, when two of the department's three professors, including Chaney, were scheduled to retire. A side-by-side comparison of the 1950 and 1958 Connecticut College course catalogs shows the extent of the curricular overhaul. A student entering Connecticut College in 1950 might not have recognized the College's 1958 course catalog. In 1950, the Connecticut College Home Economics Department had three full-time and two part-time instructors.[83] The College's 1950 course catalog listed 15 home economics courses: elementary nutrition, principles of food preparation, the house, food and nutrition of the family, management of the household, marketing, child nutrition and development, child relations, methods of teaching home economics, fieldwork in home economics, nutrition, institutional economics, problems in food preparation, individual study and investigation, and practices and procedures of the nursery school.[84] Of those courses, only child relations made it into the child development major that survived the elimination of home economics.

The 1959 Connecticut College Catalog was the first that did not display a major in home economics. Courses offered in 1959 by the child development major, into which the last remaining home economics professor had been integrated, show virtually no traces of the defunct department.[85] Child development in 1959, for example, offered the following courses: introductory anatomy and physiology (from the zoology department), chemistry of metabolism (from the chemistry department), child psychology (from the psychology department), child relations (the lone holdover from the home economics major), the family (from the sociology department), advanced child study, and individualized study.[86] By 1961, the child development major offered three additional courses: psychology of personality (from the psychology department), primitive cultures (from the sociology department), and seminar in child development.[87] None of the three new courses had been rooted in home economics.

Viewed in the context of Connecticut College's founding mission and original course offerings, the curriculum reforms of 1953 were cataclysmic. The reforms specified that as of 1958 the department of home economics would no longer exist.[88] The curricular revisions were, in the words of President Park, "a clarification of our educational tasks."[89] And indeed by 1958 the College's home economics courses and its one remaining professor had merged into child development, a department thought by Park and many Connecticut faculty members to have a more traditional academic foundation. The end result for Connecticut College was a more "intellectually pure" curriculum.[90]

Despite the rhetoric, the Connecticut College curriculum that emerged from the 1950s reforms was not a pure liberal arts program of study. The department of education stood intact, and the economics department continued to offer some commerce-oriented courses. The Auerbach Scholars retailing program, for example, that had been supported since 1938 by the State of Connecticut's leading department store, G. Fox and Company, still was a summer internship opportunity administered through the economics department, which offered courses in marketing principles and management.[91] Courses in hygiene stayed intact in the physical education department, which the College continued to offer primarily to help students fulfill a three-year sequence to ensure that students exercised their bodies as well as their minds.[92] The Connecticut College Catalog for 1959–1960 also shows courses for credit in typewriting and stenography.[93] But by 1961, the Connecticut College Catalog stated that typing and shorthand courses could be taken without credit and without charge.[94]

An Outcry from the Defenders of Home Economics

The phase-out of Connecticut College's home economics department brought a hail of criticism down on President Park from graduates of the major. The Connecticut College Archives contain a whole folder of letters critical of the move.[95] Most of the letters are reactions to Margaret Chaney's January 14, 1957 communication to home economics alumnae, in which Chaney stated that President Park "questions the value of Home Economics in a liberal arts college."[96] In her letter to home economics alumnae, Chaney had noted that her department and its supporters "have tried, with little success, to convince [Park] of the importance of Home Economics to successful family life, and of the need for training professional workers in the field."[97] Amidst the many letters of protest, the Connecticut College Archives contain just one letter of support for the decision to cut home economics. In that letter, Dorothy Chapman Cole '44 tells President Park that "the Home Ec. Dept. doesn't really belong at Conn."[98] Cole says that she found the "courses repetitive and dull" and believed that students seeking to study home economics "would be much better off attending one of the large state universities."[99]

In contrast, numerous alumnae wrote that they had chosen Connecticut College for Women because it "was the only Eastern women's college with the Home Economics major," or similarly it was "a small liberal arts college which offered home economics."[100] Cynthia Rosik, Connecticut College Class of 1955, put a finer point on it, telling Park that "Home Economics was one of the things which made Connecticut a leader among the better eastern women's colleges."[101] Alumna Dorothea Bartlett complained in 1957 to President Park that cutting home economics would remove one of Connecticut's unique features.[102] Such sentiments echoed a letter sent four years earlier in 1953 to President Park, in which Mrs. Earle W. Stamm (the wife of a Connecticut College trustee) charged, "You are changing the whole aspect of the college and I think that the alumnae will not be pleased.[103] A number of alumnae, like Bartlett, offered additional compelling rationales for saving the home economics department. Bartlett said she chose Connecticut College because she wanted to study the liberal arts and graduate equipped "to earn my own living at the end of my four years."[104] Nearly every letter of complaint to Park emphasized the excellent job preparation that the home economics major provided and referenced (or explicitly cited) the "several offers" for better pay that home economics graduates had received in comparison to their classmates who had trained in "more academic subjects" and "had to accept jobs requiring no training...or attend secretarial...schools."[105] Indeed, home economics graduates had ample employment opportunities in industry test kitchens, as dietitians, as well as in food manufacturing companies.[106] Few other fields were as committed to finding jobs for their graduates.[107]

Several other alumnae letters argued that Connecticut College's home economics department trained students for rewarding jobs in the professional sphere as well as for the important job of raising children. A former nutritionist for Beech-Nut Foods, for example, wrote that "I cannot overemphasize the value of my major to me in my present role as homemaker and mother of two children."[108] There was incredulity that a college for women could fail to offer a course of study that acknowledged "what a woman's real purpose in life is."[109] Other than home economics, "what can be more important in the education of a woman?" asked Judith Draper '38.[110] Eliminating home economics also made no sense to Carman Palmer von Bremen '38, "since the majority of graduates [of Connecticut College] marry and enter into family life?"[111] These criticisms cut to the heart of the paradox of offering home economics at a woman's college like Connecticut: on the one hand, doing so reflected progressive notions about women working to support themselves, on the other hand, justifications for home economics echoed regressive notions of republican motherhood.

President Park acknowledged nearly all of the letters of protest with a form response that cited, as justification for the decision, ten years of declining enrollments in Connecticut College's home economics classes.[112] In one of her few non-form responses, Park stated that she believed a college for women bore some responsibility to provide information on cooking and general household management; she further expressed hope that Connecticut College might establish a "kind of non-credit course" to do so.[113] While not a proponent of the home economics major, Park had been on record since 1953 as supporting courses in child development and nutrition.[114] Connecticut's Faculty Instruction Committee did in fact support keeping the child development major and nutrition course, recommending that the latter be offered in either the departments of chemistry or zoology.[115]

Deepening the Emphasis on the Liberal Arts

In addition to excising nearly all of Connecticut College's vocational courses of study, the 1952–1953 curriculum revision underscored the importance of the "Western tradition."[116] The new curriculum required students to study European history and the comparative context provided by mandatory courses in United States history or American government. The new curriculum sought to develop precision of thought through required courses in logic or mathematics, perspective and direction through courses in philosophy or religion, an understanding of the scientific method through a required laboratory science course, a facility for foreign language through one or two required language courses, acquisition of writing and analytical skills through required courses in composition and English literature, and an appreciation for art and music through required courses in either of those departments.[117]

The curriculum changes of 1952–1953 also increased the number of required courses, leaving less room for the kind of self-guided exploration of individual interests that occurred at progressive women's colleges founded after Connecticut, such as Bennington, Sarah Lawrence, and Scripps. But, as Park stated frequently, it was not Connecticut College's intention to emulate the curricula of the progressive colleges but rather to follow the older, more elite Seven Sister colleges, where academic requirements and structures had a long tradition.[118] Proponents of the new curriculum, such as English professor and alumna Gertrude Noyes '25, defended the reforms on the grounds that Connecticut's academic program would now provide coherence to students' intellectual development while also leaving ample room for exemptions and advanced placement by examination.[119] The revised curriculum, in Park's estimation, gave students more academic depth in their course of study, yet also developed their intellectual skills and the capacities they would need in adapting to a rapidly changing world.[120]

In the last year of Park's presidency, 1961–1962, Connecticut College moved to a four-course plan that had been discussed since the curriculum revision of 1952–1953. From her days as dean, Park knew well the faculty and student frustration with the five-course-per-semester plan that had been in place since Connecticut College had opened for classes in 1915.[121] Park understood that students struggled to keep up with the demands of five courses, too often turning in rushed and superficial work.[122] Faculty felt that the four-course plan, which had become the standard curriculum at Connecticut's liberal arts peers, would enable longer class meetings and foster greater depth of study.[123] Defending the new four-course curriculum, Park told an assembly of students in 1961, "these changes will make our teaching more effective...your learning less superficial...they will permit you a more secure grasp of understanding on the college courses you elect."[124] Moving to the four-course plan reinvigorated Connecticut College's curriculum and re-energized the faculty, according to future dean of faculty Gertrude Noyes.[125]

The four-course plan reduced the number of courses required for graduation from 40 to 32. Faculty hoped that the new four-course plan would bring greater vitality to the academic life of the College by enabling more seminars, independent study, and honors study—all opportunities to cultivate greater student initiative.[126] Faculty hopes were fulfilled. One tangible result of the move to the four-course plan was an immediate and dramatic increase in the number of Connecticut College students achieving academic honors.[127] Park noted in her final president's report in May 1962 that in the first year of the four-course plan the number of students on the honors list rose from 114 to 247.[128] Some, however, were skeptical that the four-course plan did little more than give professors the license to expand the scope and assignments of each course by one-fifth, thus not lessening in any appreciable way student homework, often derided as busy work.[129] Although it was still an option, few students at Connecticut College elected to take five courses ever again.[130]

In 1961, Connecticut College instituted for incoming first year students a required summer reading list of books that would serve as the basis for discussion during the opening week of the fall semester.[131] The summer reading list emphasized philosophical works, ones that would inspire students to reflect on the societal impact that scientific and technological innovations were having on the 20th century. The intent was to engage students in discussions of issues of the day and to put the incoming freshmen on notice that Connecticut College was a serious intellectual environment.[132] Chosen works for the first year of the program included C.P. Snow's *Two Cultures*, Albert Camus' *The Fall*, Barbara Ward's *Five Ideas That Changed the World*, and Walter Lippmann's *The Good Society*.[133]

In 1997, Alice Johnson, who had been Connecticut's dean of freshmen in 1961, recalled the intellectual vigor of those first discussions of C.P. Snow, noting that students exhibited palpable eagerness to critique and debate Snow's ideas.[134] The success of that first reading list brought an even more ambitious one for 1962: Arthur Koestler's *Darkness at Noon*, Andre Malraux's *Man's Fate*, William Golding's *Lord of the Flies*, and Paul Tillich's *Courage to Be*, as well as recommendations to delve into William Shakespeare's *Coriolanus*, Adolph Hitler's *Mein Kampf*, Karl Marx's *The Communist Manifesto*, Walter Rostow's *Stages of Economic Growth*, John Dos Passos' *Mid Century*, William Shirer's *The Rise and Fall of the Third Reich*, Karl Jaspers' *Future of Mankind*, and Harrison Brown's *Challenge of Man's Future*.[135] Johnson noted that the summer reading list concept caught on at colleges across the United States "faster than a prairie fire on a windy day."[136] The reading list idea was a success in part because Connecticut and other colleges, in Johnson's opinion, saw emerging in the 1960s "a new breed of student," far more lively and engaged than the 1950s variety had been.[137]

The Legacy of the Park Era Curriculum Reforms

During Park's 27 years at Connecticut College, she helped create the institution that successive generations have come to know and love.[138] The College's enrollment grew by more than 300—from 848 to 1,162—and the number of faculty increased from 94 in 1947 to 130 in 1963.[139] The College added significant facilities such as the Crozier-Williams Student Center, Warnshuis Infirmary, Hale Laboratory, and the North Dormitories.[140] Symbolically Park's departure in 1962 for the presidency of Barnard College emphasized that Connecticut College was on par with the Seven Sister colleges. Park's leadership of Connecticut also provided a model for others. A number of Connecticut faculty members under Park went on to college presidencies elsewhere, including English Professor Robert Strider to Colby College and history professor Philip Jordan to Kenyon College.[141] Graduates of the Park era recall her with a sense of awe: they remember looking up to her and aspiring to be like her.[142] Perhaps Park represented the last wave of college presidents whose position and presence in that position earned them the unquestioning respect of the students they commanded. Peggy Evans '44, who had Park as a German professor and house adviser, remembers her as demanding but caring.[143] Evans credits Park and Rosemond Tuve with helping her discover a latent love of learning that led her to earn a master's degree in English at Columbia University and eventually to write a biography of Professor Tuve.[144] Even alumni of Connecticut College from as late as the 1980s recall hearing Park spoken of with reverence.[145]

Park left Barnard in 1967 as a newlywed to serve as a vice chancellor at the University of California at Los Angeles, where her husband (Milton Anastos) taught Byzantine Greek.[146] Father Theodore Hesburgh soon thereafter selected her as the first woman to serve on the University of Notre Dame's Board of Trustees.[147] In that capacity, Park advised Notre Dame during its transition to coeducation.[148] In 1978 Praeger Press published a volume of collected essays by scholars celebrating Rosemary Park's leadership in higher education.[149]

The Connecticut College that emerged from the Rosemary Park era was an institution that had pruned some of the academic offerings that had been central at its founding. In removing the home economics program, Connecticut College let go of the field where its longest-serving president, Katharine Blunt, had achieved prominence. Also gone by the end of Park's tenure were other programs that had expressed Connecticut College's difference at its birth, such as secretarial courses. It is tempting to speculate about how founding president Frederick H. Sykes and former home economics association president Katharine Blunt would have reacted to the changes. Sykes, as well as Blunt, might have cautioned against Park's hard tack into the liberal arts curricular waters. Sykes and Blunt might have asked whether the curricular changes were made to bolster the reputation and stature of the College or whether they resulted from a genuine recognition of a changing current in women's higher education, that is, the belief that vocational programs had served their purpose and were no longer as necessary as they were in 1915.

In her last year as president, Rosemary Park expressed satisfaction that Connecticut College's revised curriculum more closely resembled the Radcliffe College she knew as a student in 1924 as well as the academic programs at Bryn Mawr, Harvard, and Pembroke (the women's college of Brown University).[150] Park's remarks left little doubt that those Seven Sister and Ivy League colleges had been the models for Connecticut to emulate during her presidency. Proponents of home economics might have said, however, that Connecticut College, through its curricular reforms of 1952-1962, became more generically a small liberal arts college with less of a plausible claim on curricular distinctiveness. The curriculum reformers might have argued in defense that having a home economics department detracted from Connecticut College's stature, in part because home economics was always seen as an inherently feminine (read inferior) field always consigned to fight an uphill battle in academe to attain the stature of the applied areas that men studied such as engineering.[151] Those critics might have asked whether Connecticut College really wanted to be associated with a field that many in higher education had long dismissed as nothing more than "glorified housekeeping."[152] Those critics might also have argued that women's higher education opportunities and employment options had expanded since 1915, rendering segregated vocational programs for women, such as home economics, an anachronism.[153]

Despite heroic attempts by the early home economics partisans, whether Ellen Richards nationally or Margaret Chaney at Connecticut College, the field could never escape limitations imposed by gender stereotypes.[154] If home economics as a discipline became regarded as a lesser area of study because it was a women's field, then Connecticut College for Women was by association a lesser college for having the major. On those grounds, it is hard to fault Rosemary Park and the Connecticut faculty for eliminating the program in favor of a purer liberal arts curriculum that more closely aligned the College with the most elite institutions of the day.

By the 1950s, none of the Seven Sister colleges offered vocational courses or programs advocated by the home economics movement. Two of the Seven Sister colleges, Smith and Vassar, had made brief dalliances into domestic science in the 1920s. Smith's Institute for Coordination of Women's Interests, founded by Ethel Puffer Howe, hoped to resolve the "intolerable choice between career and home" by developing cooperative nurseries, kitchens, laundries, and shopping arrangements.[155] But Howe's Institute at Smith lasted only six years.[156] In 1924 Vassar College created a school of euthenics focused on the development and care of the family.[157] Vassar graduate Ellen Richards defined "euthenics" as "the science of the controllable environment."[158] Central to euthenics was the belief that "social change could be produced by individuals acting decisively to alter their environment."[159] An amalgam of domestic science, economics, and sociology, euthenics would be practiced, according to Richards' vision, by a vanguard of scientifically trained women acting as social engineers.[160] Vassar's euthenics program introduced the nation's first major in child study and provided instruction in domestic architecture and furniture, food chemistry, horticulture, and hygiene.[161] Euthenics courses included "Husband and Wife," "Motherhood," and "The Family as an Economic Unit."[162] Critics of Vassar's euthenics program thought it "was a prostitution of science and smacked of vocationalism."[163] The euthenics department ran the Vassar Summer Institute for Family and Community Living as a six-week program from 1926 through 1959.[164] But as a program in a college that overwhelmingly cast its lot with the liberal arts, the euthenics department at Vassar existed at the margins of the curriculum—its courses drew few non-summer students and the program ultimately went defunct.[165]

Except for the scuttled programs at Smith and Vassar, the prevailing opinion within the Seven Sisters was that the field of domestic science was too tied to household skills to be of serious academic worth.[166] Bryn Mawr College officials, for example, declared that really intelligent women would not find enough elements of intellectual growth in domestic science to furnish a profound course of training.[167] The fact that home economics was associated with the agricultural colleges in the Midwest, which East Coast partisans deemed inferior to the elite colleges of the East, also held back the acceptance of domestic science.[168] Further complicating the situation was the fact that by the 1950s and on into the 1960s, fields such as home economics were transforming into realms no longer solely controlled by women—a morphogenesis that produced some ironic consequences.[169] Scholars such as Margaret Rossiter, for example, have noted that as men moved into the field, home economics began to receive more funding and legitimacy.[170] Occupations like social work were becoming more professionalized and more dependent on licensure and American graduate and professional schools were becoming more welcoming to women. In addition, by 1960, women were studying and working in greater numbers than ever.[171] Typing and clerical skills could be acquired after college at specialized institutions such as the Katherine Gibbs School.[172] As professional schools and careers opened to them, women did not need—as much as they had near the turn of the 20th century—the domestic arena to carve out a special sphere of influence.

Rosemary Park also seems to have realized that Connecticut College, to be taken seriously as a liberal arts college of the first rank, needed to strengthen its science programs.[173] Like Frederick Sykes, Park was a provocative thinker whose speeches tended toward visions of the future. Park saw a future constructed around science and technology.[174] She believed that the careers of the future for women would develop out of general science rather than from the gendered fields of home economics and social work that had held so much promise for women in 1915.[175] Park thought that women, especially college educated women, should be equipped to enter scientific fields; thus, she frequently took aim at the prejudiced belief that "math and science are not subjects in which girls can expect to succeed."[176] Indeed, beyond the Connecticut College campus, the new vocational training emerging in the 1950s was in science and technology. Following the Soviet Union's launch of Sputnik, Congress passed the National Defense Education Act that stressed math, science, and foreign language—all subjects that challenged home economics as a high school elective.[177] It could be argued that by emphasizing the emerging science areas, rather than the practical domestic science fields of days gone by, Connecticut College was both evolving and staying true to its mission to educate women to be of use in the world.

Park's foresight regarding science drove the decision to start Connecticut College for Men, which provided graduate programs for the growing number of male scientists working at the Pfizer and Electric Boat plants in the New London area.[178] Having men in some of the College's science classes, Park believed, would have a positive effect on women, motivating them to show that they could compete with men scholastically.[179] Having men, especially committed young scientists, in classes would also show that Connecticut College was of high enough academic quality to interest and challenge male students.[180] Despite the many accomplishments of their graduates, women's colleges, even in the late 1950s, still had to defend themselves against the ingrained notion that men's colleges were by definition superior.

Jettisoning or pushing aside the vocational courses was also a clear statement that Connecticut College was not in the realm of the so-called "finishing schools," the M.R.S.-degree colleges such as Finch, Pine Manor, or even the southern women's colleges that were widely viewed as providing an education for the cultured and decorative woman who would lead a life of gentility.[181] Such institutions, notwithstanding the unfair stereotypes of women's colleges, were always closer to being actual sites for finishing for marriage than they were serious liberal arts colleges.[182] But as strong as Connecticut College for Women became, the fact that it lacked the prestigious imprimatur of the "Seven Sisters" meant that it always inhabited the more self-conscious and insecure realm of the almost-Sisters with Douglass, Goucher, Mills, Skidmore, Wells, Wheaton, and William Smith, a realm that constantly had to prove its quality.[183]

By 1960, Connecticut College's early 20th century sisters in practical higher education—Douglass College, Simmons College, Skidmore College, and William Smith College—were also firmly established. Of that group of three, only Simmons had stayed true to its original mission and had not embraced the Seven Sisters model that meant excising the vocational in favor of the pure liberal arts. Simmons, for example, continued to maintain a school of home economics into the mid-1960s.[184] According to the 1960 Simmons College course catalogue, a Simmons education was preparation for "most of the professions which women find interesting."[185] A Simmons College student in 1960 had the opportunity to choose courses from nine different schools: business, education, home economics, library science, nursing, publication (publishing), retailing, science, or social science.[186] Douglass College also continued to offer home economics as a major in 1960.[187]

In contrast, Skidmore and William Smith, like Connecticut College, were settling further into a liberal arts curriculum. By 1962, William Smith no longer offered a home economics department.[188] But unlike Connecticut and William Smith, Skidmore continued to offer home economics.[189] Skidmore, like Connecticut, had offered courses related to marriage and family in the 1930s and 1940s, but had discontinued them as a separate program, moving them into departments such as sociology and home economics in 1954–1955.[190] Still, despite its continuing home economics program, Skidmore's roots in the Young Women's Industrial Club were less apparent with each year.[191] For colleges such as Connecticut and Skidmore that aspired to greater prestige in women's higher education, one strategy to reach that goal was to resemble, as much as possible, the Seven Sister colleges.

In fact, there is evidence that, to a large extent, insecurity about its liberal arts identity propelled the 1952–1962 curriculum reform efforts at Connecticut College. Faculty at Connecticut in the 1950s "were obsessed with establishing the intellectual credentials of [the] young college," recalled Alice Johnson in a 1997 unpublished historical account of Connecticut College in the 1950s and 1960s.[192]

Johnson's perspective on Connecticut College is not easily dismissed, because she arrived at Connecticut in 1958 from Wellesley College, not long after the first major curriculum reform in 1952–1953 but before the second wave in 1961, and stayed until her retirement in 1986.[193] To Johnson's eyes, Connecticut College's original vision of educating women to pursue careers was innovative.[194] Despite her background in the pure liberal arts field of English literature, Johnson recognized the historical significance of Connecticut's "so-called practical areas of study," that is, fields such as home economics that had been eliminated from the curriculum in the 1950s.[195] Johnson came to believe that Connecticut College, in its earliest decades, had been ahead of its time with its emphasis on women putting their liberal arts education to good use in the world.[196]

The Connecticut College for Women that Alice Johnson found in 1958, however, aspired to become the eighth sister to the Seven Sisters, with a drive that "was at times so compelling that it became education by imitation rather than by intellectual persuasion."[197] To a newcomer like Johnson, Connecticut looked like a Seven Sister college.[198] Like Wellesley, Connecticut maintained "vigorous academic standards."[199] But Johnson was "immediately impressed by how much more work professors expected of Connecticut College students than had been the case at Wellesley."[200] In Johnson's opinion, "Connecticut was still in the throes of trying to prove itself as good as, if not better than, the older women's colleges in New England."[201] Johnson noted that at Connecticut College new programs sometimes got proposed but then would be dismissed on the grounds that the Seven Sisters were not following such a course.[202] Johnson believed that Connecticut had cut majors like home economics in the 1950s "as the urge to become the eighth sister became an overwhelming desire."[203] Connecticut College's long-standing commitment to career preparation had given way to a belief that developing marketable skills could be done by a woman after graduation.[204] According to this view, career training was more appropriately acquired at specialized vocational institutions like the Katherine Gibbs School, where a woman with a B.A. could get clerical training to become an assistant to the male president of a prestigious firm.[205] If that stance toward career preparation was good enough for the Seven Sisters, then it was good enough for Connecticut College, because "To be chosen to join that illustrious group would signify that the college had at last arrived at a level of excellence commensurate with its most pressing goals."[206]

Alice Johnson found the obsession with the Seven Sister colleges difficult to appreciate because Connecticut College had struck her from the first as practicing the virtue of constant self-examination with no trace of the smugness "which permeated some of those female institutions that had been founded at a much earlier date."[207] Johnson's recollection of a self-conscious desire to be as good as the Seven Sister colleges matches the comments of numerous alumni, faculty, and administrators who described the Connecticut College they knew as always trying to keep up with older and more highly esteemed peer institutions, either the Seven Sisters or the established New England men's colleges.[208]

Figure 5.4. Dean Alice Johnson with a male student

By the beginning of the 1960s, the question Windham, Connecticut high school principal Egbert Case had posed in a 1913 letter to Elizabeth Wright (Is Connecticut like Smith or Simmons?) had taken on new meaning.[209] At the time of Connecticut College for Women's opening in 1915, the accurate answer to Principal Case would have been, Connecticut is more Smith (that is, primarily a liberal arts college) but some Simmons (with vocational majors and courses). By 1960, the answer to Case's question had changed, largely due to Connecticut's curricular movement toward pure liberal arts, a path not taken by Simmons. Simmons College was, in 1960, as it had been from the first, largely career-oriented in its programs of study for women. Smith was still a women's liberal arts college of the first rank. Curricular reform established Connecticut College solidly in the realm of Smith and the other Sister colleges.

Connecticut College's curriculum reforms of 1952 to 1962 were consistent with its founding mission in at least one essential way. The College's founders and shapers had regarded education in the liberal arts as the best preparation for a life of civic involvement. First president Frederick Sykes, for example, had emphasized that education should spur useful activity out in the world.[210] At her inauguration in

1930, Katharine Blunt had stated that "The right of women to higher education and their ability to profit by it having been proved [by the Seven Sister colleges], we are now free to experiment," free to "adapt the [Connecticut] curriculum to the special interests of women, where so far as such interests exist."[211] Blunt believed in a curriculum that differed from the Seven Sister colleges, which had largely tried to prove that women were capable of the same curriculum offered at the elite men's colleges. Like first president Frederick Sykes, Blunt wanted Connecticut College to provide women an "education related to real life.[212]

Blunt and Rosemary Park after her, as they prepared the next generation of women leaders, faced a long-standing question: should women's colleges imitate the elite men's colleges (thus providing educational equality with men) or should they take a newer, more radical approach to education?[213] Blunt (like Sykes before her) took the latter, more radical path for Connecticut College. Park, on the other hand, drew Connecticut closer to the view held by the Seven Sister colleges and its elite brother colleges, most of which like Connecticut, would become coeducational liberal arts colleges by the 1970s. Yet Park perhaps did not fully break with Blunt's path and Connecticut College's original mission but instead reinterpreted both, restating Blunt's words as "the value of college is not in just making a living but in living a life."[214] Park wanted Connecticut College to produce tough-minded and socially aware young women who were concerned with something greater than earning a living.[215] And Park believed that a liberal arts education, without supplemental vocational elements, provided women with both necessary and sufficient preparation for meaningful and productive lives after college.

The story of the elimination of home economics at Connecticut College for Women has significance beyond one campuses' experience. Connecticut's women's college peers in providing vocational courses of study (Douglass, Simmons, Skidmore, and William Smith) wrestled with similar curricular issues in the 1950s and early 1960s. Forming the backdrop to Connecticut's decade-long curriculum reform discussion was a shifting landscape of career and study opportunities for women in the United States. Fields associated with the progressive era notion of municipal housekeeping were declining as science and technology career opportunities were ascending. The removal of home economics from the curriculum at one women's college provides a lens into larger societal changes and challenges confronting women in the 1950s—a decade often characterized as one of little progress for women. To dismiss the 1950s, however, is to miss that small steps, such as the elimination of a gendered field such as home economics at colleges like Connecticut, presaged the larger steps made on campuses by the feminist movement of the 1960s and 1970s.

Notes

1   "President Harry Truman's Commission Calls for Expansion of Higher Education," from *Higher Education for Democracy: A Report of the President's Commission on Higher Education* (New York, 1947), 1, 25–29, 32–39.

2   Eastburn, "Miss Katharine Blunt, Biographical Material."

3   Rosenberg, "The Limits of Access: The History of Coeducation in America," 125.

4   Stage and Vincenti, *Rethinking Home Economics*, 77.

5   Stricker, "Cookbooks and Law Books," 490.

6   Dorothy D. Lee, "What Shall We Teach Women?" *Mademoiselle* (August 1947), 213, 354, 356, 358.

7   Sullivan, "Rosemary Park: A Study of Educational Leadership During the Revolutionary Decades," 35.

8   *Connecticut College for Women: First Annual Announcement*, 38.

9   Sullivan, "Rosemary Park," 38.

10   Noyes, *History of Connecticut College*, 143. See also Chuck Luce, "Living Legends: Rosemary Park Anastos," *Connecticut College Magazine* (Spring 1998), 32–33.

11   Ibid. See also Dorothy Shaffter File, CCA.

12   Alice Johnson, *Unpublished Memoir of Time at Connecticut College*, (1997), 42. CCA, Alice Johnson File.

13   Park served as Connecticut's acting president in 1946–1947. Her official inauguration took place on May 17, 1947. Noyes, *History of Connecticut College*. See also Sullivan, "Rosemary Park." See also "Dr. Rosemary Park Excited Over 50th Anniversary of Connecticut College," *New Haven Register* (15 January 1961); Frances Green, "Charming Scholar, Efficient Administrator is Rosemary Park," *Worcester Sunday Telegram* (20 May 1962).

14   Sullivan, "Rosemary Park."

15   Noyes, *History of Connecticut College*.

16   Ibid.

17   Luce, "Living Legends." See also "Eastburn, "Miss Katharine Blunt," Biographical Material," 7; "Connecticut College's Strategic Priorities for the Second Century: Draft 8" (2 February 2007), 40–46, which lists the opening date of each campus building.

18   Sullivan, "Rosemary Park," 28.

19   Ibid., 28.

20   Ibid., 28.

21   Ibid., 28, 36.

22   Ibid., 36.

23   Ibid., 36.

24   Ibid., 36.

25   Park, while considered one of Connecticut's most effective presidents, had less success and a shorter reign as Barnard College's president in the tumultuous later 1960s—Sullivan, "Rosemary Park."

26   Ibid., 36.

27   Rosemary Park, "Remarks to Assembly, April 27, 1961," in *Fiftieth Anniversary Celebration Publication: Connecticut College 1911–1961* (New London, CT: Connecticut College, 1961), 26.

28   Richard Goodwin, interview by author 24 April 2007 (interview in possession of author).

29   Johnson, *Unpublished Memoir of Time at Connecticut College*, 44.

30   Goodwin interview. Also Jane Bredeson (23 January 2007), Margaret Clark "Peggy" Evans (15 June 2007), and Torrey Fenton (24 April 2007), interviews by author (interviews in possession of author).

31   Sullivan, "Rosemary Park," 38.

32   Ibid.

33   The Instruction Committee is cited as the decision-making body in Rosemary Park's 14 No-
     vember 1952 letter to Margaret S. Chaney. CCA, Home Economics File.

34   Sullivan, "Rosemary Park," 39. See also Rosemary Park, "Your College Education: Our Mutual
     Responsibility," in *Fiftieth Anniversary Celebration Publication: Connecticut College 1911–
     1961* (New London, CT: Connecticut College, 1961), 19.

35   Rosemary Park, *President's Report, 1952* (New London, CT: Connecticut College for Women,
     1952), 5.

36   Ibid.

37   Ibid.

38   Ibid., 8.

39   Ibid., 9.

40   Rosemary Park, *Report of the President, 1946–1962* (New London, CT: Connecticut College,
     1962), 17.

41   *Connecticut College for Women, First Annual Announcement, 1915–1916*, 17, 32.

42   Ibid.

43   Ibid.

44   Ibid.

45   *Connecticut College Bulletin, 1939-1940* (New London, CT: Connecticut College for Women,
     30 March 1939). See also *Connecticut College Bulletin, 1925–1926* (New London, CT: Con-
     necticut College for Women, 30 March 1925); *34th Annual Catalogue of Connecticut College*
     (New London, CT: Connecticut College for Women, March 1948).

46   Margaret Chaney to Katharine Blunt (24 October 1940). CCA, Home Economics File. 1940
     enrollment figure from Irene Nye, *Chapters in the History of Connecticut College During the
     First Three Administrations, 1911–1942* (New London, CT: Connecticut College, 1943), 76.

47   Eastburn, "Miss Katharine Blunt, Biographical Material," 3–4.

48   Sykes, "The Social Basis of the New Education for Women," 227. See also Eastburn, "Miss
     Katharine Blunt, Biographical Material," 3.

49   Ibid.

50   Sarah Jane Deutsch, "From Ballots to Breadlines," in *No Small Courage: A History of Women in
     the United States*, ed. Nancy F. Cott (New York: Oxford University Press, 2000), 413–472, 441.

51   Eastburn, "Miss Katharine Blunt, Biographical Material."

52   Oral recollections of Miss Elizabeth C. Wright to Anne Taylor, 1957–58. CCA, Elizabeth
     Wright File.

53   Eastburn, "Miss Katharine Blunt, Biographical Material," 7.

54   Katharine Blunt, "Unique Characteristics of Connecticut College" (10 May 1941). CCA,
     Katharine Blunt File.

55   Ibid.

56   Eastburn, "Miss Katharine Blunt, Biographical Material," 5.

57   Linda Eisenmann, *Higher Education for Women in Postwar America, 1945–1965* (Johns Hop-
     kins University Press, 2006), 6.

58   Ibid.

59   Ibid.

60   Ibid.

61   Ibid. There are suggestions in Katharine Blunt's papers, as well as in the home economics files
     in the Connecticut College Archives, that Blunt was less than enthusiastic about a marriage
     course being part of the curriculum at a serious liberal arts college. See also Home Economics
     File, CCA.

62 Katharine Blunt to Dr. Albert Noyes, Jr. (18 December, 1939). Blunt's letter to Dr. Noyes, the chair of the Chemistry Department at the University of Rochester, emphasizes that Connecticut College's home economics courses in foods and nutrition required laboratory work and had as prerequisites courses in organic and physiological chemistry. Blunt also refers to Chaney and Ahlborn's co-authored book, "Nutrition." CCA, Home Economics File.

63 Eastburn, "Miss Katharine Blunt, Biographical Material," 3–7.

64 Ibid.

65 Ibid.

66 K.M., "Miss Blunt Cited as Distinguished Citizen," *Connecticut College Alumnae Magazine* (May 1949), 6–9.

67 Margaret S. Chaney to Faculty Instruction Committee (1 January 1946). CCA, Home Economics File. In objecting to the Ph.D. requirement for faculty, Chaney was not making a self-serving argument, for she held a Ph.D. from the University of Chicago.

68 Ibid.

69 Ibid.

70 Ibid.

71 Ibid.

72 Secretary of the faculty instruction committee to Margaret S. Chaney (9 January 1946). CCA, Home Economics File.

73 Margaret S. Chaney to President Park (1 March 1948). CCA, Home Economics File.

74 Ibid.

75 Ibid.

76 Rosemary Park to Margaret S. Chaney (2 March 1948). CCA, Home Economics File.

77 Margaret S. Chaney to Rosemary Park (29 January 1953). CCA, Home Economics File.

78 Ibid.

79 Ibid.

80 Ibid.

81 Ibid.

82 Ibid. A handwritten note on the first page of Chaney's letter states that "R.P. spoke to Miss Chaney."

83 *Connecticut College Bulletin 1950* (New London, CT: Connecticut College for Women, 1950).

84 Ibid.

85 *Connecticut College Bulletin, 1959* (New London, CT: Connecticut College, 1959).

86 Ibid.

87 *Bulletin of Connecticut College 1961* (New London, CT: Connecticut College, 15 April 1961).

88 *Bulletin of Connecticut College, 1957–1958* (New London, CT: Connecticut College, 15 April 1958).

89 Park, *President's Report, 1952,* 10.

90 Sullivan, "Rosemary Park," 39. Park does not mention the vocational courses of study in her 1952 and 1962 president's reports, the only two of those reports to raise the issue of curricular reform. But on page 14 of the 1962 president's report Park asserts that the child development major was not as attractive to current students as it had been to previous generations. Gertrude Noyes also curiously deemphasizes this aspect of curricular reform, choosing instead to give more ink in her 1982 history of the College to the shift in 1961–1962 from five courses per semester to four.

91 Eastburn, "Miss Katharine Blunt, Biographical Material." Also Jeanette Hersey, interview by author 22 January 2007 (interview in possession of author); *Bulletin of Connecticut College: Announcements for 1953–1954* (New London, CT: Connecticut College, 30 March 1953), 142.

92 *Bulletin of Connecticut College 1961*. See also "Faculty Discussion Reveals Changes of New Curriculum," *Connecticut College News* (18 February 1953), 2.

93 *Connecticut College Bulletin, 1959*.

94 *Bulletin of Connecticut College 1961*, 131.

95 CCA, Home Economics File.

96 Margaret S. Chaney to Home Economics Alumnae (14 January 1957). CCA, Home Economics File.

97 Ibid.

98 Dorothy Chapman Cole '44 to Rosemary Park (19 January 1957). CCA, Home Economics File.

99 Ibid.

100 Virginia Martin Pattison '42 to Rosemary Park (18 January 1957). See also Virginia Taber McCamey to Rosemary Park (27 January 1957). CCA, Home Economics File.

101 Cynthia Rosik to Rosemary Park (26 January 1957). CCA, Home Economics File.

102 Dorothea Bartlett to Rosemary Park (23 January 1957). CCA, Home Economics File.

103 Mrs. Earle W. Stamm to Rosemary Park (29 January 1953). CCA, Home Economics File.

104 Bartlett to Rosemary Park.

105 Marjorie J. Gosling '50 to Rosemary Park (25 January 1957). CCA, Home Economics File.

106 Stage, "Home Economics: What's in a Name?" in Stage and Vincenti, *Rethinking Home Economics*, 11.

107 Kathleen Babbitt, "Legitimizing Nutrition Education: The Impact of the Great Depression," in Stage and Vincenti, *Rethinking Home Economics*, 145.

108 Jean Kohlberger Carter '43 to Rosemary Park (22 January 1957). CCA, Home Economics File.

109 Gosling '50 to Rosemary Park.

110 Judith Draper to Rosemary Park (16 October 1958). CCA, Home Economics File.

111 Carman Palmer von Bremen to Rosemary Park (29 September 1953). CCA, Home Economics File.

112 Rosemary Park to Virginia Martin Pattison '42 (30 January 1957). CCA, Home Economics File.

113 Rosemary Park to Mrs. Daniel Draper (28 October 1958). CCA, Home Economics File.

114 Rosemary Park to Mrs. Elwood Carter, Jr. (Jean Kohlberger Carter) (25 January 1957). CCA, Home Economics File.

115 Rosemary Park to Margaret S. Chaney (19 March 1957). CCA, Home Economics File.

116 Noyes, *History of Connecticut College*, 148. See also "Faculty Discussion Reveals Changes of New Curriculum," 1–2.

117 Park, *President's Report, 1952*, 6–7.

118 Park, "Remarks to Assembly, April 27, 1961," 26.

119 Noyes, *History of Connecticut College*, 148.

120 Sullivan, "Rosemary Park," 38.

121 Park, *Connecticut College Report of the President 1946–1962*, 13–15.

122 Noyes, *History of Connecticut College*, 148. See also Park, "Remarks to Assembly, April 27 1961," 25.

123 Ibid.

124 Park, "Remarks to Assembly, April 27, 1961," 25.

125 Noyes, *History of Connecticut College*, 148.

126 Ibid., 148.

127 Park, *Report of the President, 1946–1962*, 13.

128 Ibid.

129 Johnson, *Unpublished Memoir of Time at Connecticut College*, 69.

130 Ibid.

131 Noyes, *History of Connecticut College*, 148.

132 Ibid.

133 Ibid, 149.

134 Johnson, *Unpublished Memoir of Time at Connecticut College,* 69.

135 Ibid.

136 Ibid.

137 Ibid.

138 Norman Fainstein, "Remarks at Memorial Service for President Emeritus Rosemary Park Anastos" (4 June 2004). Accessed 13 December 2006 from http://www.conncoll.edu/people/park/park_fainstein.html

139 Luce, "Living Legends." See also *Thirty-Third Annual Catalogue of Connecticut College* (New London, CT: Connecticut College for Women, 30 March 1947), 14–27; *Bulletin of Connecticut College: Catalogue Number 1962-1963, Announcements for 1963–1964* (New London, CT: Connecticut College, 15 April 1963), 9–17.

140 Charles Shain, "Introduction of Rosemary Park" (4 June 1967). CCA, Charles Shain File.

141 Noyes, *History of Connecticut College.*

142 T. Fenton interview. Also Pamela Herrup, interview by author 10 July 2007 (interview in possession of author).

143 Evans interview.

144 Ibid.

145 Eric Kaplan (6 June 2007) and Merrill (22 January 2007), interviews by author (interviews in possession of author).

146 Ibid.

147 Ibid.

148 Ibid.

149 Helen S. Astin, "Interview with Rosemary Park," in *The Higher Education of Women: Essays in Honor of Rosemary Park,* ed. Helen S. Astin & Werner Z. Hirsch (New York: Praeger Publishers, 1978), xiv–xxvii.

150 Park, "Remarks to Assembly, April 27, 1961," 26.

151 Frankfort, *Domesticity and Career in Turn-of-the-Century America,* 105.

152 Stage & Vincenti, *Rethinking Home Economics,* 15.

153 Stage and Vincenti, "Women's Place: Home Economics and Education," in *Rethinking Home Economics,* 71.

154 Ibid., 77.

155 Rosenburg, *Divided Lives,* 100. See also Sicherman, "College and Careers: Historical Perspectives on the Lives and Work Patterns of Women College Graduates," 155.

156 Ibid.

157 Dorothy A. Plum and George B. Dowell, *The Magnificent Enterprise: A Chronicle of Vassar College* (Poughkeepsie, NY: Vassar College, 1961), 63.

158 Sarah Stage, "Ellen Richards and the Social Significance of the Home Economics Movement," in *Rethinking Home Economics: Women and the History of a Profession,* 17-33, 27.

159 Ibid., 27.

160 Ibid., 23

161 Plum and Dowell, *The Magnificent Enterprise: A Chronicle of Vassar College,* 63.

162 Deutsch, "From Ballots to Breadlines," 413–472, 441.

163 Plum and Dowell, *The Magnificent Enterprise,* 63.

164 Ibid., 67.

165 Sicherman, "College and Careers" 154.

166 Stage, "Home Economics: What's in a Name?" in *Rethinking Home Economics: Women and the History of a Profession,* 8.

167 Ibid., 7. See also Stage, "Ellen Richards and the Social Significance of the Home Economics Movement," 25.

168 Stage, "Home Economics: What's in a Name?," 8.

169 Ibid.

170 Margaret Rossiter, *Women Scientists in America: Struggles and Strategies to 1940* (Baltimore: Johns Hopkins University Press, 1982).

171 Linda Eisenmann, "Educating the Female Citizen in a Post-War World: Competing Ideologies for American Women, 1945-1965, *Educational Review*, 54(2) (2002), 133–141. See also Eisenmann, *Higher Education for Women in Postwar America*, 4.

172 Johnson, *Unpublished Memoir of Time at Connecticut College.*

173 Sullivan, "Rosemary Park," 32.

174 Ibid.

175 Rosemary Park, *President's Report, 1957* (New London, CT: Connecticut College for Women, 1957), 7.

176 Ibid.

177 Virginia Vincenti, "Chronology," in *Rethinking Home Economics: Women and the History of a Profession*, 321–330, 326.

178 Astin, "Interview with Rosemary Park," xxii.

179 Ibid.

180 Ibid.

181 Amy Thompson McCandless, *The Past in the Present: Women's Higher Education in the Twentieth-Century American South* (Tuscaloosa, AL: The University of Alabama Press, 1999), 6.

182 Finishing schools bestowed the right social cache and provided training in social deportment, but were usually not four-year colleges, according to Joyce Antler's "The Educational Biography of Lucy Sprague Mitchell: A Case Study in the History of Women's Higher Education," in *Women and Higher Education in American History*, ed. John Mack Faragher and Florence Howe (New York: W.W. Norton, 1988), 43–63, 47.

183 Helen Horowitz (28 April 2007) and Mary Pat McPherson (1 November 2007), interviews by author (interviews in possession of author).

184 Claire Goodwin and Jason Wood, "A Brief History of Simmons College." Accessed 12 February 2007 from http://www.simmons.edu/resources/libraries/archives/briefhistory_text.htm. See also Poulson, "Simmons College: Meeting the Needs of Women Workers," 208–234.

185 Poulson, "Simmons College: Meeting the Needs of Women Workers."

186 Ibid.

187 Schmidt, *Douglass College: A History.*

188 Miller-Bernal, *Separate by Degree,* 88.

189 Lynn, *Make No Small Plans.* 91.

190 Ibid., 91.

191 Ibid.

192 Johnson, *Unpublished Memoir of Time at Connecticut College,* 29.

193 Alice Johnson, "Everything Changes, Nothing Changes," *Connecticut College Alumni Magazine* (Winter 1978), 21–22, 34.

194 Johnson, *Unpublished Memoir of Time at Connecticut College,* 29.

195 Ibid., 29.

196 Ibid., 31–32. Johnson admired that Connecticut had encouraged students to spend at least one semester in steady volunteer service.

197 Ibid., 30.

198 Johnson, "Everything Changes, Nothing Changes," 21–22, 34.

199 Ibid.

200 Ibid.

201 Ibid.

202 Johnson, *Unpublished Memoir of Time at Connecticut College,* 31.

203 Ibid.

204 Ibid., 46.

205 Ibid.

206 Ibid, 31. Johnson defended the strength of the physical education major, citing that its demanding science requirements had prepared not a small number of its graduates for medical school.

207 Ibid, 31.

208 Bredeson, T. Fenton, Hersey, and Kaplan interviews. Also Claire Gaudiani (5 June 2007), Lynda Munro (29 August 2007), Charlie Luce (21 April 2007), Brian Rogers (5 December 2006 and 22 January 2007), interviews by author (interviews in possession of author).

209 Egbert A. Case to Elizabeth C. Wright (5 June 1911). CCA, Elizabeth Wright File. Case had asked, "Will it [the new college] be of the nature of Simmons or of Smith?"

210 Sykes, "The Social Basis of the New Education for Women," 227.

211 Eastburn, "Miss Katharine Blunt, Biographical Material," 3.

212 Ibid., 5, 7. Oakes Ames paraphrases Blunt's view of Connecticut College's "central interest" in *The Annual Report of the President 1984/85* (New London, CT: Connecticut College, 1985), 1.

213 A question articulated by Linda Eisenmann in "Educating the Female Citizen in a Post-War World," 140.

214 Luce, "Living Legends." See also Park, "Your College Education: Our Mutual Responsibility," 15. At that talk in September 1957, Park said, "life is not just making a living. It is also living a life."

215 Rosemary Park, "Charge to the Seniors: Commencement, June 11, 1961," in *Fiftieth Anniversary Celebration Publication: Connecticut College 1911–1961* (New London, CT: Connecticut College, 1961).

CHAPTER SIX

Coeducation Comes to Connecticut College

When Connecticut College confronted the coeducation question in 1968, more was at stake than a name change for an institution that for 57 years had been known as Connecticut College for Women. The issue on the table held the prospect of forever altering the founding mission of a pioneering college that in 1911 had set out to provide higher education for women in an era when whole states, such as Connecticut, did not have a single college for women. When President Charles Shain convened Connecticut College's Summer Planning Group of eight faculty members, one of whom was dean of faculty and four of whom were department chairs, to examine the question of coeducation in 1968, his move was not without risk.[1] The issue up for study was more than an academic question, for it cut to the heart of Connecticut College's initial reason for being, and raised the possibility that the institution's signature identity would be altered irretrievably. Arguably, it is a testament to Shain's courage, accumulated political capital, and charm that he did not get sent packing by angry alumnae, faculty, and students.

The lack of immediate controversy was due in part to factors, both local and national, factors largely out of Shain's control that smoothed the way for Connecticut College to have a civil and serious discussion about coeducation. The local factors were Connecticut's move in 1959 to incorporate Connecticut College for Men, which took in part-time graduate students, many of them from Pfizer Corporation and local defense companies such as Electric Boat. The number of men enrolled in Connecticut classes increased in the 1960s when the College established exchange programs with the Coast Guard Academy and Wesleyan University.[2] Charles Shain's President's Report of 1964, for example, noted that during the 1963 and 1964 academic years a total of 18 men received the M.A. degree.[3] By 1968 men had been in Connecticut laboratories and classrooms for almost a decade and a total of 74 had received degrees from the College. Including graduate students, Wesleyan exchange students, and part-time students from local towns and the Coast Guard Academy, there were 60 men enrolled at Connecticut College in the fall of 1968.[4]

Faculty in the science departments at Connecticut College especially welcomed the opportunity to do advanced work with graduate students. The presence of men in science classes helped offset the lower enrollments those departments had experienced when the institution was solely a women's college.

Botany professor Richard Goodwin and physics professor David Fenton liked the prospect of larger classes due to the presence of men.[5] Both favored coeducation and even began to anticipate its prospect as early as 1962 when the College appointed Shain—the first man to hold the post in 34 years—as president.[6] At the time of Shain's appointment, Ruby Turner Morris, head of the economics department, sent him a telegram to ask, "where do you stand on coeducation?"[7] Indeed, coeducation as an issue was already in the air at elite northeastern single-sex colleges and universities in 1962 and may even have been in the back of Charles Shain's mind. If it was, Shain did not let on, perhaps because "he was hesitant to propose this radical notion too quickly in an all-female institution."[8]

The Coeducation Question

By 1968 coeducation had been discussed within the halls of Connecticut College for a number of years, according to numerous faculty and staff who were there in the 1960s.[9] George Willauer of English and Marion Doro of government remember Connecticut College faculty in the late 1950s and early 1960s as liberal thinkers receptive to new ideas and approaches.[10] Discussing issues that cut to the institutional core, such as coeducation, did not, according to their recollections, provoke a knee-jerk reflex to preserve the status quo, as it might have at an older or a more conservative institution.[11] The national factor influencing Connecticut College's consideration of the coeducation question was that similar conversations were occurring at Connecticut's single-sex peer institutions in the northeast. At Hamilton, Princeton, Sarah Lawrence, Vassar, Wesleyan, and Yale coeducation was on the table for discussion.[12] Faculty at Connecticut College knew that Wesleyan in 1962 had reconsidered and voted down the idea of a coordinate women's college.[13] President Shain and Associate Dean of Faculty Philip Jordan were also intimately aware of the conversations around coeducation happening at their alma mater, Princeton.[14]

The task of chairing Connecticut College's Summer Planning Group on coeducation went to Philip Jordan. Jordan's training as a historian helped him accept that the era of the late 1960s was a time of unprecedented societal change, making the higher education landscape unrecognizable in comparison to the early decades of the 20th century when Connecticut College for Women had been conceived.[15] As dean and English professor Alice Johnson observed in 1997, the 1960s created "a new world no one was truly prepared to accept."[16] Jordan, more than most, attempted to understand what that new world held for single-sex colleges like Connecticut. Jordan's service as chair of the Summer Planning Group proved useful to the College as well as to him personally. Six years after chairing Connecticut College's coeducation study group, Jordan would go on to the presidency of the formerly all male, but newly coeducational, Kenyon College, where he served from 1975 until 1995.

In his introductory cover essay contextualizing the final report of the Summer Planning Group, Jordan asserted that by 1969 single-sex colleges were a historical peculiarity of the northeastern United States.[17] The essay stopped short of calling single-sex colleges an anachronism, but that implication, and its opposite that co-education was the progressive choice, colored its subtext.[18] Jordan noted that in most of the rest of the United States, colleges and universities had long been co-educational, in most cases right from their founding.[19] In regions, such as the Midwest and West, the dominant colleges were land-grant institutions founded as coeducational institutions. The institutions in those newer regions mirrored the spirit of the times and the needs of the states in which they had developed. In the settling of those newer states on the United States' expanding western frontier, women were the necessary work partners of their husbands. Higher education for women, thus, made practical sense. Connecticut College's home region of New England, on the other hand, had been settled and organized long before anyone began to take seriously such notions as higher education, professions, and even suffrage for women.[20]

According to Jordan, the affluent easterners who defined social standards in the United States had historically viewed women as "special creatures living in a separate, luxurious women's world."[21] Under this view, women were fit objects for the affection and admiration of men, but not their equals; thus, it made no sense for women to go to college.[22] But in the world of 1968, where for one hundred years the Seven Sister colleges had irrefutably demonstrated the intellectual wor-thiness of women, and coeducational colleges, such as Cornell University were thriving elite institutions, the northeastern United States was as ready as it ever had been to reconsider its preference for single-sex education.[23]

When Charles Shain introduced the idea of a Summer Planning Group to dis-cuss coeducation, most faculty members saw the question as open, not a veiled at-tempt by the president to push his own agenda.[24] There was no sense of inevitability to the outcome of the coeducation debate, according to Jordan.[25] Connecticut's pro-fessors appreciated that Shain had placed the examination of the complicated issue in the hands of a faculty committee.[26] By contrast, Shain's two immediate predeces-sors, Rosemary Park and Katharine Blunt, though highly respected, had been seen more often than not as leading faculty processes toward particular outcomes that they wanted or expected.[27] Shain, even if he did want a certain outcome to the co-education debate—and there is no clear evidence that he did—was skillful at craft-ing a process that at least appeared open and participatory.[28]

Shain's outgoing personality tended to work toward his advantage and likely helped keep the coeducation debate at Connecticut College from becoming divi-sive. Jordan and others recall Shain as a charming man with understated charisma and deep respect for faculty decision-making processes.[29] "People liked him, trusted him, and wanted to side with him," according to those who remember the Shain era at Connecticut College.[30] Due to his "ability to listen to what students as well as faculty tried to tell him," Shain outlasted the other New England College presidents who took office between 1962 and 1964.[31] Shain also had an extraordinary recall of names and took the time to greet and talk to "the general staff of secretaries, cooks, and grounds people" at the College, with the result that they referred to him as "our friend."[32]

Although several issues drove the public discussion of coeducation at Connecticut College in 1968, numerous fears lurked near the surface of those conversations. Perhaps the greatest fear was that the College's entrance and academic standards would decline under the status quo.[33] Of paramount concern was the dwindling number of freshman applications in the late 1960s compared to the boom times of the early to mid-1960s. Applications to Connecticut College had peaked at 1,725 in 1966 and then fallen to 1,405 in 1968.[34] Verbal SAT medians had also been declining at Connecticut and other women's colleges.[35] Both downward trends were forecasted to continue at women's colleges.

A national survey of high school seniors in 1967 conducted by Princeton University had found that coeducation was most attractive to the highest achieving students, those in the top third of their high school graduating class.[36] Coeducation, the Princeton survey found, was equally as attractive to bright women as men; further, only 6.6 percent of high school girls preferred a small liberal arts college for women.[37] Anecdotal reports gathered by Connecticut College admission officers from high school personnel echoed the Princeton survey's findings.[38] It was becoming clearer to Connecticut's admission recruiting staff that the best high school students were less interested in women's colleges than their predecessors had been a generation earlier.[39] Many high school girls reported that they would not even consider a woman's college and intended to apply only to coeducational institutions.[40] If the Princeton survey did not sound the alarm bell, the experience of some of Connecticut College's peer women's colleges further down the quality and prestige food chain did. Officials at the College were aware that a handful of women's colleges had not met enrollment targets in 1968 and, as a result, were cutting budgets and letting go faculty—two things Connecticut sought to avoid.[41]

Additionally, coeducation seemed an inexorable reality within Connecticut's northeastern college milieu. Talk of co-educating the Ivy League and other elite all-male East Coast institutions was drawing enthusiasm from high school girls throughout Connecticut College's feeder-school regions.[42] The clear implication of that enthusiasm and the Princeton study's findings was that the traditional top-of-the-class applicants to Seven Sister colleges, and the step-Sisters like Connecticut, would be lured toward Amherst, Bowdoin, Princeton, Wesleyan, and Yale as soon as those institutions adopted coeducation. Underlying the Princeton survey's findings was the strong possibility that many alumnae who had chosen women's colleges like Connecticut would not have made that choice had coeducation been ubiquitous in the northeast.[43] Officials working there in 1968, especially admission director Jeanette Hersey and her associate director Jane Bredeson, were more aware than faculty of the real possibility that a single-sex Connecticut College might not attract the same high quality students that it had traditionally enrolled.[44] Hersey and Bredeson had daily conversations with prospective students, their parents, and high school guidance counselors. They knew that Connecticut College was already receiving fewer applications from top students. They also knew that the College's faculty certainly did not want classrooms populated with less capable students than the ones they had taught in earlier decades.

Alumnae survey results gathered by the Summer Planning Group underscored the important value placed on the College's academic quality. According to alumnae respondents, the most critical attribute for Connecticut College to maintain was its high academic standards; and most of the alumnae were convinced that adopting coeducation was the only way to do so.[45] Officials who watched Connecticut's budget also recognized that every aspect of the College would suffer in quality if the institution could no longer achieve its student enrollment targets. Such bottom-line factors and fears combined to loosen any existing alumnae and faculty opposition to coeducation.

There were multiple fears, however, about the men who might enroll at Connecticut College. Would a coeducational Connecticut College be able to attract men of similar academic quality to the women it had traditionally attracted? What would be the implications of a college of academically strong women and less qualified men, the so-called "Middlebury syndrome," invoked by alumnae and the Summer Planning Group's Report?[46] President Shain received angry letters from alumnae such as Madeleine Jean Huber of the Class of 1957 who asserted that "any man with the kind of grades a girl would need to get into Conn would choose Yale, Princeton, Harvard or one of the other traditional ones whose reputations are such an asset in the business world."[47] Huber speculated further about what a coeducational Connecticut College would look like: "unless you lower the academic standing (which would defeat everything the past 50 years have stood for), I honestly think one of two types [of men] will be attracted. They will either be girl crazy or so strange no nice girl would care to associate with them. Then what will become of our fine image!"[48]

Some faculty wondered if a coeducational Connecticut College would have fewer female faculty members and the resulting "subordination of women academics to men [that] exists on many coeducational campuses."[49] From its opening in 1915, when women held 59 percent of the faculty positions, Connecticut College had provided an equitable and favorable climate for women teachers and scholars.[50] The 1969 faculty gender distribution at Connecticut, for example, was 53 percent female and 47 percent male, with women comprising 50 percent of the department chairs.[51] Would that faculty gender balance disappear under coeducation, making Connecticut College virtually indistinguishable from men's colleges such as Wesleyan, or women's colleges such as Smith where men had held most of the professorships and positions of power since the beginning?[52] Not a small number of faculty felt that it would be far better to stay Connecticut College for Women than get such results. The Summer Planning Group's report urged the College to choose coeducation only if it could maintain faculty gender equity.[53]

Students, alumnae, and some faculty worried that male students would take over the majority of leadership positions and expressed similar concerns about classroom dynamics.[54] Critics of coeducation speculated that men would dominate classroom discussions and effectively silence women's voices.[55] There was also the larger issue of how a coeducational Connecticut College would continue to embody the guiding ideals of opportunity for women that had defined it from the time of its founding up through 1968.[56] That was perhaps the most difficult concern for the Summer Planning Group to address, because there was no way to know, short of fast-forwarding years into the future, the answer to that question. A no vote on coeducation would be the only sure way (albeit a blunt way) to preserve Connecticut College's historic commitment to women's education.

The minority of Connecticut College alumnae who opposed coeducation felt that "there should remain in this country some good women's colleges."[57] Faculty opponents of coeducation like English professor George Willauer agreed.[58] Coeducation's critics, such as Willauer, argued that women were still discriminated against in the United States and might need a period in their lives to "find themselves as women without suffering from the competition with men which they must face upon graduation."[59] Women's colleges could thus provide a community where students and faculty might find a kind of respite or haven from the gender discrimination operating in the rest of the world.[60]

As the proverbial eighth sister to the Seven Sister colleges, Connecticut College always had been conscious of the older, better-known members of that vaunted group of colleges. With coeducation in the air, Connecticut officials paid close attention to the developments at Vassar College, the only one of the Seven Sister colleges that would eventually choose coeducation. Connecticut officials were aware that in 1966 Yale and Vassar had conducted a study, funded by a Ford Foundation grant, to determine the feasibility and desirability of Vassar moving to New Haven to become Yale's coordinate women's college.[61] Significant opposition by Vassar alumnae and faculty prevented the idea from moving beyond the study stage.[62]

Faculty members and alumnae at Connecticut College in the 1960s recall rampant speculation as to whether the College, if asked, would spurn Yale's advances as

Vassar had.[63] In fact, Philip Jordan remembers a brief flirtation by Connecticut with Yale.[64] Senior faculty were wary of the idea, according to Jordan's recollection, because they did not welcome absorption into a large university and felt that Connecticut College would be better off charting its own course, like Vassar.[65] Such independence of spirit was consistent with Connecticut College's origins when its founders resisted Wesleyan University's entreaties to serve as a coordinate women's college.[66]

Connecticut College's Summer Planning Group considered more than just the situation at Vassar. The Group made a thorough review of the coeducation discussions occurring in 1968 at many of the northeast's oldest colleges. The Planning Group's final report refers to coeducation committee proceedings at Colgate University, Princeton, and Wesleyan and acknowledges discussions at Lafayette College, Sarah Lawrence, and Smith.[67] In 1968, coeducation seemed the "wave of the future," Charles Shain recalled two decades later.[68] The coeducation question also tapped into larger issues engaging faculty at the time, including fervent faculty debate over Betty Friedan's *The Feminine Mystique*.[69] Friedan's views on male/female relations and those of guest lecturers like international economist Gardner Patterson and Harvard sociologist David Riesman provided intellectual backdrop to the coeducation debate occurring on the Connecticut College campus, remembers Jordan

In an ironic twist on the history of both institutions, the Summer Planning Group's survey results revealed that numerous alumnae and students expressed hope that Connecticut College would expand its recently negotiated exchange agreement with Wesleyan into a coordinate college arrangement.[70] The Connecticut/Wesleyan exchange had been successful since its inception in 1967, despite the 40-mile distance between New London and Middletown. Similar to the climate of opinion at Vassar, where President Alan Simpson believed a majority of the students favored merging with Yale, the Summer Planning Group acknowledged "student preferences" for an arrangement that would presumably join Connecticut and Wesleyan.[71] How a coordinate college relationship could have been accomplished, given the distance between the two campuses, was a curious and complicated question that the Summer Planning Group prudently chose not to pursue.

Although Connecticut and Wesleyan did not try to negotiate a coordinate college agreement, there is evidence from the report issued by the Summer Planning Group that it gave consideration to the possibility of Connecticut College creating a coordinate men's college in New London, as all-male Hamilton College had with Kirkland College for women.[72] The Summer Planning Group's verdict was an emphatic no![73] Echoing Wesleyan's declaration in 1910 that a coordinate women's college was too costly, the Summer Planning Group stated: "Connecticut College simply cannot afford to build a second campus or duplicate facilities for men."[74] In dismissing the coordinate college concept, the Summer Planning Group called it an "unattractive halfway house between segregation and coeducation."[75] Campus life, the Summer Planning Group observed, was changing in revolutionary ways in the 1960s, as men and women were clamoring for fully coeducational campuses with both sexes sharing the same residence halls.[76]

Speculating about what it called the "Hamilton-Kirkland experiment," the Summer Planning Group questioned "whether the present student generation, which clearly loves to break barriers erected by their elders, will long permit the planned separation of the two colleges to stand."[77] The Planning Group was prescient in sensing that coordinate colleges were an anachronism that might fade away in the future.[78] Coordinate arrangements for men and women did in fact dissolve relatively soon thereafter at Brown University, Hamilton, and Tufts University, and eventually at Harvard University and Tulane University.

The thoroughness of the Summer Planning Group's decision-making process gave weight to its findings. During the summer of 1968, the Planning Group surveyed Connecticut College's alumnae and students. Of the College's 10,500 living alumnae, the Summer Planning Group sampled 3,969, of which 2,099 (53 percent) responded.[79] The survey results were striking in ways that defied expectations. Both the alumnae and the students of Connecticut College favored coeducation by a margin of two to one.[80] Nearly 72 percent of the alumnae voted for coeducation, although many expressed regret for "the passing of the kind of college they had loved, but at the same time accepted the necessity for change."[81] A similar majority (75 percent) said that they would continue to make gifts to a coeducational Connecticut College.[82] Amidst the resounding endorsement of a new path for their College came some ambivalence. Although more than 70 percent of alumnae responded that they would likely send a daughter to a coeducational Connecticut College, there was hesitation about sending a son there: barely half of the respondents said yes, while a quarter said no, at least not until "the program was well established."[83]

Another somewhat surprising finding of the survey was the differing attitudes of older alumnae versus younger alumnae. The oldest alumnae were the most supportive of coeducation: 75 percent of the 1930s alumnae favored coeducation compared to 68 percent of 1950s alumnae.[84] Perhaps that was because in the 1930s and 1940s there was less choice for women in selecting a college. Most of the colleges in Connecticut's primary student feeder regions (New England and the Middle Atlantic states) were single sex institutions, so you simply went, as Peggy Evans '44 observed, to one of the choices within a reasonable distance of home.[85] Many of the women in the older classes also believed that they had been pioneers in selecting Connecticut College, rather than a more established Seven Sister college, and thus felt that it would be fitting for their alma mater to be a pioneer in choosing coeducation.[86] Perhaps the 1950s alumnae of Connecticut College were slightly less favorable toward coeducation, compared to 1930s and

1940s graduates, because by the 1950s women had more geographic mobility and greater awareness of coeducational college options such as Bates, Colby, Cornell, Middlebury, Oberlin, and Swarthmore. Perhaps picking Connecticut College was a more intentional choice to select a women's college for 1950s alumnae than for 1930s and 1940s alumnae.[87] Anecdotes also suggest that 1950s alumnae were perhaps more ambivalent about the changing attitudes in the generation of students following them.[88] Regardless, two-thirds of Connecticut's youngest alumnae favored coeducation, with a number of the 1960s graduates reporting that they had nearly transferred to coeducational colleges and would certainly not have chosen a women's college in the current climate.[89]

Nearly 74 percent (1,040 of 1,402) of the students enrolled at Connecticut College in 1968 responded to the coeducation survey.[90] Seniors responded at the lowest rate (62 percent), while freshmen (the class of 1972) responded at 80 percent, the highest return rate of the enrolled classes.[91] Perhaps the most divergent finding of the student survey was the fact that 80 percent of the senior class (the Class of 1969) favored coeducation, while just 40 percent of the freshmen did.[92] Some in the Connecticut College family have speculated that the seniors, after experiencing the unglamorous "suitcase college" social life that marked women's colleges pre-coeducation, voted at a higher rate for coeducation because they wished that men had been on the Connecticut campus rather than off in Cambridge, New Haven, Middletown, and Providence.[93] Weekends at Connecticut College, before the advent of coeducation, required travel to one of the men's colleges in those cities. As a result, the Connecticut campus was a lonely place after 5 p.m. on Fridays—a fact the seniors knew all too well.[94] But what to make of the divergent views expressed by Connecticut College's freshmen? Perhaps freshmen survey respondents did not want to vote against their recent choice of a woman's college, especially after having barely experienced it—at least that has been the conclusion that lives on in the institutional memory regarding the divergent findings.[95] Social psychology theorists would also argue that voting against their still fresh choice to enroll at Connecticut College for Women would have created uncomfortable cognitive dissonance (perhaps even a response bias) for the rising sophomores who turned in surveys.

Vassar College's May 1968 decision to become coeducational helped Jordan and the Summer Planning Group contextualize and justify their recommendations for Connecticut.[96] The Summer Planning Group's summary recommendations employ a deft inversion of Vassar's founding intention, asserting that Vassar's move to coeducation fulfilled Matthew Vassar's wish to establish a college where women would receive the same education offered at the elite men's colleges.[97] The Planning Group had a point. By 1968, Vassar was entering its second century, firmly established as an elite women's college, widely seen as the equal of the Ivy League institutions for men. Coeducation for Vassar would mean that women and men would finally be getting the same high quality education together on the same campus.[98] Perhaps Jordan, or other members of the Summer Planning Group, imagined Matthew Vassar smiling at that prospect.

Making the case that coeducation would have a historically salutary effect at Vassar, a college long envied and respected at Connecticut College, was a clever ploy by the Summer Planning Group. Critics of coeducation at Connecticut, or Vassar, might have quibbled with the Planning Group's interpretations but would also have had a difficult time refuting them or reassuring those on the Summer Planning Group who worried that women's colleges were historically outmoded and that "colleges which cling to the old ways will find themselves viewed as quaint survivors of an earlier age."[99] After all, had not Vassar economics professor and women's college historian Mabel Newcomer asserted that "there is no historical evidence that the majority of women have ever preferred the separate institutions forced on them by historical circumstances?"[100]

With the Vassar vote and the results of the alumnae and student surveys as backdrops, Connecticut College's Summer Planning Group issued its final report in December 1968, concluding eight months of analysis and discussion. The Report stated that "the historical reasons for single-sex colleges are no longer operative" and went on to assert that "in our time the most desirable setting for women's higher education is one which includes men, and the College can and should serve the interests of women by subtler and more effective means than separating them from men during their college years."[101] The single sex college, in the opinion of the Summer Planning Group, erected an "artificial barrier" between its students, because men and women could only be on campus together during weekends, not during weekday classes.[102] The Summer Planning Group believed that coeducation, if properly undertaken, would bolster and advance a higher quality academic community at Connecticut College.[103] Still, the Summer Planning Group made it clear that coeducation must not lessen Connecticut College's historic commitment to the education of women.[104] The Planning Group proposed that Connecticut begin admitting men immediately.[105] Yet, in recognition of the concerns expressed by the opponents of coeducation, as well as the costs involved with integrating men into residences and other facilities, the Summer Planning Group recommended a slow and deliberate transition.[106] According to this plan, the College would add 100 to 150 men annually in the first few years, followed by gradual increases until the ratio reached 50/50—stated as a goal not a quota.[107] This matched the preferences of the students surveyed, as 67.5 percent voted for an ideal eventual enrollment of 1,000 men and 1,000 women.[108]

At the time of the coeducation announcement, President Shain told the press "in this age, a young American's education, when it is shared with the opposite sex, is superior in its basic learning conditions to an education in a single-sex environment."[109] After Connecticut's faculty voted to support the Planning Group's recommendations, the State of Connecticut's Legislature passed an act consolidating Connecticut College for Women and Connecticut College for Men under the name Connecticut College.[110]

The institutional memory at Connecticut College tends to emphasize that the College led other northeastern women's colleges toward coeducation. But the Summer Planning Group's final report indicates that Vassar had already chosen coeducation before Connecticut had concluded its investigation of the issue.[111] In fact, the Vassar faculty voted 102 to 3 for coeducation in May 1968.[112] Connecticut College's Summer Planning Group did not issue its final report until December 1968, nearly seven months after the vote at Vassar.[113] Despite the facts, the lore lingering at Connecticut College nearly 40 years later promotes the belief that the College would have forged off into coeducation whether Vassar had decided, like Smith and the rest of the Seven Sisters, to remain a women's college. But would it have? It is still worth speculating what Connecticut College would have decided had Vassar made a different choice. Would the so-called eighth sister, have had the courage to break with the Seven Sisters and go alone into higher education? The lore at Connecticut College suggests an emphatic yes, but the historical evidence is less conclusive. There are many, such as Alice Johnson, who might have said that Vassar's move gave coeducation the legitimacy of the Seven Sisters, which thus made it an acceptable choice for Connecticut.

The Transition to Coeducation

In February 1969, Connecticut College enrolled its first male undergraduate students.[114] They were two local men—both of whom were transfer students, one from Fordham University and the other from the University of North Carolina at Chapel Hill.[115] Only one of the two pioneering male students, Stephen Detmold, the son of John Detmold who worked in Connecticut College's development office, chose to live on campus. An Associated Press photograph that ran in numerous newspapers showed Stephen Detmold leaning across a desk toward a professor helping him register for classes, while two of the three onlooking female Connecticut College students evinced enthusiasm for his presence.[116] The other woman watching the scene appeared bemused. The photograph's caption read: "Big Man on Campus."[117] Over the years, the photograph has become a symbol of the entrance of men into Connecticut College, appearing in several College publications, including Gertrude Noyes' history of Connecticut College and a 1988 article reflecting on twenty years of coeducation.[118]

Figure 6.1. First male registers for class

To the President, Director of Admissions and Faculty Members:

As a Wesleyan alumnus who has been interested in Connecticut College
for many years and whose daughter has expressed an interest in the
college, may I say that if your choice of the first male under-graduate
is any indicator of future under-graduates, I shall do all my power
to keep my daughter (and son) away from your institution, that I formerly
held in high regard.

Sincerely,

a Disappointed, Discouraged,
Disillusioned Parent

Figure 6.2. A note from a parent

Stephen Detmold's pose in the photograph (and presumably his long curly
hair) irked one father of a potential future Connecticut College student, provok-
ing that father to write a disapproving note to President Charles Shain. The note,
received by the College on February 11, 1969 and signed by "a Disappointed, Discouraged, Disillusioned Parent," declared, "As a Wesleyan alumnus who has been

interested in Connecticut College for many years and whose daughter has expressed an interest in the College, may I say that if your choice of the first male under-graduate is any indication of future undergraduates, I shall do all in my power to keep my daughter (and son) away from your institution, that I formerly held in high regard."[119] There is no indication that Shain replied.

In September 1969, Connecticut College enrolled 24 male and 403 female freshmen for a ratio of 17 women for every 1 man.[120] Including the February 1969 and September 1969 transfer students the total number of male undergraduates enrolled at Connecticut College in the fall of 1969 was 40.[121] The following admission cycle brought a 500 percent increase in applications from men: 237 seeking entry to the Connecticut College Class of 1974 versus the 44 that had applied to the class of 1973.[122] The 487 new students expected to enroll at Connecticut College in September 1970 included 105 male and 372 female freshmen.[123] The number of men continued to grow. Before the end of the 1970s incoming classes at Connecticut College were 40 percent male and the entire student body was 42 percent male.[124]

Figure 6.3. Collage of articles on coeducation

A year and a half after the vote for coeducation, Philip Jordan tallied a three-page summary of the key reasons underlying Connecticut College's enthusiastic embrace of the change.[125] According to Jordan's summary, the faculty who had taught coeducational and single sex classes, and the students who had experienced Wesleyan exchange classes, judged the coeducational environment superior.[126] The faculty who had taught in coeducational and single-sex environments felt that students tended to be livelier in coeducational classes—an opinion reiterated by veteran Connecticut College faculty member Richard Birdsall nearly a decade after coeducation.[127] As for concerns regarding the possible reluctance of women to speak up or take leadership positions in the presence of men, Jordan found a widespread belief that this was unlikely to happen at colleges where men and women had similar abilities.[128] Finally, Jordan cited Carleton College, Reed College, and Swarthmore College as examples of coeducational colleges that had more rigorous academic programs and higher quality student bodies than many single sex colleges.[129] The implication was that maybe a coeducational Connecticut College would achieve similar academic rigor and quality.

Individuals who were at Connecticut College during the move to coeducation often use the word "seamless" to describe the transition.[130] For example, Gertrude Noyes' history of the College asserts, without any supporting evidence, that Connecticut made the transition to coeducation with "remarkable ease, reportedly unsurpassed by any other college."[131] Philip Jordan ties this perceived ease of transition to the fact that Connecticut College's faculty modeled the gender parity that a coeducational college should seek.[132] By contrast, Kenyon College, he later found after arriving there as president in 1975, had a harder transition to coeducation due to its paucity of female faculty and senior administrators.[133]

Connecticut College's alumnae, faculty, and students did not launch public protests like the outrage that greeted coeducation announcements twenty or more years later at Mills College, Wells College, and Wheaton College.[134] There were no lawsuits filed against Connecticut College by alumnae or parents, as occurred after trustee votes for coeducation at Randolph Macon Women's College, Wells, and Wheaton.[135] Even at Vassar, acceptance of coeducation had been more ambivalent. During his interviews for the dean of faculty position at Vassar (the post he held before becoming President of Connecticut College in 2001), Norman Fainstein, said he encountered Vassar faculty members who still harbored hopes that nearly thirty years after coeducation the College would renounce its decision and become a women's college again.[136] Alumni, faculty, and student opposition to coeducation at Connecticut College, in contrast to the public turmoil at Mills, Randolph Macon, Wells, and Wheaton, was handled like a civilized argument among relatives: it was kept in the family and away from the media.

The dominant story of coeducation at Connecticut College is of a college that was ready in 1968 to transform its original mission in a way that was evolutionary and adaptive.[137] In other words, coeducation was the next natural step in Connecticut College's development. Common characterizations of the College's mission-altering decision include "the time had come," "it was the right decision at the right time," or "we must accept change or become stagnant," said not as rationalizations masking underlying ambivalence but as genuine beliefs that Connecticut College's founding purpose fit the zeitgeist of 1911, and that the move to coeducation fit the spirit of 1969.[138] Reflecting on the ease of the transition nearly a dozen years after the decision to admit men, Charles Shain observed, "the women who said Yes, it appears, could love their version of Connecticut and make it forever part of themselves without sacrificing the imaginative power of perceiving new possessors of the same college under slightly different rules."[139]

Figure 6. 4. Philip Jordan

Another oft-mentioned explanation for the ease of coeducation at Connecticut College concerns its relative youth as an institution. Unlike Vassar, which was the oldest of the Seven Sister colleges and a name synonymous with women's education, Connecticut did not have "the weight of tradition" to consider.[140] The Summer Planning Group's Report stated the issue succinctly, "Connecticut College may enjoy an advantage over older women's colleges since its alumnae body is smaller, a larger proportion of alumnae are younger, and traditions are less hallowed."[141] In 1969 as now, Connecticut College could point to its grassroots-driven and pragmatic institutional mission. The younger, nimbler college that had fulfilled the needs of women in its home state in 1911 was adapting to fill the changing needs of students seeking higher education in 1969.

To a certain extent, Connecticut College's adaptability to the needs of changing times was embedded in its founding character, mission, and vision. Frederick
Sykes' inaugural address, for example, called for the College to look forward, not
backward.[142] In her 1943 history of Connecticut College, Irene Nye, who stood in
the faculty ranks with Sykes as the College opened in 1915, mused that "by con-
tinual change and growth an institution finds the secret of eternal youth, it is always being made."[143] Nye would likely have recognized that process of continually
making itself anew operating in Connecticut College's 1969 embrace of coeducation.

By deciding to adopt coeducation, Connecticut College, in Philip Jordan's
opinion, showed an openness to change characteristic of institutional self-
confidence.[144] English professor, dean, and 1925 alumna Gertrude Noyes saw coeducation "as an inevitable and beneficial change."[145] Government professor
Marion Doro saw the move as a natural one for a young college with an evolutionary identity.[146] Still others, who prefer to remain anonymous, say it was easier for
Connecticut College to give up its women's college past than it was, say for Vassar,
because Connecticut had never been more than a second-rate women's college
overshadowed by its better-known northeastern neighbors.[147] Perhaps this is why
some in the Connecticut College family even believed coeducation might lead the
institution to new heights. Facing the future as a coeducational college might, as
one unidentified alumna speculated, "transform the college from an excellent but
reasonably typical institution into one with a distinctive atmosphere."[148]

Deeply rooted in Connecticut College's original mission to meet a statewide
need is the undeniable reality that needs change as times change. Meeting the
needs of society, even at Connecticut College's founding moment in 1911, is what
made the institution a women's college. The State of Connecticut needed a
women's college in 1911. The people of New London were eager to have a college
in their town, so eager that they likely did not care whether it was for women,
men, or both. By 1969, the biggest issue for New Londoners relating to coeducation might have been whether a coeducational Connecticut College would keep
more students around the area on the weekends, which might result in greater
numbers venturing into town to see films, eat at restaurants, shop at stores, and in
general help invigorate the local economy. The end of the women's "suitcase college" phenomenon promised potential economic gains for New London as students stayed around campus.

The Effects of Coeducation

Every momentous decision creates winners and losers. When the Connecticut
College faculty voted by a three to one margin to embrace coeducation, the big
winners were the science and social science departments, particularly economics

and political science—subject areas favored by men and chosen less frequently by women.[149] The other winners were the faculty who believed that women's colleges were lesser institutions. For those faculty members, some of whom were women, the presence of men in the student body gave the college instant legitimacy and the prestige that it did not have as a women's college.[150] The losers were the arts departments at Connecticut College, whose decline in popularity and stature became symbolized by the departure of the American Dance Festival (ADF) ten years after coeducation. Breaking with the ADF, which had been a summer fixture on the Connecticut campus since 1948, was controversial in 1978 and reverberated negatively within the Connecticut College family for many years thereafter.[151]

Connecticut College severed ties with the ADF ostensibly for budgetary reasons. That the dance program had grown too costly for the College to maintain became the party line. Yet numerous Connecticut officials who held high campus posts in the 1970s told me, not for attribution, that the presence of the dancers—particularly the male dancers—on campus over the summer made it more difficult for Connecticut College, as a newly coeducational institution, to project a first impression that would appeal to men, especially men interested in intercollegiate athletics.[152] Presumably dance and dancers brought a too feminine summer atmosphere to Connecticut, reinforcing doubts that the College was serious about attracting men.[153] By ending its relationship with the ADF partly for this reason, the College implicitly communicated that it accepted sexist beliefs about newly coeducational former women's colleges and thus needed to demonstrate that it preferred men who played sports over men who danced.

Resource allocations in the 1970s indicate similar value judgments about the kind of men Connecticut College sought to enroll. Beyond 1969, Connecticut College invested heavily in traditional athletics.[154] According to former president Oakes Ames, when Connecticut "began to expand the athletic program in 1974, it was seen as a good way to make the College more attractive to men, and therefore to hasten the change to coeducation."[155] The change toward stronger athletics began in Ames' first year as president (1974), when he hired Charles "Charlie" Luce from Boston University to serve as the College's first director of physical education and athletics.[156] Luce, who had worked his way up from high school coaching, was an apt choice, because while he brought familiarity with the big-time of NCAA Division I athletics, he understood that at NCAA Division III colleges, such as Connecticut, the student was always a student first and an athlete second.[157] Luce grew to admire the values of the small liberal arts college, and later sent two of his children to Connecticut.[158] But when he arrived at Connecticut College in the mid-1970s, Luce knew that his charge was to enhance student athletic opportunities and facilities, especially for men. With the support of Ames and benefactors, Luce moved swiftly to remake Connecticut College's athletics program.[159]

When the subject of Connecticut College athletics comes up, invariably
Charlie Luce draws praise for "remarkable leadership" in building a sports and
recreation program at Connecticut that became the envy of other former women's
colleges such as Skidmore and Vassar.[160] Under Luce, Connecticut College followed the if-you-build-it-they-will-come philosophy in attracting male student
athletes. In 1980, the College opened a skating arena for ice hockey and followed
in 1984 with an indoor athletic center.[161] The Connecticut College Alumni Magazine's retrospective issue on the presidency of Oakes Ames cited the skating arena
and the expanded athletic center as two of the "major reason[s] for Connecticut's
success as a coeducational institution."[162] Joining the New England Small College
Athletic Conference (NESCAC) made a big difference as well. To Oakes Ames,
the most tangible symbol of Connecticut's success at coeducation was the invitation to join NESCAC and compete head to head with the region's top formerly
all-male liberal arts colleges: Amherst, Bowdoin, Colby, Hamilton, Trinity, Tufts,
and Wesleyan as well as against long coeducational Bates and Middlebury.[163]
NESCAC is widely seen as the Ivy League of NCAA Division III sports. Connecticut College's good fortune to get an invitation to join NESCAC occurred, so
the story goes, when Vassar's president turned the league down—a decision that
some at Vassar still regret.[164]

Figure 6.5. Men's soccer at Connecticut College

Athletics helped Connecticut College achieve an enrollment of 40 percent men within its first decade of coeducation and matriculate 50 percent men in the freshman class that entered in fall 1985.[165] Despite widespread agreement that its success at coeducation was propelled by athletics, there is still some concern expressed among members of the Connecticut College family about what the institution may have lost in the transition. Some assert that sports have ascended too far above the arts in the coeducational Connecticut College that began to take shape in 1969. Even thirty years after the departure of the American Dance Festival and the Connecticut College Summer School of Dance, there are alumni and faculty who question and criticize the decision to end that affiliation, blaming the move on coeducation.[166]

Defenders of athletics argue that expanding Connecticut's sports programs did more than make the College attractive to men. Athletics and fitness, they assert, began growing in popularity all over the United States starting in the 1970s, drawing not just men but also large numbers of women onto playing fields and courts at Connecticut and its peer colleges.[167] Connecticut College's move to bolster sports, thus, was consistent with developments at liberal arts colleges nationwide. Those who defend the newfound emphasis on sports as neutral or benign argue that Connecticut did nothing to minimize its arts programs, it simply followed the national trend toward athletics.[168] Others, such as professor of women's studies (and former dean of faculty) Frances Hoffmann question whether Connecticut College lurched forward into coeducation before figuring out ways to preserve, or at least honor, its women's college past.[169] Hoffmann, who spent seventeen years teaching at Skidmore College before joining the Connecticut academic community, has been struck by the paucity of stories about and recollections of Connecticut College for Women.[170] In Hoffmann's opinion, Connecticut College for Women seems to have been erased.[171] The scant evidence of Connecticut's women's college past in the way it projects an institutional identity as it approaches its centennial celebration stands in contrast with Hoffmann's experience at Skidmore.[172] Nor is Hoffmann alone in indicting Connecticut College for its tendency to forget or hide its women's college past.[173] Former president Norman Fainstein, for example, found the Connecticut College he entered in 2001 decisively coeducational with no discernable reminiscences about the good old days of its women's college past.[174]

As an example of Connecticut College's prevalent attitude toward coeducation, Hoffmann cites the way Vassar College is spoken of around the campus. Vassar, says Hoffmann, is described at Connecticut as a less-than-successful example of coeducation.[175] My conversations within the Connecticut College family corroborate Hoffmann's observation. Many of the individuals I interviewed praised

Connecticut for doing a better job than Vassar of becoming a coeducational institution; it was a theme I heard invoked repeatedly in a self-congratulatory way.[176]

I also recall from a stint in the Vassar College Admission Office from 1984 to 1987 that officials at Vassar regarded Connecticut College as having an easier time projecting a coeducational image because Connecticut was never the brand name in women's higher education that Vassar was up until 1969. At Vassar, even nearly twenty years into coeducation, there continued to be a mournful sense that coeducation had taken the College from the top tier of women's higher education to an unacceptable position in the second tier of coeducational liberal arts colleges.[177] There was a collective sense at Vassar that because Connecticut College had never been a member of the vaunted Seven Sister colleges, it had less to mourn.[178]

Perhaps also because I worked as an admission officer for Vassar when the paint had not yet dried on coeducation, I cannot let the comparison with Connecticut go by without a deeper examination of it. Former women's colleges, from my experience working at Bennington and Vassar and from what I heard during interviews with Oakes Ames, Jane Bredeson, Jeanette Hersey, Charlie Luce, Martha Merrill, and Martha Myers of Connecticut and (longtime admission officer) Nancy Rubsam of Vassar, were sensitive, even defensive, about the challenges associated with recruiting men, not just in the early days of coeducation, but even up through the late 1990s.[179] Faculty and administrators, who requested anonymity, recalled that during the presidency of alumna Claire Gaudiani it was practically forbidden to mention Connecticut College for Women publicly.[180] If Connecticut did not want to go so far as to forget its women's college past, it seemed at least under Gaudiani to relegate it into the category of subjects to avoid. And ironically, Gaudiani, in a chapter in *Challenged by Coeducation* (2006), boasts of Connecticut College's success at becoming coeducational while maintaining a commitment to women.[181]

Such mixed feelings about Connecticut's woman's college past are not surprising, given the pessimism expressed by the alumnae critics of coeducation, who in 1968 said that men would never take former women's colleges seriously.[182] Even Vassar in the late 1970s tried to poke fun at its new image with a brochure entitled "Vassar for men?" The brochure showed a cartoon drawing of a man laughing at the absurdity of the idea of men attending Vassar. By the time I worked there, Vassar's senior administration and faculty considered the brochure an embarrassment, and admission officers were instructed to discard any copies found in high school guidance files. Why was the idea of men at a former women's college like Vassar considered so odd that it would naturally invite laughter?

To answer that question is to indict societal attitudes about women and come to terms with the unfortunate fact that by 1969 not enough had changed in the United States from 1911 to make coeducation at former women's colleges like Connecticut, Skidmore, and Vassar seem as natural an institutional evolution as coeducation at former men's colleges like Amherst, Dartmouth, and Wesleyan. Scholars who have studied coeducation at colleges and universities know that such natural acceptance has been far from the case.[183] Those scholars assert that the standard pattern followed by former women's colleges has been to become, as much as possible, like the former men's colleges or even the historically coeducational colleges and universities, where male dominance in administrative, faculty, and student leadership is the norm.[184]

Success at coeducation, thus, means assimilation into the dominant model, that is, the male college model.[185] Less often considered, and perhaps even conveniently defined as failure, is the experience of colleges like Vassar where the women's college past has remained evident in a coeducational setting. Vassar, for example, has integrated men into women's traditions such as the daisy chain of outstanding seniors and the serenading of one dormitory by another.[186] Since the departure of Alan Simpson, its president in 1969, Vassar has not had a male president, and Vassar's mission statement still mentions its women's college past prominently and proudly.[187] But perhaps "failure" means something else. Perhaps the phrase "Vassar failed" serves as a kind of code for what some might label an unwanted and unforeseen consequence of coeducation at some former women's colleges: namely attractiveness to gay men.

Regardless of how proud Vassar College was of a tolerant campus community that provided welcoming and safe spaces for gay men and women, the Vassar I knew in the mid-1980s was frequently put on the defensive about "the kind of man" who would choose such an icon of women's education. Even openly gay male admission staff members at Vassar threw the "are all the men gay" question at job candidates to test how they would respond to those frequently asked questions from parents of prospective students. Given long-standing societal prejudices about homosexuality, it is not a great leap to speculate that "failure" at coeducation could mean a gay male image for a college. Was the attempt to avoid attracting "that type of man" in large numbers the unmentionable issue behind Connecticut College's decision to cut ties with the ADF? Does "Vassar failed" mean Vassar ended up with a stigmatic gay male image, one that continues to be perpetuated by college admission guidebooks?[188] In any case, the code as well as the reality of the post-coeducation images associated with the two colleges signals that Connecticut succeeded at coeducation while Vassar, if it didn't outright fail, was less successful.

How did Connecticut College "succeed" in ways that critics like Frances Hoffmann find somewhat problematic? Connecticut "succeeded" by beefing up athletic facilities and programs, through affiliations with the prestigious NESCAC, by adding to science facilities and social science programs, leading to swelling enrollments of men in economics and political science majors, by becoming a student body with a majority of women in classes but greater numbers of men in leadership positions, and by shifting the gender balance among faculty toward men in more than half of the tenured positions. A special faculty committee on pluralism reported evidence (in 2003) that such changes had occurred in the 34 years since coeducation.[189] In recruiting faculty, for example, the coeducational Connecticut sought male professors to provide role models for male students and, in the minds of some, to increase the College's prestige.[190] As a result, by 1974-1975, Connecticut had a 120 to 73 male to female majority on its teaching faculty of 193 professors.[191] Vassar went in the opposite direction, from decidedly more male faculty in 1969 to an approximate 50/50 ratio by 2000.[192] Like Connecticut, Vassar chose not to add football, but unlike Connecticut, Vassar stayed away from another high testosterone sport, ice hockey. Student leadership trends at Vassar have also exhibited closer to a 50/50 gender balance than at Connecticut.[193] Nor has Vassar joined a high-powered old-boy athletic conference like NESCAC.

Reading between the lines of the 1968 recommendations for coeducation at Connecticut is to find a tension between defending academic excellence and preserving the historic commitment to women's access to higher education. Connecticut College arguably elevated the former over the latter. In choosing coeducation, Connecticut College moved to maintain its high academic standards. The admission of men, on the other hand, soon brought into relief some of the concerns expressed by critics of coeducation such as alumna Madeleine Jean Huber '57: specifically, the issue of admission standards for men versus those for women.[194] Yet this paradox of coeducation was not Connecticut College's alone to face. One enduring perception, for example, at Connecticut, Vassar and all of the women's colleges that went coeducational is of an academic credentials gap at entrance between men and women. Just as alumnae opponents of coeducation questioned whether the College expected "to attract brighter girls by having duller boys available," some of the alumni who have experienced Connecticut as a coeducational college have stated the issue equally less charitably as "smart women and dumb men."[195] Men at Connecticut College, regardless of their academic credentials, have shown less respect for campus facilities. Early men at Connecticut were quick to destroy much of the beautiful and elegant furniture in residence hall living rooms, and what was left intact the College removed.[196] Some alumni and former campus officials tell stories of men painting moustaches on the portraits of female presidents, using dorm parlor tables and chairs for bonfires, and breaking so many windows inside the sports center that the swimming pool had to be closed temporarily.[197] Whether such antics have anything to do with incoming academic credentials or not, they tend to feed the negative stereotypes about men at Connecticut College.

The admission statistics at Connecticut College perennially show gender-based application and admission rate gaps that are now commonplace at United

States liberal arts colleges. Nationally more women than men attend college, a trend that has been growing since the year Connecticut turned coeducational: 1969. Since the turn of the new century, the male/female ratio among undergraduates nationwide has been no closer than 56/44.[198] The National Center for Education noted in 2003 that between 1969 and 2000 the share of male undergraduates in the United States declined from 58 percent to 44 percent.[199] Between the years 1969 and 2000 the raw number of male undergraduates increased by 39 percent, while the raw number of female undergraduates increased by a staggering 157 percent.[200] Between 1967 and 2000, the proportion of male high school graduates attending college decreased from 44.7 percent to 40.9 percent, while the percentage of female high school graduates attending college increased from 25.1 percent to 45.6 percent.[201] Demographics have not been favorable for colleges attempting to achieve a 50/50 male to female ratio, especially those like Connecticut that lack majors in business or engineering and do not offer fraternities. Nationally, women represent 61 percent of the students at small liberal arts colleges.[202] Numerous liberal arts colleges that have been coeducational far longer than Connecticut College, such as Dickinson College and Oberlin College, openly acknowledge the challenge of recruiting and enrolling men.[203] At those and most other colleges, the male/female enrollment ratio, whether it is 40/60 or 45/55, approximates the application ratio.

Some of the liberal arts colleges in Connecticut College's home region of New England have little trouble reaching or approaching a 50/50 male to female ratio. At formerly all-male Amherst College, for example, the Class of 2010 was 51 percent female and 49 percent male.[204] Trinity College, another former men's college, enrolled 48 percent women in its class of 2010.[205] The male/female gap, not surprisingly, is most pronounced at former women's colleges. Even after forty years of coeducation, Connecticut College struggles to approach a 50/50 male to female ratio in its student body. For almost two decades, the College's student population has hovered around 60 percent female and 40 percent male.[206] The female/male ratio in the applicant pool has varied in recent years from 66/34 to 64/36, while the enrollment ratio has ranged from 61/39 to 58/42.[207] To achieve a 40/60 male to female ratio in the freshman class, the College exercises differential (read lower) admission standards for male applicants. Male applicants are 8 percent more likely than females to get admitted.[208] Statistics available from Vassar College show similar male/female imbalances in the applicant pool and enrolling classes. The Vassar Class of 2010, for example, had a 62/38 female to male ratio—an imbalance that Vassar registrar Dan Giannini chalked up to old images not fading from the days when Vassar was perhaps the most prominent of the Seven Sister colleges.[209]

The acceptance rate gap creates an entering credentials gap along gender lines. Connecticut College's female applicants and enrollees have higher rank-in-class and grade point averages (GPA), but male applicants and enrollees have slightly higher standardized test scores.[210] Some might argue that there is no credentials gap at Connecticut, because the higher standardized test scores of males cancel out the higher grade point averages and rank-in-class of females. That argument is not persuasive. Reams of research studies show that high school achievement (GPA and class rank) is far and away the best predictor of academic success in college. Thus, women at Connecticut College arrive better prepared to meet the academic challenge. Perhaps Connecticut College can simply chalk up its gender gap to its women's college past as well as its present identity as a small liberal arts college that does not offer majors in business and engineering or have fraternities or a football team. But how relevant to 2010 high school graduates is the fact that a college was once single sex? Even some formerly all-male colleges, such as Wesleyan University, have a 60 percent female applicant pool and a 52/48 female to male ratio in their incoming freshman classes.[211]

It is ironic, and arguably a perversion of mission, that colleges such as Connecticut and Vassar—historically founded to provide opportunities for an oppressed group (women)—now provide admissions advantages to the historical oppressor group (men). The "Middlebury syndrome" of well qualified women and less qualified men feared by the 1968 Summer Planning Group is alive and well at Connecticut College.[212] Officials at Connecticut perennially wrestle with that vexing issue but take comfort in anecdotal evidence, cited by Oakes Ames and longtime faculty members like Dirk Held, that the admission gap is not obvious, or even evident, in the academic performance of men after they enroll at the College.[213]

The Legacy of Coeducation at Connecticut College

The legacy of coeducation at Connecticut College is mixed, at least according to the committee that in 2003–2004 studied pluralism at the College.[214] A Working Group on Coeducation chaired by then dean of faculty Frances Hoffmann concluded that the coeducational Connecticut College provides a "richer, more varied set of activities" beyond the classroom than were available to students during the women's college era.[215] The coeducational Connecticut College has achieved, in the words of Philip Jordan, "an indigenous social life."[216] And it happened rapidly: by 1979, students at Connecticut had established more than 50 extracurricular organizations and continuing activities.[217] Indeed, by most outward indicators the coeducational Connecticut College has been a thriving institution. The College has expanded following coeducation, increasing in size from 1,444 in 1969 to 1,880 by 2003.[218] The addition of men reversed the decline in applications, producing a 98 percent freshman application increase between 1969 and 1979.[219] Because the student body grew, male students hardly displaced female students. And consistently within NESCAC, Connecticut College has had the highest ratio of female to male athletes—although some would argue this is due mostly to the absence of football.[220]

Not all the changes brought by coeducation have been positive. Connecticut's 2003–2004 Working Group on Coeducation noted that, despite the admirable proportion of female athletes, the campus culture is drawn disproportionately to men's sports.[221] Since coeducation, men have been over-represented in student leadership positions, a fact noted as early as 1988 in an alumni magazine article touting "the success of coeducation at Conn."[222] The Working Group on Coeducation Report stated that 60 percent of Student Government Association (SGA) presidents have been men, even though the population of men at Connecticut has never exceeded 45 percent.[223] In 2002–2003, for example, men led every important campus organization, including the SGA, the judicial board that administers the honor code, and the student newspaper.[224] The fact that men are in the minority but still dominate the college's athletic culture and hold more positions of power means, in the opinion of coeducation's critics, that the institution has all the worst features of coeducational colleges.[225]

The selection of majors by students at Connecticut College also reflects gender differences found in many former men's colleges that became coeducational.[226] Male students at Connecticut tend to cluster in four social science majors regarded as suitable preparation for careers and professional graduate study in business or law. The 2003–2004 Working Group on Coeducation found that 51.4 percent of the men in the Connecticut College classes of 2000, 2001, and 2002 chose majors in economics (16.4 percent), history (12.6 percent), government (12.3 percent), and English (10.4 percent).[227] Women at Connecticut were far less represented in the pre-professional social science majors. For example, just 6.4 percent of women chose government.[228] History and economics were not even among the top five majors chosen by women.[229] Aside from government, women at Connecticut most often select majors in psychology (13.4 percent), English (8.2 percent), human development (6.3 percent), and zoology (5.4 percent).[230] That human development is a top-five major choice by women represents a tie back to Connecticut College for Women, because the major absorbed the remnants of original programs in child study and home economics.

Faculty composition at Connecticut College has moved in the direction feared by the 1968 Summer Planning Group. The percentage of male faculty has increased from 47 percent in 1969 to 62 percent in 2003-2004.[231] In 1969 the College had 50/50 parity in departmental leadership.[232] By 2003-2004, men held 63 percent of the department chair positions.[233] The Working Group noted that the faculty gender shift resulted in a ratio of 17.5 male faculty members per 100 male students and a ratio of 9.6 female faculty members per 100 female students.[234] As a result, male students at Connecticut are nearly twice as likely to be taught by a man as female students are to be taught by a woman. Connecticut's nearly two to one ratio of men to women faculty runs counter to other former women's colleges, such as Vassar, where women approach 50 percent of the faculty.[235]

Reflecting on the "lessons and legacies" of coeducation at Connecticut College, the 2003–2004 Working Group observed that "changing the composition of the student body does not automatically transform structural inequalities found in the larger society."[236] According to the Working Group, "the lesson of coeducation is that compositional changes may simply reflect and perpetuate existing systems of stratification in the society at large."[237] To address the effect of gender inequality and stratification at Connecticut College, the 2003–2004 Working Group recommended instituting programs to encourage equitable participation in campus leadership positions, paying closer attention to gender balance in faculty hiring patterns, implementing strategies to encourage students to explore major fields nontraditional for their gender, and providing support for continued development of courses and scholarship--across the curriculum—on gender and women's studies.[238]

Defenders of coeducation assert that Connecticut College did not choose to embrace the established stereotypes that so-often govern relationships between men and women on American college campuses. Connecticut College, they assert, did not go so far as to add football or fraternities and sororities, and the sports added became equally as important for men as for women. The coeducational Connecticut College prides itself on a collaborative and cooperative culture that purportedly keeps alive the best values of its women's college past and makes them available to both men and women. Defenders of coeducation believe that Connecticut College, like its formerly all-female counterparts, provides women ample examples of paths to achievement through the large number of women serving as trustees, senior administrators, and senior faculty. Furthermore, coeducation at former women's colleges shows men and women an environment of gender equity, where the traditions and the prominent alumni stories celebrate pioneering women.[239] Men, according to Connecticut, Goucher, Skidmore, Vassar, and Wheaton officials, learn to respect and value women in such an environment--and on those campuses women are relatively free of the stereotypical male attitudes and behaviors that helped fuel the feminist anger and movements that crested in the 1970s.[240]

One of the defenders of coeducation at Connecticut College is a surprising convert. Emeritus Professor of English George Willauer voted against coeducation in 1969 but has since concluded that he made a mistake.[241] While Willauer still believes in single-sex institutions, in part because his alma mater Wesleyan was a men's college when he attended it in the 1950s, he also believes that coeducation has made Connecticut College a stronger and better institution than it was as a women's college.[242] Coeducation, in Willauer's opinion, made Connecticut more vital and gave it the opportunity to redefine itself.[243] Redefinition for Connecticut College meant that maybe it could finally break free from the stigma of being a stepsister to the Seven Sister colleges and perhaps in the process grow in stature.[244] The coeducational Connecticut College is no longer in the shadow of the Seven Sisters, as it is now more commonly compared to NESCAC colleges such as Bowdoin, Middlebury, and Wesleyan, a cohort that tends to overshadow it for reasons of admissions selectivity, greater wealth, and perceived prestige. Arguably, following coeducation Connecticut College simply shed a position under one shadow for a position under another.

Notes

1   The members of the working group were: Philip H. Jordan, Jr., Associate Professor of History and Associate Dean for Academic Affairs, Chairman; Otello L. Desiderato, Professor of Psychology and Department Chairman; Robley J. Evans, Assistant Professor of English; Katherine Finney, Professor of Economics; Richard H. Goodwin, Professor of Botany and Department Chairman; William A. McCloy, Professor of Art and Department Chairman; Jeanne C. Prokesch, Associate Professor of Chemistry and Zoology; and Helen Reeve, Assistant Professor of Russian and Department Chairman. "Report of the Summer Planning Group, Summary of Recommendations," *Connecticut College Alumnae News* (December 1968), 19. Connecticut College Archives (hereafter identified as CCA), Coeducation File.

2   Park, *Report of the President, 1946–1962,* 18.

3   Rosemary Park, *Report of the President, 1963–1964* (New London, CT: Connecticut College, November 1964), 10.

4   Dorothy Desiderato, "Supplementary Data; Comments from Alumnae on Questionnaires About Coeducation" (13 February 1969). CCA, Coeducation File.

5   Richard Goodwin (24 April 2007) and David Fenton (24 January 2007), interviews by author (interviews in possession of author).

6   Ibid.

7   Alice Johnson, *Unpublished Memoir of Time at Connecticut College,* 91. Johnson was a longtime English professor and dean at Connecticut College.

8   Ibid., 91.

9   Lisa Broujas, "The Success of Coeducation at Conn," *The Connecticut College Alumni Magazine* (Summer 1988), 10-14. Also, Jane Bredeson (23 January 2007), Marian Doro (23 April 2007), and George Willauer (23 April 2007) interviews by author (interviews in possession of author).

10   Doro and Willauer interviews.

11   Ibid.

12   Philip H. Jordan, Jr., "Historic Necessity of Separate Education for Women," *Connecticut College Alumnae News* (December 1968), 15–16.

13   Johnson, *Unpublished Memoir of Time at Connecticut College,* 91-92.

14   Philip Jordan, interview by author 13 May 2007 (interview in possession of author).

15   Ibid.

16   Johnson, *Unpublished Memoir of Time at Connecticut College,* 44.

17   Jordan, "Historic Necessity of Separate Education for Women," 15–16.

18   Ibid. In *Separate by Degree* (pp. 3-4), Leslie Miller-Bernal notes that coeducation came to be seen as progressive and single-sex education anachronistic.

19   Ibid.

20   Ibid.

21   Ibid.

22   Ibid.

23   Ibid.

24   Doro and Willauer interviews.

25   Jordan interview.

26   Ibid. Also Willauer interview.

27   Goodwin interview.

28   Jordan interview.

29   Jordan and Willauer interviews. See also Johnson, *Unpublished Memoir of Time at Connecticut College.*

30   Quote of Tony Sheridan '74 in Broujas, "The Success of Coeducation at Conn," 74.

31   Johnson, *Unpublished Memoir of Time at Connecticut College,* 89.

32   Ibid., 90.

33   "Report of the Summer Planning Group, Summary of Recommendations," 19.

34   Ibid.

35   Ibid, 19.

36   Ibid.

37   Ibid. See also Charles M. Shain to Dr. A. Parks McCombs (21 February 1969). CCA, Coeducation File.

38   Bredeson interview. Also Jeanette Hersey, interview by author 22 January 2007 (interview in possession of author).

39   Ibid.

40   Ibid. Also Shain File, CCA.

41   Ibid. See also Shain to Dr. A Parks McCombs; Oakes O. Ames, *Connecticut College: Contributing to a Changing Society* (New York: Newcomen Society of America, 1987), 12.

42   "Report of the Summer Planning Group, Summary of Recommendations," 19-20.

43   Ibid. See also Dorothy Desiderato, "Recurring Themes in Alumnae Coeducation Questionnaire Comments" (11 February 1969); Desiderato, "Supplementary Data; Comments from Alumnae on Questionnaires About Coeducation."

44   Bredeson and Hersey interviews.

45   Desiderato, "Recurring Themes in Alumnae Coeducation Questionnaire Comments."

46   Ibid.

47   Madeleine Jean Huber to President Charles Shain (11 January 1969). CCA, Coeducation File.

48   Ibid.

49   "Report of the Summer Planning Group, Summary of Recommendations," 20–21.

50   *Connecticut College for Women: First Annual Announcement, 1915-1916,* 6-9. In its opening year, women comprised 10 of Connecticut's faculty members. See also Nye, *Chapters in the History of Connecticut College,* 10, 28, 29.

51   Frances Hoffman, Joan Chrisler, Dirk Held, Philip Gedeon, Manuel Lizarralde, and Frances Shields, "Working Group Report on Coeducation from Report of the Presidential Commission on a Pluralistic Community at Connecticut College" (8 August 2003). Accessed 13 December 2006 from http://www.conncoll.edu/people/president-emeritus/pluralism/html/index.htm. See also "Supplementary Data on the Decision for Coeducation at Connecticut College, Confidential until Jan. 9, 1969." CCA, Coeducation File. Note that the appendix of

Challenged by Coeducation: Women's Colleges Since the 1960s states incorrectly that the Connecticut faculty was 75% female in 1969.

52 Horowitz, *Alma Mater*.
53 Nye, *Chapters in the History of Connecticut College*, 21.
54 "Report of the Summer Planning Group, Summary of Recommendations," 20–22.
55 Ibid.
56 Ibid.
57 Desiderato, "Recurring Themes in Alumnae Coeducation Questionnaire Comments."
58 Willauer interview.
59 "Report of the Summer Planning Group, Summary of Recommendations," 20.
60 Ibid.
61 Clyde Griffen & Elizabeth Daniels, "Vassar College: A Seven Sisters College Chooses Coeducation," in *Challenged by Coeducation: Women's Colleges Since the 1960s*, ed. Leslie Miller-Bernal & Susan L. Poulson (Nashville, TN: Vanderbilt University Press, 2006), 25–47, specifically 29–30.
62 Ibid.
63 Torrey Fenton, interview by author 24 April 2007 (interview in possession of author). Also Willauer interview.
64 Jordan interview.
65 Ibid.
66 Ibid.
67 "Report of the Summer Planning Group, Summary of Recommendations, 18."
68 Broujas, "The Success of Coeducation at Conn."
69 Jordan interview.
70 "Report of the Summer Planning Group, Summary of Recommendations," 20.
71 Ibid. See also Griffen and Daniels, "Vassar College: A Seven Sisters College Chooses Coeducation," 30.
72 "Report of the Summer Planning Group, Summary of Recommendations," 18.
73 Ibid.
74 Ibid.
75 Ibid.
76 Ibid.
77 Ibid.
78 Ibid.
79 Desiderato, "Supplementary Data; Comments from Alumnae on Questionnaires About Coeducation."
80 Ibid.
81 Ibid.
82 Ibid.
83 Ibid.
84 Ibid.
85 Margaret Carpenter Evans, interview by author 15 June 2007 (interview in possession of author).
86 Jordan interview.
87 T. Fenton interview.
88 Ibid. Also Willauer interview.
89 Desiderato, "Supplementary Data; Comments from Alumnae on Questionnaires About Coeducation."
90 Ibid.

91   Ibid.

92   Ibid.

93   Bredeson, T. Fenton, and Hersey interviews. Also Elizabeth Enders, interview by author 5 June 2007 (interview in possession of author).

94   Enders and T. Fenton interviews.

95   "Report of the Summer Planning Group, Summary of Recommendations," 19–20.

96   Jordan, "Historic Necessity of Separate Education for Women," 15–16.

97   "Report of the Summer Planning Group, Summary of Recommendations," 19.

98   Ibid.

99   Ibid.

100 Ibid. Jordan quotes from page 50 of Newcomer's *A Century of Higher Education for Women*.

101 Ibid, 17–19.

102 Broujas, "The Success of Coeducation at Conn." Quote of Gertrude Noyes.

103 Ibid., 17.

104 Ibid.

105 Ibid.

106 Ibid.

107 "Report of the Summer Planning Group, Summary of Recommendations," 19.

108 Raymond K. Bordner, "Shain Optimistic About College's Decision," *The Day* (18 January 1969), 16. See also "Coeducation: A New Role for the College," *CC News* (Winter 1969). CCA. Coeducation File.

109 "Women's College Goes Coed," *The Christian Science Monitor* (January 25, 1969).

110 Noyes, *History of Connecticut College*, 178.

111 "Report of the Summer Planning Group, Summary of Recommendations."

112 Griffen and Daniels, "Vassar College: A Seven Sisters College Chooses Coeducation," 30.

113 "Report of the Summer Planning Group, Summary of Recommendations."

114 Connecticut College Press Release (February 1969). CCA, Coeducation File.

115 Ibid.

116 Broujas, "The Success of Coeducation at Conn," 11. See also "Coeducation: A New Role for the College," *CC News* (Winter 1969). CCA, Coeducation File.

117 Ibid.

118 Noyes, *History of Connecticut College*, 179. See also Broujas, "The Success of Coeducation at Conn," 11.

119 "A Disappointed, Discouraged, Disillusioned Parent," Note "to the President, Director of Admissions and Faculty Members" (Received 11 February 1969). CCA, Coeducation File.

120 News from Connecticut College, Press Release (12 September 1969). CCA, Coeducation File.

121 "The College Prexy Talks About 40 Men in a Girls' School," *Detroit Free Press* (3 December 1969). CCA, Coeducation File.

122 Connecticut College News, Press Release (25 June 1970). CCA, Coeducation File.

123 Ibid.

124 "Press Release From the Connecticut College News Office" to mark ten years of coeducation (1979?—exact date not specified). CCA, Coeducation File. See also Oakes Ames, *The Annual Report of the President, 1976* (New London, CT: Connecticut College, 1976), 4.

125 Philip H. Jordan, Jr., "Responses to Supplemental Questionnaire" (23 June 1970). CCA, Coeducation File.

126 Ibid.

127 Richard Birdsall, "Work, Love and the College Mystique," *Connecticut College Alumni Magazine* (Winter 1978), 23–24.

128 Jordan, "Responses to Supplemental Questionnaire."

129 Ibid.

130 Bredeson, Doro, and Jordan interviews.

131 Noyes, *History of Connecticut College*, 179.

132 Jordan interview.

133 Ibid.

134 Leslie Miller Bernal, "Wells College: The Transition to Coeducation Begins," in *Challenged by Coeducation: Women's Colleges Since the 1960s*, ed. Leslie Miller-Bernal & Susan L. Poulson (Nashville, TN: Vanderbilt University Press, 2006), 145–175. See also Susan F. Semel and Alan R. Sadovnik, "Coeducation at Wheaton College: From Conscious Coeducation to Distinctive Coeducation?" in *Challenged by Coeducation: Women's Colleges Since the 1960s*, 48–76; Marianne Sheldon, "Revitalizing the Mission of a Women's College: Mills College in Oakland, California," in *Challenged by Coeducation: Women's Colleges Since the 1960s*, 175–208; "Report of the Summer Planning Group, Summary of Recommendations," 20.

135 Ibid. See also "Virginia High Court to Hear Disputes Over Randolph Coed Move," *Associated Press* (23 September 2007).

136 Norman Fainstein, interview by author 24 July 2007 (interview in possession of author).

137 Bredeson and Doro interviews.

138 Desiderato, "Supplementary Data; Comments from Alumnae on Questionnaires About Coeducation."

139 Charles Shain to *Connecticut College Alumni Magazine* (Spring 1980). CCA, Coeducation File.

140 Willauer interview. Also Dirk Held (23 April 2007) and Brian Rogers (5 December 2006 and 22 January 2007), interviews by author (interviews in possession of author).

141 "Report of the Summer Planning Group, Summary of Recommendations," 20.

142 Nye, *Chapters in the History of Connecticut College*, 22.

143 Ibid., 29.

144 Jordan, "Responses to Supplemental Questionnaire."

145 Broujas, "The Success of Coeducation at Conn."

146 Doro interview.

147 Anonymous at request of the interviewees stating this opinion.

148 Unidentified alumna—in Desiderato, "Supplementary Data; Comments from Alumnae on Questionnaires About Coeducation."

149 "Supplementary Data on the Decision for Coeducation at Connecticut College, Confidential until Jan. 9, 1969."

150 Interviewees kept anonymous by request.

151 Pamela Herrup (10 July 2007), Lynda Munro (29 August 2007), Martha Myers (11 September 2007), and Jeff Oshen (1 May 2007) interviews by author (interviews in possession of author).

152 Interviewees kept anonymous by request.

153 Ibid.

154 Allen Carroll, "The Art of the Feud," *Connecticut College Alumni Magazine* (Winter 1978), 26.

155 Oakes Ames, *The Annual Report of the President, 1981–1982* (New London, CT: Connecticut College, 1982), 4. Also Ames interview.

156 Ibid. See also Ames, *Connecticut College: Contributing to a Changing Society*.

157 Charlie Luce, interview by author 21 April 2007 (interview in possession of author).

158 Ibid.

159 Ibid.

160 Ames, *Connecticut College: Contributing to a Changing Society*. Also, Hersey and Bredeson interviews.

161 Alice Johnson, "The Ames Years 1974–1988," *Connecticut College Alumni Magazine* (Spring 1988), 2–3. See also Ames, *Connecticut College: Contributing to a Changing Society*.

162 Brian C. Elowe, "Athletics" (in "The Ames Years 1974–1988") *Connecticut College Alumni Magazine* (Spring 1988), 6. Elowe graduated from Connecticut in 1981.

163 Ames, *Connecticut College, Annual Report of the President, 1981–1982*, 4.

164 Fainstein interview.

165 Ames, *Connecticut College: Contributing to a Changing Society*, 12.

166 Interviewees kept anonymous by request.

167 Ames, *Connecticut College: Contributing to a Changing Society*, 12.

168 Ames interview.

169 Frances Hoffmann, interview by author 12 June 2007 (interview in possession of author). Also Frances Hoffmann, "Women, Men and Higher Education" (Sykes Lecture, Connecticut College Reunion) (2 June 2006); Frances Hoffmann, "CCSRE Comments on 2006 Sykes Lecture" (April 2007). Both papers provided to author by Hoffmann.

170 Ibid.

171 Ibid.

172 Ibid.

173 Laurie Deredita, interview by author 31 July 2007 (interview in possession of author). Also Fainstein interviews.

174 Fainstein interview.

175 Hoffmann interview.

176 Bredeson and Hersey interviews. Also Martha Merrill, interview by author 22 January 2007 (interview in possession of author).

177 Rubsam interview.

178 Ibid. Also Willauer interview.

179 Ibid. Also Ames and Myers interviews.

180 Interviewees kept anonymous by request.

181 "Appendix 1: Statement of Six Past Presidents of Formerly Women's Colleges, 2000. Exceptional Coed Colleges: A New Model for Gender Equity," in *Challenged by Coeducation: Women's Colleges Since the 1960s*, 389–393.

182 Ruth Frerichs to Trustees (25 November 1968). CCA, Coeducation File. Frerichs was a 1947 alumna of Connecticut College for Women.

183 Hoffmann interview. Also Hoffmann, "Women, Men and Higher Education;" Hoffmann, "CCSRE Comments on 2006 Sykes Lecture." See also Miller-Bernal, *Separate by Degree*; Howe, "Myths of Coeducation," 206–220.

184 Ibid.

185 Ibid.

186 Griffen and Daniels, "Vassar College: A Seven Sisters College Chooses Coeducation."

187 "Mission Statement of Vassar College," *Vassar College Catalogue, 2007–2008* (Poughkeepsie, NY: Vassar College, 2007). The second sentence of Vassar's mission statement reads as follows: "Founded in 1861 to provide young women an education equal to that once available only to young men, the college has since 1969 opened its doors to both women and men on terms of equality."

188 "The school is 60 percent female and of the 40 percent that are male, many are gay."—quoted on page 599 in the "Vassar College" description in *The College Buzz Book (2007 Edition)* ed. Carolyn C. Wise and Stephanie Hauser (New York: Vault, Inc., 2007), 597–599. Also Vassar is ranked 16th in the "Gay Community Accepted" top-twenty ranking of the "Schools Ranked by Category" section of *The Best 351 Colleges (2004 Edition)* ed. Robert Franek, Tom Meltzer, Roy Opochinski, Tara Bray, Christopher Maier, Carson Brown, Julie Doherty, K. Nadine

Kavanaugh, Catherine Monaco, and Dinaw Mengestu (New York: Princeton Review Publishing, LLC., 2003), 38. See also the "Vassar College" description in *Students' Guide to Colleges: The Definitive Guide to America's Top 100 Schools* ed. Jordan Goldman and Colleen Buyers (New York: Penguin Books, 2005), 530–536. Also Mary Pat McPherson (1 November 2007) and Nancy Rubsam (17 August 2007), interviews by author (interviews in possession of author), McPherson is former president of Bryn Mawr College and chair of the Smith College Board of Trustees. McPherson's aunt was a friend of Connecticut College president Katharine Blunt. Longtime Vassar admission officer and 1964 Vassar alumna Nancy Rubsam noted that during her tenure in the admission office (1984–2007) it was not uncommon for prospective students to ask her and colleagues to provide an estimate of the percentage of gay male students at Vassar. She said she was often tempted to point out that to ask such an absurd question on Vassar's application would have been discriminatory. Numerous alumni of Connecticut College stated that the gay male image never attached to the College.

189 Hoffman, Chrisler, Held, Gedeon, Lizarralde, and Shields, "Working Group Report on Coeducation from Report of the Presidential Commission on a Pluralistic Community at Connecticut College."

190 Fainstein interview. Fainstein rightly criticized the sexist belief that being able to attract and hire male faculty means a college is of higher academic quality.

191 *Connecticut College Bulletin 1974–75* (New London, CT: Connecticut College, September 1974), 11–28. By contrast, in 1963, women comprised 75 of Connecticut's 130 faculty and men 55. See also *Bulletin of Connecticut College: Catalogue Number 1962-1963, Announcements for 1963–1964* (New London, CT: Connecticut College, 15 April 1963), 9–17.

192 "Appendix 1: Statement of Six Past Presidents of Formerly Women's Colleges, 2000. Exceptional Coed Colleges: A New Model for Gender Equity," 389–393.

193 Daniels and Griffen, "A Seven Sisters College Chooses Coeducation."

194 Huber to Shain.

195 Frerichs to Trustees. Also Thrya Briggs, interview by author 14 June 2007 (interview in possession of author).

196 Broujas, "The Success of Coeducation at Conn," quoting Tony Sheridan. Also Herrup, interview.

197 T. Fenton, Oshen, and Briggs interviews.

198 Tom Mortensen, "Fact Sheet: What's Wrong with the Guys." (Washington, DC: The Pell Institute for the Study of Opportunity in Higher Education, 9 August 2003).

199 Ibid.

200 Ibid.

201 Ibid.

202 Thomas J. Sheeran, "Male-Female Balance a Struggle," *AP News* (16 February 2001). See also Peter Y. Hong, "Gender Gap Growing on College Campuses," *The Los Angeles Times* (1 December 2004).

203 Ibid.

204 Thomas Parker, "Admission Report to Amherst Trustees" (12 May 2006).

205 Anja Milde, "Largest Class in Trin History Arrives," *Trinity Tripod* (12 September 2006).

206 Scott Alexander, Alex Mroszcyk-McDonald, Philip Gedeon, John Potter, Frances Shields, Dena Wallerson, and Leslie Williams, "Working Group Report on Student Recruitment and Retention, Connecticut College" (8 August 2003). Accessed 13 December 2006 from http://www.conncoll.edu/people/president-emeritus/pluralism/html/index.htm.

207 Ibid.

208 Ibid.

209 Lauren Sutherland, "Where are All the Fresh-men in the Class of 2010?" *The Miscellany News* (8 September 2006).

210 Alexander, Mroszcyk-McDonald, Gedeon, Potter, Shields, Wallerson, and Williams, "Working Group Report on Student Recruitment and Retention."

211 Katey Rich, "With More Female Applicants "Gender Gap" Widens at Wes," *The Wesleyan Argus* (28 April 2006)).

212 Desiderato, "Recurring Themes in Alumnae Coeducation Questionnaire Comments." See also "Report of the Summer Planning Group, Summary of Recommendations."

213 Ames and Held interviews.

214 Hoffman, Chrisler, Held, Gedeon, Lizarralde, and Shields, "Working Group Report on Coeducation from Report of the Presidential Commission on a Pluralistic Community at Connecticut College."

215 Alexander, Mroszcyk-McDonald, Gedeon, Potter, Shields, Wallerson, and Williams, "Working Group Report on Student Recruitment and Retention." Almost immediately the "suitcase college" phenomenon disappeared, according to an untitled 1979 (exact date not specified) Press Release From the Connecticut College News Office" to mark ten years of coeducation. CCA, Coeducation File.

216 Jordan interview.

217 "1979 Press Release From the Connecticut College News Office" to mark ten years of coeducation.

218 Ibid.

219 "1979 Press Release From the Connecticut College News Office."

220 Hoffman, Chrisler, Held, Gedeon, Lizarralde, and Shields, "Working Group Report on Coeducation from Report of the Presidential Commission on a Pluralistic Community at Connecticut College."

221 Ibid.

222 Broujas, "The Success of Coeducation at Conn."

223 Hoffman, Chrisler, Held, Gedeon, Lizarralde, and Shields, "Working Group Report on Coeducation from Report of the Presidential Commission on a Pluralistic Community at Connecticut College."

224 Ibid.

225 Hoffmann interview. See also Hoffmann, "Women, Men and Higher Education."

226 Bowen and Levin, *Reclaiming the Game: College Sports and Educational Values.*

227 Alexander, Mroszcyk-McDonald, Gedeon, Potter, Shields, Wallerson, and Williams, "Working Group Report on Student Recruitment and Retention."

228 Hoffman, Chrisler, Held, Gedeon, Lizarralde, and Shields, "Working Group Report on Coeducation from Report of the Presidential Commission on a Pluralistic Community at Connecticut College."

229 Ibid.

230 Ibid.

231 Ibid. See also "Supplementary Data on the Decision for Coeducation at Connecticut College, Confidential Until Jan. 9. 1969." According to the "Supplementary Data," women held 12 of 24 departmental chair posts and 15 of the 27 top administrative posts at Connecticut College in January 1969. For the Spring Semester of 1969, there were 83 men and 91 women on Connecticut College's teaching faculty.

232 Ibid.

233 Ibid.

234 Ibid.

235 According to the Vassar College Office of Institutional Research, women in 2003–2004 comprised 46 percent of the tenured and tenure-track faculty at Vassar. Accessed 24 March 2008 from http://institutionalresearch.vassar.edu/faculty-male.html

236 Ibid.

237 Ibid.

238 Ibid.

239 "Appendix 1: Statement of Six Past Presidents of Formerly Women's Colleges, 2000. Exceptional Coed Colleges: A New Model for Gender Equity."

240 Ibid.

241 George Willauer, "Conversion of a Skeptic," *Smith Alumnae Quarterly* (Winter 1994/95), 22–24.

242 Ibid.

243 Ibid.

244 Ibid.

CHAPTER SEVEN

Keeping the Promise to New London

From its opening day, Connecticut College for Women was more than just the State of Connecticut's one college opportunity for women; it was also New London's college.[1] At the outset, New London "invested a world of faith and love and labor in Connecticut College."[2] That the city of New London helped found Connecticut College is at the center of the best remembered and most commonly cited story about the College, that of its citizens digging into their pockets, purses, pay envelopes, and piggy banks to raise $134,000 to help launch the new institution.[3] Numerous accounts of Connecticut College's founding describe New Londoners jubilantly sounding the downtown fire siren upon reaching the $100,000 donation goal and then having a daylong celebration that included the firing of cannons and a parade.[4]

Rarely has a college opened to such fanfare and high hopes in its home community. In Connecticut College for Women's case, college and town, from the first, brought each other mutual benefit. Landing Connecticut College gave a boost in confidence and stature to New London, which had lost its past prominence as one of the cities that had vied in the 18th and 19th centuries for the title of whaling capital of America. As was true of the 19th century booster college towns, the securing of Connecticut College demonstrated that New London was a significant place, on par with Connecticut's other cities (Hartford, Middletown, and New Haven.) that had prominent colleges.

High hopes bred high expectations. Few colleges in the United States started out owing as much to their hometown as Connecticut College for Women did. Without the generosity of New Londoners, including summer resident Morton Plant whose magnanimous $1 million gift started the College's endowment, Connecticut College for Women might not have been more than the short-lived dream of Elizabeth Wright, her fellow members of the Hartford College Club, and Williams Memorial Institute principal Colin Buell. Perhaps because of the central role Connecticut College's hometown played in its founding, residents of the area, even those merely glimpsing the campus through car windows while driving by, have sometimes referred to the place as New London College or New London's college.[5]

Over the nearly 100 years of Connecticut College's existence, it has tried to give back to its home community of New London in a variety of ways, helping to fulfill the founding promise that initially united town and gown. From the beginning, for example, Connecticut College for Women's students volunteered in New London, helping organizations such as the Learned Settlement House, where students conducted science and art classes, gave piano lessons, and supervised boys and girls clubs.[6] In 1954, the College provided land at the southern edge of its campus to enable the Williams School to move from downtown New London to a more expansive facility. For a number of years thereafter, the College managed the Williams School, utilizing its classrooms for practice teaching by education majors and as observation laboratories for students studying child development.[7] Connecticut College also gave the Lyman Allyn Museum of Art the land for its site, and managed the museum between 1932 and 1982, and then more recently from 1996 to 2001.[8] Over the years, Connecticut College's studio art and art history students and faculty have helped augment the Lyman Allyn's programs and have also used the museum as a supplemental academic resource.

Investing its resources in the Williams School and the Lyman Allyn Art Museum are but two examples of Connecticut College's commitment to its local community. Yet helping a private academy such as the Williams School can be criticized as a less-than-egalitarian example of Connecticut College engaging in a community partnership. Arguably the gift of land to the Williams School was a deferred thank you for the critical contribution long-serving principal Colin Buell made to efforts to secure Connecticut College for his home city of New London. The Lyman Allyn is a regionally important museum, but Connecticut College's on-again-off-again relationship to it renders it a flawed example of the College giving back to New London.

Two other entities stand as better examples of town and college coming together. One, the Connecticut College Arboretum, has been an enduring resource for the College and the greater New London community, perhaps the best example of the college providing benefit to its local region. The other, the American Dance Festival and Connecticut College School of Dance, brought a thirty-year dose of world-class performances and arts-world fame to the campus and to New London. The presence of the Arboretum and the residency of the American Dance Festival—the latter albeit temporary—have given expression to Connecticut College's historic, and some would say inherent, responsibility to its home community while also helping shape and define the College's ongoing fulfillment of its mission.

The Connecticut College Arboretum

Early in third president Katharine Blunt's administration, Connecticut College for Women began developing an arboretum on land adjacent to the campus. The selected parcel of land had become, after the founding of the College, a favorite gathering spot for picnickers and nature lovers.[9] The College Arboretum brought together tracts on a hilltop overlooking New London and the Thames River, land that had been given to the College by generous New Londoners, land that had been passed down through generations of the Rogers and Bolles families who had originally acquired it from the Mohican tribe. Connecticut College's special library collections hold the original receipt from 1693 showing payment of "4 yards of duffels" by Thomas Bolles to Oneka, the son of Mohican Chief Uncas, for the Arboretum's land.[10] In 1931, Blunt had the foresight to see that a college arboretum might provide an attractive research facility for a botany professor and also serve as a campus and community resource.[11]

Figure 7.1. The Arboretum

Blunt was right. Starting in the 1930s, generations of Connecticut College faculty and students have studied the Arboretum's ecosystems, using the facility as an outdoor science laboratory. Countless visitors have enjoyed outings in the Arboretum's cultivated and wild spaces. Over the decades, the Arboretum has become one of the signature attributes of Connecticut College.[12] In 1979, for example, then president Oakes Ames cited the "Connecticut Arboretum...which provides students in botany, zoology, human ecology, and environmental studies with unusual opportunities for field work" as one of Connecticut College's nine most noteworthy features.[13] In 1996, all 750 acres of the Connecticut College campus became part of the

Arboretum. The campus landscape has since been managed as a plant collection following "campus as arboretum" planning principles.[14]

Figure 7.2. Students studying in the Arboretum

Professor of botany Richard Goodwin recalled in1982 how Connecticut College for Women was built on the site of the former Bolles Farm, a woodland area that had long been a favorite picnic spot for the New London community.[15] Soon after the College opened, the campus and its adjacent woodlands proved to be popular for recreational activities that drew in faculty, students, and visitors. By 1926, the College had acquired another 26 acres, giving it 64 undeveloped acres across from the west entrance to the campus, land that included a hemlock grove, a lake, a pine plantation, red maple swamps, bogs, ledges, rocky woodlands, and open fields.[16] In 1931 President Blunt recognized that establishing an arboretum could provide an opportunity for the College to fill a vacancy for a professor to head its Botany Department. Blunt subsequently convinced Connecticut College's trustees to approve an arboretum and hire an architect to draw up a plan for its grounds. Later that fall, botanist George Avery joined Connecticut College from Duke University.[17]

Figure 7.3. Professor Richard Goodwin in the Arboretum with students

In a volume recounting the first fifty years of the Arboretum's growth and development, George Avery noted that President Blunt persuaded him to come to Connecticut College by offering the dual opportunity to be a professor of botany and the founding director of the Arboretum.[18] Avery also chose to leave the larger and more prominent Duke University Biology Department for fledgling Connecticut College because he was attracted by the ground plan for the arboretum developed by the renowned architect A.F. Brinckerhoff, President of the New York Association of Landscape Architects.[19] Avery and Brinckerhoff sought to create an Arboretum that would have broad appeal and attract wide support beyond the campus. The result was the Connecticut Arboretum at Connecticut College with a membership organization called the Connecticut Arboretum Association.[20]

Dedication ceremonies for the Arboretum occurred on October 6, 1934.[21] At the time, the Arboretum consisted of 60 acres bordering the College's central campus and five acres across from the main entrance. Speaking for the College, President Katharine Blunt articulated the Arboretum's purpose: "the preservation and propagation of the native plant life of Connecticut, and the scientific arrangement of that plant life for purposes of study."[22] The Arboretum would look beyond the campus to emphasize flora native to southern New England. The fact that the Arboretum aspired from the beginning to be more than just a Connecticut College facility helped it become the valuable community resource it has been for nearly 80 years.[23]

From its birth, the Connecticut College Arboretum had to be self-sufficient. It lacked a wealthy founding patron, and Connecticut College did not have the financial means to make more than cursory investments in its development. The Arboretum's director, George Avery, was by necessity resourceful, drawing support from avid gardeners and amateur naturalists from across the state of Connecticut.[24] As a result, the Arboretum, perhaps more than any other part of Connecticut College, became intertwined with the world beyond the view from campus. Many garden clubs and women's groups pitched in to support it. For example, the Connecticut Daughters of the American Revolution in 1932 built the Arboretum's dramatic entrance of grassy steps leading down to an outdoor theater overlooking a pond.[25]

The Arboretum's chief builder, George Avery, was Connecticut College's second chair of botany. Avery replaced Caroline Black, who was the founding chairperson of the College's Botany Department. Black had joined the College's faculty at the beginning of its third academic year (1917) and had worked at building a botany program until her untimely death in 1930. It was Black's suggestion that prompted the College to split biology into distinct departments of botany and zoology, a separation that still continues to guide Connecticut College's study of the biological sciences.[26] The Connecticut College campus Caroline Black entered in 1917 was a "windy, treeless expanse of 340 acres," bordered by what she described as a "tangle of sumac and poison ivy."[27] At the request of the College's second president, Benjamin Marshall, Black began helping with the planning and the planting of the campus landscape. In the summer of 1920, for example, Professor Black supervised the transplanting of 500 shrubs from the Harkness Estate (later a state park) in Waterford to the Connecticut College campus.

Black saw potential to create a campus botanical garden that could serve as a teaching and research facility for the students and faculty of botany at Connecticut College for Women.[28] In 1928, she began transforming and cultivating five acres of overgrown land across from the College's main entrance. Many trace the Arboretum's roots to Black's botanical garden, which continued to be developed after her death.[29] Over the years, the Caroline Black Garden became a cornerstone of the Connecticut College Arboretum, a serene spot for students and staff as well as a learning laboratory for anyone interested in studying botany.[30] The Caroline Black Garden is widely considered the most attractive ornamental planting on the Connecticut College campus.[31] In 1999, the Smithsonian Institution included the Caroline Black Garden in its national Archives of American Gardens.[32]

Under George Avery's leadership, the Arboretum developed its dual character, becoming a horticultural and botanic resource for southeastern Connecticut as well as a research site for faculty and students of botany at Connecticut College.

The Arboretum provided opportunities for local garden clubs to observe and study plants and newly emerging gardening techniques.[33] The Arboretum's sweeping landscape, wooded spaces, and peaceful ponds became a favored spot for hikes and picnics by local residents. Avery and succeeding generations of biology faculty and students have used the Arboretum as a living experimental site to supplement botany lectures and textbooks. In 2006, for example, environmental studies major Jess LeClair '08 completed a survey of the stone walls in the Arboretum.[34]

Literally and symbolically the Arboretum grew over the years to express Connecticut College's connection to its home city of New London. From its inception, the Arboretum has stood at the edge of the Connecticut College campus and appeared open to all comers, whereas the more enclosed academic and residential campus may have seemed, then and now, the "college on the hill" reserved for its tuition-paying students.[35] Connecticut College has always been unusual among residential small liberal arts colleges for having such a public space within its boundaries.

After George Avery left Connecticut College in 1946 to head up the Brooklyn Botanical Gardens, Professor Richard Goodwin of the botany department took over direction of the Arboretum. Goodwin, like Avery, was a Harvard-trained botanist with a research emphasis on plant hormones.[36] One of Goodwin's chief acts was to transfer choice plants from overcrowded sections of the Caroline Black Garden to help beautify the sites of newly constructed campus buildings, such as Katharine Blunt House.[37] With his longtime botany department colleague, William Niering, Goodwin further integrated the Arboretum's resources into Connecticut College's natural science curriculum.[38] Goodwin and Niering also established a science discovery center that became a requisite field trip for local schoolchildren throughout southeastern Connecticut and southwestern Rhode Island.[39]

Historically, the Arboretum and Connecticut College have been part of the same institution. But for more than fifty years the Arboretum bore the name Connecticut Arboretum of Connecticut College. The Arboretum started out as "something of a waif," its financial support coming from its philanthropic association made up of loyal donors from around the state.[40] But as the Arboretum grew in size, reputation, and strength as an educational resource, in parallel to Connecticut College's own growth, the College asserted ownership and care for it.[41] As a result, the name changed to the Connecticut College Arboretum, making it clear that the Arboretum was owned and operated by the College, not by the state of Connecticut.[42]

Members of the Connecticut College community have long regarded their Arboretum as a treasured resource. College founder Elizabeth Wright figures into one story of efforts to protect that resource. In 1936 Wright saw a group of men drilling into a ledge in a ravine area of the Arboretum.[43] Wright leaned over the ledge and in her deep, authoritative voice requested that the men stop drilling until the College could investigate their activities.[44] The investigation found that the men were getting stone for a new College building. Wright's intervention led Connecticut College to preserve the ravine and shift to getting construction stone from another local source.[45]

Richard Goodwin's research interest in local ecology led him to convince President Rosemary Park in 1955 to purchase nearby Mamacoke Island in the Thames River.[46] Goodwin thought that Mamacoke Island could serve as a research preserve for Connecticut College, so he raised $15,000 from 250 contributors to enable the College to buy the Island from a marine construction company.[47] Showing uncanny environmental prescience, Goodwin insisted on a clause in the deed stating that Mamacoke Island could only be sold if it was first offered to the Nature Conservancy or the Connecticut Forest and Park Association for no more than $500.[48]

It did not take long for the clause to be tested. In 1957 a contractor offered Connecticut College $50,000 to lease Mamacoke Island for use as a dumping ground for sludge dredged from the Thames River.[49] Under the plan, sludge was to be dumped into a cove where Native Americans had harvested oysters for thousands of years.[50] Goodwin gleefully directed the construction firm's negotiators to the clause in the deed that ensured that Mamacoke Island would remain a natural area in perpetuity—resulting in a permanent research resource for Connecticut College and an enduring natural preserve for southeastern Connecticut.[51]

Richard Goodwin's early study of ecology and his active interest in preserving the natural world led him to help establish the Nature Conservancy in the 1950s.[52] In 1956 Goodwin became the Nature Conservancy's first president, serving two terms (1956-58 and 1964-66).[53] In fact, Goodwin was the Nature Conservancy's last volunteer president. Goodwin also established the Conservation and Research Foundation in 1953 to provide start-up grants to scientists and conservationists wishing to study and preserve the natural environment.[54] Through Goodwin's founding ties to that organization and the Nature Conservancy, which has become one of the world's leading environmental organizations, Connecticut College was at the forefront of the ensuing environmental studies movement in higher education and thus can claim a lead position among colleges and universities committed to preserving the natural world. Few colleges can claim they have a stronger environmental preservation legacy than Connecticut College's.

The work of Goodwin and Niering exemplifies how Connecticut College professors, through academic and research interests, have made positive contributions to the local community and the state that gave their institution life. Research by Goodwin and Niering showcased the importance of preserving Connecticut's freshwater marshlands.[55] That work led the Connecticut Legislature to enact some of the earliest environmental protection statutes in the United States.[56] Goodwin and Niering also publicized their research findings on the deleterious effects of herbicides in a pamphlet that focused public and legislative attention in Connecticut on roadside spraying of herbicides by utility companies.[57] That pamphlet, which President Park approved even though a utility company executive was on Connecticut College's board of trustees at the time, led companies to curtail their roadside spraying.[58]

The Connecticut College Arboretum adopted a mission statement in 1990.[59] According to the 1990 mission statement, the Arboretum operates for the benefit of Connecticut College and the community, helping prepare students and visitors for a lifetime of learning about and engagement with the natural world.[60] The Arboretum serves as a teaching and research resource, as it provides an outdoor laboratory for faculty and students in botany, conservation, ecology, natural history, and zoology.[61] Even Connecticut College art classes make use of the Arboretum as an inspirational site for drawings, paintings, and photographs, while dance and theater classes sometimes use it as a performance space.[62]

On the occasion of the Arboretum's 60th anniversary in 1991, its director Glen Dreyer characterized the valuable and unusual role the Arboretum has played historically for the College and the community, calling the Connecticut College Arboretum a living example of the natural world for people to learn from and enjoy in perpetuity.[63] Countless people on and off campus have benefited from the Arboretum. For example, each year a handful of Connecticut College seniors conduct honors research in the Arboretum and more than 25 classes draw from its resources.[64] Dreyer has stated that he can think of no other college that would be able to assemble such a "sizeable list of research reports, theses, and publications on field work conducted within walking distance of its classrooms and laboratories."[65]

The Arboretum's staff protects, sustains, and enhances the biological diversity of the Connecticut College campus, while also providing consultation on conservation matters to environmental scientists and land use planners throughout the state. Dreyer, for example, co-edited a book (released in 2005) that described ways to "green" cities and towns in the state of Connecticut.[66] The Arboretum's community educational programs continue to emphasize lessons about the environment, horticulture, and natural history. In 2004, for example, 640 people participated in continuing education programs sponsored by the Arboretum for landscape architects and professional landscape designers.[67] Each year the Arboretum gives public and private tours to hundreds of people interested in learning more about the natural world.[68] Connecticut College students provide environmental education tours of the Arboretum's native plant collection for local schools and children's organizations.[69] In 2004, those student tours brought 722 local children to the Arboretum.[70] In addition, the Arboretum maintains, develops, and interprets plant collections for teaching, research, public education, and enjoyment.[71]

During summers, it is not uncommon for the Arboretum to host productions of the great works of drama by classical playwrights such as Shakespeare, Moliere, and Aristophanes. In 2004 more than 2,500 people attended those plays.[72] For many in southeastern Connecticut, the Arboretum's play series provides a first exposure to the standout works in the history of theater.[73] The Arboretum also serves an instructional purpose through its library of botanical publications for use by visitors, including local science teachers, and Connecticut College students.[74] Nearly a quarter of the Arboretum's 450 acres that are not part of the core Connecticut College campus consists of native plant collections and natural areas. With frequent assistance from faculty, students, and community volunteers, Arboretum staff members regularly take stock of Connecticut College's plant collection.[75] By the close of 2004, for example, there were 2,671 living trees in the Arboretum, including 1,105 in the native plant collection and 1,393 forming the campus landscape.[76]

To this day, Connecticut College's Arboretum contains 200 acres of natural preserves protected from human disturbance.[77] Protection of the natural areas in the Arboretum has led to increased populations of several species of birds and animals, including pileated woodpeckers, bald eagles, Cooper's hawks, coyotes, deer, gray foxes, Fisher cats, and turkeys.[78] Connecticut College's protection and maintenance of the Arboretum's natural areas helps demonstrate its long-standing, institution-defining commitment to environmental preservation. The Arboretum is the most tangible example that environmental stewardship is a central institutional value at Connecticut College, one articulated prominently in its vision for its second hundred years.[79]

For nearly 80 years, the Arboretum has lived up to its mission statement. It has enhanced the quality of life for Connecticut College and for the citizens of the New London area, providing a resource for recreation, reflection, and renewal through contact with the natural world.[80] The Arboretum continues to increase understanding of nature through educational programs and publications about conservation, horticulture, gardening, botany, and natural history. The Arboretum is held up frequently by the College as the prime example of its mission to prepare "the next generation of citizen leaders, whose diverse responsibilities will include crafting a sustainable relationship with the natural world."[81] The Arboretum serves as an example of the extent to which a historic connection to the earth and environmental stewardship are defining values of Connecticut College.[82]

As it approaches its second century, Connecticut College believes that it stands out among peer liberal arts colleges for its "long-standing commitment to conservation and environmental studies."[83] From the outset Connecticut College offered a botany program notable for its emphasis on the conservation of local natural resources. When it introduced a major in human ecology in 1969, Connecticut College became one of the first colleges in the United States to establish a study program focused on the environment.[84] To emphasize the importance of preserving the natural world, Connecticut College since 1992 has given each graduate at commencement a white sapling to plant.[85]

A campus is the physical manifestation of a college's educational philosophy.[86] Campus aesthetics are an active demonstration of institutional mission, as physical surroundings can enhance or detract from learning.[87] In cases such as the Connecticut College campus and Arboretum, the aesthetics of a particular setting and the learning environment it creates reflect the institution's founding vision, mission, and educational values.[88] Throughout its existence, the Connecticut College Arboretum has been a special source of pride for the students who have attended, the faculty who have taught at, and the staff who have worked at the College. When asked to define what makes Connecticut College distinctive, many past and present members of the campus community point to the physical beauty of the campus setting, which is enhanced by the Arboretum.[89] There are some who believe that the physical beauty of Connecticut College's setting is its most distinctive feature.[90] Generations of students have chosen to attend Connecticut College in part due to a campus that has been judged one of the fifty most beautiful in the United States.[91]

There are some colleges that stand out for their intellectual heritage or for unifying beliefs that could transfer to other locations. But Connecticut College, despite its distinctive heritage and beliefs, is not one of them. The College's essence is defined in non-transferable ways by its location and surroundings. Few colleges have designated their whole campus an arboretum. Few colleges in the world are defined more by the physical place part of their sense of place than Connecticut College. The Arboretum is an essential part of that defining characteristic.

The American Dance Festival at Connecticut College

Numerous members of the Connecticut College family credit the American Dance Festival's summer residency from 1948 to 1978 with placing the College prominently in the national—and even international—arts scene.[92] Over the thirty years it occurred, the American Dance Festival's residency on campus came to be regarded as "the most important summertime event in modern dance."[93] By its prominence, the American Dance Festival (ADF) became a beacon shining on the College and New London, making Connecticut College the place to go in the 1950s, 1960s, and 1970s to see the latest currents in modern dance.[94]

Modern dance was still considered experimental, even radical, when the ADF partnered with Connecticut College in 1948. Throwing support behind the American Dance Festival was not the safe, uncontroversial choice expected of a staid elite college in New England. But Connecticut College was a youthful and energetic institution with a relatively young and forward-thinking woman at the helm. Connecticut's forty-year-old President Rosemary Park had the foresight in 1948 to sign on with New York University as the co-sponsor, replacing Bennington College, which had hosted the ADF since its inception in 1934.[95] Three years later, in 1951, Park persuaded Connecticut's trustees that the College should take over full sponsorship of the ADF and the Summer School of Dance.[96] Thus began the Connecticut College School of Dance and the American Dance Festival, with the College providing funding, performance spaces, classrooms, and housing for three decades.[97]

The ADF and School of Dance did not just use Connecticut's facilities for six weeks each summer; the Festival and School became entwined with the College's faculty, students, and programs. Ruth Bloomer of the Connecticut College physical education department (which until the 1970s offered the College's only dance courses), for example, served as the first co-director of the ADF with her former teacher, the famous dance choreographer Martha Hill.[98] Connecticut students took classes in the School of Dance, and College faculty and New London-area residents attended ADF performances by the artistic-boundary-pushing likes of Alvin Ailey, Merce Cunningham, Paul Draper, Martha Graham, Erich Hawkins, Doris Humphrey, Jose Limon, Pilobolus, Paul Taylor, and Twyla Tharp.[99]

Each summer the Connecticut College School of Dance attracted approximately 300 students from more than 40 states and nearly 20 foreign countries.[100] For six weeks students came to New London to engage in intensive study of anatomy, choreography, dance analysis and education, notation, stagecraft, technique, music for dance, and theater production.[101] The first five weeks of each summer program consisted of dance classes, supplemented by weekly evening lectures and performances given by distinguished artists and teachers, such as Martha Graham, Martha Hill, and Jose Limon.[102] The Connecticut College School of Dance billed itself as a "laboratory for study and experimental production in which the student works for six weeks as apprentice to a group of artists and teachers."[103] The School of Dance sought to attract students and teachers of dance, professional dancers, musicians, and others interested in arts study and education.[104] Dance students became immersed, according to School of Dance co-director Ruth Bloomer, "in this heady mixture of doing—making, seeing—feeling, redoing...focused totally in one direction if only for a brief period of time."[105] The School of Dance's approach enabled students to dig "deeply into [their] own resources, stimulated on the way by others in the same state," resulting in "an exhilaration rarely met."[106] This approach also enabled even the youngest students to feel as if they were being regarded seriously as artists and dancers.[107]

The American Dance Festival always occurred during the sixth and final week of the School of Dance's summer program.[108] But it was the ADF weeks that brought the world to New London. The School of Dance and the ADF turned the Connecticut College campus into a summer arts colony, making it a cousin to Tanglewood in the Berkshires and Yaddo in Saratoga Springs. The ADF brought dancers, composers, writers, and musicians to New London.[109] Audiences saw many groundbreaking dance pieces, often glimpsing the premiere performance of a production that later became a standard in the modern dance repertoire.[110] Between 1948 and 1978, the ADF attracted to New London the world leaders in modern dance, and the Summer School of Dance annually brought high school-age students, among its 300 participants, and vast audiences to the Connecticut College campus.[111]

Figure 7.4. School of Dance students

The presence of the ADF enabled Connecticut College to develop a strong undergraduate dance program.[112] When the Summer School of Dance and the ADF began in 1948, Connecticut College offered dance through its physical education department. By the 1970s, the College had attracted to its dance faculty accomplished teachers such as Martha Myers and offered B.A. and M.F.A. programs in dance.[113] In 1976, Connecticut College had 233 undergraduates enrolled in dance classes and 28 students majoring in dance.[114] The ADF became an integral feature of Connecticut College's dance program, as the dance department could boast that its majors spent a minimum of one semester in residence at the Festival.[115]

Hosting the ADF summer residency also gave Connecticut College cachet among patrons of the arts in New York and New England. Alumni recall seeing notice of the festival and its performances in the summer weekend arts sections of *The New York Times* and feeling proud that their alma mater was associated with a star performing arts organization.[116] For some, the ADF defined Connecticut College's image in the larger world as Connecticut College and the ADF became "virtually synonymous."[117] By association with the ADF and the arts aficionados it attracted, Connecticut College's own performing arts programs achieved higher visibility.[118] The ADF affiliation provided bragging rights. Connecticut College may have been younger and less widely known than the Seven Sister colleges, but none of them could tout the ADF affiliation.

Figure 7.5. ADF dancers practicing

The ADF residency not only gave New London area residents the opportunity to see performances normally just available in New York or Boston, but it also brought tourists to the region, visitors whose spending enriched the coffers of local businesses. The mere presence of the ADF during the summer months enlivened the New London arts scene and became a tangible example of Connecticut College's commitment to providing cultural uplift to its local community.[119] The ADF, for example, held year-round community outreach programs, consisting of movement classes, workshops, and dance concerts in southeastern Connecticut and Rhode Island.[120] The ADF also held free classes and short demonstrations on New London streets, in shopping centers, and in recreation halls.[121] The presence of the ADF also became a local source of pride, as an August 14, 1964, editorial in New London's *The Day* shows: "New London is the summer capital for the world of modern dance, a distinction unchallenged since the School of Dance was established in 1948 on the campus of Connecticut College."[122] Yet, unfortunately, when the American Dance Festival left for North Carolina in 1978 and the Connecticut College Summer

School of Dance closed, New London lost that distinction forever in the dance and performing arts worlds.[123]

By the mid-1970s, the ADF residency was becoming a financial drain on Connecticut College's budget. Crowds had diminished over the years. There was a growing sense on campus that perhaps the ADF had lost its luster and was not worth the College's continued investment.[124] Connecticut College had always subsidized the ADF. But as ticket sales decreased, the ADF changed from a break-even proposition to a net expense on the College's balance sheet. In 1975, for example, the Summer School of Dance and the ADF reported an $11,000 deficit, while the College had a $50,000 budget shortfall of its own.[125] By 1976, the College estimated that it spent a total of $50,000 each summer to support the ADF.[126] Faced with years of red ink from the ADF, the Connecticut College Board of Trustees authorized President Oakes Ames in December 1976 to require the ADF to provide $15,000 toward the College's $50,000 annual outlay for its operating costs.[127]

In the negotiations that led Connecticut's Board to settle on the $15,000 figure, the College had started by asking the ADF to pay $27,400 to offset the personnel, facilities maintenance, and air conditioning expenses associated with the summer festival.[128] That request startled the ADF's leadership, because the amount was more than five times the College's usual rent charges of $5,000 per summer.[129] Dropping the requested ADF contribution down to $15,000 was a compromise move to show Connecticut College's interest in keeping the Festival.[130]

The College's insistence on more than $5,000 per year in rent from the ADF started a feud between it and the Festival's director, Charles Reinhardt.[131] Reinhardt alleged that Connecticut College's request for three times its usual rent of $5,000 signaled a change in priorities.[132] He labeled that change a lessening of Connecticut College's commitment to the arts and scoffed at the $15,000 rent request, asserting that the ADF's presence was worth $500,000 in annual advertising and public relations for the College.[133] Reinhardt called Connecticut's estimate of $50,000 in annual ADF expenses an "accounting trick," arguing that costs for building maintenance and security were ones the College would have to pay in the summer with or without the ADF.[134] There were equally strong feelings on Connecticut College's side of the disagreement. College officials believed that it was not right to divert funds provided through the tuitions paid by its undergraduates enrolled from September to May to a six-week summer program of little benefit to those undergraduates.[135] Connecticut College's mission, so the argument went, was to educate undergraduates during September through May, not to operate a summer program.

Figure 7.6. Poster for the ADF's 20th season at Connecticut College

For a year Connecticut College and the ADF reached a compromise. Connecticut College agreed in early 1977 to cover $35,000 of the estimated $50,000 annual operating costs, and the ADF agreed to contribute $5,250.[136] Showing the importance of the ADF to the region, two organizations focused on expanding cultural opportunities in the State of Connecticut stepped up to provide $9,000 of the remaining $9,750 needed to finance the 1977 season.[137] Connecticut's Commission on the Arts contributed $7,500 and the Southeastern Connecticut Chamber of Commerce pledged $1,500, because both organizations wanted the ADF to remain in the state.[138] An anonymous donor pitched in the remaining $750.[139]

The wrangling with Connecticut College over rent prompted ADF director Reinhardt to seek autonomy for his organization. Reinhardt's move in 1975 to incorporate the ADF as a legal entity, separate from Connecticut College, laid the foundation for the ADF to consider its options, including the prospect of moving away from Connecticut College and New London.[140] Reinhardt treated the funding compromise of 1977 as a temporary rapprochement. Within months of that compromise, the ADF had established a committee to consider alternative host sites to Connecticut College and New London. During the fall of 1977, the ADF's site selection committee entertained eleven serious offers for future host sites, one of which was Connecticut College.[141]

In October 1977, Reinhardt and the ADF's site selection committee announced the elimination of eight contenders, including Connecticut College, leaving three finalists: Duke University, the University of Massachusetts at Amherst, and the University of Wisconsin at Milwaukee.[142] Speaking for the College, President Oakes Ames expressed disappointment, saying the loss of the ADF would be especially hard for Connecticut's dance program.[143] At the same time, Ames also reemphasized that the College felt that it had made the best offer it could to keep the Festival.[144] From Charles Reinhardt's perspective, Connecticut College had lost out because the three remaining finalist sites had shown greater commitment to the ADF.[145] Reinhardt was not just speaking about the institutional commitment of Connecticut College, for he had long maintained that New London and its surrounding communities had failed to support the ADF adequately.[146] The editorial board of New London's *The Day* agreed, lamenting the New London community's inadequate response to the possibility of losing the ADF.[147] Action to keep the festival should have occurred, in *The Day's* opinion, as soon as Reinhardt began to make noise about moving elsewhere.[148]

Near the end of October 1977, Charles Reinhardt announced that the American Dance Festival would move to Duke University in Durham, North Carolina, beginning with the 1978 season.[149] Duke's winning proposal included the pledge of a $1 million endowment for the ADF.[150] But it was not just the money that lured the ADF to Duke University, it was also the outpouring of enthusiasm and support from North Carolina's leaders in the arts, education, business, and politics.[151] Chief among the ADF's cheerleaders and supporters was Duke University's President Terry Sanford, who as governor of North Carolina had helped create the state-supported North Carolina School of the Arts in Winston-Salem.[152] Reinhardt expressed excitement regarding Duke and Durham's joint commitment to the ADF and took a shot at Connecticut, asserting that "in New London there was an old town-and-gown separation that we could not bridge."[153] The choice of Duke and Durham has been an enduring one, as the ADF remains there more than 30 years later.

Second-guessing, sour grapes, and recriminations followed the ADF's departure. The party line at the College was that both Connecticut College and the Festival had come to the mutual conclusion that it was time to part. William Churchill, special assistant to President Oakes Ames, told Connecticut College's student newspaper, *College Voice*, that "the Festival is not, in its present form, what it used to be in the golden days of Martha Graham and Jose Limon."[154] Taking Churchill's statement a few steps further, the *College Voice* reporters asserted that "the time is ripe to move on, and it is time for Connecticut to develop its own program that is more suited to the needs of the College and the community."[155] The *College Voice* article did not speak for everyone in the Connecticut College family. Many officials at Connecticut College felt betrayed by Reinhardt and the ADF. Those College officials felt that the institution deserved gratitude and loyalty from the ADF for subsidizing the program during all the lean years when modern dance was emerging and building an audience.[156] Thirty years of funding by Connecticut College, according to this view, should not have been interpreted by the ADF's leadership as an expectation, or an entitlement, for ongoing support in perpetuity.[157] Although the haggling over rent payments became the public issue in contention, many at Connecticut agreed with President Ames that the ADF's decision in 1975 to incorporate had "pulled the festival and the College apart," perhaps irreparably.[158] Many in the college community felt that the ADF belonged to Connecticut College, due to the historical and financial relationship, and were hurt by Reinhardt's move to incorporate it.[159]

From Charles Reinhardt's perspective, incorporation was simply a business decision that would make the ADF better able to attract financial support from patrons.[160] Plus, in Reinhardt's estimation, the ADF "belong[ed] to the dance world, not Connecticut College."[161] Reinhardt also justified the move south to Duke University on the grounds that the ADF needed a home where dance as an art form and the Festival as an event would be considered more of a priority by its host institution.[162] Despite a successful 29-year run for the Festival in New London, Reinhardt chose to dwell on the lean later years. For example, he blamed the unremarkable box office receipts collected in the Festival's last decade on the small size of Connecticut College's Palmer Auditorium, which seated fewer than 2,000.[163] Even as he looked forward to a new home in Durham, North Carolina, Reinhardt insisted that the small space at Connecticut College and the lack of support by New Londoners had been the cause of the Festival's attendance problems, not any decline in interest in modern dance.[164]

There were some in New London who did not lament the departure of the American Dance Festival, dismissing it as "an elitist happening up on the hill."[165] Others in the college community criticized the ADF for becoming "so high powered that students could no longer get the personal attention they needed."[166] Still, others went so far as to say that the ADF's programs had devolved into an unwieldy and incoherent "smorgasbord."[167] Yet even critics of the ADF would likely agree that its departure removed an arts beacon that had shone on New London for thirty years, the likes of which has never returned.

Connecticut College responded to the closing of the School of Dance and the loss of the ADF with plans for a new summer arts program that would include dance, theater, and studio art. For its inaugural summer, the new arts program brought in the Bill Evans Dance Company of Seattle for a three-week residency of workshops and performances.[168] College officials hoped that the replacement summer arts program would draw 300 students to the campus and would enrich the New London community with classes in movement, exercise for dance, ballet, jazz, and modern dance.[169] But while Connecticut College successfully undertook an alternative program to replace the ADF, that new program never approached generating the excitement and notoriety that the Summer School of Dance and the American Dance Festival brought to the campus and to New London.[170] Within a decade the program ceased.

To the city of New London the loss of the ADF was both cultural and financial. New London officials estimated that the School of Dance and the ADF brought $1.5 million annually in economic benefit to the city and the surrounding towns in southeastern Connecticut.[171] At the time of the ADF's departure from Connecticut College, New London city manager C. Francis Driscoll called the loss "devastating."[172] "It will be a terrible cultural loss to the area," said Marilyn Glassman, chair of the Friends of the American Dance Festival.[173]

Critics of the College's hard-nosed negotiations with the ADF asserted that it was shortsighted and would result in a loss of prestige for Connecticut College in the arts world. Veteran art professor David Smalley observed at the time of its departure that "the Dance Festival was dropped on Connecticut College from heaven" and had brought hard-to-replace expertise in arts management that had benefited all of the arts departments at the College.[174] Following the departure of the ADF, faculty critics like Smalley blamed President Ames for demonstrating a lack of initiative to find a comparable replacement.[175] Critics alleged that College priorities had shifted away from the arts toward athletics and the sciences.[176]

Thirty years later, the critics wonder why Connecticut College did not seek to attract gifts to endow the ADF's summer residency and take its annual expense off the College's ledgers.[177] The critics assert that Ames and the trustees should have sought external-funding sources for the ADF, some of which might have brought new supporters to the College. Critics point to the lost opportunity for publicity for Connecticut College through notices of the ADF's performances that ran in the *New York Times* Friday arts section during summers.[178] Critics also lament the loss of a signature affiliation that, they argue, helped solidify Connecticut College as one of the best small liberal arts colleges for the study of dance and associated performing arts such as theater.[179]

Those who still stand behind Connecticut's tough negotiation stance toward Charles Reinhardt argue that the ADF's residency, like all programs of the College, needed periodic evaluation to determine its worth to the institution.[180] Supporters of Ames' hard line, and Ames himself, also cite factors that could not be discussed easily in public, factors relating to Connecticut College's relatively recent, at the time, decision to admit men.[181] One such factor was the tension between the ADF's summer dominance of the Connecticut College campus and the newly coeducational college's self-consciousness about the image it presented to prospective male students.[182]

Connecticut College's evolving and still insecure identity as a coeducational college in the 1970s led its officials frequently to consider how decisions would affect its ability to attract male students to the campus.[183] Admission dean Jeanette Hersey believed that "a good many people were turned away from Connecticut, because" the presence of the ADF created the impression that the College "was too arty a place."[184] While the ADF residency had made Connecticut more prominent, it had done so in a way that was now seen as counterproductive to the coeducational image the College wanted to project.[185] Thus, the negotiation with the ADF became an instance where the College's appeal to men factored heavily into the posture its officials took.

Thirty years after the departure of the ADF, with the move to coeducation fading into the distant memory for most members of the Connecticut College family, there are few occasions when the issue of what the College might have lost in the transition gets raised.[186] Recollections of the ADF decision tend to bring out the issue of sports versus the arts at the coeducational Connecticut College. Supporters of the ADF contend that its departure coincided with the ascension of athletics as the College moved to attract men and prove that it could achieve a fully coeducation campus, not merely turn it into Connecticut College for Women with some men.[187] According to the extreme version of this critical view, the emphasis on sports that began in the 1970s has so far overshadowed the significance of the arts at Connecticut College that many would have a hard time believing that a performing arts organization like the ADF once helped define the College to the world.[188] The critics allege that the College did not have to choose between arts and sports.[189] With the continued presence of the ADF, it could have had both.

The performing arts departments at Connecticut College and its arts reputation were not the only losers when the ADF departed. The arts communities of New London and southeastern Connecticut lost a steady annual trail of prominent artists to an area perennially in the shadow of much larger New England cities.[190] Supporters of the arts believe that the world-renowned dancers, by their examples, invigorated nearby arts communities and raised the sights of countless children who saw the ADF's performances or attended the Summer School of Dance.[191]

The presence of the ADF, it could be argued, never provided New London with a tangible benefit rivaling that of the Arboretum or the many hours of volunteer service contributed by Connecticut College students. But it is shortsighted to look at the ADF with just a hardheaded, bottom-line cost and benefit perspective or even just through the prism of Connecticut College's transition to coeducation. The value of the ADF to Connecticut College and New London must be measured in ways other than the conventional concrete calculus of success and failure.

The ADF brought great psychic and symbolic benefit to New London. The ADF was a marquee presence that put the southeastern Connecticut arts community on the national map. Like the founding of Connecticut College within its city limits, the presence of the ADF in New London raised civic pride, anchoring the historic whaling city as a destination of significance. Never before and never since has Connecticut College sponsored a continuing program that brought such notice to its home city. On those grounds, the College's partnership with the ADF stands as a short-lived example, but one with an enduring memory, of an attempt, intentional or not, by Connecticut College to fulfill the hopes New Londoners had on that day in 1911 when they paraded in the streets celebrating their new college.

Inherent in the founding story of Connecticut College is the persuasive notion that the institution, in no small part, owes its existence to its hometown. Stated simply, the College has a responsibility to New London. How that responsibility translates into action has been open to interpretation over the past one hundred years. There have been some who have believed that Connecticut College, by its very existence in New London, is a resource of permanent value to its local community. According to this view, Connecticut College showed adequate gratitude, when it honored the many townspeople of New London who gave so generously, by naming one of the original buildings New London Hall and by using local stone to construct the campus.[192]

The Connecticut College Arboretum then, as a special feature not found on many college campuses, including those not as beholden to their hometown, more than helps fulfill the promise that Connecticut College held for all the New Londoners whose contributions in 1911 turned the institution from dream into reality. Furthermore, not only has Connecticut College established permanent community-enhancing entities like the Arboretum, but it has also provided additional resources for New Londoners through occasional special programs, such as the American Dance Festival, and the countless hours of voluntary community service performed by its students over nearly one hundred years.

There is another view, one that holds Connecticut College to an even deeper level of commitment to its hometown of New London. The root of this interpretation of the promise inherent in Connecticut College's founding story is the belief that the College's existence and prosperity would not be possible without New London. According to this interpretation, the College must not stand apart from New London like a rich and haughty neighbor and must never turn its back on its city when that city is hurting. This idea that Connecticut College owes its city an enduring, active commitment came into conflict with the other view, that New London benefits simply by the presence of the College, in the late 1990s during the presidency of Claire Gaudiani '66, a fascinating and confounding period in the College's history that gets recounted and analyzed in the following chapter.

Notes

1   Agnes Underwood, interview by author 26 October 2007 (interview in possession of author).

2   "Timely Views by the Commentator," *New London Telegraph* (22 March 1917).

3   According to *The New London Telegraph's* Commentator (22 March 1917), the funds invested in Connecticut College for Women had been "Millionaires' money, storekeepers' money, mechanics' money, laborers' money—money from the pay envelopes of street car men, the railroaders, the purse of the seamstress: one wonderful gift, perhaps you will recall, of a week's labor of a poor woman of the washtub; newsboys' money, school girls' pocket money—thousands and tens of thousands of New London money, the money of New London's rank and file."

4   Ibid. See also Noyes, *History of Connecticut College*; Nye, *Chapters in the History of Connecticut College*; and Buell, "Thames College: An Account of the Struggle by a Yale Graduate to Found a Woman's College in Connecticut," 751.

5   Casey Wilkinson Zahn, interviews by author August 2005 and November 2007 (interviews in possession of author). Norwich, Connecticut native Zahn told me that she and her childhood friends in the 1960s tended to refer to Connecticut College as New London College.

6   "The College in the Community: Students Carry on Work at Settlement House," *Connecticut College News* (1956).

7   Rosemary Park, "College to Supervise Secondary School, *Connecticut College Alumnae News* (March 1954), 3–4.

8   Ibid.

9   Nye, *Chapters in the History of Connecticut College*, 72.

10 Dan Clem, "Living Laboratory: The Connecticut College Arboretum Celebrates Its 75th Year," *CC: Connecticut College Magazine* (Summer 2006), 32–37.

11 George Avery, "Early Historical Highlights," in *The Connecticut College Arboretum: Its First Fifty Years* (New London: Connecticut College, 1982), 3–8.

12 Oakes Ames (5 June 2007) and Lisa Brownell (22 January 2007), interviews by author (interviews in possession of author).

13 *Connecticut College, Report of the President, 1977–1978* (New London, CT: Connecticut College), 6.

14 *Arboretum* (Brochure) (New London: Connecticut College, 2004).

15 Richard H. Goodwin, "The Connecticut Arboretum: Its Establishment and Growth," in *The Connecticut College Arboretum: Its First Fifty Years* (New London: Connecticut College, 1982), 9–31.

16 Avery, "Early Historical Highlights."

17 Ibid.

18 Ibid.

19 Ibid.

20 Ibid.

21 Ibid.

22 Ibid.

23 Avery, "Early Historical Highlights."

24 Ibid.

25 Nye, *Chapters in the History of Connecticut College*, 73.

26 *Trees of the Connecticut College Campus* (Brochure) (New London: Connecticut College, 2000).

27 *Caroline Black Garden* (Brochure) (New London: Connecticut College Arboretum, Summer 2001).

28 *Trees of the Connecticut College Campus.*

29 *Caroline Black Garden.*

30 Ibid.

31 Ibid.

32 Ibid.

33 Avery, "Early Historical Highlights."

34 Clem, "Living Laboratory."

35 Brownell interview. Brownell, who grew up in nearby Waterford, noted that New London residents often referred to Connecticut College as the "college on the hill," a term used to emphasize its physical and symbolic distance from them.

36 Richard Goodwin, interview by author 24 April 2007 (interview in author's possession). Goodwin and Avery knew each other from graduate school at Harvard.

37 *Arboretum.*

38 Goodwin, "The Connecticut Arboretum: Its Establishment and Growth." See also Richard H. Goodwin, *The Connecticut College Arboretum: Its Sixth Decade and a Detailed History of the Land* (New London: Connecticut College, 1991).

39 Ibid.

40 Ibid.

41 Ibid.

42 Ibid.

43 Ibid.

44 Ibid.

45 Ibid.

46 Ibid.

47 Ibid. See also Clem, "Living Laboratory."

48 Ibid.

49   Ibid.
50   Ibid.
51   Ibid.
52   Ibid.
53   Ibid.
54   "Goodwin, 96, Environment Pioneer, Dies," *The Day* (10 July 2007).
55   Ibid.
56   Ibid.
57   Ibid.
58   Ibid. Also Goodwin interview.
59   Goodwin, *The Connecticut College Arboretum.*
60   Ibid.
61   Ibid.
62   *Trees of the Connecticut College Campus.*
63   Glen D. Dreyer, "Foreword," in Goodwin, R.H. *The Connecticut College Arboretum: Its Sixth Decade and a Detailed History of the Land* (New London: Connecticut College, 1991), v.
64   Clem, "Living Laboratory."
65   Dreyer, "Foreword."
66   "Sprucing up the Arbo," *CC: Connecticut College Magazine* (Winter 2007), 6.
67   *Connecticut College Arboretum Annual Report 2004.* (New London: Connecticut College Arboretum, 2004).
68   Ibid.
69   Ibid.
70   Ibid.
71   Goodwin interview.
72   Ibid.
73   Ibid.
74   Ibid.
75   Ibid.
76   Ibid.
77   *Arboretum.*
78   Clem, "Living Laboratory."
79   *Strategic Priorities for the Second Century: Draft 8* (New London: Connecticut College, 2 February 2007).
80   *Arboretum.*
81   Ibid.
82   Lee Higdon, interview by author 24 April 2007 (interview in possession of author). Also Brownell interview.
83   Ibid.
84   Untitled, unsigned draft of letter to "The Day" (1969), from Connecticut College Archives. Coeducation File. See also "Leaving the Land Behind," *The Hartford Courant* (12 July 2007).
85   "Living Tradition," *Yankee*, Vol. 69, Issue 5 (June 2005).
86   Richard Ekman, "Creating Campus Appeal: Architecture's Effect on the Message Conveyed About an Institution," *University Business* (December 2007), 40–41. When he wrote the article, Ekman was president of the Council of Independent Colleges.
87   Thomas A. Gaines, *The Campus as a Work of Art* (New York: Praeger, 1991); D.R. Kenney, R. Dumont, & G. Kenney, *Mission and Place: Strengthening Learning and Community Through*

Campus Design (Westport, CT: Praeger Publishers, 2005); George D. Kuh, "Appraising the Character of a College," *Journal of Counseling & Development,* 71, (1993), 661–668.

88　Ekman, "Creating Campus Appeal."

89　Thyra Briggs (14 June 2007), Torrey Fenton (24 April 2007), Martha Merrill (22 January 2007 and 30 October 2007), Jeff Oshen (1 May 2007), and Brian Rogers (5 December 2006 and 22 January 2007), interviews by author (interviews in possession of author).

90　Frances Hoffman, interview by author, 12 June 2007 (interview in author's possession).

91　Gaines, *The Campus as a Work of Art.*

92　The ADF section is informed by interviews conducted by the author with Oakes Ames (5 June 2007), Jane Bredeson (23 January 2007), Thyra Briggs, Lisa Brownell, Laurie Deredita (31 July 2007), Norman Fainstein (24 July 2007), Pam Herrup (10 July 2007), Jeanette Hersey (22 January 2007), Charlie Luce (21 April and 31 August 2007), Lynda Munro (29 August 2007), Martha Myers (11 September 2007), Jeff Oshen, Brian Rogers, and Susan Young (31 July 2007) (all interviews in possession of author). Sources will be identified except when the individual(s) providing the information requested confidentiality.

93　Tim Murphy, "American Dance Festival Won't Return to College," *The Day* (7 October 1977), 1.

94　Noyes, *History of Connecticut College,*168. Also Oshen interview.

95　Ibid., 168.

96　Jack Anderson, "American Dance Festival—Mecca has Moved South," *New York Times* (18 June 1978).

97　Noyes, *History of Connecticut College,*" 167

98　"ADF in Retrospect," *Connecticut College Alumni Magazine* 53 (Winter 1978), 5–8.

99　Ibid., Noyes, *History of Connecticut College,*" 167-168.

100　"School of Dance Names Faculty for Ninth Season," *Connecticut College News* 2 (April 1956).

101　*Bulletin of Connecticut College School of Dance, Tenth Season, July 8 to August 18, 1957* (New London, CT: Connecticut College, 1957). CCA, American Dance Festival (ADF) File.

102　Ibid.

103　Ibid.

104　*Bulletin of Connecticut College School of Dance, Tenth Season, July 8 to August 18, 1957.*

105　Ruth Bloomer, "Ten Years of Modern Dance," *Connecticut College News* 3 (February 1958), 3–4.

106　Ibid.

107　Young interview. Susan Young attended the School of Dance in 1969, during the summer before her senior year of high school. She appreciated how the School encouraged her independence and enabled her to explore artistic areas of interest.

108　Ibid.

109　Noyes, *History of Connecticut College,*" 168.

110　Ibid.

111　Ibid.

112　Myers interview.

113　Ibid. See also Noyes, *History of Connecticut College,*" 194–195.

114　"Connecticut College News Office Press Release" (10 November 1976).

115　Ibid.

116　Oshen and Herrup interviews.

117　Oshen interview. See also Anderson, "American Dance Festival—Mecca has Moved South."

118　Ibid. Also Briggs and Herrup interviews.

119　Myers and Brownell interviews.

120　"Bring Back the ADF," *Pundit* (18 November 1976).

121　Terry Byrne, "New London's Dance Dilemma," *New York Times* (September 25, 1977).

122 Noyes, *History of Connecticut College*," 194.

123 Myers and Oshen interviews.

124 Bredeson interview. George Willauer, interview by author 23 April 2007 (interview in possession of author).

125 Michael J. Whalen, "New London Still in Mind as Host to Dance Festival," *The Hartford Courant* (26 November 1976).

126 No title or author, *The Day* (6 December 1976). CCA, ADF File.

127 Ibid.

128 Anna Kisselgoff, "Dance Festival in New London Seeks New Site," *The New York Times* (15 November 1976).

129 Ibid.

130 Ibid.

131 Allen Carroll, "The Art of the Feud," *Connecticut College Alumni Magazine* (Winter 1978), 2–4, 26.

132 Kisselgoff, "Dance Festival in New London Seeks New Site."

133 Ibid.

134 Byrne, "New London's Dance Dilemma."

135 Viki Fitzgerald and Amy Kest, "American Dance Festival Steps Out, "*College Voice* (21 October 1977).

136 "Matching Grants Encourage Festival to Remain at College for Season," *Connecticut College News* (Winter 1977)).

137 "Board Backs Ames on his Festival Stand," *The Day* (6 December 1976).

138 "Matching Grants Encourage Festival to Remain at College for Season."

139 Ibid.

140 Byrne, "New London's Dance Dilemma."

141 "American Dance Festival Advised to Seek New Site, *The New York Times* (11 October 1977).

142 Murphy, "American Dance Festival Won't Return to College."

143 Ibid.

144 Ibid.

145 Ibid.

146 Ibid.

147 "Opinion of the Day, New Opportunities for Conn College," *The Day* (14 October 1977).

148 Ibid.

149 Anna Kisselgoff, "American Dance Festival is Lured to Duke with $1 Million Pledge," *The New York Times* (31 October 1977).

150 Ibid.

151 Ibid.

152 Ibid.

153 Anderson, "American Dance Festival—Mecca has Moved South."

154 Fitzgerald and Kest, "American Dance Festival Steps Out."

155 Ibid.

156 bid.

157 Ibid. Quote of Fred Grimsey, Connecticut's Director of Theater Services, who had been with the ADF since 1969. According to the article, "Mr. Grimsey does feel that Conn subsidized the American Dance Festival in the 'lean years,' when modern dance was just getting off the ground, and should not have been expected to do so any longer."

158 Byrne, "New London's Dance Dilemma."

159 Carroll, "The Art of the Feud."

160 Byrne, "New London's Dance Dilemma."

161 Ibid.

162 Fitzgerald and Kest, "American Dance Festival Steps Out."

163 Ibid.

164 Ibid.

165 Byrne, "New London's Dance Dilemma."

166 Ibid.

167 Anderson, "American Dance Festival—Mecca has Moved South." Quote of Laurie Cameron, Coordinator of Summer Dance Activities at Connecticut College.

168 "College Plans Program to Offset Festival Loss," *The Day* (25 February 1978).

169 Ibid.

170 Myers interview.

171 Michael J. Whalen, "Official Calls Festival Loss Devastating," *Hartford Courant* (12 November 1976).

172 Ibid.

173 Fitzgerald and Kest, "American Dance Festival Steps Out, "

174 Carroll, "The Art of the Feud."

175 Ibid.

176 Ibid., 26. Art Department Chairman David Smalley stated fears of "a move to make Connecticut more like Hobart and Trinity—big on the sciences and athletics and weak in the arts."

177 Myers interview. Myers, who continued to have an affiliation with the ADF after it left Connecticut College, also alleges that the ADF never received the $1 million endowment promised by Duke University officials.

178 Ibid. Also Fainstein, Munro, and Oshen interviews.

179 Ibid.

180 Hersey, Luce, Bredeson, and Ames interviews.

181 Ibid.

182 Ibid.

183 Ibid.

184 Carroll, "The Art of the Feud," 26.

185 Hersey, Luce, Myers interviews.

186 Hoffmann and Fainstein interviews.

187 Interviewees kept anonymous by request.

188 Ibid.

189 In elevating sports, Connecticut College embraced the New England small college model of former men's institutions such as Amherst, Bowdoin, and Williams, institutions that became its peers in NESCAC.

190 Myers interview.

191 Ibid. Also Munro and Oshen interviews.

192 Reference to the College using local stone for construction of its buildings—Brownell interview.

CHAPTER EIGHT

The Bold and Controversial Gaudiani Years (1988–2001)

Claire Gaudiani was a pioneering president for Connecticut College from the moment of her appointment: the only graduate (class of 1966) to lead the institution. Serving as president of her alma mater was a self-described labor of love for Gaudiani, one that engendered "a special sense of responsibility to the College because of all that the faculty gave to [her]" as a student.[1] In her October 1988 inaugural address, Gaudiani referred to herself as "the first daughter called to lead the family enterprise."[2] She saw herself returning home to help Connecticut College "stretch to connect its traditions to innovations." She declared that she wanted the community to feel its own strength through collective effort.[3] At that historic moment, Gaudiani stated her high ideals and grand dreams for alma mater, and the College she took over greeted her with high hopes.

A year before becoming Connecticut College's eighth president, Gaudiani had received the alumni medal, an honor bestowed only on the institution's most devoted and accomplished graduates. No doubt the search committee that selected her had also been impressed by her many board memberships and consulting relationships with prominent organizations such as the National Endowment for the Humanities and the Dana, Exxon, Hazen, and Rockefeller foundations. A Ph.D. in French literature who had authored three books, Gaudiani held an appointment in the University of Pennsylvania's French department in addition to helping found and direct the Joseph H. Lauder Institute for International Studies at Penn's Wharton School of Business.[4] The appointment of the administrative director of a small institute, rather than the more traditional choice of a college dean or provost, signaled that Gaudiani might bring to Connecticut College an entrepreneurial as well as an academic mindset.

Ambition, Energy, and Innovation

From the outset, Claire Gaudiani did not fail to deliver on the high expectations the Connecticut College family held for its first daughter president. Like an entrepreneur, she generated ideas for innovative initiatives and incited an air of momentum. Gaudiani raised more than $100 million to support existing and new academic and co-curricular programs and facilities. The funds she raised made possible $60 million in campus expansion and renovation and also helped launch six interdisciplinary academic centers that gave depth to the curriculum and in-

vigorated the intellectual life of Connecticut College.[5] During the thirteen years
Gaudiani led Connecticut College (1988–2001), aggressive fundraising alongside
a record-setting stock market, propelled by the worldwide dot-com boom, quintu-
pled the College's endowment from $31 million to $168 million.[6] Gaudiani's high
visibility, through the speeches she gave and articles she wrote, raised the national
profile of Connecticut College and established her as a leading voice for innovation in the liberal arts. The New England Association of Schools and Colleges accrediting board, for example, called her a "visionary president."[7] John DiBiaggio,
former president of Tufts University and Michigan State University, said she provided a conscience for higher education.[8]

Gaudiani's dynamism and all the attention it drew to Connecticut College
paid off in more than fundraising, publicity, and endowment growth. The College
achieved a higher stature relative to its peers. Connecticut College ascended in the
U.S. News and World Report annual college rankings from 41 within the national
small liberal arts college bracket to the top 25, peaking at 24.[9] The College has
never ranked as high since Gaudiani's departure; for example, Connecticut ranked
44 in the 2008 survey.[10] From the beginning Gaudiani saw her role as chiefly to
provide a collective vision and direction, to inspire a spirit of confidence about the
future, "to articulate a vision for Connecticut College, to connect the College's
traditions to the changing outside world, " to move alma mater forward to the
"forefront of liberal education," to be an institution that led its peers, not one
that followed.[11] In looking toward the future of higher education, she speculated
that most institutions would "brace themselves," while Connecticut College
would help shape the future.[12] Connecticut College, she believed, could achieve a
new profile for itself by creating a national model of excellence, one that rein-
vented liberal arts education for a new generation of students.[13] Gaudiani's rhetoric was ambitious and reflected the bold hopes and ambitious ideals that many
incoming leaders, especially those who see themselves as change agents, hold out
for their institutions. Her conception of what Connecticut College's trustees
wanted in selecting her was leadership that transcended critical presidential tasks
such as fundraising, management, and public relations.[14] And she intended to deliver by capturing the imagination of the Connecticut College community.[15]

Another guiding principle for Gaudiani's presidency was her belief that leaders, if they are profoundly committed to their ideals, are neither passive nor concerned about being loved by everyone.[16] As a result, she pushed her initiatives
rapidly and aggressively. Within a decade, Connecticut College had established six
innovative interdisciplinary centers that emphasized international studies, service
learning, and experiential learning. Critics and proponents alike credited the centers with giving Connecticut College greater intellectual strength and rigor.[17] By
1998 she had implemented two strategic plans that, among other initiatives, as-

pired to give every student the opportunity to have a funded internship and a travel research and immersion program (TRIP) experience in another country. And she had led Connecticut College through its largest-ever capital campaign. Students, faculty, alumni, and staff, at least in the beginning years of Gaudiani's presidency, drew inspiration from her drive to propel Connecticut College ever higher.[18] However, some thought that Gaudiani's pace of change was too fast. The New England Association of Schools and Colleges accrediting board, for example, recommended in 1996 that the College take "a period of reflection about the progress that has been made."[19] Yet in that report, the accrediting board also expressed "enormous admiration" for Gaudiani's visionary leadership.[20]

Figure 8.1. Former president Claire L. Gaudiani

Within the Connecticut College family there still lingers admiration and gratitude for Gaudiani's accomplishments. "She made alumni feel proud to have gone
there," is an oft-repeated statement about the Gaudiani years.[21] The fact that she was
an alumna gave her a long honeymoon with Connecticut College's off-campus constituencies. Alumni and other benefactors tend to favor presidents who are charismatic big-picture promoters of their institution and themselves. Gaudiani's self-
promotion brought mutual benefits—because in promoting herself as a dutiful and
successful exemplar of the place, she was also promoting Connecticut College. Even
Gaudiani's critics, and there are many—especially among faculty who lived through
her presidency—laud her strength as an innovative thinker whose visions were attractive, even contagious. For example, Emeritus Professor of Government Wayne
Swanson told a reporter in 1999 that "she has done an awful lot to improve the position of the College, there's no denying that," but then he went on to level criticisms
of Gaudiani's harsh management style.[22] Numerous Connecticut officials and
alumni describe her as the charismatic pied piper type with the ability to recognize
that Connecticut College needed a galvanizing persuasive leader after the quieter
presidency of Oakes Ames from 1974 to 1987.[23]

As Connecticut College's leader, Claire Gaudiani tried to live her beliefs, expressed in 1992 and 1996, that college presidents must actively engage in the life
of the classroom, faculty lounge, library, and athletic fields in an effort to avoid the
killing bureaucracy that creates paper-pushing presidents only tangentially connected to the real mission of the institution.[24] Gaudiani believed that a president's
vision should entice the community to engage in fresh thinking and "blue-sky
speculation."[25] If after the stasis of Ames years (1974–1987) the trustees wanted a
correction to an aggressive and energetic style, that's what they got in bushels, for
better and for worse, in Gaudiani.

During her early years in office, Gaudiani practically had her way with the
press. She drew positive coverage even during an era of harsh invective hurled at
colleges and universities by critics like William Bennett, Allan Bloom, Dinesh
D'Souza and Charles Sykes.[26] A 1992 article on Connecticut College in *The
Chronicle of Higher Education*, for example, showcased Gaudiani's strategic plan,
noting that the College was reducing waste and duplication and undertaking aggressive investment management strategies to grow the $50 million endowment to
$100 million.[27] In a time of retrenchment for higher education, the *Chronicle* por-
trayed Connecticut College as thriving through careful growth and prudently es-
chewing a complicated superstructure that would need undoing in tough times.[28]
Gaudiani, according to the article, had encouraged administrators to juggle multiple responsibilities and had led a new strategic plan that emphasized diversity, eth-
ics, internationalism, and balance between the arts and sciences. The article's one
negative note was a stray comment that, while some faculty and staff felt that the

strategic plan had brought coherence to the College, others thought it reeked too much of corporate management.[29]

Eighteen years later, there are not a few within the Connecticut family who wonder if the College got intoxicated on the positive press that Gaudiani spun so masterfully in her first ten years as president. Examined in full, Gaudiani's presidency has analogies to the classical fable of Icarus and Daedalus. Like Icarus, Gaudiani, it could be argued, flew too close to the sun and saw her wax wings melt before she fell back to earth amidst a vote in 2000 by three-quarters of tenured faculty calling for her immediate resignation. But before the tumultuous end to her presidency, Gaudiani tried to repay her alma mater's historical debt to its home city, hoping that doing so would inspire colleges across America to reach out and improve their local communities.

Focusing Connecticut College Beyond Its Campus

By the time Claire Gaudiani returned to lead her alma mater, the historic relationship between Connecticut College and New London had been inverted. When New London had led Connecticut College into being, it was a prosperous and growing city, not simply languishing in the fading glow of its past significance as an 18th and 19th century whaling port. At the birth of Connecticut College in 1911, New London had the wealth, civic energy, and stature to rally its residents to contribute $134,000 to help launch the state of Connecticut's first women's college. Nearly eighty years later, Connecticut College was the thriving child and New London was the ailing parent. Many factors had contributed to those changing circumstances. In the 1960s, construction of Interstate 95 physically cut Connecticut College and its city off from each other.[30] The trolley line that had linked Connecticut College to downtown New London gave way to the four-lane Mohegan Avenue, which resembled an interstate highway more than a neighborhood street.[31] The shipbuilding and defense industries that had once sustained New London began to shed jobs, ten thousand in all. Middle class residents fled to nearby towns, "depressing [New London's] real estate market and devastating [its] tax base."[32] By the 1990s, New London's downtown streets were a collection of empty storefronts and decrepit historic buildings.[33]

Between 1911 and Gaudiani's inauguration in 1988, Connecticut College had held itself mostly aloof from New London.[34] Gaudiani's speeches and writings indicate that she was bothered by the unfortunate fact that her college had become the rich institution on the hill looking down at a poor city with decaying schools, decades of job losses, and a big list of unfulfilled promises that had left a moribund downtown commercial district.[35] Within ten years, Gaudiani would become a leading booster of her home city's fortunes, promoting what she called "team New London," providing, in her words, the "moral juice" to propel economic development and social justice.[36] Gaudiani would make it her mission to help revitalize Connecticut College's home city and change its image for the better.[37]

Gaudiani saw an institutional responsibility, even a moral imperative, for Connecticut College to give of its bountiful resources not just to the city that had made its existence and prosperity possible but also to the larger world beyond the view from campus. She believed it incumbent on her position to "take a leadership role in the development of programs that would demonstrate and enhance the ways the college community embodies [its] values."[38] Connecticut College's institutional genetic code contained, in Gaudiani's opinion, a commitment to the common good.[39] She had reason to feel that way. Preparing students for an active interest in community affairs had been articulated as a chief value of the College as early as 1917 by founding president Frederick Sykes in his farewell commencement address.[40] Several of Sykes' successors, including Katharine Blunt, Rosemary Park, and Oakes Ames, continued that emphasis.[41] Thus it was historically fitting that contributing to society, starting with the College's own backyard, became the defining theme of Gaudiani's presidency.

Reaching out to New London was critical but not sufficient. Gaudiani also interpreted Connecticut College's outward-looking mission as a charge to engage with the whole world. She often spoke of the coming "global decade" and "the internationalization of everyday life" and work.[42] She outlined plans for Connecticut to lead other liberal arts colleges in preparing students "to meet citizens of other cultures on their own terms" and "in their own language[s]."[43] Gaudiani believed in an education that "promotes an understanding of local, regional, national, and international communities, and encourages involvement in them."[44] Using her bully pulpit, Gaudiani exhorted faculty and students to study abroad in developing countries, not just the usual spots in Europe.[45] She contended that encounters with the developing world would prepare students to know and help others from backgrounds and communities radically different from the relatively advantaged places from which most of them came.[46] Gaudiani hoped that by the year 2004 a majority of graduating seniors would have completed an overseas internship, preferably in a developing country.[47] Students, according to this vision, would graduate with the knowledge and skills necessary to "pursue any career in an international arena" and be able to conduct a business meeting in their non-native language.[48] Gaudiani's emphasis on foreign language fluency harkened back to second president Benjamin Marshall's call at his inauguration in 1917 for Connecticut College to graduate students able to write and speak French, German, or Italian.[49]

To help realize her global vision, Gaudiani established the interdisciplinary Toor Cummings Center for International Studies and the Liberal Arts.[50] Gaudiani intended the Center for International Studies and the Liberal Arts

(CISLA) to stand as "a national model of excellence in international education and the liberal arts."[51] In establishing CISLA, Gaudiani led Connecticut College toward a globalized curriculum and an emphasis on cultural literacy before those waves crested in higher education.[52] CISLA helped raise Connecticut College's institutional profile, placing the College in the vanguard of institutions attracting corporate and foundation patrons to fund globally oriented curricular and co-curricular innovations.

The two strategic plans Gaudiani forged during her presidency promoted a union between the liberal arts and local and global citizenship, with the intention to educate students who saw themselves as agents of change with a moral obligation to work for greater equality of opportunity in society. She believed it was Connecticut College's job to help students to know, understand, and help others beyond themselves.[53] Connecticut College, in Gaudiani's view, should prepare its students to imagine and help bring about a better future.[54] Her 1999 president's message stated that the Connecticut College "community makes us people who bring hope to others—with knowledge and compassion, with analytical skills and a commitment to justice."[55] "We should not only talk about a just society," she told a reporter in 1999, "but we should be applying...our heads and hearts and hands to create opportunities for a just society to live and breathe around us."[56] When she looked toward the future of Connecticut College, Gaudiani envisioned an increasingly diverse faculty that augmented its scholarly research with experience living in public housing projects and threatened neighborhoods.[57] She envisioned a culturally diverse liberal arts curriculum that would connect volunteer service to learning in the classroom and lab and help students "develop modern civic virtues."[58] She envisioned a Connecticut College in 2004 that would have built and sustained relationships with the diverse communities in the larger world around it.[59]

Gaudiani saw many fronts for Connecticut College to demonstrate the value of making contributions to society, but none more important than New London. To emphasize the importance of community outreach, Gaudiani and Connecticut College's social science faculty worked to create and fund a new center that would integrate service learning into the academic program.[60] The Holleran Center for Community Action and Public Policy represented Gaudiani's dream of making Connecticut College a pioneer in community engagement.[61] With the establishment of the Holleran Center in 1996, Gaudiani put Connecticut College at the forefront of the service-learning movement that was sweeping through higher education in the 1990s. As she pushed Connecticut to develop into a "college with a conscience," one that fostered a campus ethos of non sibi (not for oneself), Gaudiani became "an articulate national spokesperson on the intersection of justice, economic prosperity, and the common good."[62]

At a conference on college teaching at Miami (Ohio) University in 1995, Gaudiani asserted the Deweyan notion that learning should be conceptual/theoretical and relational/experiential.[63] She brought the message back to Connecticut College's founding tension between the purely academic and the vocational, as she described representative examples of her college's service-learning courses. She cited a botany course on the theory and use of electron microscopy that involved teaching New London high school students how to use the intricate instrument. She described how an environmental studies class taught to New London middle school students skill-building approaches to science, such as how to run tests, develop hypotheses, and check results. And Gaudiani cited her own "Literature, Service and Social Reflection" course, focused on readings and discussions that would educate students to have a better understanding of how to participate in a civil society.[64] There and elsewhere, Gaudiani argued that service learning enables students to explore links between their academic studies and community problems, thereby giving them the opportunity to learn to function as citizen-leaders in whatever communities they enter after graduation. Connecticut College's 1999–2001 Catalog, for example, opened with Gaudiani's "Message from the President" that "a liberal arts education aims to prepare men and women for a lifetime of learning, service and leadership."[65] Gaudiani wanted a service ethos to pervade her campus, starting with the students selected by the admission office. Whether an applicant had engaged in community service became a critical element in the review of candidates for admission to the College.[66] The education that students want and deserve, according to Gaudiani, transcends worldly success and marketable skills.[67] Students, she insisted, want to be transformed, and thus Connecticut College made service learning a key element in providing that "transforming education."[68]

During Gaudiani's tenure, Connecticut College encouraged and touted service-learning projects, such as one student's independent study project to renovate an abandoned firehouse in downtown New London.[69] Gaudiani articulated quite forcefully the idea that a service-learning curriculum would ensure that "the best-educated young people in the country understand what it takes to build a community," and thus would be equipped to "move from ideals and knowledge in a book to really improving the quality of life for all citizens."[70] Gaudiani believed that getting involved in initiatives beyond its campus fulfilled Connecticut College's historical and "moral obligation to [its] community and an educational responsibility to [its] students."[71] Those obligations and responsibilities were ones Gaudiani felt personally. "It's easy to talk about social justice and community," she said in 1999. "But people—particularly young people—want to know, 'what are you doing to make that real?'"[72] Her vision for alma mater mirrored John Dewey's concept of schools or colleges as community institutions that actively engaged their students in solving real world problems and helped create civil society by promoting participatory democracy.[73] Gaudiani's ideas also echoed legendary University of Chicago president William Rainey Harper's view that colleges could serve as the "prophets of...democracy."[74]

Speaking at a conference at Santa Clara University in 2000 Gaudiani told the audience that she brought the perspective of a president of a small liberal arts college perched on a beautiful hill overlooking a small and struggling city.[75] Proud as she was of alma mater, Gaudiani said she was troubled because despite the money raised and the new programs and new buildings added to campus, Connecticut College had not, until recently under her direction, attempted to transform its home city of New London, the community that helped give it life in 1911.[76] Colleges and universities, Gaudiani went on to say, are uniquely positioned to help create fundamental and transforming change in American cities.[77] Furthermore, because academic institutions are among the most privileged institutions in the country, they have power as well as a responsibility to advocate for social justice. Academic institutions, she reminded the audience, are major beneficiaries of philanthropy, thus they themselves have an obligation to be philanthropic.[78] Academic institutions, like her own, she said, teach by example, not just in classrooms. In closing, Gaudiani underscored her point by invoking the words of the prophet Jeremiah, "make the peace of the city your concern...for in its peace, ye shall have peace."[79]

In Gaudiani's opinion, the rapid growth of American cities and towns in the 20th century had wrought an increasingly fragmented and uncivil society; addressing this problem, she argued, should be of deep concern to liberal arts colleges. The small liberal arts college could be a leading agent for positive societal change and the reestablishment of civil society, according to Gaudiani, because the small liberal arts college provides a human-sized community and a laboratory for developing models of citizenship.[80] Gaudiani argued that Connecticut College was especially well suited to undertake this task, because it could draw upon an 80-year-old honor code that connected rights to virtues in individuals, an 80-year commitment to volunteerism, and a historic commitment to gender equality and evolving gender relations, as exemplified by its founding vision and later move to coeducation.[81] Gaudiani further argued that Connecticut College, through its service-learning curriculum, could serve as a small-scale model of civil society. In her opinion, "since its founding in 1911, the College had distinguished itself as a "living laboratory of democratic civil society."[82] The essential character of Connecticut College, Gaudiani believed, had been shaped by its honor code, volunteer spirit, commitment to gender equality, and secular history.[83]

Reconnecting Connecticut College to New London

In 1996 Connecticut College came to the aid of a neighboring institution, the Lyman Allyn Art Museum.[84] The Allyn Museum had been built as the fulfillment of Harriet Allyn's 1932 gift for a community museum for New London and had been constructed adjacent to the south end of the Connecticut College campus.[85] The Lyman Allyn had been managed off and on by Connecticut College but had been independent since 1982.[86] Gaudiani regarded the move as good for New London, because a valuable cultural institution in the city would be getting support and sustenance. Having the Lyman Allyn under the Connecticut tent also benefited the College through the establishment of a museum studies program and expansion of resources available to the College's art and art history programs.[87]

Taking on management of the Lyman Allyn Art Museum was a neighborly move to help a local institution, and was just the beginning. Gaudiani still sought a project undertaken in the spirit of non sibi that would proclaim to the world that Connecticut College really cared about its backyard. She found it in 1997 when Connecticut College Downtown opened as a storefront satellite campus.[88] Connecticut College's downtown initiative would show a commitment to the redevelopment of New London, serve as a national example of collegiate action for social justice, fulfill the 1990 and 1996 mission statements calling for involvement in local and regional communities, and demonstrate that the College could be a "responsible institutional citizen," a constructive force in its "home City of New London."[89] According to its promotional brochure, Connecticut College Downtown provided opportunities for civic engagement, economic investment, and learning through service.[90] Students at the downtown campus served as interns and volunteers in New London-area public schools, prisons, and businesses.[91] The downtown center also provided meeting space for community groups, established a micro loan program, helped develop strategies to reduce truancy in New London schools, and coordinated lunchtime theater and speaker programs.[92]

Creating a nexus between the Connecticut College campus and downtown New London was an enlightened initiative rooted in the College's founding mission. Here was an opportunity to revive what had become a dormant partnership between Connecticut College and New London. Like founding president Frederick Sykes, Gaudiani's head was "in the clouds," and she believed that "the good that counts is good in action."[93] Like Sykes, Gaudiani was a bold visionary, a change agent whose imaginings about Connecticut College's future required vigorous, and sometimes uncomfortable, thought and action on the part of its faculty and students. Her strengths were most apparent in the symbolic frame of leadership, and she had a penchant for grand gestures that would attract media attention.[94] And initially Gaudiani won much attention and praise for her efforts to apply Connecticut College's resources and connections toward assistance to New London. Speaking of redevelopment plans for downtown New London, the editorial board of the city's newspaper, *The Day*, wrote, "Ms Gaudiani deserves enormous credit" and predicted that "this is just the beginning of the flowering of this city of New London and the benefits that blossoming will have for the whole region."[95]

Connecticut College Downtown was indeed just the beginning. Gaudiani proceeded to convince the board of trustees to contribute $2.6 million in institutional funds toward historical rehabilitation and new construction in New London.[96] In 1999, Connecticut College took a further step into New London, leasing 22,000 square feet in the Mariner Square building for shared use with Rensselaer Polytechnic Institute (RPI).[97] Connecticut College was to utilize the downtown New London classroom facilities by day and RPI's Southeastern Connecticut Graduate Center was to occupy them at night.[98] Gaudiani portrayed the partnership with RPI as an opportunity for Connecticut College students to gain access to cutting-edge technologies not generally available at liberal arts colleges.[99] The RPI partnership also represented a critical turn of directions for Gaudiani, because the Mariner Square project stepped beyond curriculum-based community outreach and engagement and put Connecticut College in the business of economic redevelopment. Trustees supported both of those outreach agendas, but faculty, from the beginning, were less sanguine regarding the New London redevelopment initiatives.[100] Despite faculty concerns, Gaudiani pushed ahead, convinced that the RPI partnership would enliven downtown New London.[101] Gaudiani and her chief aides at Connecticut College expected Mariner Square to fill within two years, but leases were slow to develop and much of the space in the building stayed vacant.[102] Gaudiani's critics took note and began fearing that the project was not a prudent use of college funds.[103]

Gaudiani subsequently convinced the boards of Connecticut College and the New London Development Corporation—of which she was president from 1997 through 2002—to execute a complicated loan and purchase deal to enable conversion of a historic downtown building into apartments for the College's students.[104] The trustees of both organizations and Gaudiani believed that living in the downtown apartments would give Connecticut College students the opportunity to understand the needs of New London and contribute to its betterment.[105] The hoped-for result would be a living and learning center that would knit Connecticut College and its city closer together.[106] Along with the RPI partnership, the downtown apartments would provide a laboratory to test whether "a diverse group of citizens [can] work together to make social justice and economic development two sides of the same coin."[107]

It is hard to fault Gaudiani's idealistic vision. But her execution of that vision, especially as it morphed from student engagement through the Holleran Center to economic redevelopment, was flawed and, from its inception, controversial among faculty. While favorable global financial conditions drove endowment growth and Gaudiani basked in the glow of Connecticut College's successful capital campaign, faculty grumbling about her tone deafness toward collegial governance and her autocratic leadership style remained a campus undercurrent. Then the stock market took a dive as the dot-com bubble burst and large deficits appeared on Connecticut College's balance sheet. As they confronted budgetary red ink and faced the immediate prospect of teaching classes at the downtown satellite campus, many faculty began to express concern that the College was evolving in ways that they did not deem appropriate. Generally faculty had supported reconnection to New London via the student community service projects undertaken through the Holleran Center and Connecticut College Downtown. But putting funds into economic redevelopment efforts that diluted the residential nature of the College struck many on campus as straying from mission as well as financially risky.[108]

Furthermore, the economic redevelopment of New London felt to many like a pet project of Gaudiani's, not a necessary move to secure safer campus borders or make better first impressions on campus visitors.[109] For example, Trinity College in Hartford, Clark University in Worcester, and the University of Pennsylvania in Philadelphia undertook economic redevelopment near their campuses in the 1990s in part because decay in surrounding neighborhoods had spurred declines in admission interest and campus safety.[110] At Clark and the University of Pennsylvania, economic redevelopment efforts in neighborhoods contiguous to the campus served the additional purpose of providing convenient and affordable housing for faculty.[111] There was no evidence that economic redevelopment of New London was necessary to stimulate applications to Connecticut College, make an already safe campus safer, or expand affordable faculty housing options.[112] Connecticut College's redevelopment efforts in New London occurred largely because Gaudiani thought it was the right thing for her alma mater to do.[113]

Gaudiani's Vision Comes Undone

In May of 2000, 78 of Connecticut College's 105 tenured faculty members signed a petition calling for Claire Gaudiani's resignation.[114] In the estimation of New London's *The Day*, the faculty petition was "not the work of a handful of malcontents, but rather an action undertaken soberly by overwhelming numbers of faculty" at the College.[115] *The Day* found it ironic that Gaudiani had "a substantial national reputation for leadership, but...her relationship with her own faculty is poor."[116] Chief among faculty concerns was Gaudiani's infrequent and insufficient consultation with them on key decisions, such as the $2.6 million investment of College funds in downtown New London.[117] The faculty saw Connecticut College Downtown and the RPI partnership as capricious projects forced on them by Gaudiani.[118] Connecticut College faculty members were especially dismayed by plans to hold classes in downtown New London. As far as most of them were concerned, the College's classroom facilities on its residential hilltop campus made it unnecessary to establish a satellite center in downtown New London. Faculty felt that the downtown campus made Connecticut College seem like a commuter college, rather than a residential liberal arts institution. Connecticut faculty worried that the College's mission of residential education might be creeping away from their stewardship.[119] Students also were dubious about the prospect of a downtown residential campus, fearing that it might "take away from the College's close-knit community."[120] Gaudiani, on the other hand, saw it as vitally important to make a living demonstration of the College's outreach and engagement agenda by coming down the hill into New London.[121]

The petition calling for Gaudiani's ouster had followed a quieter effort a week earlier in which a handful of professors met privately with Gaudiani and asked her to resign.[122] Because they feared retribution against their non-tenured junior colleagues, only senior professors met with Gaudiani. The senior faculty members who approached Gaudiani privately did so to offer her the opportunity to avert the spectacle of a public call for her resignation. Gaudiani's response was chilly, remembers one veteran professor who was there.[123] She rebuffed their efforts, setting in motion the public faculty petition, which for the same reasons as the private meeting involved only tenured faculty.

In response to the faculty petition, Connecticut College's trustees issued a statement of solid support for Gaudiani. Trustee chair Duncan N. Dayton lauded Gaudiani for making the College "stronger than ever before," citing as one example the fact that Connecticut College had become the 12th most selective liberal arts college in the nation.[124] Up to the point of the faculty no-confidence vote, Gaudiani had received the strong backing of trustees and alumni leaders who applauded her energetic efforts to bring national attention to their college. One board member (Frank Turner) called Gaudiani one of the "five truly transforming college presidents" of the last twenty-five years.[125] Gaudiani survived the faculty resignation petition in part because she had the backing of trustees, yet also because she had weathered a previous faculty denouncement in the late fall of 1998, when faculty had voted 63 to 2 to condemn Gaudiani for "acting in bad faith" for refusing to place a piece of faculty legislation on the agenda for a trustee meeting.[126] That and other actions led some faculty members to label her a hypocrite, whose speeches celebrated the values of democracy and civil society while her approach to running the College was autocratic.[127] Gaudiani often shrugged off faculty criticism as de rigueur for an academic setting, once telling a reporter that "you can't make an electric motor run without things rubbing together...There has to be some spark and sparkle. That doesn't mean (the relationship) is antagonistic.

What it means is that the institution is moving forward. The only time you have total peace is in a coffin, or with a machine with no motor."[128]

The latter half of the year 2000 was a time of tumult at Connecticut College. Accusations of non-collaborative, imperial, top-down decision-making flew. Rumors swelled of large future budget deficits, worse than the ones the College had endured in the past year.[129] Many blamed the College's financial problems on Gaudiani's choice to invest in the revitalization of downtown New London.[130] Staff and faculty were especially displeased to learn that the College would stop filling vacant positions and cease offering early-retirement packages.[131] Faculty resented being asked to cut expenses while the College maintained what they saw as a bloated and overpaid administrative staff.[132] Some also wondered if Gaudiani's dual chief executive roles at Connecticut College and the NLDC involved an unethical conflict of interest.

In the fall of 2000 deeper budget cuts transpired at Connecticut College. More than 200 students at the 1,600-student college marched to protest closure of two dining halls, reduced hours at the sports center, and a tenfold increase in fees for the health service.[133] On the evening of the march, 1,000 students grilled Gaudiani about the budget cuts.[134] Coinciding with the on-campus disaffection for Gaudiani was the gathering storm off-campus around the New London Development Corporation (NLDC), of which she was president.[135] The NLDC was embroiled in a battle with individual homeowners over eminent domain laws—a case that eventually became the landmark *Kelo vs. New London* decided by the United States Supreme Court in 2005.[136] Throughout the controversy, in which Gaudiani stood on the side of developers against individual homeowners, buckets of negative ink were written about her, and by association, Connecticut College.[137]

To the relief of much of its faculty, students and staff, Gaudiani announced in October 2000 her resignation from Connecticut College, effective following her sabbatical for the spring semester of 2001.[138] The trustees issued a statement of full support and admiration for Gaudiani, noting her many accomplishments as president and asserting that her departure after the sabbatical had been in the planning stages for several months.[139] Years later Gaudiani claimed that she and Connecticut College's trustees had begun discussing her retirement as early as 1999, although few of her detractors believe that.[140]

Assessing the Gaudiani Era

Whether Claire Gaudiani's departure from Connecticut College was planned or coerced is not the central issue of her case. The important question is why did she depart embroiled in so much controversy? A persuasive argument could be made that Gaudiani's presidency broke down due to the unfortunate entanglement of her service-learning agenda with efforts to achieve economic redevelopment in

New London. Her attempts to engage students more fully with New London be-came a casualty of her controversial involvement in the New London Develop-ment Corporation. Her dual role as president of both Connecticut College and the New London Development Corporation created tensions that led to conflicts, as growing numbers of faculty questioned whether what was good for the NLDC was also good for the college.

To this day, even Gaudiani's detractors concede her ability to articulate a compelling vision for Connecticut College. Her effectiveness at achieving a decade of endowment growth, freshman application increases, and rising national recog-nition derived from her abilities as a symbolic leader.[141] She understood and culti-vated what she labeled "the enormous power leaders have over the imagination" of their constituents.[142] Some have remarked that Gaudiani might have been more appropriately a consultant for Connecticut, an agent to assess its strengths and weaknesses and then help devise a vision that others of a more collegial tempera-ment would implement to move the College forward. Not surprisingly, Gaudiani acknowledged in 1992 that she approached the process of devising the College's strategic plan with the mindset of a consultant.[143]

Others say Gaudiani never met a trendy idea she didn't like. She lacked, in the words of one faculty member, what Winston Churchill called the ability to know the difference between the few good ideas she should follow and the many bad ones she should discard.[144] Still, although many of Gaudiani's major initiatives for Con-necticut—from service learning to globalization to interdisciplinary centers—were, if not fads, far from path-breaking in higher education, she was skillful at sweeping others up in her energy and applying the force of her persuasive powers. Creating a community service center, for example, was a defining achievement for Gaudiani and Connecticut College. But, admirable as it was, the Holleran Center was hardly a novel undertaking that distinguished Connecticut College from peer colleges. Be-tween 1985 and 2000, there were hundreds of community service centers founded on campuses all over the United States. Many of those other colleges, some of them New England neighbors to Connecticut, integrated community service into their curricular programs and made their local neighborhoods a central institutional pri-ority.[145] For example, Clark University undertook initiatives to revitalize the Worcester, Massachusetts neighborhoods and schools around its campus. Clark's $6 million investment in Worcester included housing incentives to encourage faculty and staff to live in nearby neighborhoods as well as the offer of free tuition for all students admitted from an eight-block area near its campus.[146] Trinity College in-vested $5.9 million to create a job center, expand neighborhood watch programs, build boys and girls clubs, and develop a cluster of schools on the site of a former bus garage.[147] Trinity's initiatives in Hartford, Connecticut also helped integrate urban studies issues into its traditional liberal arts curriculum.[148]

Where Gaudiani tripped, and ultimately fell, was in negotiating the tension between administrative and faculty decisionmaking.[149] Although she acknowledged that her 1990 strategic plan for Connecticut College was the product of "a collegial mind" and she wrote in 1996 that a president "can only benefit from listening to people," Gaudiani, in the later years of her presidency, did not live up to her stated ideals.[150] In the estimation of numerous Connecticut College faculty members, Gaudiani violated a basic tenet of small college governance by often failing to respect the advice and consent process of collaborative decision-making expected in a highly collegial environment.[151] "A lot of her ideas are very good, Connecticut psychology professor Joan Chrisler told the *Hartford Courant* in 1997, "but she doesn't have the patience to go through the faculty governance structure."[152] Her "notion of shared governance is, she decides what to do and then shares it with us—that is, tells us," added Connecticut sociology professor J. Alan Winter.[153] The faculty demonstrated their displeasure with Gaudiani's governance style by voting against Connecticut College Downtown and the RPI partnership even after the fact.[154]

Twenty-twenty hindsight from the vantage point of 2001, or even 2009, suggests that Gaudiani's top-down, big initiative leadership style was a mismatch with the collegial atmosphere of a small college that wrote into its 1990 and 1996 mission statements that it "maintains a strong commitment to shared governance among students, faculty, staff, and trustees."[155] Connecticut College faculty sometimes found it hard to cope with the harsh way she dealt with people.[156] In its accreditation report of 1997, the New England Association of Schools and Colleges noted, for example, a largely "dispirited" faculty and a workplace at Connecticut College where many faculty and staff felt disenfranchised.[157] Regardless of her intentions, Gaudiani's actions suggested to Connecticut College faculty members that she devalued free and open debate, and merely paid lip service to collegial persuasion and consensus building. Faculty expected her to adhere to a shared governance model, because shared governance has been an enduring central value of Connecticut College, one written into most of its mission statements. When Gaudiani failed repeatedly to meet that expectation, she lost the legitimacy on which leadership rests and her days were numbered as Connecticut College's president.[158]

Top-down, change-oriented management is always risky at a small college, but it is sometimes allowed, or at least overlooked, in times of dire crisis and usually forgiven if the outcomes of the decisions made are positive. When their decisions go badly, non-collaborative presidents find themselves with few allies and scant defenses against faculty detractors who begin throwing around derogatory terms such as autocrat and dictator. Such became the case, according to faculty, in Gaudiani's final years.[159] When situations devolve to such a point, presidents rarely survive and institutions, as Connecticut College did, require time to repair.[160]

Gaudiani's public rhetoric demonstrated a clear understanding of the persuasion to consensus model of collegial leadership. "It is the president's job," Gaudiani wrote in 1992, "to set the stage for responsible and inclusive planning and decision making."[161] Presidents, she wrote in 1996, have success at bringing a vision to life when the people in the college's community believe that they have helped shape that vision.[162] Similarly, Gaudiani told a reporter from the *Christian Science Monitor* in 1992 that "leaders almost never exercise power...they need to lead in ways that creates a vision that motivates people."[163] That same year Gaudiani wrote that "good presidents also must be good academic leaders," who speak not just from a compelling personal vision, but out of wisdom derived from their constituents."[164] Her writings indicated that Gaudiani recognized that faculty at colleges like Connecticut are the "critical, self-perpetuating strength and its greatest natural resource," that she expected to continue to learn from faculty, as she had as a student, that she understood that effective leaders cannot simply order change but must persuade and build consensus.[165] But her actions after a few years in office demonstrated disconnect with her words.

Small single-focus institutions like Connecticut College are highly participatory and grounded in a history of collegial decision-making.[166] Discussion of key initiatives at faculty meetings or before the faculty senate can serve as a symbol of cooperation between the faculty and the administration as well as a signal that the president comprehends and respects how decisions are made at the institution.[167] Without widespread faculty support and acceptance, the actions of change agents like Gaudiani do not become internalized in the everyday workings of such institutions or have lasting impact on their evolving mission.[168] That kind of coalition building and consensus gathering rarely happened under Gaudiani, according to Connecticut College faculty.[169] Despite her claims in 1992 and 1996 that a president "can only benefit from listening to" "the college community [and] exemplify[ing] community values," Gaudiani, in the opinion of many faculty members, exhibited a profound disdain for faculty opinions.[170] Faculty laughed at the absurdity of a downtown classroom building shared with RPI, but faculty also felt, with a sense of resignation, that it did not matter what they thought.[171]

Just three years before Connecticut College's faculty revolted in 2000, the Harvard Graduate School of Education (HGSE) held up Gaudiani's leadership of strategic planning processes as a model.[172] An HGSE case study, entitled "Community-Centered Planning at Connecticut College," lauded the participatory nature of Connecticut's 1994 strategic plan, citing praise by College administrators for Gaudiani's ability to harness the good ideas of many people and make the campus constituencies believe "it is your plan, not mine."[173] Perhaps the situation was different at Connecticut College in 1994 than in 2000. Maybe six years into her presidency Claire Gaudiani's leadership commanded a greater degree of respect and allegiance within the Connecticut College community. There is evidence that it may have. Numerous alumni, faculty, and staff say that had Gaudiani left in 1998, at the end of the successful capital campaign, when her detractors were in the minority, she would have been hailed by most at the College as a heroic president, taking her place among the revered ranks of Katharine Blunt and Rosemary Park.[174]

Yet given how divergent the rancorous reality of Gaudiani's collapse in 2000 was from the model president depicted in the 1997 Harvard Case Study, it is tempting to wonder if the HGSE's case study was another example of Gaudiani's masterful ability to generate promotional press for herself and Connecticut College. Perhaps distance from the inner workings of the Connecticut College campus made it easier to see Gaudiani as an exemplary and visionary leader. Those closer to campus were no doubt puzzling over a poignant question posed by one of Gaudiani's harsher critics, Sociology Professor J. Alan Winter, who asked in 1999, "how is it...that a president who has raised salaries, raised the prestige of the College, and improved the quality of the student body nonetheless is widely disliked by the faculty?"[175] Whatever the answer to that question, there may have been some embarrassment among the case study writers at the Harvard Graduate School of Education when it became clear that few faculty saw Gaudiani as the collaborative decision maker described in the HGSE case study.

The Gaudiani case exhibits a breakdown in what some organizational theorists call the "loosely coupled" governance system that operates on most college campuses in the United States.[176] In the loosely coupled systems and the organized anarchies that predominate in college governance structures, not everyone will know what is going on at every moment.[177] The situation at colleges is the opposite of the highly organized, but restrictive and controlled, professional bureaucracies often found in corporations and governmental institutions.[178] The breakdown in Connecticut College's loosely coupled system occurred when Gaudiani was off pursuing her agenda for restoring the College's historic connection to New London. While in her dual role as president of Connecticut College and the New London Development Corporation, Gaudiani acted as if presidential initiative and vision were uncoupled from faculty approval of alterations in curriculum and acquisitions of facilities. Either Gaudiani did not recognize that president-driven change and faculty approval of that change usually involves a loose, and sometimes even a tight coupling, or she did not care.

Gaudiani's headline grabbing style cut both ways off campus too. Despite her frequent championing of social justice, Gaudiani found herself responding to critics who accused her and the NLDC of insensitivity to the working class residents of New London's Fort Trumbull neighborhood.[179] By the year 2000, stories about the New London Development Corporation's battle with Fort Trumbull residents ran almost daily in Connecticut papers, especially in New London's *The*

Day. The NLDC's plans called for razing the homes of Fort Trumbull residents and replacing them with upscale housing and national chain stores. Fort Trumbull residents were literally the proverbial "little guys" battling against the forces of power and money to keep their property from being bulldozed.[180] A number of Fort Trumbull residents dug in against the NLDC's attempts to buy their property or seize it through eminent domain.[181] The holdouts in the neighborhood charged that eminent domain amounted to "legalized theft."[182] A group of Connecticut College students called the NLDC's plans an attempt to turn New London into a "factory made cookie-cutter city" and labeled the New London Development Corporation the "New London Destruction Company."[183] There was even more outrage in Fort Trumbull and among Gaudiani's detractors when the New London Neighborhood Alliance made her an honorary member.[184]

The press often portrayed Gaudiani as cozy with Pfizer, the proposed chief tenant of the development the NLDC was pushing.[185] That her husband, David Burnett, was a top executive at Pfizer, in charge of its corporate university, did not help Gaudiani's moral authority in New London or on campus. It did not help that she justified the NLDC's plans with the observation that, in most cases of forward progress in America someone has "left skin on the street."[186] Nor did it help when her vision began to be parodied, using her words against her, that is, her stated desire to turn New London into "a world-class hip little city."[187] The "skin on the street" and "hip little city" quotes became infamous in New London and still get repeated derisively by Gaudiani's most vehement critics.[188]

New London city officials also questioned her methods. Many in New London thought that Gaudiani pushed faster than the city could respond. Echoing faculty concerns, some city leaders criticized Gaudiani for steamrolling the NLDC, for pushing ahead with her own agenda without consulting the appropriate city officials or going through the proper channels.[189] According to former New London mayor Jane Glover, Gaudiani failed to "understand that the municipal side takes a lot longer than the think-up side."[190] Gaudiani's action-oriented impatience may have lent itself to garnering headlines and winning trustee support, but it alienated New London officials accustomed to a more deliberate pace of decision-making and change. "You either get on board her train, and it usually costs you somehow to get on board, or you find yourself under it and you get run over," said former president of the Southeastern Connecticut Chamber of Commerce William Moore.[191]

Perhaps Gaudiani's heart was in the right place; who can fault any powerful official for advocating a social justice agenda to help a poor community? But all too often her public actions as head of the NLDC lent itself to caricature as a puppet of Pfizer and a symbol of wealth and power out of touch with the common man she so vehemently championed. Actions that contradicted her words made it all too easy to question whether Gaudiani was ever truly a selfless proponent for the good of her city or simply just another self-promoting C.E.O. spouting self-serving idealistic rhetoric.[192] The constant display in Connecticut newspapers of her authoritarian, get-out-of-my-way style resulted in a loss of integrity in New London.[193] That forceful and dramatic style of leadership also led her to burn through numerous senior administrators, few of whom outlasted her presidency.[194]

Leaving aside all of Gaudiani's stylistic mistakes as head of the NLDC, it is arguable that when Connecticut governor John Rowland asked her in 1997 to manage incoming state funds to the City of New London he put her in a position to take the fall if redevelopment initiatives failed. Rowland, who resigned in 2004 amid a federal investigation into graft allegations, may have intentionally deflected responsibility and criticism of the high stakes New London project from himself to Gaudiani. As former New London mayor and NLDC board member Jane Glover observed in 1999, if the hoped for turnaround "doesn't materialize, New Londoners aren't going to blame intransigent politicians. They are going to blame Claire Gaudiani."[195]

Many have looked back on Claire Gaudiani's presidency and wondered whether she was too focused on New London at the expense of Connecticut College. Her zeal for New London resulted in some awkward moments for the College. For example, in 1999 Gaudiani told a reporter from England's *The Economist* that Yale University's president (Richard Levin) should spend at least a third of his time on New Haven matters.[196] Gaudiani later apologized for that remark, which must have struck her detractors as unnecessarily brash and ill advised. On the other hand, supporters of her bold style likely cheered her on for calling out the rich and powerful Yale. Certainly she had proponents who believed that she had "incredible skill in steering the college where it should be going," and felt that "she [was] a genius [who] will work her heart and soul to the nub for the good of the school, and yet is criticized at every turn."[197] But she had many more critics such as faculty and staff who saw her investment of $2.6 million in College funds in New London, especially at a time of frequent budget shortfalls, as an unforgivably bad decision.[198]

Recriminations about the Gaudiani era linger among some members of the Connecticut College family. There is still bitterness over the salary freezes and employee benefits cuts necessitated by the $10-$20 million budget deficit left in her wake, bitterness that a $10 million gift in 2000 (the largest to that point for the College) had to be used to plug holes in the budget.[199] Bitterness is especially sharp in reference to the $551,500 severance package Gaudiani received.[200] Some Connecticut College professors and staff saw the severance package as an expensive but necessary payout to get Gaudiani to leave.[201] But psychology professor Joan Chrisler spoke for many at Connecticut College when she told the *Chronicle of Higher Education* that "it seems very unfair to those of us who remain with her legacy."[202] Critics have also noted, with some irony, that Gaudiani actually did create the lean and mean organization she had championed in 1992, yet unlike her idealized visions, the lean and mean Connecticut College she left behind was a campus scarred by cost-cutting and public embarrassment.[203] Hard feelings about both took some time to subside.

There are some on the Connecticut College campus who question Gaudiani's motives regarding community service and social justice programs. Those critics suggest that Gaudiani showed little interest in the College's many small, un-sexy, yet substantial community outreach programs; for example, the College's commitment to enabling New London residents, including those at the lowest income levels, to attend the children's program operated by the human development department.[204] Other quiet initiatives—such as Connecticut College's long-standing commitment to environmental sustainability—has made it a place (Gaudiani's critics argue) that tries to be an incubator of goodness based on principle rather than a desire for publicity.[205] Her critics contend that Gaudiani seemed always to be seeking to promote the big-idea initiatives that would attract publicity to her and the College.[206] Some believe Gaudiani's chief motivation for redevelopment of New London was always to raise the profile of Connecticut College.[207] There are also some who suggest that Gaudiani romanticized her alma mater's historical relationship with New London.[208] According to this line of criticism, having a New London address has never added to the Connecticut College's appeal, and putting too much emphasis on ties to its home city makes the College seem provincial rather than national.[209]

Although the Connecticut College Board of Trustees stood by Gaudiani publicly through her resignation, behind the scenes they took steps to address the breakdown in communication between her and the faculty. Barbara Shattuck Kohn, Connecticut's trustee chair at the time, told the *Chronicle of Higher Education* in 2005 that in the hurly burly of Gaudiani's later years the board created a faculty-trustee liaison committee to provide a forum for the discussion of campus problems.[210] At the same time, another committee of trustees and faculty met independently to discuss campus issues of concern before they reached a crisis point. Board chair Kohn also decided that it was appropriate to have a standing discussion with Gaudiani every Monday so she could monitor campus happenings.[211]

Faculty who prefer to remain anonymous scoff at such trustee band-aid, attempts at damage control and pin nearly as much blame for the Connecticut College Downtown debacle on the board of trustees as on Gaudiani. Faculty critics of the trustees assert that the Connecticut board should have been censured or forced to resign over the mess they allowed Gaudiani to make of the College's finances.[212] The faculty critics of the trustees still find it unforgivable that Connecticut's endowment funded the downtown initiatives, especially given the opportunity cost—when the College loaned $1 million from its endowment to downtown development projects at 10 percent interest rates, the endowment funds were expected to earn 18 to 22 percent.[213] And more than just her faculty critics are still angry about the $10 million gift that got used to paper over the budget holes Gaudiani's New London initiatives created. On the other hand, some administrative staff members at Connecticut College question why the faculty waited so long to stand up against Gaudiani's financial mismanagement. More than a few longtime administrators speculate that the faculty cut Gaudiani slack because she had reduced teaching loads and raised faculty salaries considerably in the first half of her presidency.[214] As the old higher education cliché goes, the easiest way for a president to silence faculty critics is to give them a raise, reduce their teaching load, or both.

By the time it occurred, the faculty vote for Gaudiani's resignation had become a kind of "garbage can" solution driven by a kind of magical belief that all would be better if they threw her away and started over with someone new.[215] Being new and from the outside did help Gaudiani's successor. From the outset of his presidency, Norman Fainstein, the former dean of faculty at Vassar College, struck a tone of openness and collegiality with Connecticut College's faculty. The appointment of the impeccably-faculty-credentialed Fainstein sent a symbolic message to Connecticut College's professors: here is someone like you, who likely understands and respects small college governance.

By contrast, Gaudiani had come back to Connecticut College from a small center at the University of Pennsylvania's Wharton School of Business, not from a small liberal arts college.[216] Ironically, a few years before her appointment as president, Gaudiani had applied to be dean of faculty at Connecticut College and was deemed unworthy of serious consideration, in part because she was a non-tenured senior fellow in romance languages at Penn, not a senior faculty member.[217] Perhaps Gaudiani had carried too much the large university approach and attitude with her to Connecticut College. Her establishment of six interdisciplinary academic centers on the Connecticut campus and plans for a downtown campus were straight out of the "university as metropolis" model that she saw work successfully at Penn's Wharton School.[218] She failed to understand that large university structures and solutions do not always graft easily onto small colleges.

Soon after replacing Gaudiani, Norman Fainstein proceeded to withdraw Connecticut College from its investments in New London. Fainstein curtailed plans to move faculty, classes, and students into the Connecticut College Downtown facilities and closed them—although the College is still paying on the 15-year lease Gaudiani signed for space in Mariner Square.[219] Paying that lease has been a financial liability for the college, because the Mariner Square building has rarely approached full occupancy. Reportedly the College also lost money when it sold off the rest of its downtown properties.[220] Fainstein also calmed the faculty and restored collegial decisionmaking. Still, as much as Fainstein succeeded at repairing Connecticut College, he was perhaps too much the antithesis of Gaudiani. Fainstein won over Gaudiani's faculty critics, but not those among the trustees and alumni who continued to appreciate her visionary qualities. Fainstein's critics saw his leadership as un-imaginative. At the beginning of his fifth year (2005), Fainstein announced his intention to return full-time to the Connecticut College faculty in September 2007 following a year's sabbatical. His resignation did not come as a complete surprise to the Connecticut College community, as it was also rumored that the trustees were not planning to renew his contract.

Had she not overreached through the New London redevelopment efforts, Gaudiani might have been one of Connecticut College's most successful and revered presidents. Serving on the board of New London Development Corporation rather than as its president might have kept her more attuned to faculty needs on campus. Had she lent symbolic support to the NLDC's goals instead of getting entangled as its leader, Gaudiani might have achieved engagement with New London in a way that was historically consistent with the college's mission and not at odds with faculty wishes. Listening more closely to faculty might have enabled her to better calibrate her level of involvement in New London community affairs and live up to her view that "leaders need to be primarily in service to the people and values of the organization that they lead."[221] Her motives for the redevelopment of New London might then have been better understood as a reconnection with the College's founding mission and vision. Gaudiani's divided leadership of the two entities, however, unfortunately gave much fodder to critics who asserted that she let her enthusiasm for New London's redevelopment efforts distract her focus away from her stewardship of Connecticut College. It is tempting to speculate that a combination of Gaudiani's big-idea, symbolic frame leadership (a vision that galvanizes alumni financial support and trustee confidence) and Fainstein's attention to faculty authority and collegial decisionmaking might have made for the ideal presidency at Connecticut College from 1988 to 2001.

Effective presidents of small colleges must exhibit respect for collegial decision-making, they must recognize the value of political persuasion, and they must understand that creating lasting change for an institution requires patience, and is as often the result of many seemingly insignificant acts as it is of big splashy initiatives.[222] Even Gaudiani knew that patience was not her strong suit. In the early months of her presidency, she remarked to the president of the Connecticut College Alumni Association, "I am congenitally impatient…I will need to remember to pace myself to ensure that we are making progress toward new institutional goals in ways that are comfortable for at least most of the college community."[223]

She should have read that statement back to herself periodically throughout her presidency. Lurching forward with bold initiatives can work in large complex universities where a president, with solid trustee support, is more ruler (even benevolent dictator) than the small college ideal of first among equals.[224]

At small, faculty-driven, collegial liberal arts colleges, such as Connecticut College, the faculty body often flinches reflexively against quick decisions and rapid changes. There is often an instinct to conserve what has been determined to be good and enduring about the institution. Calls for change, especially by a president who has not built a visible coalition of broad faculty support, can signal disrespect for the institution and the individuals who have built it. College presidents must recognize the limits of their authority and work within those boundaries if they wish to accomplish anything meaningful and lasting for the institutions they lead. Unfortunately for Connecticut College, Gaudiani went beyond those boundaries in coupling the redevelopment of New London to Connecticut College.

The Gaudiani Legacy

Claire Gaudiani's detractors and supporters agree that, through her outreach and economic revitalization efforts, she tried to advance a vision for how development in New London could achieve economic opportunity and social justice for the residents of one of Connecticut's poorest cities.[225] Despite leaving amidst controversy and conflicts, Gaudiani still garners praise in some Connecticut College alumni circles as well as from some of the senior officials who served in her administration.[226] Many alumni continue to laud her for making good on her intention to provide a collective vision and direction for the college, and for inspiring a spirit of confidence about its future.[227]

Since leaving Connecticut College, Gaudiani has written books on sustaining civil society (*The Greater Good*), the tradition of American giving (*Generosity Rules*), as well as several articles, including one on women and philanthropy.[228] She holds a faculty appointment at New York University's Center for Philanthropy and Fund Raising.[229] She sits on the boards of the Luce Foundation, MBIA, Inc., and Worcester Polytechnic Institute and speaks frequently on issues related to the public good, particularly the responsibility of individuals to share with others less fortunate than themselves.[230] She also maintains a remarkably revealing and self-promotional personal web site apart from her faculty biography on the New York University web site.[231]

Although Gaudiani's vision of a fully functioning downtown campus for Connecticut College was short-lived, the College's curriculum continues to offer students numerous points of engagement with New London. For example, art history professor Abigail Van Slyke and her students gave tours for and curated a 2005–2006 exhibit at the Lyman Allyn Art Museum entitled "Commerce and Culture:

Architecture and Society on New London's State Street."[232] The exhibit grew out of Van Slyke's senior seminar of the same title in which students traced the development of New London's State Street between 1850 and 1950, and ultimately emerged with a deeper understanding of their College's home city.[233] Community engagement opportunities are also available through courses offered by the departments of anthropology, English, environmental studies, gender and women's studies, government, human development, psychology, sociology, and theater.[234]

Gaudiani's outreach legacy most visibly endures in the Holleran Center for Community Action and Public Policy, which provides Connecticut College students and faculty opportunities to make contributions to New London.[235] The Holleran Center has put engagement and outreach at the forefront of Connecticut College's mission as it approaches its second century. In fact, the College's most recent mission statement and marketing slogan proclaim that it is an institution "putting the liberal arts into action."[236] Toward that end, the Holleran Center makes $2,000 grants to encourage faculty to integrate community learning into courses with themes of social justice, economic opportunity, and youth development.[237] The Holleran Center also awards certificates in community action to students who complete the required course work, an internship, and a senior project. In its first ten years of operation, the Holleran Center awarded 133 such certificates.[238]

The autobiographical section of Claire Gaudiani's personal web site reveals a lifelong devotion to her Roman Catholic faith and emphasizes that her Catholicism has always been central to her identity. For example, in her senior year at Connecticut, Gaudiani became the first Roman Catholic to head the College's religious fellowship organization.[239] She told a reporter in 1999 that her retreats for rejuvenation occasionally consist of "a week at a convent just to pray, ponder, and write."[240] Indeed, it does not take much of a leap of analysis to see elements of the Jesuit credo (for others, not for self) running through Gaudiani's thirteen-year tenure as president of Connecticut College. And Gaudiani makes no apologies for the role her Catholic faith played in the decisions she made as president of her alma mater.[241] Many of Gaudiani's guiding views and professional decisions have been, she acknowledges, informed by her strong Catholic faith.[242] Perhaps there was always a mismatch between the secular Connecticut College (one of America's few elite private colleges to have no religious background to its mission and history) and the faith-inspired Gaudiani. The speeches she gave and the initiatives she promoted while at Connecticut College seem, with the benefit of the passing of time that brings reflection, more appropriate for a Catholic rather than a secular institution— or perhaps for a college that had been more explicitly built on Deweyan (learning by doing) principles. And indeed Gaudiani's Deweyan visions of Connecticut College as an experiential and community-focused institution struck more than a few members of the faculty as a misinterpretation of the College's mission.[243]

The Claire Gaudiani years at Connecticut College continue to be ripe for scrutiny. Viewed in relation to the College's founding mission and vision, Gaudiani deserves no small amount of admiration for laboring to reconnect Connecticut College's historical ties to New London and for working to renew the College's focus on the world beyond its campus. As an alumna, she understood better than most that practical elements have always cemented Connecticut College's liberal arts foundation, that the grassroots founding and the campus setting give literal and figurative expression to the notion that it is a college not just looking out toward the larger world and facing its home community but part of it. Gaudiani's case is cautionary and instructive, however, because the partially realized outreach vision she had might have been fully realized had it not become entangled with the controversies generated by her leading role in the economic redevelopment of New London.

Notes

1   Ellen Hofheimer Bettmann and Claire L. Gaudiani, "A Talk Between Presidents," *Connecticut College Alumni Magazine* (Summer 1988), 1–7.

2   Claire L. Gaudiani, "Tradition and Innovation," *The Inaugural Address of Claire L. Gaudiani, President of Connecticut College, October 1 1988* (New London, CT: Connecticut College, 1988). Connecticut College Archives (hereafter identified as CCA), Claire Gaudiani File. Also Claire Gaudiani, interview by author 5 June 2007 (interview in possession of author).

3   Bettmann and Gaudiani, "A Talk Between Presidents," 7.

4   Gaudiani biographical information in the program of *The Inaugural Address of Claire L. President of Connecticut College, October 1 1988.*

5   Stan DeCoster, "An Apostle Charges Ahead," *The Day* (6 June 1999). I found this and other articles on Claire Gaudiani and the New London Development Corporation in the Special Collections of Connecticut College's Charles Shain Library. All newspaper articles referenced in this chapter are available either in the Special Collections at Connecticut College or in the Claire Gaudiani File of the Connecticut College Archives.

6   Editorial Board, "Conflict at Connecticut College," *The Day* (8 June 2000).

7   Robert A. Frahm, "Taking Charge of Education," *Hartford Courant* (12 October 1997).

8   Ibid.

9   "*U.S. News* Rankings Through the Years," *The Chronicle of Higher Education* (2007). Accessed 24 January 2008 from http://chronicle.com/stats/usnews/index.php?category=Liberal+Arts+Colleges#about. Connecticut College ranked 24 in 1999. See also *A Decade of Achievement at Connecticut College* (New London, CT: Connecticut College, 1999), which cites Connecticut's rise in the rankings from 41 to 24. CCA, Gaudiani File.

10   Jennifer Grogan, "CGA Ranks High in New College Report," *The Day* (20 August 2007).

11   Claire Gaudiani, "Developing a Vision," in *Leadership Transitions: The New College President*, ed. Judith Block McLaughlin (San Francisco: Jossey-Bass Publishers, Spring 1996), 59–70. Quote from Claire Gaudiani, "Lemon Spritzers and Thank You Notes: A New Job Description for College Presidents," *Educational Record* (Spring 1992), 52–55; Laurel Shaper Walters, "Teamwork Builds College's Future," *Christian Science Monitor* (28 February 1992).

12   Bettmann and Gaudiani, "A Talk Between Presidents," 3.

13   Ibid.

14 Gaudiani, "Lemon Spritzers and Thank You Notes: A New Job Description for College Presidents," 54.

15 Gaudiani, "Developing a Vision."

16 Frahm, "Taking Charge of Education."

17 Thyra Briggs (14 June 2007), Dirk Held (23 April 2007), Martha Merrill (22 January 2007), and Lynda Munro (29 August 2007), interviews by author (interviews in possession of author).

18 DeCoster, "An Apostle Charges Ahead." Also Liz Cheney (9 May 2007), Anthony and Elizabeth Enders (5 June 2007), Eric Kaplan (6 June 2007), Charlie Luce (21 April 2007), and Daniel Parrish (27 September 2007), interviews with author (interviews in possession of author). Also Merrill interview.

19 Ibid.

20 DeCoster, "An Apostle Charges Ahead."

21 Anthony and Elizabeth Enders, Briggs, Kaplan, and Merrill interviews. Also Torrey Fenton (24 April 2007) and Jeff Oshen (1 May 2007) interviews by author (interviews in possession of author).

22 Ibid.

23 Doro, Enders, Fenton, Luce, Merrill, Munro, Oshen, Rogers interviews.

24 Gaudiani, "Lemon Spritzers and Thank You Notes: A New Job Description for College Presidents." See also Gaudiani, "Developing a Vision."

25 Gaudiani, "Developing a Vision."

26 William J. Bennett, *The De-Valuing of America: The Fight for our Culture and our Children* (New York : Summit Books, 1992). See also Allan Bloom, *The Closing of the American Mind : How Higher Education has Failed Democracy and Impoverished the Souls of Today's Students* (New York : Simon and Schuster, 1987); Dinesh D'Souza, *Illiberal Education : The Politics of Race and Sex on Campus* (New York : Maxwell Macmillan International, 1991); Charles J. Sykes, *ProfScam : Professors and the Demise of Higher Education* (Washington, D.C. : Regnery, 1988).

27 Liz McMillen, "Connecticut College's Strategic Plan Helps it Stay Lean and Mean," *The Chronicle of Higher Education* (3 June 1992), A27–28.

28 Ibid.

29 Ibid.

30 Jefferson Decker, "President and Planner," *University Business* (March 1999), 34–39. Also Brian Rogers, interview by author 22 January 2007 (interview in possession of author).

31 Carol W. Kimball, "Taking the Trolley to New London," *The Day* (7 August 2007), B3.

32 Decker, "President and Planner."

33 Heather Vogell, "Conn's Step Into New London Marches to Others' Beat," *The Day* (4 April 1999).

34 Decker, "President and Planner," 34.

35 Claire L. Gaudiani, "Day One, Day Two (Imaging the Future), Day Three (Social Justice), Day Four (Learning to Serve, Serving to Learn)" (2000). Accessed 20 September 2006 from http://www.collegevalues.org/diaries.cfm?a=0&cat=70. See also Robert A. Hamilton, "In New London, Creating Jobs, Building a Buzz for Renewal," *New York Times* (9 May 1999).

36 Decker, "President and Planner," 34.

37 Vogell, "Conn's Step Into New London Marches to Others' Beat."

38 Gaudiani, "Lemon Spritzers and Thank You Notes: A New Job Description for College Presidents," 54–55.

39 Gaudiani interview.

40 Frederick H, Sykes, "Commencement Address," *Connecticut College News*, 20 June 1917.

41   Oakes Ames, *Annual Report of the President, 1984-1985* (New London, CT: Connecticut College, 1 September 1985). See also Rosemary Park, "Charge to the Seniors: Commencement, June 11, 1961," in *Fiftieth Anniversary Celebration Publication: Connecticut College 1911–1961* (New London, CT: Connecticut College, 1961), 28.

42   Gaudiani, "Tradition and Innovation: Inaugural Address."

43   Bettmann and Gaudiani, "A Talk Between Presidents," 3.

44   "Connecticut College Mission Statement (Amended 24 February 1990 and 7 December 1996)," *Connecticut College Catalog, 1999–2001* (New London, CT: Connecticut College, 1999), 4.

45   Gaudiani interview. Also Marion Doro (23 April 2007) and George Willauer (23 April 2007), interviews by author (interviews in possession of author).

46   Ibid.

47   Claire L. Gaudiani, "Of Heart and Mind: External Forces in Higher Education" (1994). Accessed 20 September 2006 from http://www.clairegaudiani.com/Writings/pages/OfHeartAndMind2.aspx. See also Claire L. Gaudiani, "Of Heart and Mind: The College and the City," *Connecticut College Magazine* (Fall 1994).

48   Ibid. Also Rogers interview.

49   Benjamin Marshall, *Inaugural Address* (23 November 1917), CCA, Benjamin Marshall File.

50   *A Decade of Achievement at Connecticut College.*

51   Ibid.

52   Ibid.

53   Gaudiani, "Of Heart and Mind: External Forces in Higher Education." See also Gaudiani, "Of Heart and Mind: The College and the City."

54   Ibid.

55   Gaudiani, "A Message From the President," 3.

56   Decker, "President and Planner," 36.

57   Gaudiani, "Of Heart and Mind: External Forces in Higher Education." See also Gaudiani, "Of Heart and Mind: The College and the City."

58   Ibid. See also Claire Gaudiani, "In Pursuit of Global Civic Virtues" (Remarks at the 1991 Annual Meeting of the Connecticut College Alumni Association), *Connecticut College Alumni Magazine* (Winter 1992), 1.

59   Ibid.

60   Carolyn Battista, "The Holleran Center at 10," *CC: Connecticut College Magazine* (Fall 2006), 28–31.

61   Claire L. Gaudiani, "Learning to Serve, Serving to Learn;" Address at 15th Annual Lilly Conference on College Teaching, Miami University, Oxford, Ohio (18 November 1995). Accessed 27 November 2006 http://www.clairegaudiani.com/Writings/pages/LillyConference.aspx

62   John DiBiaggio and Elizabeth Hall to the Editor (defending Gaudiani), *Chronicle of Higher Education* (15 October 2000), B 12. DiBiaggio was president of Tufts University and Hall was Executive Director of Campus Compact at Brown University. See also "Learning to Serve, Serving to Learn."

63   Gaudiani, "Learning to Serve, Serving to Learn." See also John Dewey, "My Pedagogic Creed," *School Journal* (January 1897), 77–80; Benson, Harkavy, and Puckett, *Dewey's Dream.*

64   Gaudiani, "Learning to Serve, Serving to Learn."

65   Claire Gaudiani, "A Message From the President," *Connecticut College Catalog, 1999–2001* (New London, CT: Connecticut College, 1999), 3.

66   Ibid.

67   Gaudiani, "Day One, Day Two (Imaging the Future), Day Three (Social Justice), Day Four (Learning to Serve, Serving to Learn)."

68   Ibid.

69 Heather Vogell, "A Man With a Plan: College Project Evolves into Firehouse Renovation," *The Day* (10 January 1999).

70 Decker, "President and Planner," 36.

71 Decker, "President and Planner," 34–39.

72 Ibid.

73 Dewey, "My Pedagogic Creed." See also Benson, Harkavy, and Puckett, *Dewey's Dream*, 42.

74 Dewey, "My Pedagogic Creed." See also Benson, Harkavy, and Puckett, *Dewey's Dream*. See also "The University and Democracy" in William Rainey Harper, *The Trends in Higher Education* (Chicago: University of Chicago Press, 1905), 1–34. Harper argued that "the university is the messiah of democracy, its anticipated deliverer" and declared that the "university is the prophet of this democracy."

75 Gaudiani, "Day One, Day Two (Imaging the Future), Day Three (Social Justice), Day Four (Learning to Serve, Serving to Learn)."

76 Ibid.

77 Ibid.

78 Ibid.

79 Ibid.

80 Decker, "President and Planner," 36.

81 Gaudiani, "Of Heart and Mind: External Forces in Higher Education."

82 Gaudiani, "Day One, Day Two (Imaging the Future), Day Three (Social Justice), Day Four (Learning to Serve, Serving to Learn)." See also Gaudiani, "A Message From the President."

83 Gaudiani, "Of Heart and Mind: External Forces in Higher Education."

84 Beth Dufresne, "At the Lyman Allyn a Pulse Beats Again," *The Day* (5 May 1999).

85 Ibid.

86 Ibid.

87 Ibid.

88 Decker, "President and Planner," 36. See also Robert A. Hamilton, "New London, New Vision," *Connecticut College Magazine* (Spring 1998), 22–27.

89 Gaudiani, "Day One, Day Two (Imaging the Future), Day Three (Social Justice), Day Four (Learning to Serve, Serving to Learn)." See also "Connecticut College Mission Statement (Amended 24 February 1990 and 7 December 1996);" Hamilton, "New London, New Vision."

90 "New London, New Vision" (Brochure) (1999). CCA, Claire Gaudiani File.

91 Decker, "President and Planner," 36.

92 Ibid. See also Heather Vogell, "Gaudiani Unveils Plans for Social Progress," *The Day* (28 April 1999).

93 Nye, *Chapters in the History of Connecticut College*, 23, 26. Sykes, "The Social Basis of the New Education for Women," 226–242.

94 Ibid. Also Lee G. Bolman and Terence E. Deal, *Reframing Organizations: Artistry, Choice, and Leadership* (San Francisco: Jossey-Bass, 2003).

95 Editorial Board, "Towards a River of Dreams," *The Day* (15 February 1998),

96 Ibid. See also Heather Vogell, "Conn College May Invest More in City," *The Day* (11 December 1998).

97 Dan Pearson, "Conn, RPI Plan High-Tech Learning Center in New London," *The Day* (15 December 1999).

98 Ibid.

99 Ibid.

100 Laurie Deredita, interviews with author 31 July and 4 September 2007 (interviews in possession of author). Deredita is director of special collections at Connecticut College and oversees the New London Development Corporation (NLDC) collection, which is a repository of in-

formation on Gaudiani's outreach efforts to New London. Also Doro, Held, Rogers, and Willauer interviews.

101 Ibid.

102 Deredita interviews.

103 Ibid. Also Bredeson, Doro, Held, Rogers, and Willauer interviews.

104 Dan Pearson, "Conn College OKs Housing in Downtown," *The Day* (3 October 1999).

105 Ibid.

106 Ibid.

107 Hamilton, "In New London, Creating Jobs, Building a Buzz for Renewal."

108 Bredeson, Deredita, Doro, Held, Rogers, and Willauer interviews.

109 Ibid.

110 Vogell, "Conn's Step Into New London Marches to Others' Beat." Also Ira Harkavy, interview by author 17 January 2008 (interview in possession of author); Harold Wingood, interview by author 12 November 2007 (interview in possession of author). Harkavy played a central role in Penn's outreach and redevelopment efforts in West Philadelphia. Wingood was Clark's chief enrollment officer from 1994–2008.

111 Vogell, "Conn's Step Into New London Marches to Others' Beat." Also Harkavy and Wingood interviews.

112 Bredeson, Held, Merrill, Rogers, and Willauer interviews.

113 Gaudiani interview.

114 Julianne Basinger, "Under Fire From Students and Professors, President of Connecticut College Quits," *The Chronicle of Higher Education* (27 October 2000), A40.

115 Editorial Board, "Conflict at Connecticut College."

116 Ibid.

117 David Fenton, interview by author 24 January 2007 (interview in possession of author). Also Held interview. See also Judy Benson, "Some Faculty Seek to Ouster Gaudiani," *The Day* (9 May 2000).

118 Doro, Held, Rogers, and Willauer interviews.

119 Deredita, Fenton, Held, Rogers, Sheridan, and Willauer interviews.

120 D. Pearson, "Conn Student Group Opposes Razing Fort Homes," *The Day* (1 March 2000).

121 Gaudiani, "Day One, Day Two (Imaging the Future), Day Three (Social Justice), Day Four (Learning to Serve, Serving to Learn)." Also Gaudiani interview.

122 Benson, "Some Faculty Seek to Ouster Gaudiani."

123 Held interview.

124 Judy Benson, "Conn Trustee Dayton Throws Strong Support to Gaudiani," *The Day* (13 May 2000).

125 Trish Brink, "Claire L. Gaudiani to Step Down as President of Connecticut College" (13 October 2000). Accessed 28 March 2007 from http://www.conncoll.edu/news/articles/buildarticle.cgi?971461467.txt)

126 DeCoster, "An Apostle Charges Ahead."

127 Ibid.

128 Ibid.

129 Ibid.

130 Erin Strout, "The Trustees Tipping Point: When Does a Governing Board Say Enough is Enough and Fire the President?" *Chronicle of Higher Education* (6 May 2005), A27.

131 Ibid.

132 Editorial Board, "Conflict at Connecticut College."

133 Basinger, "Under Fire From Students and Professors, President of Connecticut College Quits." The College's enrollment had not yet grown to 1,900.

134 Ibid.

135 Julianne Basinger, "A Promoter of Town-Gown Cooperation Finds Development May Be Her Undoing," *The Chronicle of Higher Education* (2 June 2000), A41–42.

136 Cindy Anderson, "A House Divided: A Story About Eminent Domain," *Yankee Magazine* (January/February, 2007). See also John Riley, "When David Meets Goliath," *InfoWars.com* (8 May 2005). Accessed 28 March 2007 from http://www.infowars.com/articles/ps/eminent_ domain_david_vs_goliath.htm; Carola Von Hoffmannstahl-Solomonoff, "Land Grabbers Stew," *Deep qt* (21 September 2005). Accessed 28 March 2007 from http://www. users.cloud9.net/~drs/deep_qt/deepqt_maindish.html.

137 Colin McEnroe, "A Heart-Breaking Work of Staggering Self-Reinvention," *The Hartford Courant* (18 October 2005).

138 Basinger, "Under Fire From Students and Professors, President of Connecticut College Quits."

139 Brink, "Claire L. Gaudiani to Step Down as President of Connecticut College."

140 Strout, "The Trustees Tipping Point: When Does a Governing Board Say Enough is Enough and Fire the President?"

141 Bolman and Deal, *Reframing Organizations: Artistry, Choice, and Leadership.*

142 Decker, "President and Planner," 37. See also Gaudiani, "Developing a Vision."

143 Walters, "Teamwork Builds College's Future."

144 Held interview.

145 Vogell, "Conn's Step Into New London Marches to Others' Beat."

146 Ibid.

147 Ibid.

148 Ibid.

149 Donald Kennedy, "Making Choices in the Research University," in *The Research University in a Time of Discontent*, ed. J.R. Cole, E. G. Barber, & S. R. Graubard (Baltimore, MD: The Johns Hopkins University Press, 1994), 85–114.

150 Gaudiani, "Developing a Vision." See also Walters, "Teamwork Builds College's Future."

151 Birnbaum, *How Colleges Work* and Robert Birnbaum, "The Latent Functions of the Academic Senate: Why Senates Do Not Work But Will Not Go Away." *Journal of Higher Education* (July/August 1989), 423–443; Peter D. Eckel and Adrianna Kezar, "The Challenges Facing Academic Decision making: Contemporary Issues and Steadfast Structures," in *The Shifting Frontiers of Academic Decision Making: Responding to New Priorities, Following New Pathways*, 1–14. Also interviews with numerous Connecticut faculty.

152 Frahm, "Taking Charge of Education."

153 Ibid.

154 Benson, "Some Faculty Seek to Ouster Gaudiani."

155 DeCoster, "An Apostle Charges Ahead." See also "Connecticut College Mission Statement (Amended 24 February 1990 and 7 December 1996)."

156 Ibid. Quoting Connecticut College government professor Wayne Swanson.

157 Ibid.

158 Ibid. See also Eckel and Kezar, "The Challenges Facing Academic Decision Making: Contemporary Issues and Steadfast Structures;" Hartley and Wilhelm Shah, "The Tenuous Legitimacy of Ad-hoc Decision-making Committees."

159 Numerous individuals not identified by request.

160 Birnbaum, *How Colleges Work.*

161 Gaudiani, "Lemon Spritzers & Thank You Notes: A New Job Description for College Presidents," 55.

162 Gaudiani, "Developing a Vision."

163 Walters, "Teamwork Builds College's Future." See also Gaudiani, "Developing a Vision."

164 Gaudiani, "Lemon Spritzers & Thank You Notes: A New Job Description for College Presidents," 53, 54.

165 Ibid. See also Bettmann and Gaudiani, "A Talk Between Presidents."

166 Birnbaum, *How Colleges Work*. See also Eckel, "The Role of Shared Governance in Institutional Hard Decisions: Enabler or Antagonist?"

167 Birnbaum, "The Latent Functions of the Academic Senate: Why Senates Do Not Work But Will Not Go Away."

168 Burton R. Clark, *The Distinctive College* (Chicago: Aldine Publishing Company, 1970). See also Burton R. Clark, "The Organizational Saga in Higher Education," *Administrative Science Quarterly* (June 1972), 178–184; Peter D. Eckel, "The Role of Shared Governance in Institutional Hard Decisions: Enabler or Antagonist?" *Review of Higher Education* (Fall 2000), 15–39.

169 Willauer and Held interviews; and Margaret "Peggy" Sheridan interview by author 2 May 2007 (interview in possession of author).

170 Gaudiani, "Developing a Vision." See also Gaudiani, "Lemon Spritzers & Thank You Notes: A New Job Description for College Presidents." Also Fenton, Held, Sheridan, and Willauer interviews.

171 Frahm, "Taking Charge of Education." Also Fenton, Held, Sheridan, and Willauer interviews.

172 Joseph P. Zolner, "Community-Centered Planning at Connecticut College," *Harvard Graduate School of Education Case Study* (Cambridge, MA: Harvard University, 1997), 1–12. CCA, Gaudiani File.

173 Ibid.

174 Briggs, Doro, Enders, Kaplan, Luce, Merrill, and Willauer interviews.

175 DeCoster, "An Apostle Charges Ahead."

176 Birnbaum, *How Colleges Work*. See also Birnbaum, "The Latent Functions of the Academic Senate: Why Senates Do Not Work But Will Not Go Away;" Eckel & Kezar, "The Challenges Facing Academic Decision Making: Contemporary Issues and Steadfast Structures;" K.E. Weick, "Educational Organizations as Loosely Coupled Systems," *Administrative Science Quarterly* (March 1976), 1–19.

177 Birnbaum, *How Colleges Work*. See also Birnbaum, "The Latent Functions of the Academic Senate: Why Senates Do Not Work But Will Not Go Away."

178 H. Mintzberg, "The Professional Bureaucracy," In *Structures in Fives: Designing Effective Organizations* (Englewood Cliffs, NJ: Prentice Hall, 1993), 189–213.

179 Heather Vogell, "Redevelopment Plan Lacks Contingencies for the Needy," *The Day* (2 January 1999).

180 Riley, "When David Meets Goliath."

181 Heather Vogell, "Fort Trumbull Residents Say They Want to Stay Put," *The Day* (6 January 1999).

182 Ibid.

183 Dan Pearson, "Conn Student Group Opposes Razing Fort Homes," *The Day* (1 March 2000).

184 Dan Pearson, "Gaudiani Honor is Focus of Discord," *The Day* (28 December 1999).

185 Anderson, "A House Divided." See also Tim Cavanaugh, "Endgame in New London, or, Another Successful Five-year Plan," *Reasononline* (8 June 2006). Accessed 28 March 2007 from http://www.reason.com/news/printer/117322. Riley, "When David Meets Goliath;" Von Hoffmannstahl-Solomonoff, "Land Grabbers Stew."

186 Anderson, "A House Divided." See also McEnroe, "A Heart-Breaking Work of Staggering Self-Reinvention."

187 Judy Benson, "NLDC Gets Praise, Criticism for Plan at Public Meetings," *The Day* (27 April 1998).

188 McEnroe, "A Heart-Breaking Work of Staggering Self-Reinvention."

189 Frahm, "Taking Charge of Education."

190 Decker, "President and Planner," 39.

191 DeCoster, "An Apostle Charges Ahead."

192 D.J. Julius, J.V. Baldridge, & J. Pfeffer, "A Memo from Machiavelli," *Journal of Higher Education* (March/April 1999), 113–133.

193 Morgan McGinley, "Gaudiani Must Learn Leadership in Public Realm," *The Day* (2 November 1997).

194 Deredita, Held, and Luce interviews.

195 Decker, "President and Planner," 38.

196 Ibid.

197 Eleanor B. Gray to the editor, "Spoiled Little Children on the Hill," *The Day* (18 June 2000).

198 Deredita, Held, and Willauer interviews. See also Basinger, "Under Fire From Students and Professors, President of Connecticut College Quits."

199 Editorial Board, "Conflict at Connecticut College."

200 Julianne Basinger, "Connecticut President's Golden Parachute Angers Faculty Members," *Chronicle of Higher Education* (22 November 2002), 31.

201 Numerous individuals not identified by request.

202 Basinger, "Connecticut President's Golden Parachute Angers Faculty Members."

203 McMillen, "Connecticut College's Strategic Plan Helps it Stay Lean and Mean."

204 "College Students and Faculty Provide 'the Finest Preschool Education.'" Accessed 21 December, 2007 from http://aspen.conncoll.edu/camelweb/alumni/news/?id1=3922. Also Interview subjects who requested anonymity.

205 Ibid.

206 Ibid.

207 Robert Fromer, "The Pfizer Conspiracy: A Failure of Government," Letter to Governor Jodi Rell, 16 December 2004. Accessed 28 March 2007 from http://pages.cthome.net/ryoung0/

208 Interviewees who requested anonymity.

209 Ibid.

210 Strout, "The Trustees Tipping Point: When Does a Governing Board Say Enough is Enough and Fire the President?"

211 Ibid.

212 Interviewees who requested anonymity.

213 Vogell, "Conn College May Invest More in City."

214 Editorial Board, "Conflict at Connecticut College."

215 Eckel and Kezar, "The Challenges Facing Academic Decision making: Contemporary Issues and Steadfast Structures."

216 Decker, "President and Planner," 35.

217 Held interview.

218 W.T. Mallon, "Centers, Institutes, and Academic Decision-making: Addressing "Suburban Sprawl" Through Strategies for "Smart Growth," in *The Shifting Frontiers of Academic Decision Making: Responding to New Priorities, Following New Pathways*, 15–34. Also numerous interviews with Connecticut College faculty members.

219 Deredita and Luce interviews.

220 Deredita interviews.

221 Walters, "Teamwork Builds College's Future."

222 Birnbaum, *How Colleges Work*.

223 Bettmann and Gaudiani, "A Talk Between Presidents."

224 Birnbaum, *How Colleges Work*.

225 Carey, Deredita, Doro, Merrill, Rogers, and Willauer interviews.

226 Briggs, Carey, Enders, Kaplan, Luce, Merrill, and Oshen interviews.

227 Briggs, Kaplan, Merrill, and Oshen interviews.

228 Claire Gaudiani, *The Greater Good: How Philanthropy Drives the American Economy and Can Save Capitalism* (New York: Henry Holt/New York Times Books, 2003) and *Generosity Rules: A Guidebook for Giving* (Lincoln, Nebraska: iUniverse, 2007). See also "How American Women's Philanthropy Helped Build Economic Growth and Democratic Society," In *The Transformative Power of Women's Philanthropy*, ed. M Taylor and S. Shaw-Hardy (San Francisco: Jossey-Bass Publishers, 2005), 23–38.

229 ClaireGaudiani.com, "Resume." Accessed 28 March 2007 from http://www.clairegaudiani.com/pages/Resume.aspx.

230 Kari Haskell, "A Sense of Duty Takes Shape During Dinnertime Discussion" (Profile of Claire Gaudiani), *New York Times* (6 January 2008), 20. In this profile, Gaudiani describes how at a young age she developed a concern for the needy.

231 ClaireGaudiani.com. Accessed 20 September 2006 from http://www.clairegaudiani.com/pages/Home.aspx

232 "Commerce and Culture: Architecture and Society on New London's State Street," *CC: Connecticut College Magazine* (Fall 2005), 15.

233 Ibid.

234 *Connecticut College 2005–2007 Catalog* (New London, CT: Connecticut College, 2005).

235 Battista, "The Holleran Center at 10," 30, 31.

236 *Connecticut College's Strategic Priorities for the Second Century: Draft 8.*

237 Ibid.

238 Ibid.

239 Bettmann and Gaudiani, "A Talk Between Presidents."

240 DeCoster, "An Apostle Charges Ahead."

241 Gaudiani interview. See also Gaudiani, "Day One, Day Two (Imaging the Future), Day Three (Social Justice), Day Four (Learning to Serve, Serving to Learn)."

242 Ibid.

243 Sources anonymous by request.

CHAPTER NINE

Connecticut College on the Edge of Its Second Century

Colleges and universities are expressions of faith in selected idealistic notions.[1] In the United States, visionaries and pragmatists have founded thousands of colleges on the premise that individual lives and society at large will be improved, and maybe even transformed, through the pursuit of knowledge and truth.[2] The founding of Connecticut College for Women mirrored such notions, resting upon the belief that women in the state of Connecticut needed an indigenous option for higher education. The founders of Connecticut College had clear answers to the key questions that define institutional purpose: whom do we serve (women), how do we serve them (a liberal arts curriculum with some vocational courses of study), what is our reason for being (to fill a need in a state), why are we here (to provide a high quality and useful education for women, a growing college-going population that had few options in 1911)?[3] Connecticut College was built on high ideals, born of a mission for the greater good, according to former president Claire Gaudiani.[4] Connecticut College's clear founding purpose reflected what some theorists call the internal compass function of mission.[5] Having such clarity of mission at the moment of its origin can enable an institution to retain its bearings and not lose its way as it develops.[6]

The founding of a college has parallels to a social movement: each depends on the sense of purpose created when a group of individuals is drawn to a particular cause.[7] Frequently the establishment of a new college depends on a powerful charismatic individual or a group of true believers—in Connecticut College's case Elizabeth Wright, the Hartford College Club, Colin Buell, Morton Plant, and Frederick Sykes—wholly invested in realizing a shared vision.[8] Founders are critical shapers of an institution's values and purposes and central definers of the nature of its activities; founders provide an answer to the question what does the institution do?[9] At their origination, institutions tend to articulate clearly their reasons for being, often stating a founding purpose that expresses how the particular college is special and distinctive.[10] Even at institutions that adapt into new forms, the story of the founding reminds everyone why the college exists and what it historically has aspired to accomplish. Inherent in the founding purpose, mission, and vision is, figuratively speaking, the institution's genetic code.

Connecticut College: A Distinctive College with an Organizational Saga?

Institutions that are distinctive in their mission and character have an organizational saga that expresses their unique purpose, according to sociologist Burton Clark.[11] Usually introduced by an individual or a group of individuals with a mission, the organizational saga gives expression and form to what the institution has been, what it is today, and by extrapolation what it will be in the future.[12] Organizational sagas do not develop in passive institutions that merely adapt to meet the changing demands of the market or in institutions that simply show obeisance to some higher governing authority.[13] Organizational sagas are more prone to develop in mission driven institutions, like small liberal arts colleges that emphasize consistency over change.[14] Burton Clark constructed his concepts of the organizational saga and the distinctive college through an examination of three particular, and one could argue peculiar, liberal arts colleges: Antioch College, Reed College, and Swarthmore College.[15] Clark chose those three colleges because each developed and expressed strong clarity of purpose, either at its founding or during key transformational moments.[16] Would Clark find the kind of clarity of purpose that makes for a discernable organizational saga (and a distinctive college) were he to examine Connecticut College's first one hundred years?

Figure 9.1. An aerial view of the campus

The answer to that question is up for debate. Certainly Connecticut College for Women had a strong founding purpose and was distinctive within its geographic region when college-going patterns were more localized. But it is arguable that Connecticut College's move to coeducation in 1969 was an adaptation of the type inconsistent with a strong organizational saga, that is, an adaptation driven by institutional necessity to meet the changing demands of society. On the other hand, given Connecticut's founding purpose to meet the higher education needs of women in its home state, one could assert that adapting to meet an emerging societal need (coeducation) was inherent in, and thus an updated expression of, the College's organizational saga.

Figure 9.2. Students on Tempel Green before Blaustein Humanities Center

Whether or not one agrees that organizational sagas are most salient in distinctive institutions, Clark has provided a useful frame for examining colleges such as Connecticut. Especially apt is Clark's notion of initiation, the first stage in an organizational saga's development, the point at which institutional mission and vision are articulated by a founder, such as Connecticut College's first president Frederick Sykes, or recast due to crisis, or altered due to a readiness for change—such as coeducation at Connecticut—that redefines an established institution.[17] In the second stage of its development, the organizational saga gets fulfilled by a core group of true believers, usually senior faculty, who are frequently aided by successive generations of students who internalize the saga and keep it alive.[18] The true believers are necessary, because the vision of the charismatic leader—expressed in the initiation phase—will not endure without a band of devotees invested in promoting the vision after the leader departs.[19] In the case of Connecticut College, the founding visions of President Frederick Sykes and trustee Colin Buell endured in the curriculum until the 1950s, and are still expressed in the College's recent marketing slogan that espouses the notion of "putting the liberal arts into action."[20] Yet in the case of Connecticut's reconnection to New London under Claire Gaudiani, no band of devotees fulfilled her vision, because as she departed in 2001 the implementation of that vision was in tatters, requiring subsequent withdrawal from downtown New London initiatives as a financial self-preservation move.

An organizational saga can provide a powerful sense of unity to a college, becoming a strong self-fulfilling belief underlying its internalized institutional image and its projected public image.[21] The conviction that it was providing educational access for the women of a whole state gave Connecticut College for Women a unifying founding purpose and a sense of uniqueness in its home region. Yet organizations, including liberal arts colleges such as Connecticut College, tend to over-claim uniqueness, emphasizing that they are institutions unlike others.[22] To be sure, every college has an individual ethos, the elements that distinguish it from others with similar surface characteristics.[23] And therein is the complicated, and sometimes contradictory, part. Some colleges resist projecting their uniqueness for fear that doing so will restrict their identity and will confine their appeal to a limited, and perhaps unsustainable, market segment in higher education. Other colleges eschew distinctiveness because they get intoxicated by the belief that they can be excellent in everything they do. Both are potentially misguided courses of action.

To understand what makes Connecticut College distinctive in 2010 requires looking back to numerous places in its past to find the roots of its character. Although it is a young college, not yet one hundred years old, there are enduring aspects to Connecticut College, "things that," as Frederick Sykes said in his 1917 farewell address, "do not die while memory lasts," things that are evocative of the history lived over nearly one hundred years at what started as Connecticut College for Women and became coeducational Connecticut College.[24] A good start is Connecticut College's own history, beginning with the founding vision and mission. For example, much is revealed about Connecticut College by the opportunities it provided to an underdog population (women) at its founding, the dramatic and beautiful setting that intentionally looked out toward the world beyond the campus from the beginning, the rigorous liberal arts core supplemented by vocational training that prepared women to do useful work outside the home, and the pioneering spirit that sought to offer women the practical kind of education they sought in the progressive era. In aggregate, those historically defined characteristics helped set Connecticut College for Women apart from its distaff peers.

Each of Connecticut's early shapers (Frederick Sykes, Colin Buell, and Katharine Blunt) articulated a vision for Connecticut College that was no mere copy of the Seven Sisters or a female version of the New England men's colleges. Yet as Connecticut College has moved forward into coeducation, the visions of those early leaders have been obscured. Often it seems as if Connecticut College's sense of its heritage reaches back no further than to the era of Rosemary Park. Perhaps this is because the institutional memory is selective, wanting to forget the vocational edges to the curriculum that Park eradicated. Perhaps this is because the idea of preparing women to work, an idea that was progressive in 1911, seems quaint to a coeducational college that engages men and women as equals in the classrooms and laboratories and prepares them to enter the same occupational fields. Yet a closer look reveals that the views of Sykes, Buell, and Blunt—although not identified explicitly—still animate the spirit of Connecticut College. Connecticut still is largely as they saw it, a college whose students are gaining a useful education, not one cloistered in rarefied air above the ground of the real world, but one connected to it through the programs of the Arboretum, the Holleran Center for Community Service, the Center for International Studies, the preschool the College operates, and the physical proximity to the Lyman Allyn Art Museum—all entities that provide opportunities for Connecticut students to live the College's stated mission of putting the liberal arts into action as contributing citizens of a global society.[25]

In the Connecticut College family, there is a minority view regarding the institution's history that warrants acknowledgment. According to this view, since 1969 Connecticut College has shied away from its women's college past, engaging in a kind of over-correction to prove that it is truly coeducational. If that charge is even partially true, Connecticut College might benefit by determining what, if anything, was sacrificed. Were sports elevated above the arts? Are women still represented prominently among faculty and student leaders? Was it an irreparable loss to cut ties with the American Dance Festival? Has Connecticut College for Women been relegated to historical artifact status? The College's last five mission statements, for example, have not mentioned the education of women explicitly.[26] Is that due to an intentional desire to avoid calling attention to its women's college past, or perhaps due to an implicit acknowledgment that special attention to the education of women is so well understood in Connecticut College's heritage that it does not need to be spelled out?[27]

From its founding, Connecticut College has been anything but a static institution. Instead it has had an evolving identity. In less than a century the College has filled a gap in educational opportunity for women, embraced coeducation before many of its peers, and has established itself as a leading liberal arts college. The elements that made Connecticut College the successful institution it was before coeducation in 1969—an emphasis on a high quality yet practical education and an energetic embrace of the future—continue to enrich it. For example, Connecticut College recognized early that international perspectives and environmental studies could enrich the curriculum, and showed that joining service to learning could invigorate undergraduate education and help assist communities beyond the campus grounds. More recently, Connecticut College's willingness to break paths has produced some high profile failures. Connecticut officials still flinch at the mention of Claire Gaudiani's efforts to revitalize New London. Those economic redevelopment initiatives, while they generated temporary good will, ultimately brought the College bad press and budget deficits. Nearly a decade after the debacle, the bad memories have faded everywhere but on the Connecticut College campus and the streets of New London. Regardless of the outcome, Gaudiani's visions were inspired and altruistic if not always executed properly. Just because Gaudiani was not entirely successful in her outreach and economic redevelopment efforts does not mean that Connecticut College should never try to achieve a similar reconnection with New London again.

Organizations like Connecticut College are grounded in the shared assumptions of the individuals participating in them—and identified by norms, attitudes, symbols, institutional ideology, interpretations, legends, myths, and stories.[28] The stories institutions tell to establish their uniqueness are not always themselves unique, but rather similar, representative types of tales.[29] For example, like Pitzer College and Reed College, Connecticut College sometimes emphasizes its secular origins and historical avoidance of Greek fraternal organizations.[30] Whether unique or not, a college's history, tradition, and values help determine its character, while providing material for the institutional memory that goes forward.[31]

One indication that Connecticut College lacks a recognizable organizational saga is the low awareness members of its community have of its history. Some things about Connecticut College's history are well known. For example, there is near complete awareness that Connecticut was once a women's college. Nearly everyone in the Connecticut family knows that the College became coeducational somewhere between 1967 and 1972, although not everyone can identify 1968 and 1969 as the pivotal years for that decision and its implementation. What is less well known about Connecticut is its founding story. It is not widely known, for example, that Connecticut's founding was related to Wesleyan University. Almost no one has ever heard of Colin Buell. And few know much about its institution-shaping first president Frederick Sykes.

A majority of the people I interviewed remarked that until they read the summary in my introductory letter, they had never heard of Elizabeth Wright and had no idea that Wesleyan's decision to cease admitting women led to the founding of their alma mater. Professor Richard Goodwin expressed this widespread obliviousness to Connecticut's history in a March 2007 letter to me that stated, "I joined the faculty at Connecticut College in 1944...[and] retired in 1976...but have continued to be involved with the College in one way or another ever since...Quite frankly I lived my life and developed my career with no particular appreciation of the College's 'founding story.'"[32] Former president Norman Fainstein reported that it was at least a year into his tenure before he heard of Elizabeth Wright and the Hartford College Club.[33] Vassar College, from which Fainstein came to Connecticut, has, in his opinion, a much stronger grasp of its institutional history as well as less ambivalence about claiming its women's college past.[34]

There is slightly more awareness of Connecticut College's historical ties to New London. Those aware of New London's grassroots campaign to raise $100,000 know the story from Gertrude Noyes' 1982 history of the College. That New Londoners collectively made such a generous founding gift is perhaps the best known tale of the past that gets handed down from generation to generation of students, faculty, staff, and alumni. Reinforcement of the story exists in the presence of New London Hall—one of Connecticut College's oldest and most prominent buildings. A close runner-up for best-known story is Morton Plant's $1 million gift, perhaps because of the building on Connecticut College campus named for Plant, and because a relatively recent alumni magazine article recounted the colorful tale of how that magnanimous donation occurred.[35]

Aside from Connecticut's admissions and public affairs departments, whose job it is to communicate the College's history, only the most loyal and involved alumni, and veteran faculty members at Connecticut, can recount both the Wesleyan and New London stories and talk knowledgeably about Elizabeth Wright, the Hartford College Club, Frederick Sykes or Colin Buell. The fact that ignorance of Connecticut College's history is so widespread among its extended family is telling.[36] Low awareness of its history suggests that a college does not depend on unifying stories or lore to create bonds among alumni or to perpetuate a clear sense of its institutional identity or saga. Perhaps Connecticut College lacks a commonly understood and repeatedly told organizational tale or saga because its mission has evolved and adapted, rather than stayed static, over nearly 100 years. Perhaps having an evolving mission is what defines Connecticut College at its core and thus paradoxically forms its distinctive saga and character. Or perhaps Connecticut College's relative youth makes it less self-conscious of its history and less interested in yoking itself to a past that must be celebrated or venerated.

There are some who look at Connecticut College's history and see some contradictory elements. Connecticut College's founding can be interpreted as the response to a slippage back on progress for women, making it a kind of compensatory founding; that is, compensating the women of the state of Connecticut for something they lost when Wesleyan University shut them out.[37] According to this view, the fact that Connecticut College developed out of a repair and recovery for women, rather that an initiation of some new opportunity—as was the case with the Seven Sisters—built into the College's institutional psyche and temperament an inherent reluctance to trumpet its women's college past.[38] Another skeptical take on Connecticut asserts that for an institution that was supposed to be the college for women in its state, it has never been a local place in character, or emphasis, and has shown a paradoxical eagerness to forget its women's college past.[39]

There are others in the Connecticut family who believe that the College's past is only marginally relevant.[40] According to this view, Connecticut should emphasize what it is now, not what it has been in the past.[41] The College should look forward, not back, show itself to be a place going places, a college with an evolutionary history and identity, not an institution inhibited by the legacy of its past.[42] This does not mean that Connecticut College does not know what it is, but rather that it knows that its history (as a nimble, evolving institution) has been a basis for change, not an impediment.[43]

There is an explanation less kind to Connecticut College, articulated by individuals who prefer anonymity. According to this view, Connecticut College's history is that of a second-rate institution, the proverbial redheaded stepsister to its more elite peers.[44] This has led to a negative institutional self-image and a sense, even if it is not explicitly articulated, that it is better to be the lesser cousin to the prestigious Seven Sisters or NESCAC than to stand on one's own and risk oblivion.[45] If the past is less than glorious, so goes this view, why recall it, why not look forward to potentially better days?[46] Perhaps Connecticut College so eagerly embraced coeducation and all the institutional adjustments it entailed due to a desire to emerge from the shadow of the Seven Sisters and be a better known and more highly regarded college.

There are some misconceptions about Connecticut College for Women that might not exist if there were a stronger understanding of its history. For example, not a few people think that Connecticut was a college where rich girls went to get their so-called "M.R.S. degree."[47] That view is inaccurate as well as insulting to the women who chose to attend Connecticut College because it provided a pioneering opportunity to get an excellent liberal arts education and prepare for newly emerging careers. There is no evidence that graduates of Connecticut College for Women were any more or less likely than their Seven Sister counterparts to marry. In fact, the Connecticut College women who studied home economics were quite successful at finding jobs after graduation, so much so that home economics faculty such as Margaret Chaney likely agreed with what M. Carey Thomas famously said about Bryn Mawr graduates, "our failures only marry."[48] Regardless, before the women's liberation movement of the 1960s and 1970s, the majority of college women at every institution, including the Seven Sister colleges, were eager for marriage, seeing it as the next step in their lives.

Although declining marriage rates among Seven Sister alumnae fed fears of race suicide in the progressive era that begot Connecticut College for Women, there is no evidence that founders Elizabeth Wright, Frederick Sykes, and Colin Buell saw preparation for marriage as a prominent goal of the College. Furthermore, Katharine Blunt, who never married, was less than enthusiastic about the marriage class taught by Connecticut College's home economics department in the 1930s and 1940s.[49] Blunt sought to have the home economics major emphasize scientific training rather than domesticity.[50] And finally, no M.R.S.-degree-oriented college would have passed the curricular reforms that in the 1950s pruned home economics from Connecticut College for Women's list of majors.

Some alumni and staff wish that Connecticut College had a different name, one not so frequently confused with the Connecticut state colleges and universities.[51] "Conn College" and "Conn" have been nicknames perennially popular with students and alumni. But the invocation of Conn results, more often than not, in Connecticut College getting mistaken for UCONN, that is, the University of Connecticut.[52] A few former Connecticut administrators told me that more than once in the last thirty years the College's leadership has tried to eliminate or minimize all references to "Conn" or "Conn College" in official publications.[53] Those who lament that Connecticut College's name has cookie-cutter, regional state college overtones wish that the College had kept its original name: Thames College.[54] Thames College, some argue, would have been a more distinctive name yet still would have served as a sufficient identifier of the College's home region. True enough. But if the founders had unequivocally wanted to pay homage to the local community's central role in establishing the College, the most appropriate name might have been New London College.

Still, all the disenchantment with the College's name would probably surprise Elizabeth Wright, Colin Buell, and Morton Plant were they still alive. Connecticut College's founders did not anticipate the name confusion, because in 1911 there was no University of Connecticut in Storrs. At its founding, the name Connecticut College had power that Thames College or New London College lacked. The name Connecticut College for Women held the force of a whole state, and as such that name proclaimed the founding promise that Elizabeth Wright and the Hartford College Club sought to fulfill for their home region by giving it what it lacked: a college for women.

Connecticut College's ambivalence about its name is indicative, some say, of an overall institutional inferiority complex. That they have to clarify the name on their diploma makes many Connecticut College alumni wish that they could claim a college name like Swarthmore or Tufts that does not invite mix-ups with other institutions. Yet having a name that spurs mistaken identities is not a problem peculiar to Connecticut College. The names Trinity, Wesleyan, and Wheaton beg the question which one? Washington University and the University of Pennsylvania (Penn) are often thought to be the University of Washington and Penn State—so much so that Washington University appends "in Saint Louis" to most of its communications and the Penn bookstore sells a t-shirt proclaiming "Not Penn State."

If the collective Connecticut College family had a firmer sense of the College's history and distinctive personality, the name confusion might seem an inconsequential annoyance. But when institutional history and identity are a muddle, the name confusion becomes another reminder that the College has not projected a consistent, coherent, and proud story of itself to the world. Acceptance and celebration of its full history, including the women's college years and the confusing name, might go a long way toward Connecticut College emerging out of the shadows cast by other more prominent institutions in its home region of New England. Success at emerging from its perennial shadows may depend ultimately on Connecticut College closing the wealth gap between it and its New England peer colleges—at least that is the consensus view on and off campus. Certainly lack of resources is a problem for Connecticut College, and a major contributor to its second-tier status. But no amount of wealth will buy Connecticut College a coherent, consistent, and proud story of what it has been since it was conceived in 1911. No amount of additional wealth will give Connecticut College a discernable organizational saga and a recognizable institutional niche. Pinning its hopes on amassing wealth is simply another outward looking strategy. Looking inward to identify its particular institution-defining characteristics might be an effective complementary strategy.

What Defines Connecticut College?

To understand an institution like Connecticut College is to grasp what makes it special.[55] Whether special or distinctive, all organizations have a culture.[56] For leaders especially, it is essential to comprehend an institution's organizational culture, because culture always influences decisions.[57] Strategies arise from the heritage and the purposes of an organization, because both are as idiosyncratic as fingerprints.[58] Organizational culture, especially at collegial small colleges such as Connecticut, is the glue that holds together an institution, expressing the values and beliefs shared by its members.[59] For example, shared governance is a central tenet of Connecticut

College's organizational culture.[60] Leaders who have violated that basic cultural value have, as Claire Gaudiani found out, engendered vehement opposition.

Faculty, staff, and alumni of Connecticut College describe the campus culture as friendly and supportive.[61] Some say it has always felt more Midwestern relaxed than Eastern neurotic and competitive.[62] Alumni say that Connecticut College takes bright students who have not been academic superstars and pushes them toward higher intellectual heights.[63] Faculty members report that Connecticut students are sharp and industrious but not the intellectually self-confident risk takers that they imagine populate classrooms at Swarthmore and Wesleyan.[64] Aside from that criticism, Connecticut College faculty members claim to be more or less satisfied with their students. Long gone, they say, are the early days of co-education when there was a noticeable gap (what the committee that studied the coeducation question in 1968 called the "Middlebury syndrome") between the very able women and the too frequently less able men.[65] Yet there is still grumbling in some corners of campus about an alleged post-coeducation ascendance of athletics and jocks over arts and artists.[66] Some Connecticut faculty also lament that men now hold more than 50 percent of the tenured positions, that male students, despite comprising just 40 percent of the campus population, tend to hold more leadership positions than the women, and that only one of Connecticut's last five presidents has been a woman.[67]

When pressed to isolate the College's special strengths, Connecticut officials point to programs in environmental studies (supported by the Arboretum); a stand-out emphasis on international study, including courses in hard-to-find languages such as Italian; a tradition of participatory shared governance that engages students in decision making processes; an honor code whose chief feature is un-proctored exams; a long-standing commitment to volunteerism in the community; and the curricular innovations wrought by six interdisciplinary centers that orient students toward using their knowledge to make contributions out in the world. Connecticut College is also a young college with an evolving identity, not one chained to the past; it is a coeducational college that has valued women and tried to integrate men fully rather than treat them as an add-on; it has emphasized the need to study the environment and the increasingly international world; it has always maintained strong arts programs; and it embraced interdisciplinary study before most of its peer colleges did.[68] This collection of features provides a beginning answer to the question, what sets Connecticut College apart from its New England peers?

Many at Connecticut College see it as an undervalued underdog, and indeed there is a bit of a pleasant surprise quality to the institution that makes for a potentially appealing contrast to the stereotype of the long-established, self-satisfied, elite college of the northeast.[69] Connecticut College is much younger than all of its NESCAC peers and arguably more humble and more nimble, as it lacks the anchoring weight of tradition ubiquitous elsewhere. A case in point is the near unanimous view that the move to coeducation was relatively seamless and uncontroversial, in part because Connecticut College for Women was not solidified in the popular imagination as one of the representational icons of women's higher education like Vassar. Virtually everyone connected to Connecticut agrees that the time had come for coeducation in 1969 and that the College has never looked back with regret.

Organizational culture is reflected in what is done, how it is done, and who is doing what at colleges such as Connecticut.[70] Interpreting an organization's culture helps determine whether shared mission or strong personalities hold the place together.[71] Katharine Blunt, Rosemary Park, and Claire Gaudiani exemplify leaders whose strong and forceful personalities were always bound up in and hard to separate from the goals and aspirations of the Connecticut College they led. Yet in two of those three cases (Blunt and Park), the forceful leader had the unquestioned moral authority necessary to represent the culture. Holding that moral authority made Blunt and Park successful. Losing it tripped up Gaudiani. An institution's culture can also be influenced by the culture of its peer system.[72] In the case of Connecticut College, its institutional peers have always exerted a strong—some would say too strong—influence. This has been so even as the peer groups have changed from the Seven Sisters, during Connecticut's women's college years, to the colleges of the New England Small College Athletic Conference (NESCAC) since 1969. Having a strong peer system has been both a blessing and a curse for Connecticut College.

Unlike Burton Clark's three distinctive colleges (Antioch, Reed, and Swarthmore), each of which defined itself against the generic mass of small colleges, Connecticut College has from its beginning benefited from its proximity and claims of similarity to an elite set of regional peers. Connecticut College is blessed to be located in the one region of the United States where private higher education reigns supreme: New England. Aside from its picturesque campus and setting, arguably the greatest asset of this 1,900-student liberal arts college is not its teaching-oriented faculty, not its average class size under 20 students, not its 750-acre arboretum, not its six innovative interdisciplinary academic centers, but rather Connecticut College's strong associations with the other, and in most cases more prestigious and wealthier, market-leading small liberal arts colleges of the northeastern United States.

From the founding inspiration of a woman disgruntled at Wesleyan University, through its women's college years (1911-1969), when it was often called the "eighth sister" to the historic Seven Sisters, to the present day when it participates in NESCAC, Connecticut College has always been able to define, or at least legitimize, its institutional quality by association with the best small colleges in its home region.

For example, Connecticut College officials and alumni are quite content to claim the NESCAC "brand" that stands for high quality academics and athletics.[73] Many an older and better-endowed small college in the American Midwest, South, or West (such as Denison University, Trinity University, and Whitman College) might gladly trade for the associations that adhere to Connecticut College's history and location. One tangible benefit of Connecticut's associative strengths is that its peer group does not need to engage in the aggressive tuition discounting that burdens budgets at many liberal arts colleges outside of the northeast. An under-endowed institution like Connecticut College would be at a greater competitive disadvantage if it had to discount tuition to keep up with richer peers.

When they describe and promote their college, members of the Connecticut College community tend to overemphasize the generic aspects that can be found at any good small liberal arts college. There is a reflex-like tendency to rely on the fact that Connecticut is "one of those" New England colleges, part of a well-understood brand that needs little promotion. Connecticut College's approach has been like most of its peers in New England, the only region in the United States where there is a sense that simply being another excellent liberal arts college (even a generic one) is a sufficient brand identity. Were it not located in New England, Connecticut College's murky sense of what constitutes its institutional character and competitive advantage might spell trouble. Relying too much on the advantages of its region leaves Connecticut College a partially realized institution, one yet to mine the benefits that might accrue from determining and projecting its distinctive character. Perhaps if Connecticut communicated its distinctive qualities more clearly and boldly it might attract more ethnic and geographic diversity as well as more students there by choice rather than as an acceptable backup to other colleges deemed to be of higher academic quality and prestige.

Unlike Connecticut College, some colleges are intentionally less cognizant of their peers.[74] Such distinctive colleges develop an air about them manifest in a strong sense of community that can even border on a cult.[75] There is a palpable conviction at such institutions that it is a little universe set apart from the larger world and inhabited by the lucky few.[76] To some extent every college is its own unique universe. But Connecticut College, due to its associative qualities, original outward-looking mission, and strong historical ties to New London, has not become a cultish, hermetically sealed universe unto itself. The sealed universe characteristic of Burton Clark's distinctive college, exemplified especially by the now nearly defunct Antioch, is perhaps the one aspect of the distinctive college that is the most alien to Connecticut College.

Critics of Clark's notion of the distinctive college with a discernable organizational saga question its applicability beyond small, single-purpose colleges such as Antioch, Reed, and Swarthmore.[77] Rapidly growing or complex institutions, such as region-serving public universities, for example, are not fertile ground for an organizational saga to develop, because at such places it is difficult, nigh impossible, to get an overview that can be shaped into a unified whole.[78] And component colleges of a large university that construct their own organizational saga do so at the risk of conflicting with the larger parent entity.[79] There is an additional risk of developing a singularly distinctive institutional personality. Too strong an institutional personality can foster resistance to change, even when change is necessary for survival.[80] For example, some might argue that Connecticut College benefited in entering coeducation from its lack of an overly strong and distinctive personality. The majority at the College in 1968 believed that coeducation was necessary for Connecticut to survive at the institutional quality level to which it had become accustomed. Resistance to change, at that point, might have imperiled Connecticut College's mission to provide academic excellence. Unlike Vassar, which was steeped in women's college traditions and had arguably a better claim on the label distinctive college, Connecticut had less to unmake and reconstruct as it entered coeducation as a less than distinctive college.

Connecticut College's Evolving Mission

An institution's mission is a shared definition of its function and purpose.[81] The primary components of institutional mission are distinctiveness (is the purpose special, unique, or differentiated from others?), consensus (do members share a common definition of the mission?), and consistency (are programs and activities in line with the stated mission?).[82] Institutional missions are not static; they evolve imperfectly like expressions of a living faith.[83] The mission of an institution like Connecticut College is not a particular idea that holds constant, but rather an evolving sense of purpose that comes to be embraced over time.[84] Examining the evolution of mission at one institution, such as Connecticut College, provides a lens for understanding that particular college and others like it. This is so because mission distinguishes the activities that conform to institutional imperatives and those that do not.[85] Mission gives expression to the beliefs and values of an institution's members, providing a clear overall purpose that guides and reinforces priorities and produces greater institutional cohesion, showing what behaviors are valued, and guiding institutions toward what they should be doing.[86] A clear mission and a sense of shared purpose can inspire and motivate while also communicating an institution's characteristics, values, and history.[87]

Connecticut College's most recent mission statement, developed in 2006, is succinct: "Connecticut College educates students to put the liberal arts in action as citizens in a global society."[88] Accompanying Connecticut College's mission statement are six additional institutional core values. Those core values are: (1) academic excellence; (2) diversity, equity, and shared governance; (3) education of the whole person; (4) adherence to common ethical and moral standards; (5) community service and global citizenship; and (6) environmental stewardship.

Connecticut College's mission statement and core values are admirable and an attempt to express distinctiveness.[89] But globalism has become something of a cliché in higher education; it is nearly impossible to name a college that is not attempting to prepare its graduates for success in a global society.[90] Likewise, Connecticut College's emphasis on "putting the liberal arts into action" is not unlike Oberlin College's "learn, make a difference," Grinnell College's "strong tradition of social responsibility and action," and Wellesley College's mission to "provide an excellent liberal arts education for women who will make a difference in the world."[91] Arguably, Connecticut College's mission statement uses different words to say what most high quality liberal arts colleges are saying about themselves in the first decade of the 21st century.

Figure 9.3. View looking out from the college over Long Island Sound

Connecticut College has also restated its institutional vision as it approaches its centennial celebration in 2011.[92] The first component of the College's vision is the rigorous pursuit of knowledge. The third component is to provide a residential experience that gives students an opportunity to shape their campus community around a shared set of values.[93] Neither the first nor the third vision element is a surprise, given Connecticut College's original intention in 1911 to provide first-rate instruction in the liberal arts and its subsequent establishment of an honor code. What is notable is the second element of Connecticut's new institutional vision, which proclaims a commitment to educating the entire person.[94] In attempting to do so, Connecticut College states that it aspires to put the ethical, moral, and physical development of each student on the same plane as intellectual development.[95] This intention seems a dramatic departure from the College's founding mission and vision, which simply addressed intellectual development, preparation for useful service, and education for citizenship. There was no mention of ethical, moral, and physical development in 1915.[96] Is the emphasis on physical development a nod to the growth of athletics at Connecticut College post-coeducation and thus an example of an evolving rather than a static mission? Or was the entire person concept implicit in the College's original emphasis on cultivating service and citizenship? The evidence suggests the answer to those questions is perhaps. In either case, the entire person concept raises some historical mission tension for Connecticut College.

To make its vision for 2011 a reality, Connecticut College has embarked on a drive for $200 million in additional capital.[97] If the campaign is successful, the expected result is for more vibrant intellectual life on campus; stronger and more innovative education in the sciences; improved capacity for campus internationalization, including an "intercultural commons;" a stronger and more diverse faculty; revitalized athletic opportunities; and internship and advising programs that foster exploration beyond the classroom.[98] This all reads like standard fare as far as institutional aspirations go. No doubt Connecticut College will be stronger financially at the end of a $200 million fundraising campaign, but it is questionable whether it will be any more distinctive. Perhaps distinctiveness is less critical for Connecticut College than getting more resources to keep pace with its well-heeled and more prestigious New England small college peers.

Researchers who study mission in higher education assert that what mission does is more important than what mission says.[99] Mission is not necessarily what the college says about itself in publications or mission statements but rather what the college expects to do now and in the future.[100] Accordingly, colleges should worry less about crafting mission statements that say what the college purports to be and should focus more on actions that show what the college expects to do.[101] Effective missions show congruence between the stated mission and institutional actions.[102] For example, it is not enough for Connecticut College to espouse the value of environmental stewardship and develop a policy on sustainability. What matters more is the actual implementation of energy efficient processes and green building practices around its campus. Likewise, aspiring to a campus community with greater ethnic diversity is admirable, but actual progress in changing student and faculty demographics is what matters. Without supporting tangible actions, mission statements are just collections of platitudes.[103]

Well-crafted mission statements do not guarantee that an institution's programs and activities will be consistent with its stated mission. Mission statements sometimes are inconsistent with actions: witness the growing phenomenon of self-described liberal arts colleges where the majority of students major in vocational subjects like business administration.[104] Connecticut College is not one of those inconsistent institutions, thanks to Rosemary Park's efforts in the 1950s to excise the home economics major and secretarial courses from the curriculum.

Institutional missions in higher education exhibit striking continuity over time but must sometimes shift to fit changing circumstances—for example, Connecticut College's move to coeducation—in which case, the institution may struggle to redefine its purpose.[105] Salient missions are ones that external observers notice and then describe in the same terms used by the institution's students, faculty, and alumni.[106] It is worth asking whether external observers reading Connecticut's 2006 mission and value statements would recognize a differentiated purpose that sounds like the College's. Or would those observers consider Connecticut College's mission statement another generic example of a New England small liberal arts college? Moreover, in 1950, for example, was Connecticut College for Women's sense of self more congruent with how others saw it than it is now? The answers to those three questions seem to reside in the uncertain territory of "maybe"; and when it comes to mission, distinctive colleges do not inhabit uncertain territory.

Mission statements also have normative value; they exist because they are expected to in the realm of higher education.[107] Mission statements respond to the-everyone-is-doing-it-so-why-shouldn't-we impulse. Mission statements also have utility and political value because they signal to key external constituencies, such as benefactors, that the institution shares their values and goals.[108] For that reason, colleges such as Connecticut often clarify mission and vision statements prior to launching fundraising campaigns.[109]

A high level of mission agreement, founded on consensus and consistency, is generally the mark of a successful institution.[110] Effective institutions have a clear mission and show openness to opportunity.[111] At its founding in 1911, Connecticut College had the kind of clear mission agreement that provides an institution with purpose and meaning.[112] Later, in 1968 Connecticut College showed that it was open to opportunity and possibility when adopting coeducation and forever altering its mission. There is a risk, however, in too much mission agreement and consistency. Sometimes an unwavering mission can be an inhibiting factor that stalls adaptations to changing circumstances. The perils of mission consistency are especially pronounced when institutions limit themselves to choices consistent with their mission, despite a recognized need to adapt or change to survive.[113] Healthy institutions are generally not ones where resistance to change is the favored and unexamined default response. This was the potential institutional pothole Connecticut College avoided by examining the coeducation question care-fully and subsequently voting to preserve its founding commitment to academic quality by admitting men.

Future Challenges for Connecticut College

Lack of institutional wealth puts Connecticut College at a competitive disadvantage. Connecticut College has the smallest endowment in NESCAC: $225 million, compared to funds near or above $1 billion at Amherst, Bowdoin, Middlebury, and Williams.[114] Many in the Connecticut family consider the modest endowment the College's greatest weakness.[115] While there is widespread agreement that lack of institutional wealth has held the College back during its first hundred years, there is great optimism that the new century will bring Connecticut's financial resources up to the level of its peers. Because it has always been the poor cousin to other New England small liberal arts colleges, the fruits of a $200 million capital campaign will have a more transformative effect at a college like Connecticut. Having greater financial resources will enable Connecticut College to pay better faculty salaries, approach or achieve need blind admission, and upgrade facilities.

While most of its NESCAC peers have similar wish lists for larger endowments, Connecticut College's needs are especially acute because—as the endowment laggard—it is too tuition dependent for comfort. Within the last decade, for example, Connecticut College had to increase enrollment from 1,600 to 1,900 primarily for revenue reasons.[116] By most financial measures, be it faculty salaries or the capacity to afford need-blind admission, Connecticut College is below the median in NESCAC and also below the median when compared to the likes of Carleton, Grinnell, Haverford, Oberlin, Pomona, Reed, and Vassar.

On the other hand, some marvel at the level of quality and prominence Connecticut College has achieved despite its resource limitations.[117] Connecticut, for example, does not hurt for paying customers—annually receiving 4,000 to 5,000 applications for a freshman class of 475. Consistently, 60 percent of the College's students pay the full price and nearly 90 percent graduate.[118] Connecticut College's percentage of full-pay students matches most of its NESCAC peers, but is high when compared to national liberal arts colleges beyond the East Coast. Again, this is a function of a New England address and propinquity to centers of wealth in the Boston to Washington corridor. But Connecticut College can only progress so far relying on a plurality of well-heeled northeastern customers to offset its meager endowment. Demographic projections show stagnant future population growth for the northeast, as the United States' population center shifts south and west, and as the country moves toward a college-going ethnic minority majority. The colleges that successfully navigate those demographic changes will be the ones that establish a strong financial resource base and appeal to an ethnically diverse student population.

Connecticut officials recognize that strengthening the College's financial foundation is of paramount importance as the centennial celebration approaches. The appointment of Lee Higdon in 2006 as Connecticut College's tenth president signaled an emphasis on finances. Higdon forged a strong fundraising record as president of the College of Charleston and came to higher education following a career as an investment banker with Salomon Brothers. Initially, Higdon's appointment raised some eyebrows among faculty because his highest degree is an M.B.A. not a doctorate. Still, even faculty traditionalists at the College recognize—or at least are resigned to—the reality that Connecticut, as the poor cousin in NESCAC, needs a president who can go out and get resources to strengthen the academic program. Also on Higdon's side is the reality that American higher education has found that scholarly thinker-in-chief presidents do not always make effective fundraisers.

Higdon is following a president (Norman Fainstein) with greater resemblance to a thinker-in-chief. Fainstein—bringing three MIT degrees—joined Connecticut College in 2001 from Vassar, where he had been dean of faculty and a sociology professor. Fainstein's presidency restored calm and financial equilibrium to the campus after the freewheeling later years of Claire Gaudiani had left Connecticut College with a $10 million to $20 million budget deficit and controversial entanglements in downtown New London.[119] Fainstein righted the financial course of Connecticut and reestablished collegial decisionmaking, but he failed to convince enough alumni, trustees, and faculty that he had the right set of qualities to lead the College through a centennial fundraising campaign.[120] Thus, Fainstein's resignation was not unexpected, nor was it widely lamented.[121]

Since his arrival, Lee Higdon has energized Connecticut's campus and alumni. He has been a ubiquitous presence around campus, especially at athletic contests.[122] He openly speaks of building a student culture at Connecticut that fosters future alumni support of the College.[123] His efforts are working. The Connecticut College Class of 2007, for example, achieved a record level of participation (93 percent) in the class gift fund.[124] Attitudes within the Connecticut College family toward Higdon's leadership range from the opinion that he is the right president at the right time to "let's wait and see."[125] But even the wait-and-see camp seems guardedly optimistic. While faculty members tend toward the latter cautious view, Connecticut's alumni and senior staff are especially enthusiastic, seeing Higdon's past presidential experience as an asset, and applauding his emphasis on expanding the College's resource base.[126]

Another major challenge for Connecticut College is to increase the ethnic diversity of its community. Despite years of effort, Connecticut College has rarely enrolled an incoming class with more than 20 percent students of color in it—a track record that trails most of its New England liberal arts peers. Wesleyan University, for example (sometimes called "diversity university"), routinely enrolls one-third freshmen of color.[127] By contrast, the dominant image, and arguably the reality, of the Connecticut College student, is of a white affluent suburban north-easterner seeking a small New England college where s/he can get some intellectual polish while continuing to play sports, hang out with others clad in preppy apparel, and earn a degree from a "good school." To the extent that Connecticut's image tilts toward that of a country club where the students drive fancier cars than the faculty and staff, it can be off-putting to students of more modest means.[128] Many of the non-white students at Connecticut College likely come from towns and high schools quite different from the ones attended by most of its white students. Lower income students of color may be reluctant to enter what appears to be a privileged world where those who lack wealth are conspicuous.

Connecticut College has the will to increase the ethnic diversity of its campus community, as witnessed by recent appointments of individuals of color to its top two student affairs positions.[129] But when it comes to attracting students and faculty of color, Connecticut College (due to its low endowment) lacks the wallet to compete with wealthier rivals such as Amherst, Bowdoin, Vassar, and Wesleyan, all colleges that can offer need-blind admission, larger financial aid packages, and higher faculty salaries. Need-blind admission, especially, will be essential if Connecticut College wants to attract more of the talented students of color sought by its peer institutions. Higher salaries will help Connecticut College increase the ethnic diversity of its faculty and maintain the quality of its teaching and research core mission.

As Connecticut College faces future challenges, perhaps it will be unrealistic to expect that the College will want to, or need to, articulate a distinctive vision that sets it apart. Trying to do so might even be a dubious endeavor, given the generic shared aspects that knit together so many high quality small colleges in New England.[130] Some believe that it would be more fruitful for Connecticut to determine the distinctive qualities of the students who choose to study there rather than work to define what constitutes the College's institutional distinctiveness.[131] Certainly that is an approach Connecticut can take. But even if Connecticut College determines what kind of student it enrolls, the College may still gain from knowing if its signature type of student has made an intentional choice to be there, based on certain defining characteristics of the College that set it apart from others. However it chooses to approach the task of clarifying and articulating its difference, Connecticut College has much to benefit from shaking off its institutional inferiority complex, reveling in its own particular character, and recognizing its remarkably rapid ascent into the upper ranks of national liberal arts colleges. Perhaps the impending centennial celebration will enable Connecticut College to reconnect to—and more fully embrace—its history and thus take essential steps toward understanding, declaring, and owning the essential elements and strengths that distinguish it from its peers.[132]

Notes

1   Hartley, *A Call to Purpose*, 5.

2   Ibid.

3   Clark, *The Distinctive College*. See also Matthew Hartley & Lawrence Schall, "The Endless Good Argument: The Adaptation of Mission at Two Liberal Arts Colleges," *Planning for Higher Education* (June–August 2005), 5–11; Hartley.

4   Claire Gaudiani, interview by author 5 June 2007 (interview in possession of author). Also Lisa Brownell, interview by author 22 January 2007 (interview in possession of author).

5   Hartley, *A Call to Purpose*.

6   Ibid.

7   Ibid.

8   Clark, *The Distinctive College*. See also Hartley, *A Call to Purpose*.

9   Hartley & Schall, "The Endless Good Argument," 6. See also Ellen E. Chaffee, "Successful Strategic Management in Small Private Colleges," *The Journal of Higher Education* (March–April 1984), 212–241.

10 Ibid. See also Clark, *The Distinctive College*.

11 Ibid.

12 Clark, "The Organizational Saga in Higher Education," 178–184. See also Clark, *The Distinctive College*.

13 Burton R. Clark, "Belief and Loyalty in College Organization," *The Journal of Higher Education* (June 1971), 499–515.

14 Ibid.

15 Clark, *The Distinctive College* and "Belief and Loyalty in College Organization." I know Reed College well, having served as its dean of admission since January 2002. Clark's chapters on Reed still ring true.

16 Ibid.

17 Ibid. See also Clark, "The Organizational Saga in Higher Education."

18 Clark, "Belief and Loyalty in College Organization."

19 Clark, *The Distinctive College* and "Belief and Loyalty in College Organization."

20 Connecticut College's notion of putting the liberal arts into action echoes Sykes' and Buell's views that Connecticut College for Women would prepare women to be useful in the world.

21 Clark, *The Distinctive College*, "Belief and Loyalty in College Organization," and "The Organizational Saga in Higher Education."

22 Joanne Martin, Martha S. Feldman, Mary Jo Hatch & Sim B. Sitkin, "The Uniqueness Paradox in Organizational Stories," *Administrative Science Quarterly* (September 1983), 438–453.

23 George D. Kuh, "Ethos: Its Influence on Student Learning," *Liberal Education* (Fall 1993), 22–32.

24 Frederick H. Sykes, "Students of Dear C.C.," *Connecticut College News* (June 20, 1917). Connecticut College Archives, Frederick Sykes File.

25 "College Students and Faculty Provide "The Finest Preschool Education."" Accessed 21 December, 2007 from http://aspen.conncoll.edu/camelweb/alumni/news/?id1=3922

26 "Connecticut College Mission Statement," *Connecticut College Annual Report, 1986-1987* (New London, CT: Connecticut College, 1987). See also "Connecticut College Mission Statement" (Revised October 2004), *Connecticut College 2005-2007 Catalog* (New London, CT: Connecticut College, 2005), 3–4.

27 Vassar College, by contrast, mentions women's education explicitly in its institutional mission, stating that it was "founded in 1861 to provide young women an education equal to that once available only to men, the college has since 1969 opened its doors to both men and women on

terms of equality." *Vassar College Catalogue* (Poughkeepsie, NY: Vassar College, 2007). Some wonder whether forgetting the women's college past at Connecticut has been intentional— Laurie Deredita (31 July 2007), Norman Fainstein (24 July 2007), and Frances Hoffmann (12 June 2007), interviews by author (interviews in possession of author).

28 Birnbaum, *How Colleges Work*. See also Warren Bryan Martin, "Adaptiveness and Distinctiveness," *Journal of Higher Education* (March-April 1984), 286–296; and William G. Tierney, "Organizational Culture in Higher Education: Defining the Essentials," *The Journal of Higher Education* (January-February 1988), 2–21.

29 Martin, Feldman, Hatch & Sitkin, "The Uniqueness Paradox in Organizational Stories."

30 George Willauer, interview by author 23 April 2007 (interview in possession of author). See also William Trufant Foster, "Reed College: Neither Hallowed nor Hampered by Tradition," from an unpublished biography (1950), Reed College Library, Special Collections; will of Amanda Reed, 27th Clause, Creating Reed Institute (4 September 1901), Reed College Library, Special Collections. Amanda Reed's will states that Reed College must "forever be and remain free from sectarian influence, regulation or control, permitting those who may seek its benefits to affiliate with such religious societies as their consciences may dictate"; Robert Knapp, "Religion at Reed," Draft Statement for Reed College Web Site (25 July 2007), in possession of author; "Pitzer College, History and Mission." Accessed 26 March 2008 from http://www.pitzer.edu/about/mission.asp.

31 George D. Kuh, "Appraising the Character of a College," *Journal of Counseling & Development* (July/August 1993), 661–668.

32 Richard Goodwin to author (6 April 2007).

33 Fainstein interview.

34 Ibid.

35 Catherine Phinizy, "The Bighearted Millionaire," *Connecticut College Alumni Magazine* (Spring 2000), 22–27.

36 Hoffmann interview. Also Frances Hoffmann, "Women, Men and Higher Education" (Sykes Lecture, Connecticut College Reunion) (2 June 2006); Frances Hoffmann, "CCSRE Comments on 2006 Sykes Lecture," (April 2007). Both papers provided to author by Hoffmann.

37 Sally Schwager (6 May 2007) and Margaret "Peggy" Sheridan (2 May 2007), interviews by author (interviews in possession of author). Schwager is a professor at the Harvard Graduate School of Education, where she teaches a course entitled "The History of Women's Education in the United States." In addition to our conversation, Professor Shwager shared a syllabus for the Fall 2006 edition of that course.

38 Sheridan interview.

39 Fainstein interview. Also Hoffmann, "Women, Men and Higher Education;" Hoffmann, "CCSRE Comments on 2006 Sykes Lecture."

40 Brownell interview. Also Thyra Briggs, interview by author 14 June 2007 (interview in possession of author).

41 Ibid.

42 Marion Doro (23 April 2007), Jeanette Hersey (22 January 2007), Jeff Oshen (1 May 2007), interviews by author (interviews in possession of author). Also Willauer interview.

43 Philip Jordan, interview by author 13 May 2007 (interview in possession of author). Also Doro interview.

44 Interviewees not identified to protect their identity. Also, Lynda Munro provided the "red-headed stepsister" analogy, although she was not one of those labeling Connecticut's history as that of a second-rate institution.

45 Interviewees not identified to protect their identity.

46 Ibid.

47 Finishing school is a misunderstood term, unfortunately used to put down women's colleges. True finishing schools were not senior colleges but rather pre-college institutions for wealthy girls, not intending to study at college. Finishing schools bestowed the right social cache and provided training in social deportment. In its earliest years, Los Angeles' Marlborough School was an example of a finishing school, according to Joyce Antler's "The Educational Biography of Lucy Sprague Mitchell: A Case Study in the History of Women's Higher Education," in *Women and Higher Education in American History*, ed. John Mack Faragher and Florence Howe (New York: W.W. Norton, 1988), 43–63, 47. For example, when Lucy Sprague Mitchell entered Radcliffe, she became only the second Marlborough graduate before 1900 to attend college.

48 Helen L. Horowitz, *The Power and Passion of M. Carey Thomas* (Champaign, Illinois: University of Illinois Press, 1999), 385.

49 Katharine Blunt to Dr. Albert Noyes, Jr. (18 December, 1939).

50 Ibid.

51 Sources (several) not identified by request.

52 Briggs, Brownell, Hersey, Munro, and Oshen interviews. Also Patricia Carey (23 January 2007), Pamela Herrup (10 July 2007), Martha Merrill (22 January 2007), and Brian Rogers (5 December 2006 and 22 January 2007), interviews by author (interviews in possession of author).

53 The individuals who relayed this information asked to remain anonymous.

54 Ibid.

55 Kuh, "Ethos: Its Influence on Student Learning" and "Assessing the Character of a College."

56 Birnbaum, *How Colleges Work*.

57 Tierney, "Organizational Culture in Higher Education."

58 Chaffee, "Successful Strategic Management in Small Private Colleges."

59 Birnbaum, *How Colleges Work*.

60 Connecticut College's "Strategic Priorities for the Second Century: Draft 8" (February 2, 2007), 38–39.

61 Elizabeth Cheney (9 May 2007), Anthony and Elizabeth Enders (5 June 2007), Charlie Luce (21 April 2007), and Agnes Underwood (26 October 2007), interviews by author (interviews in possession of author). Also Kaplan, Munro, and Willauer interviews.

62 Jane Bredeson, interview by author 23 January 2007 (interview in possession of author). Also Hersey interview. These regional characterizations are stereotypes to be sure.

63 Briggs and Underwood interviews.

64 Several current and emeritus faculty members who requested anonymity.

65 The "Middlebury syndrome" is explained in Dorothy Desiderato's "Recurring Themes in Alumnae Coeducation Questionnaire Comments" (11 February 1969). Connecticut College Archives, Coeducation File.

66 Sources (several) not identified by request.

67 Frances Hoffman, Joan Chrisler, Dirk Held, Philip Gedeon, Manuel Lizarralde, and Frances Shields, "Working Group Report on Coeducation from Report of the Presidential Commission on a Pluralistic Community at Connecticut College" (8 August 2003). Accessed 13 December 2006 from http://www.conncoll.edu/people/president-emeritus/pluralism/html/ index.htm

68 Linda Eisenmann (11 June 2007), Claire Gaudiani (5 June 2007), Eric Kaplan (6 June 2007), interviews by author (interviews in possession of author). Also Merrill interview.

69 Bredeson, Carey, Eisenmann, Hersey, Kaplan, Luce, and Rogers interviews. Also Torrey Fenton, interview by author 24 April 2007 (interview in possession of author).

70 Tierney, "Organizational Culture in Higher Education."

71 Ibid.

72   Birnbaum, *How Colleges Work.*

73   Lee Higdon, interview by author 24 April 2007 (interview in possession of author). Also Cheney, Fainstein, Gaudiani, Luce, and Munro interviews. Cheney '92 is associate director of alumni relations at Connecticut and Munro '76 is a trustee.

74   Clark, *The Distinctive College.*

75   Clark, *The Distinctive College*, "Belief and Loyalty in College Organization," and "The Organizational Saga in Higher Education."

76   Ibid.

77   Richard C. Richardson, Jr., "Belief and Loyalty in College Organizations: Comment," *The Journal of Higher Education* (June 1971), 516–520.

78   Ibid.

79   Ibid.

80   John R. Thelin, "Life and Learning in Southern California: Private Colleges in the Popular Culture," *History of Education Quarterly* (Spring 1975), 111–117.

81   Barbara Sporn, "Managing University Culture: An Analysis of the Relationship Between Institutional Culture and Management Approaches," *Higher Education* (July 1996), 41-61.

82   Peter T. Ewell, "Institutional Characteristics and Faculty/Administrator Perceptions of Outcomes: An Exploratory Analysis," *Research in Higher Education*, 30 (1989), 113–136. See also Nancy Fjortoft & John C. Smart, "Enhancing Organizational Effectiveness: The Importance of Culture Type and Mission Agreement," *Higher Education* (June 1994), 429–447.

83   Hartley, *A Call to Purpose.*

84   Ibid.

85   Lawrence M. Schall, "Swarthmore College: The Evolution of an Institutional Mission" (Ed. D. dissertation, University of Pennsylvania, 2003). See also Christopher C. Morphew & Matthew Hartley, "Mission Statements: A Thematic Analysis of Rhetoric Across Institutional Type," *The Journal of Higher Education* (May/June 2006), 456–471.

86   Hartley, *A Call to Purpose.* See also Kuh, "Ethos: Its Influence on Student Learning" and Hartley and Schall, "The Endless Good Argument."

87   Morphew & Hartley, "Mission Statements: A Thematic Analysis of Rhetoric Across Institutional Type."

88   "Connecticut College's Strategic Priorities for the Second Century: Draft 8" (February 2, 2007), 38.

89   Ibid, 39.

90   A survey of mission statements found on college web sites, for example, shows that Dickinson College and Middlebury College seek to "engage the world," Macalester College's mission puts a "special emphasis on internationalism," Clark University seeks to educate "contributing citizens of the world," and Amherst College harkens back to its 1821 motto, Terras irradient: "Let them give light to the world." Accessed 2 February 2008 from http//www.dickinson.edu/; http://middlebury.edu/academics/catalogs/catalog/about_midd/m...; http://www.macalester. edu/about.html; http://www.clarku.edu/aboutclark/mission.htm; https:cms.amherst.edu/ aboutamherst/mission/node/7854

91   The Oberlin College view book and stationery from 1998-2005 displayed the slogan "learn, make a difference": "Core values of Grinnell College." Accessed 2 February 2008 from http://www.grinnell.edu/offices/president/missionstatement/core/; "Wellesley College: The College." Accessed 2 February 2008 from http://www.wellesley.edu/Welcome/college.html.

92   Connecticut College, "Strategic Priorities for the Second Century: Draft 8," 3, 38–39.

93   Ibid.

94   Ibid.

95 Ibid.

96 *Connecticut College for Women: First Annual Announcement, 1915–1916.*

97 "Connecticut College's Strategic Priorities for the Second Century: Draft 8," 8–10. "Connecticut College Launches $200 million Campaign" (27 October 2008). Accessed 2 April 2009 from http://aspen.conncoll.edu/news/4701.cfm?var1=campaign

98 Ibid, 12, 37.

99 Richard Chait, "College Mission Statements," *Science* (7 September 1979), 957. See also Hartley, *A Call to Purpose.*

100 Kuh, "Appraising the Character of a College."

101 Chait, "College Mission Statements."

102 Fjortoft & Smart, "Enhancing Organizational Effectiveness." See also Chait, "College Mission Statements" and Morphew & Hartley, "Mission Statements: A Thematic Analysis of Rhetoric Across Institutional Type."

103 Chait, "College Mission Statements."

104 Delucchi, 'Liberal Arts' Colleges and the Myth of Uniqueness," 414–426.

105 Ibid.

106 Kuh, "Appraising the Character of a College."

107 Morphew & Hartley, "Mission Statements: A Thematic Analysis of Rhetoric Across Institutional Type."

108 Ibid.

109 "Connecticut College's Strategic Priorities for the Second Century: Draft 8."

110 Fjortoft & Smart, "Enhancing Organizational Effectiveness."

111 Martin, "Adaptation and Distinctiveness."

112 Fjortoft & Smart, "Enhancing Organizational Effectiveness."

113 Ibid. See also Birnbaum, *How Colleges Work.*

114 "2007 NACUBO Endowment Study," National Association of College and University Business Officers, (2008). See also "785 College and University Endowments," *The Chronicle of Higher Education* (1 February 2008), A14–A17.

115 Herrup, Kaplan, Luce, Munro, Sheridan, and Underwood interviews. Also James Garvey (19 January 2007) and Dirk Held (23 April 2007), interviews by author (interviews in possession of author).

116 Held, Luce, and Merrill interviews.

117 Eisenmann, Higdon, Munro, Rogers, and Sheridan interviews.

118 Higher Education Data Sharing Consortium (HEDS) statistics on financial aid recipients and graduation rates for Connecticut College.

119 Bredeson, Held, Munro, and Rogers interviews.

120 Sources not identified by respect.

121 Ibid.

122 Stan DeCoster, "Keeping up with Lee Higdon," *CC: Connecticut College Alumni Magazine* (Fall 2006), 20–25.

123 Higdon interview.

124 Eric Cardenas, "Commencement May 20, 2007 'Dream Big,'" *Connecticut College Magazine* (Spring 2007). See also Gary Ng, "Alumni Giving Hits New Record," *The College Voice* (28 September 2007), 1, 4. Ng emphasizes the "inspirational leadership of President Lee Higdon" in motivating the Class of 2007 to surpass the previous record of 73% participation set by the Class of 1995. More recently, Mandy Barrett, president of Connecticut College's Class of 2008, challenged her class to surpass the Class of 2007's 93% gift participation rate—see "Giv-

ing Back." Accessed 21 December 2007 from http://www.conncoll.edu/advancement/seniors/news.html

125 Numerous interviewees who asked to remain anonymous.

126 Carey, Herrup, Merrill, and Munro interviews.

127 "Wesleyan University," in *Students' Guide to Colleges: The Definitive Guide to America's top 100 Schools,* ed. Jordan Goldman and Colleen Buyers (New York: Penguin Books, 2005), 585–592.

128 Brownell, Carey, and Merrill interviews.

129 Mary Howard, "Bengochea Joins CC Community in a Path-breaking Role, *CC: Connecticut College Alumni Magazine* (Summer 2006), 8. See also Lauren Morrow, "Student and Residential Life Get New Staffers," *The College Voice* (14 September 2007), 1,3. Dean of College Community Armando Bengochea is a native of Cuba and Dean of Students Jocelyn Briddell is African American.

130 Higdon interview.

131 Carey interview.

132 Merrill interview.

BIBLIOGRAPHY

"ADF in Retrospect," *Connecticut College Alumni Magazine* 53 (Winter 1978), 5–8.

Scott Alexander, Alex Mroszcyk-McDonald, Philip Gedeon, John Potter, Frances Shields, Dena Wallerson, and Leslie Williams, "Working Group Report on Student Recruitment and Retention, Connecticut College," (8 August 2003). Accessed 13 December 2006 from http://www.conncoll.edu/people/president-emeritus/pluralism/html/index.htm

David F. Allmendinger, Jr., "Mount Holyoke Students Encounter the Need for Life Planning, 1837–1850," *History of Education Quarterly*, (Spring 1979), 27–46.

David F. Allmendinger, Jr., "New England Students and the Revolution in Higher Education," *History of Education Quarterly* (Winter 1971), 381–389.

David F. Allmendinger, Jr., *Paupers and Scholars: The Transformation of Student Life in Nineteenth-Century New England* (New York: St. Martin's, 1975).

Oakes Ames, *The Annual Report of the President, 1976* (New London, CT: Connecticut College, 1976).

Oakes Ames, *The Annual Report of the President, 1981–1982* (New London, CT: Connecticut College, 1982).

Oakes Ames, *The Annual Report of the President 1984/85* (New London, CT: Connecticut College, 1985).

Oakes O. Ames, *Connecticut College: Contributing to a Changing Society* (New York: Newcomen Society of America, 1987).

Cindy Anderson, "A House Divided: A Story About Eminent Domain," *Yankee Magazine* (January/February, 2007).

Jack Anderson, "American Dance Festival—Mecca has Moved South," *New York Times* (18 June 1978).

Joyce Antler, "After College What?": New Graduates and the Family Claim," *American Quarterly* (Autumn 1980), 409–434.

Joyce Antler, "The Educational Biography of Lucy Sprague Mitchell: A Case Study in the History of Women's Higher Education," in *Women and Higher Education in American History*, ed. John Mack Faragher and Florence Howe (New York: W.W. Norton, 1988), 43–63.

Rima D. Apple, "Liberal Arts or Vocational Training?: Home Economics Education for Girls," in *Rethinking Home Economics: Women and the History of a Profession*, ed. Sarah Stage and Virginia B. Vincenti (Ithaca, NY: Cornell University Press, 1997), 79-95.

Helen S. Astin, "Interview with Rosemary Park," in *The Higher Education of Women: Essays in Honor of Rosemary Park*, ed. Helen S. Astin & Werner Z. Hirsch (New York: Praeger Publishers, 1978), xiv–xxvii.

Charles D. Atkins to Frederick Sykes (17 August 1916). CCA, Frederick Sykes File.

George Avery, "Early Historical Highlights," in *The Connecticut College Arboretum: Its First Fifty Years* (New London: Connecticut College, 1982), 3–8.

Kathleen R. Babbitt, "Legitimizing Nutrition Education: The Impact of the Great Depression," in *Rethinking Home Economics: Women and the History of a Profession*, ed. Sarah Stage and Virginia B. Vincenti (Ithaca, NY: Cornell University Press, 1997), 145–162.

Mandy Barrett, "Giving Back." Accessed 21 December 2007 from http://www.conncoll.edu/advancement/seniors/news.html.

Dorothea Bartlett to Rosemary Park (23 January 1957). CCA, Home Economics File.

Julianne Basinger, "Connecticut President's Golden Parachute Angers Faculty Members," *Chronicle of Higher Education* (22 November 2002), 31.

Julianne Basinger, "A Promoter of Town-Gown Cooperation Finds Development May Be Her Undoing," *The Chronicle of Higher Education* (2 June 2000), A41–42.

Julianne Basinger, "Under Fire From Students and Professors, President of Connecticut College Quits," *The Chronicle of Higher Education* (27 October 2000), A40.

Carolyn Battista, "The Holleran Center at 10," *CC: Connecticut College Magazine* (Fall 2006), 28–31.

Annette K. Baxter, "Preface," in *The Clubwoman as Feminist: True Womanhood Redefined, 1868-1914*, ed. Karen J. Blair (New York: Holmes and Meier, 1980), xi–xv.

William J. Bennett, *The De-Valuing of America: The Fight for our Culture and our Children* (New York: Summit Books, 1992).

Judy Benson, "Conn Trustee Dayton Throws Strong Support to Gaudiani," *The Day* (13 May 2000).

Judy Benson, "NLDC Gets Praise, Criticism for Plan at Public Meetings," *The Day* (27 April 1998).

Judy Benson, "Some Faculty Seek to Ouster Gaudiani," *The Day* (9 May 2000).

Lee Benson, Ira Harkavy, and John Puckett, *Dewey's Dream: Universities and Democracies in an Age of Education Reform* (Philadelphia: Temple University Press, 2007).

Ellen Hofheimer Bettmann and Claire L. Gaudiani, "A Talk Between Presidents," *Connecticut College Alumni Magazine* (Summer 1988), 1–7.

Richard Birdsall, "Work, Love and the College Mystique," *Connecticut College Alumni Magazine* (Winter 1978), 23–24.

Robert Birnbaum, *How Colleges Work: The Cybernetics of Academic Organizations and Leadership* (San Francisco, CA: Jossey-Bass Publishers, 1988).

Robert Birnbaum, "The Latent Functions of the Academic Senate: Why Senates Do Not Work But Will Not Go Away." *Journal of Higher Education* (July/August 1989), 423–443.

Karen J. Blair, *The Clubwoman as Feminist: True Womanhood Redefined, 1868–1914* (New York: Holmes and Meier, 1980).

J. Bleak, "Charging Into the Market: Governance Challenges Created by the Fit and Fitness of Commercial Activities," in *The Shifting Frontiers of Academic Decision Making: Responding to New Priorities, Following New Pathways*, ed. Peter D. Eckel (Westport, CT: Praeger, 2006), 35–54.

Allan Bloom, *The Closing of the American Mind: How Higher Education has Failed Democracy and Impoverished the Souls of Today's Students* (New York: Simon and Schuster, 1987).

Ruth Bloomer, "Ten Years of Modern Dance," *Connecticut College News* 3 (February 1958), 3–4.

Katharine Blunt, "Address at Connecticut College for Women's Twenty-fifth Anniversary Celebration" (12 & 13 October 1940) in Warrine Eastburn, "Miss Katharine Blunt Biographical Material," 8. CCA, Katharine Blunt File.

Katharine Blunt, "Inaugural Address" (16 May 1930) in Warrine Eastburn, "Miss Katharine Blunt Biographical Material," 3. CCA, Katharine Blunt File.

Katharine Blunt to Dr. Albert Noyes, Jr. (18 December, 1939).

Katharine Blunt, "Unique Characteristics of Connecticut College" (10 May 1941). CCA, Katharine Blunt File.

"Board Backs Ames on his Festival Stand," *The Day* (6 December 1976).

Louise S. Boas, *Women's Education Begins: The Rise of the Women's Colleges* (Norton, MA: Wheaton College Press, 1935).

Lee G. Bolman and Terence E. Deal, *Reframing Organizations: Artistry, Choice, and Leadership* (San Francisco: Jossey-Bass, 2003).

Daniel J. Boorstin, "Higher Education in Place of Higher Learning," in *The Americans: the Colonial Experience* (New York: Vintage Books, 1958), 178–184.

Daniel J. Boorstin, "Culture with Many Capitals: The Booster College," In *The Americans: The National Experience* (New York: Vintage Books, 1965), 152–161.

Daniel J. Boorstin, "A Higher Learning for All," in *The Americans: The Democratic Experience* (New York: Vintage Books, 1973), 478–490.

Raymond K. Bordner, "Shain Optimistic About College's Decision," *The Day* (18 January 1969), 16.

William G. Bowen and Sarah A Levin, *Reclaiming the Game: College Sports and Educational Values* (Princeton, NJ: Princeton University Press, 2003).

David Breneman, *Liberal Arts Colleges: Thriving, Surviving, or Endangered?* (Washington, DC, Brookings Institution, 1994).

"Bring Back the ADF," *Pundit* (18 November 1976).

Trish Brink. "Claire L. Gaudiani to Step Down as President of Connecticut College," (13 October 2000). Accessed 28 March 2007 from http://www.conncoll.edu/news/articles/buildarticle. cgi?971461467.txt).

Lisa Broujas, "The Success of Coeducation at Conn," *The Connecticut College Alumni Magazine* (Summer 1988), 10–14.

John S. Brubacher & Willis Rudy, *Higher Education in Transition: A History of American Colleges and Universities* (3rd ed.) (New York: Harper & Row, 1997).

Colin S. Buell, "Appeal to Fellow Graduates of Yale on Behalf of Connecticut College for Women's Endowment Committee" (March 1914). CCA, Colin Buell File.

Colin S. Buell, "Appeal to the People of Connecticut and Statement of Policy by the Trustees of Thames College" (3 June 1911). CCA, Colin Buell File.

Colin S. Buell to Edward D. Robbins (21 April 1911). CCA, Colin Buell File.

Colin S. Buell, "Letter of Appeal to Fellow Graduates of Yale" (March 1914). CCA, Colin Buell File.

Colin S. Buell, "New London Should Try to Bring College Here" *The Day*, (13 September 1910). CCA, Colin Buell File.

Colin Buell, "Rome Was Not Built in a Day" (1915). CCA, Colin Buell File.

Colin S. Buell, "Thames College, a College for Women to be Located in New London, Connecticut" (undated, 1911?), 4–5. CCA, Colin Buell File.

Colin S. Buell, "Thames College: An Account of the Struggle by a Yale Graduate to Found a Woman's College in Connecticut," *Yale Alumni Weekly* (21 April 1911), 751. CCA, Colin Buell File.

Colin S. Buell, "Thames College, A College for Women to be Located in New London, Connecticut" (no date, estimated 1911). CCA, Colin Buell File.

Bulletin of Connecticut College, 1957–1958 (New London, CT: Connecticut College, 15 April 1958).

Bulletin of Connecticut College: Announcements for 1953–1954 (New London, CT: Connecticut College, 30 March 1953).

Bulletin of Connecticut College 1961 (New London, CT: Connecticut College, 15 April 1961).

Bulletin of Connecticut College: Catalogue Number 1962–1963, Announcements for 1963-1964 (New London, CT: Connecticut College, 15 April 1963).

Bulletin of Connecticut College School of Dance, Tenth Season, July 8 to August 18, 1957 (New London, CT: Connecticut College, 1957). CCA, American Dance Festival (ADF) File.

Wallace Buttrick to Elizabeth Wright (25 March 1910) CCA, Elizabeth Wright File.

Terry Byrne, "New London's Dance Dilemma," *New York Times* (25 September 1977).

"Calls it First Woman's Century," *Buffalo Courier* (31 March 1913). CCA, Frederick Sykes File.

"A Canadian President for Connecticut College" (no author, no date) 31. CCA, Frederick Sykes File.

Eric Cardenas, "Commencement May 20, 2007 'Dream Big,'" *Connecticut College Magazine* (Spring 2007).

Caroline Black Garden (Brochure) (New London: Connecticut College Arboretum, Summer 2001).

Allen Carroll, "The Art of the Feud," *Connecticut College Alumni Magazine* (Winter 1978), 2–4, 26.

Jean Kohlberger Carter '43 to Rosemary Park (22 January 1957). CCA, Home Economics File.

Egbert A. Case to Elizabeth C. Wright (5 June 1911). CCA, Elizabeth Wright File.

Catalogue of William Smith College 1918–1919 (Geneva, New York: Hobart College, 1918). HWS Archives.

Tim Cavanaugh, "Endgame in New London, or, Another Successful Five-year Plan," *Reasononline* (8 June 2006). Accessed 28 March 2007 from http://www.reason.com/news/printer/117322.

Ellen E. Chaffee, "Successful Strategic Management in Small Private Colleges," *The Journal of Higher Education* (March-April 1984), 212–241.

Richard Chait, "College Mission Statements," *Science* (7 September 1979), 957.

Margaret S. Chaney to Faculty Instruction Committee (1 January 1946). CCA, Home Economics File.

Margaret S. Chaney to Home Economics Alumnae (14 January 1957). CCA, Home Economics File.

Margaret Chaney to Katharine Blunt (24 October 1940). CCA, Home Economics File.

Margaret S. Chaney to President Park, (1 March 1948). CCA, Home Economics File.

Margaret S. Chaney to Rosemary Park (29 January 1953). CCA, Home Economics File.

Margaret B. Chaney, "Memorial Resolution—Miss Elizabeth C. Wright" (February 1963).

Burton R. Clark, *The Distinctive College: Antioch, Reed & Swarthmore* (Chicago: Aldine Publishing Company, 1970).

Burton R. Clark, "Belief and Loyalty in College Organization," *The Journal of Higher Education* (June 1971), 499–515.

Burton R. Clark, "The Organizational Saga in Higher Education," *Administrative Science Quarterly* (June 1972), 178–184.

Dan Clem, "Living Laboratory: The Connecticut College Arboretum Celebrates Its 75th Year," *CC: Connecticut College Magazine* (Summer 2006), 32–37.

Geraldine Joncich Clifford, "Women's Liberation and Women's Professions: Reconsidering the Past, Present, and Future," in *Women and Higher Education in American History*, ed. Faragher and Howe (New York: W.W. Norton, 1988), 165–182.

"Coeducation: A New Role for the College," *CC News* (Winter 1969). CCA, Coeducation File.

Dorothy Chapman Cole '44 to Rosemary Park (19 January 1957). CCA, Home Economics File.

"The College in the Community: Students Carry on Work at Settlement House," *Connecticut College News* (1956).

"College Founder, Honorary Trustee Dies at Age of 93," *Conn Census* (8 May 1958). CCA, Frances Scudder Williams File.

"College Plans Program to Offset Festival Loss," *The Day* (25 February 1978).

"College President Sykes Asked to Resign; May Fight Trustees' Attempt to Remove Him," *The Day* (14 March 1917).

"The College Prexy Talks About 40 Men in a Girls' School," *Detroit Free Press* (3 December 1969). CCA, Coeducation File.

"College Students and Faculty Provide "the Finest Preschool Education."" Accessed 21 December, 2007 from http://aspen.conncoll.edu/camelweb/alumni/news/?id1=3922.

"College Trustees Voted to Secure Eggleston Land," *The Day* (22 September 1913).

"The Commentator's Column," *The New London Telegraph* (22 March 1917).

"The Commentator's Column: Being Personal Opinions on Events, Conditions and People Here and Elsewhere," *New London Telegraph* (Fall 1917).

"Commerce and Culture: Architecture and Society on New London's State Street," *CC: Connecticut College Magazine* (Fall 2005), 15.

"Conflict at Connecticut College," *The Day* (8 June 2000).

Walter W. Conklin, "Would Reorganize College Trustees," Letter to the Editor, *The Day* (19 March 1917).

"Connecticut and Wesleyan Plan Resident Student Exchange," *CC News* (Spring 1968).

Connecticut College Announcement 1917–1918 (New London, CT: Connecticut College for Women, 20 June 1917).

Connecticut College Announcement 1918–1919 (New London, CT: Connecticut College for Women, 29 March 1918).

Connecticut College Arboretum (Brochure) (New London: Connecticut College, 2004).

Connecticut College Arboretum Annual Report 2004. (New London: Connecticut College Arboretum, 2004).

Connecticut College Bulletin, 1925–1926 (New London, CT: Connecticut College for Women, 30 March 1925).

Connecticut College Bulletin, 1939–1940 (New London, CT: Connecticut College for Women, 30 March 1939).

Connecticut College Bulletin 1950 (New London, CT: Connecticut College for Women, 1950).

Connecticut College Bulletin, 1959 (New London, CT: Connecticut College, 1959).

Connecticut College Bulletin 1974–75 (New London, CT: Connecticut College, September 1974).

Connecticut College Catalog for 1924–1925 (New London, CT: Connecticut College for Women, 30 March 1925).

Connecticut College 2005–2007 Catalog (New London, CT: Connecticut College, 2005).

The Connecticut College for Women (New London, CT: Connecticut College for Women, 1911).

Connecticut College for Women, Preliminary Announcement: Foundation, Organization, Site, and Plans (New London, CT: Connecticut College for Women, 1914).

Connecticut College for Women First Annual Announcement, 1915–1916 (New London, CT: Connecticut College for Women, 1915).

"Connecticut College Mission Statement," *Connecticut College Annual Report, 1986–1987* (New London, CT: Connecticut College, 1987).

"Connecticut College Mission Statement" (Amended 24 February 1990 and 7 December 1996).

"Connecticut College Mission Statement" (Amended 24 February 1990 and 7 December 1996), *Connecticut College Catalog, 1999–2001* (New London, CT: Connecticut College, 1999), 4.

"Connecticut College Mission Statement" (Revised October 2004), *Connecticut College 2005–2007 Catalog* (New London, CT: Connecticut College, 2005), 3–4.

"Connecticut College News Office Press Release" (25 June 1970). CCA, Coeducation File.

"Connecticut College News Office Press Release" (10 November 1976).

"Connecticut College Office of Press Relations" (15 February 1963). CCA, Elizabeth Wright File.

"Connecticut College Press Release" (February 1969). CCA, Coeducation File.

Connecticut College, Report of the President, 1977–1978 (New London, CT: Connecticut College, 1978).

"Connecticut College's Strategic Priorities for the Second Century: Draft 8," (2 February 2007).

Jill Kerr Conway, "Perspectives on the History of Women's Education in the United States," *History of Education Quarterly* (Spring 1974), 1–12.

"Core values of Grinnell College." Accessed from http://www.grinnell.edu/offices/president/missionstatement/core/

John W. Creswell, *Educational Research: Planning, Conducting, and Evaluating Quantitative and Qualitative Research* (Upper Saddle River, NJ: Pearson/Merrill Prentice Hall, (2nd ed.) 2005).

The Day (6 December 1976). CCA, ADF File.

Margery W. Davies, *Woman's Place is at the Typewriter: Office Work and Office Workers, 1870-1930* (Philadelphia, PA: Temple University Press, 1982).

A Decade of Achievement at Connecticut College (New London, CT: Connecticut College, 1999).

Jefferson Decker, "President and Planner," *University Business* (March 1999), 34–39.

Stan DeCoster, "An Apostle Charges Ahead," *The Day* (6 June 1999).

Stan DeCoster, "Keeping up with Lee Higdon, *CC: Connecticut College Alumni Magazine* (Fall 2006), 20–25.

Michael Delucchi, "Liberal Arts" Colleges and the Myth of Uniqueness," *The Journal of Higher Education* (July-August 1997), 414–426.

Dorothy Desiderato, "Recurring Themes in Alumnae Coeducation Questionnaire Comments," (11 February 1969). Connecticut College Archives, Coeducation File.

Dorothy Desiderato, "Supplementary Data; Comments from Alumnae on Questionnaires About Coeducation" (13 February 1969). CCA, Coeducation File.

Daniel DeSouza, Julie Kozaczka, Nicole Lew, Abigail A. Van Slyck, "Home Away From Home: Dormitory Design at Connecticut College," Exhibition, 6 December 2004 –7 January 2005. CCA, Campus Architecture File.

Sarah Jane Deutsch, "From Ballots to Breadlines," in *No Small Courage: A History of Women in the United States*, ed. Nancy F. Cott (New York: Oxford University Press, 2000), 413–472.

John Dewey, "My Pedagogic Creed," *School Journal* (January 1897), 77–80.

John DiBiaggio and Elizabeth Hall to the Editor, *Chronicle of Higher Education* (15 October 2000), B 12.

"A Disappointed, Discouraged, Disillusioned Parent," Note "to the President, Director of Admissions and Faculty Members," (Received 11 February 1969). CCA, Coeducation File.

"Dr. Rosemary Park Excited Over 50th Anniversary of Connecticut College," *New Haven Register* (15 January 1961).

"Dr. Sykes to Head Woman's College, *The Day* (14 February 1913). CCA, Frederick Sykes File.

Judith Draper to Rosemary Park (16 October 1958). CCA, Home Economics File.

Glen D. Dreyer, "Foreword," in Goodwin, R. H. *The Connecticut College Arboretum: Its Sixth Decade and a Detailed History of the Land* (New London: Connecticut College, 1991), v.

Dinesh D'Souza, *Illiberal Education: The Politics of Race and Sex on Campus* (New York: Maxwell Macmillan International, 1991).

Warrine Eastburn, "Miss Katharine Blunt, Biographical Material." CCA, Katharine Blunt File.

Peter D. Eckel, "The Shared Decision Making in Shared Programs: The Challenges of Interinstitutional Academic Programs," in *The Shifting Frontiers of Academic Decision Making: Responding to New Priorities, Following New Pathways*, ed. Peter D. Eckel (Westport, CT: Praeger, 2006), 55–74.

Peter D. Eckel and Adrianna Kezar, "The Challenges Facing Academic Decision making: Contemporary Issues and Steadfast Structures," in *The Shifting Frontiers of Academic Decision Making: Responding to New Priorities, Following New Pathways*, ed. Peter D. Eckel (Westport, CT: Praeger, 2006), 1–14.

"Towards a River of Dreams," *The Day* (15 February 1998).

Linda Eisenmann, "Educating the Female Citizen in a Post-War World: Competing Ideologies for American Women, 1945–1965, *Educational Review*, 54(2) (2002), 133–141.

Linda Eisenmann, *Higher Education for Women in Postwar America, 1945–1965* (Baltimore: Johns Hopkins University Press, 2006).

Richard Ekman, "Creating Campus Appeal: Architecture's Effect on the Message Conveyed About an Institution," *University Business* (December 2007), 40–41

Charles W. Eliot, "The Woman that Will Survive," *A Late Harvest* (Boston: The Atlantic Monthly Press, 1924)—originally published in *The Delineator* (August 1914).

Brian C. Elowe, "Athletics" (in "The Ames Years 1974–1988") *Connecticut College Alumni Magazine* (Spring 1988), 6.

Equal Franchise League, "A Disavowal," (1917). CCA, Frederick Sykes File.

Peter T. Ewell, "Institutional Characteristics and Faculty/Administrator Perceptions of Outcomes: An Exploratory Analysis," *Research in Higher Education*, 30 (1989), 113–136.

"Faculty Discussion Reveals Changes of New Curriculum," *Connecticut College News* (18 February 1953), 2.

Norman Fainstein, "Remarks at Memorial Service for President Emeritus Rosemary Park Anastos" (4 June 2004). Accessed 13 December 2006 from http://www.conncoll.edu/people/park/park_fainstein.html

Viki Fitzgerald and Amy Kest, "American Dance Festival Steps Out, "*College Voice* (21 October 1977).

Nancy Fjortoft & John C. Smart, "Enhancing Organizational Effectiveness: The Importance of Culture Type and Mission Agreement," *Higher Education* (June 1994), 429–447.

William Trufant Foster, "Reed College: Neither Hallowed nor Hampered by Tradition," from an unpublished biography, (1950), Reed College Library Special Collections.

"A Founder of College, Mrs. S. H. Williams," *Connecticut College 1958* (Summer 1958), 4.

"Founder of Connecticut College Writes First Novel," Exposition Press, News Release (1950). CCA, Elizabeth Wright File.

Robert A. Frahm, "Taking Charge of Education," *Hartford Courant* (12 October 1997).

"Frank Valentine Chappell, Former Regatta Day Chief, Is Dead at the Age of 86," *The Day* (19 February 1962). CCA, F.V. Chappell File.

Roberta Frankfort, *Collegiate Women: Domesticity and Career in Turn-of-the-Century America* (New York: New York University Press, 1977).

Estelle Freedman, "Separatism as Strategy: Female Institution Building and American Feminism, 1870-1930," *Feminist Studies*, (Autumn 1979), 512–529.

Ruth Frerichs to Trustees (25 November 1968). CCA, Coeducation File.

Robert Fromer, "The Pfizer Conspiracy: A Failure of Government," Letter to Governor Jodi Rell, December 16, 2004. Combatting (sic) Eminent Domain Abuse in Connecticut, http://pages.cthome.net/ryoung0/ (accessed March 28, 2007).

Betty Fussell, "From Cloisters to Cantilevers: A Brief History of Connecticut College Architecture," *Connecticut College Alumnae News* (December 1951), 3-8.

"F.V. Chappell Says Dr. Sykes' Charge is Unqualified Falsehood," *The Day* (17 March 1917).

Thomas A. Gaines, *The Campus as a Work of Art* (New York: Praeger, 1991).

ClaireGaudiani.com. Accessed 20 September 2006 from http://www.clairegaudiani.com/pages/Home.aspx

Claire L. Gaudiani, "Day One, Day Two (Imaging the Future), Day Three (Social Justice), Day Four (Learning to Serve, Serving to Learn)" (2000). Accessed 20 September 2006 from http://www.collegevalues.org/diaries.cfm?a=0&cat=70.

Claire L. Gaudiani, "Developing a Vision," in *Leadership Transitions: The New College President*, ed. Judith Block McLaughlin (San Francisco: Jossey-Bass Publishers, Spring 1996), 59–70.

Claire L. Gaudiani, *The Greater Good: How Philanthropy Drives the American Economy and Can Save Capitalism* (New York: Henry Holt/New York Times Books, 2003) and *Generosity Rules: A Guidebook for Giving* (Lincoln, Nebraska: iUniverse, 2007).

Claire L. Gaudiani, "How American Women's Philanthropy Helped Build Economic Growth and Democratic Society," in *The Transformative Power of Women's Philanthropy*, ed. M Taylor and S. Shaw-Hardy (San Francisco: Jossey-Bass Publishers, 2005), 23–38.

Claire L. Gaudiani, "In Pursuit of Global Civic Virtues" (Remarks at the 1991 Annual Meeting of the Connecticut College Alumni Association), *Connecticut College Alumni Magazine* (Winter 1992), 1.

Claire L. Gaudiani, "Learning to Serve, Serving to Learn;" Address at 15th Annual Lilly Conference on College Teaching, Miami University, Oxford, Ohio (18 November 1995). Accessed 27 November 2006 http://www.clairegaudiani.com/Writings/pages/LillyConference.aspx

Claire L. Gaudiani, "Lemon Spritzers and Thank You Notes: A New Job Description for College Presidents," *Educational Record* (Spring 1992), 52–55.

Claire L. Gaudiani, "A Message From the President," *Connecticut College Catalog, 1999–2001* (New London, CT: Connecticut College, 1999), 3.

Claire L. Gaudiani, "Of Heart and Mind: External Forces in Higher Education" (1994). Accessed 20 September 2006 from http://www.clairegaudiani.com/Writings/pages/OfHeartAndMind2.aspx.

Claire L. Gaudiani, "Of Heart and Mind: The College and the City, " *Connecticut College Magazine* (Fall 1994).

ClaireGaudiani.com, "Resume." Accessed 28 March 2007 from http://www.clairegaudiani.com/pages/Resume.aspx.

Claire L. Gaudiani, "Tradition and Innovation," *The Inaugural Address of Claire L. President of Connecticut College, October 1 1988* (New London, CT: Connecticut College, 1988). Connecticut College Archives, Claire L. Gaudiani File.

"Gay Community Accepted" in "Schools Ranked by Category" section of *The Best 351 Colleges (2004 Edition)* ed. Robert Franek, Tom Meltzer, Roy Opochinski, Tara Bray, Christopher Maier, Carson Brown, Julie Doherty, K. Nadine Kavanaugh, Catherine Monaco, and Dinaw Mengestu (New York: Princeton Review Publishing, LLC., 2003), 38.

Laura Drake Gill, "Address of Welcome at the Meeting in 1908," *ACA Publications*, 3 (18) (1908).

Jean Glasscock, *Wellesley College 1875–1975: A Century of Women* (Wellesley, MA: Wellesley College, 1975).

Jordan Goldman and Colleen Buyers, *Students' Guide to Colleges: The Definitive Guide to America's top 100 Schools* (New York: Penguin Books, 2005).

"Goodwin, 96, Environment Pioneer, Dies," *The Day* (10 July 2007).

C. Goodwin & J. Wood, "A Brief History of Simmons College," (2002). Retrieved 7 February 2007 from http://www.simmons.edu/resources/libraries/archives/briefhistory.htm.

Richard H. Goodwin, "The Connecticut Arboretum: Its Establishment and Growth," in *The Connecticut College Arboretum: Its First Fifty Years* (New London: Connecticut College, 1982), 9–31.

Richard H. Goodwin, *The Connecticut College Arboretum: Its Sixth Decade and a Detailed History of the Land* (New London: Connecticut College, 1991).

Lynn D. Gordon, "Co-education on Two Campuses: Berkeley and Chicago, 1890–1912," in *Woman's Being, Woman's Place: Female Identity and Vocation in American History*, ed. Mary Kelley (Boston: G.K. Hall & Co., 1979), 171–193.

Lynn D. Gordon, Review: "Female Gothic: Writing the History of Women's Colleges" (*Alma Mater: Design and Experience in Women's Colleges From Their Nineteenth Century Beginnings to the 1930s* by Helen Horowitz), American Quarterly (Summer 1985), 299–304.

Lynn D. Gordon, *Gender and Higher Education in the Progressive Era* (New Haven, CT: Yale University Press, 1990).

Sarah H. Gordon, "Smith College Students: The First Ten Classes, 1879–1888," *History of Education Quarterly* (Summer 1975), 147–167.

Marjorie J. Gosling '50 to Rosemary Park (25 January 1957). CCA, Home Economics File.

Patricia A. Graham, "Expansion and Exclusion: A History of Women in American Higher Education," *Signs: Journal of Women in Culture and Society* (Summer 1978), 759–773.

Julia Grant, "Modernizing Mothers: Home Economics and the Parent Education Movement, 1920–1945," in *Rethinking Home Economics: Women and the History of a Profession*, ed. Sarah Stage and Virginia B. Vincenti (Ithaca, NY: Cornell University Press, 1997), 55–76.

Eleanor B. Gray to the editor, "Spoiled Little Children on the Hill," *The Day* (18 June 2000).

Frances Green, "Charming Scholar, Efficient Administrator is Rosemary Park," *Worcester Sunday Telegram* (20 May 1962).

Clyde Griffen & Elizabeth Daniels, "Vassar College: A Seven Sisters College Chooses Coeducation," in *Challenged by Coeducation: Women's Colleges Since the 1960s*, ed. Leslie Miller-Bernal & Susan L. Poulson (Nashville, TN: Vanderbilt University Press, 2006), 25–47.

Jennifer Grogan, "CGA Ranks High in New College Report," *The Day* (20 August 2007).

Beverly G. Guy-Sheftall, "Black Women and Higher Education: Spelman and Bennett Colleges Revisited," *The Journal of Negro Education* (Summer 1982), 278–287.

Beverly Guy-Sheftall, "Diversity and Women's Colleges," in *A Closer Look at Women's Colleges* (1999). Accessed 10 February 2007 from (http://www.ed.gov/pubs/WomensColleges/ chap4fin.html.

Arthur Twining Hadley to Elizabeth C. Wright (16 April 1910). CCA, Elizabeth Wright File.

G. Stanley Hall, *Adolescence*, Volume II (New York: D. Appleton, 1904).

Robert A. Hamilton, "In New London, Creating Jobs, Building a Buzz for Renewal," *New York Times* (9 May 1999).

Robert A. Hamilton, "New London, New Vision," *Connecticut College Magazine* (Spring 1998), 22–27.

William Rainey Harper, "The University and Democracy" in *The Trends in Higher Education* (Chicago: University of Chicago Press, 1905), 1–34.

W.W. Harris, "College's Fate Hangs in Balance," *The Day* (20 March 1917). CCA, Frederick Sykes File.

William Welton Harris, "Some Personal Reminiscences of Dr. Sykes," *Connecticut College News* (26 October 1917). CCA, Frederick Sykes File.

Matthew Hartley, *A Call to Purpose: Mission-Centered Change at Three Liberal Arts Colleges* (New York: RoutledgeFalmer, 2002).

Matthew Hartley & Lawrence Schall, "The Endless Good Argument: The Adaptation of Mission at Two Liberal Arts Colleges," *Planning for Higher Education* (June-August 2005), 5–11.

Matt Hartley & S.R. Wilhelm Shah, "The Tenuous Legitimacy of Ad-hoc Decision-making Committees," in *The Shifting Frontiers of Academic Decision Making: Responding to New Priorities, Following New Pathways*, ed. Peter D. Eckel (Westport, CT: Praeger, 2006), 75–92.

Irene Harwath, Mindi Maline, and Elizabeth DeBra, "Women's Colleges in the United States: History, Issues, and Challenges" (1997). Accessed 26 October 2006 from http://www.ed.gov/offices/OERI/PLLI/webreprt.html

Kari Haskell, "A Sense of Duty Takes Shape During Dinnertime Discussion" (Profile of Claire Gaudiani), *New York Times* (6 January 2008), 20.

Hugh Hawkins, "The Making of the Liberal Arts College Identity," *Daedalus* (Winter 1999), 1–25.

B. Hinman, "Ground-breaking at Wake Forest," *Wake Forest Magazine*, (1975). Accessed 8 March 2007 from http://www.wfu.edu/history/HST_WFU/groundbreaking.html.

Richard H. Hirsch, "Generating Ideals and Transforming Lives: A Contemporary Case for the Residential Liberal Arts College," in *Distinctively American: The Residential Liberal Arts College*, ed. Steven Koblik & Stephen R. Graubard (New Brunswick, NJ: Transaction Publishers, 2000), 173–194.

Frances Hoffmann, "CCSRE Comments on 2006 Sykes Lecture," (April 2007). Paper provided to author by Hoffmann.

Frances Hoffmann, "Women, Men and Higher Education" (Sykes Lecture, Connecticut College Reunion) (2 June 2006). Paper provided to author by Hoffmann.

Frances Hoffman, Joan Chrisler, Dirk Held, Philip Gedeon, Manuel Lizarralde, and Frances Shields, "Working Group Report on Coeducation from Report of the Presidential Commission on a Pluralistic Community at Connecticut College" (8 August 2003). Accessed 13 December 2006 from http://www.conncoll.edu/people/president-emeritus/pluralism/html/index.htm.

Peter Y. Hong, "Gender Gap Growing on College Campuses," *The Los Angeles Times* (1 December 2004).

Helen Horowitz, *Alma Mater: Design and Experience in the Women's Colleges from Their Nineteenth-Century Beginnings to the 1930s* (New York: Knopf, 1984).

Helen L. Horowitz, "The Great Debate: Charles W. Eliot and M. Carey Thomas," in *Yards and Gates: Gender in Harvard and Radcliffe History*, ed. Laurel Thatcher Ulrich (New York: Palgrave MacMillan, 2004), 129–137.

Helen L. Horowitz, *The Power and Passion of M. Carey Thomas* (Champaign, Illinois: University of Illinois Press, 1999).

"How College Controversy Appears in Other Cities," *The Day* (19 March 1917). CCA, Frederick Sykes File.

Mary Howard, "Bengochea Joins CC Community in a Path-breaking Role, *CC: Connecticut College Alumni Magazine* (Summer 2006), 8.

Florence Howe, "Myths of Coeducation," in *Myths of Coeducation: Selected Essays, 1964-1983* (Bloomington: Indiana University Press, 1984), 206–220.

Madeleine Jean Huber to President Charles Shain, (11 January 1969). CCA, Coeducation File.

Scott Jaschik, "President Quits at Case Western," *InsideHigherEd.com* (17 March 2006). Accessed 24 February 2008 from http://www.insidehighered.com/news/2006/03/17/case.

William D. Jenkins, "Housewifery and Motherhood: The Question of Role Change in the Progressive Era," in *Woman's Being, Woman's Place: Female Identity and Vocation in American History*, ed. Mary Kelley (Boston: G.K. Hall & Company, 1979), 142–153.

Alice Johnson, "The Ames Years 1974-1988," *Connecticut College Alumni Magazine* (Spring 1988), 2-3.

Alice Johnson, "Everything Changes, Nothing Changes," *Connecticut College Alumni Magazine* (Winter 1978), 21–22, 34.

Alice Johnson, *Unpublished Memoir of Time at Connecticut College,* (1997), 42. CCA, Alice Johnson File.

Joan Marie Johnson. *Southern Women at the Seven Sister Colleges: Feminist Values and Social Activism, 1875-1915.* Athens: University of Georgia Press, 2008.

Philip H. Jordan, Jr., "Historic Necessity of Separate Education for Women," *Connecticut College Alumnae News* (December 1968), 15–16.

Philip H. Jordan, Jr., "Responses to Supplemental Questionnaire" (23 June 1970). CCA, Coeducation File.

D.J. Julius, J.V. Baldridge, & J. Pfeffer, "A Memo from Machiavelli," *Journal of Higher Education* (March/April 1999), 113–133.

Rosalind A. Keep, *Fourscore Years: A History of Mills College* (Oakland: Mills College, 1931).

Elaine Kendall, *Peculiar Institutions: An Informal History of the Seven Sister Colleges* (New York: G.P. Putnam's Sons, 1975).

Donald Kennedy, "Making Choices in the Research University," in *The Research University in a Time of Discontent*, ed. J.R. Cole, E. G. Barber, & S. R. Graubard (Baltimore, MD: The Johns Hopkins University Press, 1994), 85–114.

D.R. Kenney, R. Dumont, & G. Kenney, *Mission and Place: Strengthening Learning and Community Through Campus Design* (Westport, CT: Praeger Publishers, 2005).

Linda K. Kerber, "Why Should Girls Be Learn'd and Wise?": Two Centuries of Higher Education for Women as Seen Through the Unfinished Work of Alice Mary Baldwin," in *Women and Higher Education in American History*, ed. John Mack Faragher and Florence Howe (New York: W.W. Norton, 1988), 18–42.

Carol W. Kimball, "Taking the Trolley to New London," *The Day* (August 7, 2007), B3.

Anna Kisselgoff, "American Dance Festival is Lured to Duke with $1 Million Pledge," *The New York Times* (31 October 1977).

Anna Kisselgoff, "Dance Festival in New London Seeks New Site," *The New York Times* (15 November 1976).

Robert Knapp, "Religion at Reed," Draft Statement for Reed College Web Site (25 July 2007). In possession of author.

Louise W. Knight, "The Quails," (B.A. honors thesis, Wesleyan University, 1972).

Ann Heubeck Knipp and Thaddeus P. Thomas, *The History of Goucher College* (Baltimore, MD: Goucher College, 1938).

Sally Gregory Kohlstedt, "Single-Sex Education and Leadership: The Early Years of Simmons College" in *Women and Education Leadership*, ed. Sari Knopp Biklen and Marilyn B. Branningan (Lexington: MA: Lexington Books, 1980), 93–112.

George D. Kuh, "Appraising the Character of a College," *Journal of Counseling & Development* (July/August 1993). 661–668.

George D. Kuh, "Ethos: Its Influence on Student Learning," *Liberal Education* (Fall 1993), 22–32.

Dorothy D. Lee, "What Shall We Teach Women?" *Mademoiselle* (August 1947), 213, 354, 356, 358.

Henry Lefavour, "The Utilitarian in Higher Education," *ACA Publications*, 3 (6), 1903.

The Liberal Arts at Connecticut College (New London, CT: Connecticut College, 2007).

"Living Tradition," *Yankee*, Vol. 69, Issue 5 (June 2005).

Bradley J. Longfield, "Review of David Potts' *Wesleyan University, 1831–1910: Collegiate Enterprise in New England*," *The Journal of American History* (March 1995), 1709–1710.

Chuck Luce, "Living Legends: Rosemary Park Anastos," *Connecticut College Magazine* (Spring 1998), 32–33.

Mary C. Lynn, *Make No Small Plans: A History of Skidmore College* (Saratoga Springs, NY: Skidmore College, 2000).

K.M., "Miss Blunt Cited as Distinguished Citizen," *Connecticut College Alumnae Magazine* (May 1949), 6–9.

Alice Maggin, "Five Years of Change," *Connecticut College Magazine*, July/August, 1993, 19–22.

Bryan Mahan, "To the Committee Appointed to Select a Site, and to Establish a Women's College in Connecticut" (5 November 1910). CCA, Elizabeth Wright File.

W.T. Mallon, "Centers, Institutes, and Academic Decision-making: Addressing 'Suburban Sprawl' Through Strategies for 'Smart Growth,' in *The Shifting Frontiers of Academic Decision Making: Responding to New Priorities, Following New Pathways,* ed. Peter D. Eckel (Westport, CT: Praeger, 2006), 15–34.

Kenneth L. Mark, *Delayed by Fire: The Early Years of Simmons College* (Privately Published, 1945).

William C. Marra and Sara E. Polsky, "Lack of Confidence: Faculty of Arts and Sciences Votes, 218–185–18, to Express Lack of Confidence in Summers," *The Harvard Crimson* (16 March 2005).

Janet E. Marthers, "Feminism and the Daughters of the American Revolution: 1890–1920" (M.A. thesis, Reed College, 2005), Reed College Library Thesis Tower.

Joanne Martin, Martha S. Feldman, Mary Jo Hatch, & Sim B. Sitkin, "The Uniqueness Paradox in Organizational Stories," *Administrative Science Quarterly* (September 1983), 438–453.

Warren Bryan Martin, "Adaptiveness and Distinctiveness," *Journal of Higher Education* (March-April, 1984), 286–296.

"Matching Grants Encourage Festival to Remain at College for Season," *Connecticut College News* (Winter 1977).

Nancy Barr Mavity, "To Honor Dr. Sykes," *Connecticut College Alumni Magazine* (December 1951), 10, 11.

Beverly McAnear, "College Founding in the American Colonies," *The Mississippi Valley Historical Review* (June 1955), 24–44.

Virginia Taber McCamey to Rosemary Park (27 January 1957). CCA, Home Economics File.

Amy Thompson McCandless, *The Past in the Present: Women's Higher Education in the Twentieth-Century American South* (Tuscaloosa, AL: The University of Alabama Press, 1999).

Colin McEnroe, "A Heart-Breaking Work of Staggering Self-Reinvention," *The Hartford Courant* (18 October 2005).

Morgan McGinley, "Gaudiani Must Learn Leadership in Public Realm," *The Day* (2 November 1997).

Liz McMillen, "Connecticut College's Strategic Plan Helps it Stay Lean and Mean," *The Chronicle of Higher Education* (3 June 1992), A27–28.

Michael S. McPherson & Morton O. Shapiro, "The Future Economic Challenges for the Liberal Arts Colleges," in *Distinctively American: The Residential Liberal Arts College*, ed. Steven Koblik & Stephen R. Graubard (New Brunswick, NJ: Transaction Publishers, 2000), 47–75.

Anja Milde, "Largest Class in Trin History Arrives," *Trinity Tripod* (12 September 2006).

Leslie Miller-Bernal, *Separate by Degree: Women Students' Experiences in Single-Sex and Coeducational Colleges* (New York: Peter Lang Publishing, 2000).

Leslie Miller-Bernal, "Wells College: The Transition to Coeducation Begins," in *Challenged by Coeducation: Women's Colleges Since the 1960s,* ed. Leslie Miller-Bernal & Susan L. Poulson (Nashville, TN: Vanderbilt University Press, 2006), 145–175.

Leslie Miller-Bernal & Susan L. Poulson (eds.), "Appendix 1: Statement of Six Past Presidents of Formerly Women's Colleges, 2000. Exceptional Coed Colleges: A New Model for Gender Equity," in *Challenged by Coeducation: Women's Colleges Since the 1960s,* ed Leslie Miller-Bernal & Susan L. Poulson (Nashville, TN: Vanderbilt University Press, 2006), 389–393.

Leslie Miller-Bernal and Susan L. Poulson, *Challenged by Coeducation: Women's Colleges Since the 1960s* (Nashville, TN: Vanderbilt University Press, 2006).

H. Mintzberg, "The Professional Bureaucracy," In *Structures in Fives: Designing Effective Organizations* (Englewood Cliffs, NJ: Prentice Hall, 1993), 189–213.

"Miss Elizabeth Wright Dies; College Founder, First Bursar," *Conn Census* (28 February 1963). Connecticut College Archives (hereafter identified as CCA), Elizabeth Wright File.

Mission Statements of Amherst College, Clark University, Dickinson College, Middlebury College, and Macalester College. Accessed from http//www.dickinson.edu/; http://middlebury.edu/academics/catalogs/catalog/about_midd/m...; http://www.macalester.edu/about.html; http://www.clarku.edu/aboutclark/mission.htm; https:cms.amherst.edu/aboutamherst/ mission/node/7854.

"Mission Statement of Vassar College," *Vassar College Catalogue* (Poughkeepsie, NY: Vassar College, 2007).

Christopher C. Morphew & Matthew Hartley, "Mission Statements: A Thematic Analysis of Rhetoric Across Institutional Type," *The Journal of Higher Education* (May/June 2006), 456–471.

Lauren Morrow, "Student and Residential Life Get New Staffers," *The College Voice* (14 September 2007), 1,3.

Tom Mortensen, "Fact Sheet: What's Wrong with the Guys." (Washington, DC: The Pell Institute for the Study of Opportunity in Higher Education, 9 August 2003).

"Mrs. Williams is Retiring From Board," *The Day* (21 May 1949).

Starr J. Murphy to Elizabeth Wright (22 March 1910), CCA, Elizabeth Wright File.

Tim Murphy, "American Dance Festival Won't Return to College," *The Day* (7 October 1977), 1.

Natalie A. Naylor, "The Ante-bellum College Movement: A Reappraisal of Tewksbury's Founding of American Colleges and Universities," *History of Education Quarterly* (Autumn 1973), 261–274.

Blake Nedel, "The Early History of Reed College or, "How Your Dorm Got its Name, in 10,000 Words or Less,"" in *The 2001 Reed College Student Body Handbook* (Portland, OR: Reed College Student Senate, 2001), 2–8.

Paul Neely, "The Threats to Liberal Arts Colleges," in *Distinctively American: The Residential Liberal Arts College*, ed. Steven Koblik & Stephen R. Graubard (New Brunswick, NJ: Transaction Publishers, 2000), 27–45.

Mabel Newcomer, *A Century of Higher Education for Women* (New York: Harper, 1959).

"New London, New Vision" (Brochure) (1999). CCA, Claire Gaudiani File.

News from Connecticut College, Press Release, (12 September 1969). CCA, Coeducation File.

Gary Ng, "Alumni Giving Hits New Record," *The College Voice* (28 September 2007), 1, 4.

Crandall J. North to William North Rice (14 January 1908). WUA, William North Rice File.

"Notes to File, Miss Elizabeth C. Wright, Retired Bursar," (19 March 1959). CCA, Elizabeth Wright File.

"Notes From College Row: Right Again," *The Wesleyan Alumnus* (October 1968), 4.

Gertrude E. Noyes, *History of Connecticut College* (New London: Connecticut College, 1982).

Irene Nye, *Chapters in the History of Connecticut College During the First Three Administrations, 1911-1942* (New London: Connecticut College, 1943).

Irene Nye, John E. Wells, and David D. Leib, "Faculty Resolution in Regard to Mr. Buell" (7 February 1931). CCA, Colin Buell File.

Lynn K. Nyhart, "Home Economists in the Hospital," in *Rethinking Home Economics: Women and the History of a Profession,* ed. Sarah Stage and Virginia B. Vincenti (Ithaca: Cornell University Press, 1997), 125–144.

"Opinion of the Day, New Opportunities for Conn College, *The Day* (14 October 1977).

Oral recollections of Miss Elizabeth C. Wright to Anne Taylor, 1957–58. CCA, Elizabeth Wright File.

Joseph C. Palamountain, Jr. *Such Growth Bespeaks the Work of Many Hands: The Story of Skidmore College* (New York: The Newcomen Society of North America, 1976).

Patricia A. Palmieri, "From Republican Motherhood to Race Suicide: Arguments on the Higher Education of Women in the United States, 1820-1920," in *Educating Women Together: Coeducation in a Changing World*, ed. Carol Lasser (Urbana and Chicago: University of Illinois Press, 1987), 49–64.

Patricia A. Palmieri, *In Adamless Eden: The Community of Women faculty at Wellesley* (New Haven, CT: Yale University Press, 1995).

Patricia A. Palmieri, "There was Fellowship: A Social Portrait of Academic Women at Wellesley College, 1895-1920," *History of Education Quarterly* (Summer 1983), 195–214.

Rosemary Park, "Charge to the Seniors: Commencement, June 11, 1961," in *Fiftieth Anniversary Celebration Publication: Connecticut College 1911–1961* (New London, CT: Connecticut College, 1961), 28.

Rosemary Park, "College to Supervise Secondary School, *Connecticut College Alumnae News* (March 1954), 3–4.

Rosemary Park, *President's Report, 1952* (New London, CT: Connecticut College for Women, 1952).

Rosemary Park, *President's Report, 1957* (New London, CT: Connecticut College for Women, 1957).

Rosemary Park, "Remarks to Assembly, April 27, 1961," in *Fiftieth Anniversary Celebration Publication: Connecticut College 1911–1961* (New London, CT: Connecticut College, 1961), 26.

Rosemary Park, *Report of the President, 1946–1962* (New London, CT: Connecticut College, 1962).

Rosemary Park, *Report of the President, 1963–1964* (New London, CT: Connecticut College, November 1964).

Rosemary Park, "Your College Education: Our Mutual Responsibility," in *Fiftieth Anniversary Celebration Publication: Connecticut College 1911–1961* (New London, CT: Connecticut College, 1961), 19.

Rosemary Park to Mrs. Elwood Carter, Jr. (Jean Kohlberger Carter) (25 January 1957). CCA, Home Economics File.

Rosemary Park to Margaret S. Chaney (2 March 1948). CCA, Home Economics File.

Rosemary Park to Margaret S. Chaney (19 March 1957). CCA, Home Economics File.

Rosemary Park to Margaret S. Chaney (14 November 1952). CCA, Home Economics File.

Rosemary Park to Mrs. Daniel Draper (28 October 1958). CCA, Home Economics File.

Rosemary Park to Virginia Martin Pattison '42 (30 January 1957). CCA, Home Economics File.

Thomas Parker, "Admission Report to Amherst Trustees" (12 May 2006)—copy provided by Amherst College trustee, Colin Diver.

Virginia Martin Pattison '42 to Rosemary Park (18 January 1957).

Dan Pearson, "Conn College OKs Housing in Downtown," *The Day* (3 October 1999).

Dan Pearson, "Conn, RPI Plan High-Tech Learning Center in New London," *The Day* (15 December 1999).

Dan Pearson, "Conn Student Group Opposes Razing Fort Homes," *The Day* (1 March 2000).

Dan Pearson, "Gaudiani Honor is Focus of Discord," *The Day* (28 December 1999).

Catherine Phinizy, "The Bighearted Millionaire," *Connecticut College Alumni Magazine* (Spring 2000), 22–27.

"Pitzer College, History and Mission." Accessed 26 March 2008 from http://www.pitzer.edu/about/mission.asp.

Dorothy A. Plum and George B. Dowell, *The Magnificent Enterprise: A Chronicle of Vassar College* (Poughkeepsie, NY: Vassar College, 1961).

David B. Potts, "American Colleges in the Nineteenth Century: From Localism to Denominationalism," *History of Education Quarterly* (Winter 1971), 363–380.

David B. Potts, *Wesleyan University, 1831–1910: Collegiate Enterprise in New England* (New Haven: Yale University Press, 1992).

Susan L. Poulson, "Simmons College: Meeting the Needs of Women Workers," in *Challenged by Coeducation: Women's Colleges Since the 1960s,* ed. Leslie Miller-Bernal and Susan L. Poulson (Nashville, TN: Vanderbilt University Press, 2006), 208–234.

"President Harry Truman's Commission Calls for Expansion of Higher Education," from *Higher Education for Democracy: A Report of the President's Commission on Higher Education* (New York, 1947), 1, 25–29, 32–39.

"President Sykes Comments on Action of Trustees," *The Day* (19 April 1917).

"President Sykes Gives Reasons Why His Trustees Oppose Him," *The Day* (15 March 1917).

"Press Release From the Connecticut College News Office" to mark ten years of coeducation (1979?—exact date not specified). CCA, Coeducation File.

"Prof. Colin S. Buell, '77, Dies; Principal of W.M.I. and Connecticut College Trustee," *The Day* (31 January 1938). CCA, Colin Buell File.

Will of Amanda Reed, 27th Clause, Creating Reed Institute (4 September 1901), Reed College Library Special Collections.

Files of William Reeves and Frederick Sykes, CCA.

"Report of the Summer Planning Group, Summary of Recommendations," *Connecticut College Alumnae News* (December 1968). Connecticut College Archives (hereafter identified as CCA), Coeducation File.

William North Rice, Draft of Letter to Elizabeth Wright (14 July 1910). WUA, William North Rice File.

William North Rice to Elizabeth Wright (22 July 1910). WUA, William North Rice File.

William North Rice to Miss Bass (16 June 1909). WUA, William North Rice File.

William North Rice to Miss Moore (9 January 1909) WUA, William North Rice File.

William North Rice to Mrs. Cummings (4 March 1909). WUA, William North Rice File.

Katey Rich, "With More Female Applicants 'Gender Gap' Widens at Wes," *The Wesleyan Argus* (28 April 2006)*)*.

Richard C. Richardson, Jr., "Belief and Loyalty in College Organizations: Comment," *The Journal of Higher Education* (June 1971), 516–520.

John Riley, "When David Meets Goliath," *InfoWars.com* (8 May 2005). Accessed 28 March 2007 from http://www.infowars.com/articles/ps/eminent_domain_david_vs_goliath.htm;

Richard E. Ritz, *A History of the Reed College Campus and its Buildings* (Portland, OR: The Trustees of the Reed Institute, 1990).

David W. Robson, "College Founding in the New Republic, 1776–1800," *History of Education Quarterly* (Autumn 1983), 323–341.

Brian Rogers, "From the Beginning," in *Connecticut College: The Long View,* ed. Lisa Brownell, William Mercer, Catherine Phinizy, and Brian Rogers (New London, CT: Connecticut College, 1999), 15–32

Rosalind Rosenberg, *Divided Lives: American Women in the Twentieth Century* (New York: Hill and Wang, 1992).

Rosalind Rosenberg, "The Limits of Access: The History of Coeducation in America," in *Women and Higher Education in American History,* ed. John Mack Faragher and Florence Howe (New York: W.W. Norton, 1988), 107-129.

Cynthia Rosik to Rosemary Park (26 January 1957). CCA, Home Economics File.

Margaret Rossiter, *Women Scientists in America: Struggles and Strategies to 1940* (Baltimore: Johns Hopkins University Press, 1982).

Margery S. Rowe '19, "To Dr. Sykes: 'Lives of Great Men all Remind Us, We Can Make Our Lives Sublime,'" *Connecticut College News* (20 June 1917).

Frederick Rudolph, *The American College and University: A History* (New York: Alfred A. Knopf, 1962).

Frederick Rudolph, *Mark Hopkins and the Log: Williams College, 1836–1872* (New Haven, CT: Yale University Press, 1956).

John L. Rury, "Vocationalism for Home and Work: Women's Education in the United States, 1880-1930," *History of Education Quarterly* (Spring, 1984), 40.

Lawrence M. Schall, "Swarthmore College: The Evolution of an Institutional Mission" (Ed. D. dissertation, University of Pennsylvania, 2003).

George P. Schmidt, *Douglass College: A History* (New Brunswick, NJ: Rutgers University Press, 1968).

"School of Dance Names Faculty for Ninth Season," *Connecticut College News* 2 (April 1956).

Sally Schwager, "Taking Up the Challenge: The Origins of Radcliffe," in *Yards and Gates: Gender at Harvard and Radcliffe*, ed. Laurel Thatcher Ulrich (New York: Palgrave MacMillan, 2004), 92–103.

Secretary of the faculty instruction committee to Margaret S. Chaney (9 January 1946). CCA, Home Economics File.

Reverend Joseph H. Selden, "Frederick Sykes Memorial Service Address," *Connecticut Colleges News* (26 October 1917). CCA, Frederick Sykes File.

Susan F. Semel and Alan Sadovnik, "Coeducation at Wheaton College: From Conscious Coeducation to Distinctive Coeducation?" in *Challenged by Coeducation: Women's Colleges Since the 1960s*, ed. Leslie Miller-Bernal and Susan L. Poulson (Nashville, TN: Vanderbilt University Press, 2006), 48–76.

"785 College and University Endowments," *The Chronicle of Higher Education* (1 February 2008), A14–A17.

Edward W. Sheldon to Morton Plant (15 January 1913).

Marianne Sheldon, "Revitalizing the Mission of a Women's College: Mills College in Oakland, California," in *Challenged by Coeducation: Women's Colleges Since the 1960s*, ed. Leslie Miller-Bernal and Susan L. Poulson (Nashville, TN: Vanderbilt University Press, 2006), 175–208.

Charles Shain to *Connecticut College Alumni Magazine* (Spring 1980). CCA, Coeducation File.

Charles Shain, "Introduction of Rosemary Park" (4 June 1967). CCA, Charles Shain File.

Thomas J. Sheeran, "Male-Female Balance a Struggle," *AP News* (16 February 2001).

Barbara Sicherman, "College and Careers: Historical Perspectives on the Lives and Work Patterns of Women College Graduates," in *Women and Higher Education in American History*, ed. Faragher and Howe (New York: W.W. Norton, 1988), 130–164.

Karen Manners Smith, "New Paths to Power: 1890-1920," in *No Small Courage*, ed. Nancy F. Cott (New York: Oxford University Press, 2000), 353–412.

Barbara M. Solomon, *In the Company of Educated Women: A History of Women and Higher Education in America* (New Haven, CT: Yale University Press, 1985).

Barbara Sporn, "Managing University Culture: An Analysis of the Relationship Between Institutional Culture and Management Approaches," *Higher Education* (July 1996), 41–61.

"Sprucing up the Arbo," *CC: Connecticut College Magazine* (Winter 2007), 6.

Sarah Stage, "Ellen Richards and the Social Significance of the Home Economics Movement," in *Rethinking Home Economics: Women and the History of a Profession*, ed. Sarah Stage and Virginia B. Vincenti (Ithaca, NY: Cornell University Press, 1997), 17–33.

Sarah Stage, "Home Economics: What's in a Name?" in *Rethinking Home Economics: Women and the History of a Profession*, ed. Sarah Stage and Virginia B. Vincenti (Ithaca, NY: Cornell University Press, 1997), 1-14.

Sarah Stage and Virginia B. Vincenti, *Rethinking Home Economics: Women and the History of a Profession* (Ithaca: Cornell University Press, 1997).

David M. Stameshkin, *The Town's College: Middlebury College, 1800–1915* (Middlebury, VT: Middlebury College Press, 1985).

Mrs. Earle W. Stamm to Rosemary Park (29 January 1953). CCA, Home Economics File.

Frank Stricker, "Cookbooks and Law Books: The Hidden History of Career Women in Twentieth-Century America," in *A Heritage of Her Own: Toward a New Social History of American Women*, ed. Nancy F. Cott and Elizabeth Hofkin Pleck (New York: Simon & Schuster, 1979), 476–498.

Erin Strout, "The Trustees Tipping Point: When Does a Governing Board Say Enough is Enough and Fire the President?" *Chronicle of Higher Education* (6 May 2005), A27.

Erich M. Studer-Ellis, "Springboards to Mortarboards: Women's College Foundings in Massachusetts, New York, and Pennsylvania," *Social Forces* (March 1995), 1051–1070.

Laura Suchan, "Useful Ornaments: Form and Function at an Ontario Ladies College," Presentation at the History of Education Society's Annual Conference, St. Petersburg, Florida (7 November 2008).

"Suit for Slander to be Brought Against Dr. Sykes; Yonkers Man Who Interests Self in College Affairs Got Sykes His Job," *Waterbury Herald* (25 March 1917).

Patricia Sullivan, "Rosemary Park: A Study of Educational Leadership During the Revolutionary Decades" (Ph.D. dissertation, Boston College, 1982).

"Supplementary Data on the Decision for Coeducation at Connecticut College, Confidential until Jan. 9, 1969." CCA, Coeducation File.

Lauren Sutherland, "Where are All the Fresh-men in the Class of 2010?" *The Miscellany News* (8 September 2006).

Charles J. Sykes, *ProfScam: Professors and the Demise of Higher Education* (Washington, D.C.: Regnery, 1988).

Frederick H. Sykes, "Commencement Address," *Connecticut College News* (20 June 1917).

Frederick H. Sykes, "Industrial Arts Education and Industrial Training," *Teachers College Record* (September 1911), 197.

Frederick H. Sykes to Mrs. George Fenner (9 June 1917), CCA, Frederick Sykes File.

Frederick H. Sykes, "Students of Dear C.C.," *Connecticut College News* (20 June 1917). CCA, Frederick Sykes File.

Frederick H. Sykes, "The Social Basis of the New Education for Women," *Teachers College Record* (May 1917), 227.

Donald Tewksbury, *The Founding of American Colleges and Universities Before the Civil War* (New York: Archon, 1965).

John R. Thelin, *A History of American Higher Education* (Baltimore: Johns Hopkins University Press, 2004).

John R. Thelin, "Life and Learning in Southern California: Private Colleges in the Popular Culture," *History of Education Quarterly* (Spring 1975), 111–117.

34th Annual Catalogue of Connecticut College (New London, CT: Connecticut College for Women, March 1948).

Thirty-Third Annual Catalogue of Connecticut College (New London, CT: Connecticut College for Women, 30 March 1947).

William G. Tierney, "Organizational Culture in Higher Education: Defining the Essentials," *The Journal of Higher Education* (January-February 1988), 2–21.

"Timely Views by the Commentator," *New London Telegraph* (22 March 1917).

Nancy Tomes, "Spreading the Germ Theory: Sanitary Science and Home Economics, 1880–1930," in *Rethinking Home Economics: Women and the History of a Profession*, ed. Sarah Stage and Virginia B. Vincenti (Ithaca, NY: Cornell University Press, 1997), 34-53.

"Towards a River of Dreams," *The Day* (15 February 1998).

Trees of the Connecticut College Campus (Brochure) (New London: Connecticut College, 2000).

Trustee Files of Colin Buell, F.V. Chappell, Oliver Gildersleeve, George S. Palmer, and Henry P. Wright. CCA.

"2007 NACUBO Endowment Study," National Association of College and University Business Officers, (2008).

Untitled, unsigned draft of letter to "The Day," (1969), from Connecticut College Archives. Co-education File. See also "Leaving the Land Behind," *The Hartford Courant* (12 July 2007).

"*U.S. News* Rankings Through the Years," *The Chronicle of Higher Education* (2007). Accessed 24 January 2008 from http://chronicle.com/stats/usnews/index.php?category=Liberal+Arts+Colleges#about.

"Vassar College," in *The College Buzz Book (2007 Edition),* ed. Carolyn C. Wise and Stephanie Hauser (New York: Vault, Inc., 2007), 597–599.

Vassar College Faculty Demographics, 2003-2004, Vassar College Office of Institutional Research. Accessed 24 March 2008 from http://institutionalresearch.vassar.edu/faculty-male.html

"Vassar College" in *Students' Guide to Colleges: The Definitive Guide to America's Top 100 Schools* ed. Jordan Goldman and Colleen Buyers (New York: Penguin Books, 2005), 530–536.

Virginia B. Vincenti, "Chronology of Events and Movements Which Have Defined and Shaped Home Economics," in *Rethinking Home Economics: Women and the History of a Profession*, ed. Sarah Stage and Virginia B. Vincenti (Ithaca, NY: Cornell University Press, 1997), 321–330.

"Virginia High Court to Hear Disputes Over Randolph Coed Move," *Associated Press* (23 September 2007).

Heather Vogell, "Conn College May Invest More in City," *The Day* (11 December 1998).

Heather Vogell, "Conn's Step Into New London Marches to Others' Beat," *The Day* (4 April 1999).

Heather Vogell, "Fort Trumbull Residents Say They Want to Stay Put," *The Day* (6 January 1999).

Heather Vogell, "Gaudiani Unveils Plans for Social Progress," *The Day* (28 April 1999).

Heather Vogell, "A Man With a Plan: College Project Evolves into Firehouse Renovation," *The Day* (10 January 1999).

Heather Vogell, "Redevelopment Plan Lacks Contingencies for the Needy," *The Day* (2 January 1999).

Carman Palmer von Bremen to Rosemary Park (29 September 1953). CCA, Home Economics File.

Carola Von Hoffmannstahl-Solomonoff, "Land Grabbers Stew," *Deep qt* (21 September 2005). Accessed 28 March 2007 from http://www.users.cloud9.net/~drs/deep_qt/deepqt_maindish.html.

Laurel Shaper Walters, "Teamwork Builds College's Future," *Christian Science Monitor* (28 February 1992).

"WDD, For the National Cyclopedia of American Biography" (1 December 1935). CCA, Frederick Sykes File.

Glenn Weaver, *The History of Trinity College: Volume I* (Hartford, CT: Trinity College Press, 1967).

Governor Frank Weeks to Elizabeth C. Wright (13 May 1910). CCA, Elizabeth Wright File.

K.E. Weick, "Educational Organizations as Loosely Coupled Systems," *Administrative Science Quarterly* (March 1976), 1–19.

Roberta Wein, "Women's Colleges and Domesticity, 1875–1918," *History of Education Quarterly* (Spring 1974), 31–47.

"Wellesley College: The College." Accessed from http://www.wellesley.edu/Welcome/college.html.

Michael J. Whalen, "New London Still in Mind as Host to Dance Festival," *The Hartford Courant* (26 November 1976).

Michael J. Whalen, "Official Calls Festival Loss Devastating," *Hartford Courant* (12 November 1976).

F.C. Wilcox, "Piety and Profit in College Building," *The Journal of Higher Education* (March 1937), 147–149.

George Willauer, "Conversion of a Skeptic," *Smith Alumnae Quarterly* (Winter 1994/95), 22–24.

Nancy Woloch, *Women and the American Experience* (Boston: McGraw Hill, 2006).

"Women's College Goes Coed," *The Christian Science Monitor* (January 25, 1969).

"Women's College President Talks," *New Haven Union* (April 6, 1913). CCA, Frederick Sykes File.

"Women's Education Amply Advanced for Experiment in Meeting Special Needs, Says Dr. Blunt at Inaugural, *The Day* (16 May 1930). CCA. Katharine Blunt File.

Thomas Woody, *A History of Women's Education in the United States, Volume II* (New York: The Science Press, 1929).

Elizabeth C. Wright, "A College for Women in Connecticut," Report to the Hartford College Club (July 1910). CCA, Elizabeth Wright File.

Elizabeth C. Wright, "Report of Women's College to the Hartford College Club," (14 May 1910). CCA, Elizabeth Wright File.

Elizabeth C. Wright to Colin Buell (12 March 1911). CCA, Elizabeth Wright File.

Elizabeth Wright to Colin Buell (8 July 1913). CCA, Colin Buell. File.

Elizabeth C. Wright to Professor William North Rice of Wesleyan (26 July 1910), CCA, Elizabeth Wright File.

Elizabeth C. Wright to Mr. Nelson Wild (July 1911). CCA, Elizabeth Wright File.

Winona Young, Marion Kofsy, Esther Batchelder, Sadie Coit, Ruth Trail, Luise Ansley, Juline Warner, Alice Horrax, Marenda Prentis, "Students' Mass Meeting Passes Resolutions: Appreciate President Sykes' Work with and Attitude Towards Students Body," *Connecticut College News* (20 June 1917).

Robert Zemsky, Gregory R. Wegner, & William F. Massey, *Remaking The American University: Market-Smart And Mission-Centered* (New Brunswick, NJ: Rutgers University Press, 2005).

Joan G. Zimmerman, "Daughters of Main Street: Culture and the Female Community at Grinnell, 1884–1912, in *Woman's Being, Woman's Place: Female Identity and Vocation in American History*, ed. Mary Kelley (Boston: G.K. Hall & Company, 1979), 154–170.

Joseph P. Zolner, "Community-Centered Planning at Connecticut College," *Harvard Graduate School of Education Case Study* (Cambridge, MA: Harvard University, 1997), 1–12. CCA, Gaudiani File.

INDEX

HISTORY OF
SCHOOLS &
SCHOOLING

THIS SERIES EXPLORES THE HISTORY OF SCHOOLS AND SCHOOLING
in the United States and other countries. Books in this series examine the
historical development of schools and educational processes, with special
emphasis on issues of educational policy, curriculum and pedagogy, as
well as issues relating to race, class, gender, and ethnicity. Special
emphasis will be placed on the lessons to be learned from the past for
contemporary educational reform and policy. Although the series will
publish books related to education in the broadest societal and cultural
context, it especially seeks books on the history of specific schools and on
the lives of educational leaders and school founders.

For additional information about this series or for the submission of
manuscripts, please contact the general editors:

Alan R. Sadovnik   Susan F. Semel
Rutgers University-Newark   The City College of New York, CUNY
Education Dept.   138th Street and Convent Avenue
155 Conklin Hall   NAC 5/208
175 University Avenue   New York, NY 10031
Newark, NJ 07102

To order other books in this series, please contact our Customer Service
Department:

800-770-LANG (within the U.S.)
212-647-7706 (outside the U.S.)
212-647-7707 FAX

Or browse online by series at:

www.peterlang.com